National Theatre Connections 2023

TEN PLAYS FOR YOUNG PERFORMERS

(Circle Dreams Around) The Terrible, Terrible Past

Innocent Creatures

Is My Microphone On?

Is This Good Enough?

Model Behaviour

Old Times

Samphire

Strangers Like Me

The Heights

Tuesday

Edited by

NATIONAL THEATRE

T0333425

methuen | drama

LONDON · NEW YORK · OXFORD · NEW DELHI · SYDNEY

METHUEN DRAMA
Bloomsbury Publishing Plc
50 Bedford Square, London, WC1B 3DP, UK
1385 Broadway, New York, NY 10018, USA
29 Earlsfort Terrace, Dublin 2, Ireland

BLOOMSBURY, METHUEN DRAMA and the Methuen Drama logo are
trademarks of Bloomsbury Publishing Plc

First published in Great Britain 2023

Typeset by RefineCatch Limited, Bungay, Suffolk
Printed and bound in Great Britain

To find out more about our authors and books visit www.bloomsbury.com
and sign up for our newsletters.

Contents

National Theatre Connections

Connections is the National Theatre's annual nationwide youth theatre festival – a celebration of new writing, partnership and, above all, young people. Every year Connections gives youth theatres and school theatre the unique opportunity to stage new plays written specifically for young people by some of the most exciting playwrights writing today, and to perform them in leading theatres across the UK.

New plays are at the heart of Connections – stories for and about young people that challenge them to experience life in someone else's shoes, and transport them to different times, places and emotional landscapes. Through our 2023 portfolio, a young person might travel thousands of years into the future, or into a parallel universe; they might explore the climate emergency or the impact of grief, or journey into a dream. We are proud to be able to share this incredible collection of plays, and that, through this anthology, these plays continue to be permanently available to schools, colleges and youth theatres.

At the beginning of their rehearsal process, companies take part in the Connections Directors' Weekend – an opportunity for the directors to work with the playwright of their chosen play and a leading theatre director. Notes from these workshops accompany the plays in this anthology, giving an insight into the playwrights' intentions, creative inspiration and practical suggestions for exploring the text.

In 2023, over 280 companies from across the UK will take up the challenge of staging a brand-new Connections play, with over 6,000 young people aged 13–19 involved in every aspect of theatre-making. Connections offers a space for young people to be creative, to express themselves and to connect with other young theatre-makers, both in their local area and across the country.

Connections is not just the National Theatre's programme: it is run in collaboration with fantastic theatres across the UK who are equally passionate about youth theatre. Our Partner Theatres work with every company to develop and transfer their production, and we hope the festivals will celebrate the brilliant work that has been created, and amplify the voices of young people.

We hope you enjoy this year's plays.

Kirsten Adam
Head of Young People's Programmes
November 2022

Introduction

It is autumn 2022 and the dominant narrative in the UK is that we are at the start of an energy crisis. However, as I hopped from room to room at this year's Directors' Weekend (which, for the uninitiated, is the weekend the 300 or so directors from all over the UK taking part in Connections get to meet their writer and creatively scrutinise their play for a whole day) I marvelled as I witnessed young and old, seasoned and first-timers, tentative and bold, professionals from the world of learning and participation throw themselves wholeheartedly into the activities and exercises created for them by their respective National Theatre directors as they interrogated the plays laid bare before them. They bounced off the walls, threw balls at each other from point-blank range, jumped, dodged, closed their eyes and committed to trust, strummed guitars, asked questions, searched for answers, made lists, created landscapes, struck poses, threw shapes and forged ideas. In the words of one of the playwrights, what I was watching was unlimited and unadulterated creative playfulness, inspired by the words, images, characters and events unleashed by this year's Connections plays. It was exhilarating to behold, as it exploded our collective imaginations and it became unequivocally clear that, when it comes to the ten plays in this anthology, they are fuel rods generating an abundance of powerful positive energy – set to sweep through the rehearsal rooms, school halls, drama studios and theatres up and down the whole of the UK and beyond. So when it comes to the engine room of creativity, there's no lack of energy there, quite the contrary.

Once again, each of the ten playwrights in this collection takes the two simple questions of who we are and who might we be if we dared to be our true selves, runs with them, re-fashions them and engages with them to produce work that fires, builds, heals, scales and changes all who come into direct contact with these timely texts – metaphorically and, in some cases, quite literally.

Take a deep breath, open your eyes wide, and your mind and arms wider still, as I invite you to dive into this collection and embrace it wholeheartedly, on every level, and let the play begin.

Ola Animashawun
Connections Dramaturg and National Theatre Associate.
November 2022

Connections 2023 Portfolio

We are happy to let you have details of the Connections 2023 plays. The slate includes eight new plays, and two plays that were originally part of previous Connections cycles.

A note on casting

At National Theatre Connections we think long and hard about every play that we put into the portfolio. The writers whose plays make up our portfolios offer their plays as stories about humanity, and we want the plays to be for everyone, and to tell stories about a wide range of experiences, from around the world. We are proud to continue to offer plays that challenge young people to experience life in someone else's shoes, and transport them to different times, places and emotional landscapes.

We encourage our playwrights to keep the casting options for their plays as open as possible. For all plays in the portfolio, all parts can be played by D/deaf and disabled performers and, apart from where the playwright states otherwise, by actors of any gender or ethnicity. If your group doesn't exactly match the apparent casting requirements of a play in terms of race, ethnicity or gender, and you would like to produce it, we would still encourage you to do so. Any queries or changes regarding casting should be checked with the Connections team and we will advise accordingly.

Where locations are specified, rather than being preoccupied with accents, we recommend focusing your energies on finding the emotional truth of these settings. The exception in the 2023 portfolio is *Samphire*, in which some characters speak in a Suffolk dialect.

Synopses

(Circle Dreams Around) The Terrible, Terrible Past *by Simon Longman*

Cast size: flexible, with a suggested minimum cast size of 8
Recommended for ages 14+

A play about being young in the fields and towns that feel far away from where things might be happening; a play about the expectations of life and the circularity of human existence.

Someone has a recurring dream. It's a bit weird. There are fish, chickens, cows, who all look and sound like people – people who look kind of familiar. And there's a butcher, killing people. And the dream feels like a circle – going round and round and back to the start again. They can't get free of it – it's like a line eating its own arse.

Which means we're stuck in their dream too, watching it with them. We see the fields and rivers they visit in the half light. And raves they've been to with people jumping out of the windows and losing their legs. And the careers adviser from school advising jobs such as being a water carrier, or a chimney sweep, or a candlestick maker or a fishmonger. They dream about the past mainly, a past that they don't belong to but the past wants to belong to them. It's forcing its way inside, so that their future looks like the past.

See? It's a bit weird. It always starts with someone selling someone some crabs and it all gets progressively surreal from there. And there doesn't seem to be any way out.

Content guidance:

- Strong language.
- A brief reference to substance abuse.
- One brief, mildly sexually explicit conversation.
- The following are seen within the context of a dream: a dead body covered in blood, and weapons including an axe, a meat cleaver and a bolt gun.

We will share specific guidance around use of an axe, bolt gun and meat cleaver onstage.

Innocent Creatures *by Leo Butler*

Cast size: minimum of 8
Recommended for ages 15+

A play about the future, both imminent and far far away. Soon, very soon, Big Ben will be underwater surrounded by ice floes – which is where we meet Enid and Mia at the start of the play. They each have an ice floe, as they wait to be rescued by the robots in helicopters and taken to the Holiday Inn to be reprogrammed. But on second thoughts that's not for Mia: she'd rather die than be rescued/captured and have a chip implanted in her neck, and proceeds to plunge into the icy water and sink to the bottom of the ocean. This is a world where the robots are in charge and humans are made from recycled laptops, Kindles and iPads. All the men were killed long ago – they were far too hairy. No one is allowed to refer to having had parents on pain of an electric shock – that's how the reprogramming happens.

Fast forward another thousand years and Enid is still going strong, living in the rainforest that is overflowing with animals – tigers, monkeys, horses, bears, trap-door spiders and earwigs; you name it, it's there in abudance. But the people only eat the vegetation – well, you wouldn't kill an innocent creature for food would you? Fast forward thousands and thousands of years more and the sun is scorching hot as it's about to explode and emit its last ray, signalling the end of Planet Earth along with it, and Enid is still going strong: she's happy, she's got her pet hamster for company and Mia's suddenly dropped in to say hello, after being brought back to life a few hundred years earlier by the robots. The last sunset will be beautiful, worth hanging around for to see.

Content guidance:

- This is a sci-fi play set in the near and distant future, and features characters who are robots or part android. Within this context, the play features discussion of characters being 'exterminated' and 'gas chambers'; violence to an animal (which is revealed to be robotic); a character cutting open their wrists to reveal wires; and a character's eyes being gouged out and replaced with implants.
- Strong language.

Is My Microphone On? *by Jordan Tannahill*

Cast size: minimum of 7, no maximum
Recommended for ages 13+

How do we move forward from here? Young people will no longer be able to avoid the consequences of climate change. They speak to the adults in the audience, holding them to account, questioning the choices that have not been made, the ones that children will be forced to make, and what kind of future they stand to inherit.

Content guidance:

- Strong language.

In 2023 *Is My Microphone On?* will also be produced by youth theatre groups across Sweden, as part of Länk's national festival, culminating in performances on 22 April – Earth Day.

Is This Good Enough? *by Avaes Mohammad*

Cast size: flexible cast size, with 30 named characters
Recommended for ages 13+

A contemporary take on *The Conference of the Birds* (a twelfth-century epic Persian poem by Sufi poet Farid ud-Din Attar) meets seventies cult film classic *The Warriors*. Young people from all over the city, all the different tribes, the Rude Boys, the Party Girls, the Footballers, the Chess Players, the Skateboarders, the Drug Runners and the Uniformed Schoolkids are all converging in the park one cold winter's midnight: summoned there by the mysterious and enigmatic Cyroe. No one really knows who Cyroe is, or has ever really met him. All they do know is that when Cyroe calls, you answer. Eager to learn Cyroe's message for them, what they don't know, but are about to find out, is that far from having the 'answer' to what they might all be looking for, Cyroe is going to send them on a treacherous quest – across deserts, up mountains, over frozen wastelands and a long dangerous rock faces – where they will face their worst nightmares and darkest fears in an attempt to find the answer for themselves and discover the true meaning of leadership.

Content guidance:

- Includes references to drug use.

Model Behaviour *by Jon Brittain*

Cast size: 9
Suitable for all ages

A fast-paced comic, white-knuckle ride through the rollercoaster of personal (playground) politics played out against the backdrop of the world stage.

When Mr Smallwood announces that his politics year group are going to spend an entire day role playing what it's like to be a delegate at the United Nations, the keenest pupil in the class, Ronni, is of course delighted. Everyone else in the class isn't and (with perhaps the only exception being Sarah, who never says anything) they all quickly exhibit their contempt for the project, as they take it in turns at adopting varying degrees of cynicism. This manifests as a rainbow of negativity including disinterest, disdain, and the desire to destroy, disrupt and to liberally undermine everything at will.

What should be one of Ronni's most memorable days at school – a personal triumph as she displays her diplomatic and intellectual prowess for the benefit of the whole of humanity – instead looks set on course to explode into a thermo-nuclear car crash of a day – in outer-space and cyber-space – all thanks to her typical and totally predictable classmates . . . who have never ever taken anything seriously in their whole lives. Apart from Sarah that is, and perhaps if people paid a little more attention to her and took the time to discover that she does actually say things, just very quietly, and if Ronni could perhaps learn to follow as well as lead . . . well, perhaps, maybe the future could be bright – glowing with hope and not radiation.

Content guidance:

- Some moderate language.

Old Times *by Molly Taylor*

Cast size: 14
Recommended for ages 14+

A play about stigmatism, friendship and justice. Stefi and Zafer are twins about to turn eighteen; they have finally reached adulthood. However, life is throwing up complications; Zafer is fighting illness, and Stefi is scared the past is about to turn around and bite them. Five years ago, their old school crew were involved in the murder of a policeman. Except only one of them was accused and convicted, well-known troublemaker and 'bad kid' Tom Joy. The rest of the gang kept shtum and weren't even implicated, but it tore their friendship group apart, and the town has never forgotten the notorious crime. So when Stefi hears Tom Joy has been released from prison, and she starts receiving spooky calls from an unknown number, she knows it's time to get the group back together so they can get plan strategy, talk survival and get their story straight. Stefi has a plan to protect them all. But when she gathers the seven friends back together under false pretences, the ghosts from the past are reborn. Who was really responsible for the crime? Who betrayed whom? Do they deserve retribution? And will they ever be able to move on?

Content guidance:

- References to cancer.
- Moderate language and two instances of strong language.
- Reference to the stabbing of a character (unseen, offstage).
- A brief reference to substance abuse.

We will share specific guidance around the use of a knife onstage.

Samphire *by Shamser Sinha*

Cast size: 21 characters, recommended minimum cast size of 12
Recommended for ages 16+

A play about school, special educational needs, love, independence and life in rural Suffolk. Alicia is neurodiverse due to her mother's substance abuse when she was pregnant with Alicia. However, she does not want her neurodiversity to define her. Alicia now lives in a children's home, and Jake lives in a shed. They are a couple, though Jake shows way more affection to his dog (a lurcher) than he ever does to Alicia. They rob farms for animals to eat. But when they steal a piglet from Chelle's dad's farm it's a big mistake – a bridge too far and their dreams of a house share in Leiston and working in the local nuclear power station are put in jeopardy. A Suffolk story. A rural story. A story with dogs, marshlands, prejudice, detention, emotional blocks, frustrations, neo-fascists, flirting, fallings-out, threats of police action and a demon dog. Jake and Alicia are no ordinary couple – they're special and they don't belong . . . allegedly.

Content guidance:

- One instance of strong language.
- References to masturbation.
- Violence against an animal, portrayed in a non-naturalistic way.
- Reference to the death of a child (unseen, offstage).
- References to drug and alcohol abuse.
- Discussions around consent.
- Within the play there is a brief scene featuring an extremist group, who use some Islamophobic language.

Strangers Like Me *by Ed Harris*

Cast size: minimum of 15
Recommended for ages 14+

A play about grief, masculinity, relationships and friendship. Elbow's best friend Hamster has died, suddenly, unexpectedly. So Elbow is now grieving . . . right? But what is grieving? How do you do it? And what happens if you get it wrong? Privately, Elbow is beginning to feel they weren't even as close as everyone makes out. So it would be better if everyone just left Elbow alone – Mum, Dad, his stupid big brother Donut, but especially all those annoying kids at school pretending they really care . . . writing poems, singing songs and holding a vigil at Elbow and Hamster's favourite meeting place. Who do they think they are? Come to think of it, who do any of us think we are . . . deep down? Elbow doesn't know. Elbow just knows there's a strange feeling inside, or the absence of a feeling, or the feeling of horrible, horrible nothingness – which can only be dealt with through anger.

Content guidance:

- Play explores responses to the death of a friend of the lead character (unseen, off stage).
- Strong language.
- In a non-naturalistic scene, one character – who is the embodiment of part of the lead character's psyche – has their tongue ripped out. It is then reattached later in the play.

The Heights *by Lisa McGee*

Cast size: 14 named characters, minimum cast size of 8
Recommended for ages 13+

This is a play about stories. Lillie is a teenager who lives on the Heights Estate. A place where nothing ever happens, except in Lillie's head. Lillie's not like most people, definitely not. For starters, she never goes out, but sits in her bedroom window on the sixth floor of her tower block, watching the world and the people in it go by – though sometimes some of those same people enter her world. As she sits, she makes up stories. Some of these stories are sad, some are happy, some are funny and some are just wonderful. However, whatever they are, they are just stories. Aren't they? No one would play catch in the middle of the street with a loaded gun, or use the same gun to frighten a stranger as they slept in their bed. And no one could give birth to a baby made of glass, or murder their twin brother over an argument about what they should spend their money on if they won the lottery. . . would they? Surely these are all just stories, dark, curious, beguiling figments of Lillie's fertile imagination aren't they?

Content guidance:

- Strong language.
- Some infrequent moments of violence – these include one character choking another, and a scene where a character is tied up and gagged. In a non-naturalistic scene, there is a description of a glass baby shattering and causing a character's arms and legs to bleed.

Tuesday *by Alison Carr*

Cast size: 9–50, any gender
Suitable for all ages

Tuesday is light, playful and nuanced in tone. And a little bit sci-fi.

The play centres on an ordinary Tuesday that suddenly turns very weird indeed when a tear rips across the sky over the school yard. Not only that, but it starts sucking up pupils and staff while at the same time raining down a whole new set of people. But, then, that's what happens when parallel worlds collide!

Confusion reigns as the 'Us' and 'Them' try to work out what is going on. How are Ash and Magpie identical? Can Billy cope with having his sister back? Who is Franky?

Eventually, though, cracks appear between the two groups. As the air here starts to disagree with the 'Them', the race is on to try to get things back to how they were and safely return everyone to the universe they came from.

The play touches on themes of friendship, sibling love, family, identity, grief, bullying, loneliness and responsibility. And in the process we might just learn something about ourselves as well as some astronomical theories of the multiverse!

Content guidance:

- Discussion of the death of a character (unseen, off stage).

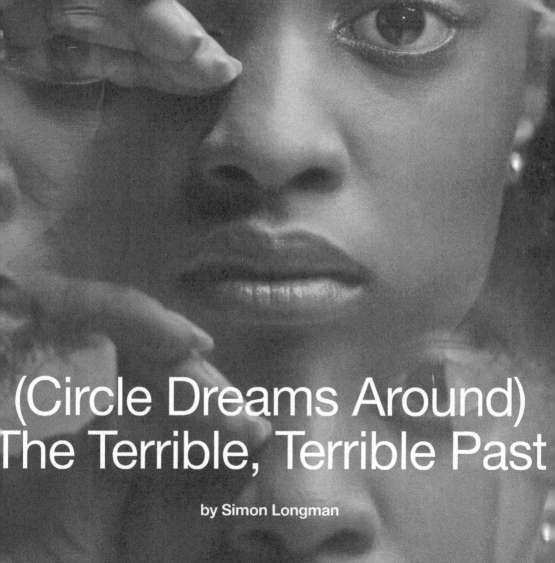

(Circle Dreams Around)
The Terrible, Terrible Past

by Simon Longman

Simon Longman is a playwright from the West Midlands. His plays include *Patient Light* for Eastern Angles; *Island Town* for Paines Plough; *Gundog* for Royal Court; *Rails* for Theatre by the Lake; *White Sky* for Royal Welsh College of Music & Drama/ Royal Court; *Sparks* for Old Red Lion; and *Milked* for Pentabus Theatre Company. He is the recipient of the forty-ninth George Devine Award for Most Promising Playwright and has previously won the Channel 4 Playwrights' Scheme. His work has been translated and produced internationally. He is represented by Judy Daish Associates.

Notes about the play

The play is for an ensemble, but some specific characters crop up throughout the play.

Each line is numbered throughout, so you know who is saying what in each scene. This doesn't mean that every character needs to be played by a different person – you can double, triple, etc. up throughout.

Lines marked > can be assigned to anyone.

A . in between lines is a pause. The more the space, the longer the pause.

The important props are mentioned in the script, so they should be in the play. Beyond that, it's up for grabs.

The space can be as messy or clean as you like. The play is a dream – some dreams are cluttered, some are big open spaces.

Scenes Five, Nine, Twelve, Twenty, Twenty-Three are voice-only scenes. The voice should be distant, maybe a little echoed. It could be the same voice throughout, or multiple voices. Have a play around with it to see what sounds interesting.

An important thing about the animal characters:

> *Absolutely* NO ONE *should be playing the animals like they're actual animals. So no one should be forced to flap their arms about pretending to be a chicken. Or flapping about on the floor like a fish. (If I had to do that when I was younger, or even now, or any point in my life from now on, I would die of embarrassment.)*

> *So no literal animal impressions allowed.*

> *The animals should be played like they are humans.*

> *Think of it like someone going to a fancy-dress party they don't want to go to as a chicken, and therefore putting in not a huge amount of effort to dress like a chicken. They might have a costume-shop chicken outfit on. Or a homemade beak. Or if they are playing a cow, then maybe their clothes have got black and white spots on. You know, that kind of thing.*

Apart from that, anything is up to anyone.

Scene One: Another Beginning and Another End

Two people. One is holding a shoe.

1   It always ends with a shoe and me trying to explain it. So I do. I say:

I always have weird dreams.

They're circles. The go round and round. Which is a bit disorientating. Because you're like, oh we're back to the start again. I can't get free of it.

And gets me thinking about circles.

2   What about them?

1   Like, what is a circle? Really? A line forced round and back to where it started. A line eating itself. A line stuck, completely, hopelessly, up its own arse.

It's like, me, here, but if I bent over and shoved my head up my own bumhole. Me as a circle. And I'd be pretty depressed because of that.

And like I asked my friend once whether they dream in circles too. And they said they didn't used to, but as they got a bit older, they do.

I asked another friend and they said the same thing.

Then I asked them what they dreamt about.

And they said just weird stuff that comes back around again and again.

Like I do. You know?

2   Think so.

1   Yeah. But also – Like –

In these dreams I feel like me. But I'm not me. You know? I can see me, but I'm not me, physically, in the dream. I'm someone else. But I know it's me.

And the thing that scares me the most is: who's looking at me? Who's walking around my head, hiding in the folds of the skin of my brain, making me watch my own dreams?

And the landscapes. The fields and rivers and towns I visit in the space behind my closed eyes. It's the past. Forcing itself inside me. A past I don't belong to but a past that wants to belong to me so much that it makes everything a circle that I can't get out of.

2   How does it start?

1   It starts with me, but it's not me, but it is me, selling someone some crabs in a fish shop.

2   Ha. That's weird.

1   Yeah it starts quite fun. But always ends with a funeral and the sky shattering.

There's a very thin line between a dream and a nightmare. Like there's a very thin line between the past and the future.

Isn't there?

They are alone.

1   You've gone again.

We're back to the start. Always are. Round and round. I knew I was still asleep.

Scene Two: Fishmonger, Crab, Crab, Crab, Crab . . .

Two people in a fishmongers.

3   I mean. It's a fish. Dunno what more you want.

4   Yeah but there's, like, different fishes though?

3   Yeah.

4   Yeah.

3   Yeah so?

4   Look my mum just gave me this list and says I've got to get a certain type of fish.

3   Yeah. Which one then?

4   I dunno I lost the list. I remember the fish started with a C.

3   Cod.

4   No that one.

They point.

3   That one?

4   Yeah.

3   That's a crab.

4   Crabs are fish aren't they?

3   No.

4   What? Oh. What are they?

3   They're crabs.

4   Like lobsters and that?

3   I guess.

4   Right wow so my mum's probably not looking for that then.

3   No.

4   Does start with a C though. God this is hard. Who'd want to buy fish? Who'd want to sell fish? Who'd want anything to do with fish? Fish are *gross*.

.

4   But I mean that's just me. Like it's cool you work in a fish shop. I couldn't work here. The smell is awful. Smells like what I imagine death would smell like. Well, I mean, sort of is what death smells like because all the fish and stuff are literally dead. But you'd finish for the day and you'd have that smell in your hair and clothes and stuff so you'd think you'd died too. So for that reason I couldn't work here. You know what I mean?

.

3   Choose a fish.

4   Um yeah. Let's just have the crab. Close enough.

3   How many?

4   Twenty?

3   Twenty?

4   Yeah.

3   You want twenty crabs?

4   Yeah. No. What? Oh I dunno. This is impossible. How many's normal?

3   One each.

4   For each person eating?

3   Obviously.

4   Alright I'll have two.

3   One for you one for your mum?

4   No three. One for my brother and all. He's eating too. And my dad.

3   So. Four?

4   Mum, my brother and my dad. Three.

3   And you.

4   And me what?

3   You're eating too.

4   Oh yeah I'm eating too.

3   So, four?

4   No Mum, my brother and my dad. That's three.

3 AND YOU!

4 Oh right right right yeah me. Sorrysorrysorry. Yeah. Three please.

3 FOUR!

4 Four yeah four. Ha.

They bag up some crabs. Someone comes in. The person waiting for their crabs looks around at the new person.

4 Hi.

5 Um. Alright?

4 Yeah.

They turn away. Then back again.

4 Did you see the person walking around with the axe outside?

5 Um. No?

4 I did. On the way here. There's a person with an axe walking around town. Looks mad.

5 Um. Okay?

3 Here.

They turn back and take the bag that's being held out to them.

4 Oh. Thanks.

They look inside the bag.

4 Alright crabs? Haha. Hey imagine if I brought one of those crabs back to life. Like, nurtured it back to life. Be like Jesus of the fish. Haha. I'd love that. Resurrect a crab. Resurrect all the crabs! Imagine that. I'd have crabs. Loads of crabs. Proper crabs like. Not like, the ones you get in your pubes. Real crabs. That'd be class. I'd send them after my enemies. They'd chop them all up. Just nipping everyone to death. I'd like that a lot. Would you?

3 I dunno what to say to that.

4 Yeah don't worry I'm sure not many would.

Um. Thanks.

They turn to go. Stop.

4 Sometimes I think I can bring animals back to life. That's all I meant. I'd love that I think. Being a vet. I'd love that. But everyone tells me I'm not clever enough so I've given up before I've even tried. That's okay isn't it? That's just the way of the world.

Anyway. Watch out for the man with the axe. Bye.

They leave.

They other two look at each other.

5   Um so – Hey! Hello. Yeah I – I wanted to –

Scene Three: What?

A few people in a park, after school.

6   See try and work that one out. I'm like, not sure, what it means. There's some layers there, I guess. Right? We're talking a, I dunno, like, fish shop? Right? Like a butcher's. But for fish. I dunno what you call them. Fish butcher's. And crabs? Dunno what crabs mean. Not even my star sign. Weird dream right?

7   I remember picking up a crab when I was a kid and throwing it into the sea as far as I could.

6   The stuff with the axe too is weird.

7   Sometimes I'd stamp on them.

8   That's messed up.

7   Was a kid. You do weird shit when you're a kid don't you?

8   Yeah I guess. I used to dig holes in the garden and stick my head in them. Stayed like that for hours, pretending to be a worm.

7   Ha.

6   Like I feel like I looked different.

7   When?

6   In the dream.

8   It's called a fishmonger's, by the way. Not a fish butcher's.

6   Oh yeah course.

Someone walks past them carrying a bloody meat cleaver, dragging a body covered in blood. They watch. The person passes, a trail of blood left behind.

8   Hey you know that careers adviser guy.

7   Who?

8   Remember that guy that came in to school to tell you what you might want to be in the future.

6   Oh yeah.

8 Yeah he told me I should actually *be* a fishmonger. I was like, mate, I don't even eat fish. I hate them. They actively *freak* me the *fuck* out.

7 He told me to be a water carrier.

6 He told me that too! What is that?

7 You carry water about.

6 What like you're a walking tap?

7 Yeah think so. Looked it up and it's not been a job for hundreds of years.

8 Why's he telling everyone to do old dead jobs?

9 He told me I should get into making candlesticks.

8 He's mad. What about you?

10 Chimney sweep. I was like, I'll sweep your chimney, mate.

6 What's that mean?

10 Means, like, I'd, like, dunno, sweep him up. Send him up the chimney.

7 What?

10 I dunno sounded better in my head. I don't wanna be a chimney sweep. I absolutely hate vertical tunnels. And that was one of the questions too. Do you like spending time in small tube-like spaces that go up, brackets: vertical tunnels? And I was like, no.

.

9 Hey did you see that kid just then?

7 Yeah.

9 Can't believe how dead they looked just then all chopped up.

8 Think it was Sam.

6 Wait, isn't their dad a butcher?

9 Yeah think so.

6 And they got *butchered.* I mean, that's quite ironic, isn't it?

Scene Four: Ironic Chicken

A few people eating food, outside.

11 I dunno. Like, the only ironic thing I can really think of is if a fish walks into a fish shop place and – No! A shark. Right. A shark walks into a fish market. And buys a shark fin for its tea. And then it gets it back to its fish house and cooks it but while it's in the pot it looks at the fin properly and it's like like, oh wait that's my fin I remember when they cut that off me.

12   Is that ironic?

13   I thought ironic was the same thing as sarcastic?

11   Yeah they are but a bit different.

12   How?

11   Like if I said oh you don't know what ironic means but say it sarcastically like this: oh you don't know what ironic means.

12   What?

11   I actually don't know sorry.

13   No like. It's this. Ironic is – Like. Um. Oh like whoever invented, like, traffic lights. Yeah?

12   That's not ironic.

13   I'm not finished. So the person that invented traffic lights didn't have a driver's licence.

11   So they couldn't drive?

13   Yeah they couldn't drive. So they never *experienced* their invention.

11   Ohhhhh. Cool.

13   You get it?

11   Yeah. Like the person that invented hotdogs was actually a dog?

13   No.

11   Like the person that invented toothpaste was actually a giant brush?

13   What?

11   Or tooth?

A chicken falls from the sky. It is dead. Someone picks it up.

11   Oh I've got / another one!

12   / It's a chicken.

11   So like, if a pig, like, um /

12   / Does no one care that a chicken just nearly fell on us? /

11   / got on a bus and – No wait! If a cow, like, butchered a butcher?

13   Yeah kind of.

12   Hello?

11   No no no. If a pig sold bacon to other pigs.

12   Can people hear me?

13   If a pig sold bacon –

11   To other pigs that would be ironic?

12   Am I dead?

13   Yeah. Yeah that's ironic. Because the pig is bacon.

12   Does no one care about the dead chicken?

11   What about it? Just died flying in the sky. Get over it.

12   Chickens can't fly.

11   Yeah they can they've got wings.

12   They're flightless.

11   Why'd you care?

12   Someone had to have thrown this or something?

11   Maybe it fell off a plane.

12   What?

13   Yeah maybe the chicken was on a plane and then fell off.

12   What?

13   Chicken was on a plane and it fell off.

12   What?

11   The *chicken* was on a *plane* and it fell *off*.

12   I don't understand why you think chickens go on planes.

13   Oh my God we really can't explain it any clearer.

They check their phone for the time.

11   Shit we're gonna be late for Freddie's funeral.

13   Throw that chicken away, you can't bring a dead chicken to a funeral.

They leave. The person holding the chicken remains. Looks down at the chicken.

12   This doesn't make any sense.

They drop it on the floor and leave.

Someone dressed as a chicken comes in and picks up the chicken; they look down at it in their hands.

14   You nearly made it, didn't you?

Oh well.

I'll miss you.

Sometimes I think such horrible thoughts. They burn so brightly sometimes I think I want to scream. When I think about my body I think about how we're meant to taste really good. I don't understand. I've tried eating myself and it hurt and didn't taste good. But I guess I wasn't cooked. I suppose I could eat you.

But I don't want to eat my brother.

I'll just assume that we must taste nice to commit mass murder for.

I'll bury you. I noticed that they were doing something similar with a human. I'll watch then copy that.

They look up at the sky.

14   Do you want to wake up yet?

If you do, I'm sorry, you won't for a while, if you ever do.

Scene Five: We're in It Now

An empty space. A voice.

> Circles. Try not to forget that.
> We're in it now.
> We're all in it now and there's not going to be much we can do to get out of it.
> The past likes a circle. A circle is its favourite shape.
> It also likes pushing itself into everyone.
> In the slow time between night and morning.
> That's where it loves to be so it's the first thing people have to look at when they wake up.
> Or think they've woken up.
> Look. There's a half light. Can you see it? Coming in through the gap in the clouds. I wake up in a field, flicker my eyes open and see the dawn rest heavily on the horizon. I am cold and shivering and I've lost one of my shoes. I've got a headache and my phone screen is smashed. I look at my friend and they look at me and say:

Scene Six: Half Awake

Two people in a field. Hungover.

15   I don't think we should drink that much again.

1   Yeah. Why've I only got one shoe on?

15   Dunno. You lost it. I think I remember you losing it.

1   Why are we in a field?

15   Another thing I can't explain to be honest with you.

A farmhand comes in.

2   Oh. Hello. What – Who are you?

15   Why you dressed like that? You are farmer or something?

2   Um. Yeah a bit. Well, yeah. Not a bit. I am a farmer. This is – my land.

15   Yours?

2   Well, my family's.

15   So you want us to go?

2   No I don't. I'd happily have loads of people in these fields. Friends and that. If I had any. But I would go yeah because my dad likes shooting trespassers with a shotgun.

15   He can't do that.

2   He can do anything, he's rich. You better go. Because you both seem really nice. And I hate my dad. Do you know how many trespassers he's killed?

15   None, hopefully.

2   Nah it's not none. It's like, hundreds.

15   Why's he not in jail?

2   I dunno really. Keeps paying people off. He's a landowner so he can do what he wants.

15   Not now though. He can't do that *now*.

2   Try telling him that. He says things were better in the good old days. So that's where he likes to spend his time. You better go. Where's your shoe?

1   Lost it I think.

2   Well, if it turns up I'll – I'll try and get it back to you. Or something. Do you live in town?

1   Yeah.

2   Yeah yeah okay I'll look for your shoe and then if I find it, I'll get it to you somehow. Where'd you –

They see something on the horizon.

2   Oh shit that's my dad. You better go. Follow the field till you get to the gate. Then go through the next two fields. Be careful in the second one because there's a bull who is angry because it's horny but can't get any but that's not important right now so once you get through that you'll be at the river. Swim across avoiding the sharks /

15   / What? /

2   / and then you'll be on a footpath which'll take you home.

15   Did you say sharks?

2   My dad put them in there to stop trespassers. Told you he was a psycho.

1   I thought I woke up?

2   I would go now. God I hate him. He's making me be a farmer even though I absolutely hate everything about the outdoors and – Sorry this isn't important right now either. You gotta go otherwise you'll get shot. If I find your shoe I'll get it back to you.

1   Um. Thanks.

They look at each other a moment. The other person has already made to leave. They stop.

15   Are you coming?

1   Yeah sorry. Just – Do I know you?

2   Don't think so. I don't know anyone. I kind of don't exist. I mean, look at me. I'm not dressed for the present, am I?

1   No. Guess so.

2   Go. I'd hate to see you get shot.

They go. The farmhand watches them go. The farmhand pinches themselves. Nothing happens.

They pinch themselves again and a load of apples fall from the sky.

2   Always the same. Wish finding the shoe was that easy. Maybe this time.

They pinch themselves and another chicken falls from the sky. It is dead.

2   Nope. There's that dead chicken again.

Scene Seven: Apples, Apples, Apples, Apples, etc., etc., etc.

Some people gather apples.

16 I wouldn't mind so much if I liked apples, you know? But I hate them.

17 Think if you were picking up stuff you liked for a living you would eventually hate it.

16 Nah I wouldn't. I wouldn't get bored of picking up, I don't know, puppies? Would I?

17 I think you would.

18 Yeah the novelty would quickly wear off. You'd miss the apples because they don't move around or bite you.

16 I don't think so. Puppies are amazing. I'd just pick them up and cuddle them.

17 Then where'd they go?

16 I dunno my job's just picking them up. Like I don't know where these apples go do I?

17 They go to shops and people eat them.

18 Imagine if people ate your puppies.

16 Shut up. Shut up with your horrible, horrible thoughts.

They pick apples for a bit.

Someone picks up the dead chicken that fell from the sky.

19 Um. There's a dead chicken here.

16 Gross.

19 What do we do with it?

18 Leave it. Our job is apple picking not chicken picking.

19 Oh. Yeah suppose.

They drop the chicken on the ground. Look up. Look around. Look confused.

19 Um. I dreamt this. Me – Me picking apples like this.

16 Boring dream.

19 I know. We just pick apples. Forever. And the weirdest thing is that they're aren't any trees so I've no idea where they're coming from.

Someone comes in holding a bloody cleaver, dragging a body. They cross the space, then leave. The others keep picking – they don't seem to care that much.

18   Bit weird that you didn't mention that would happen in your dream.

19   The dead body?

18   Yeah.

19   Yeah I was thinking that. I don't remember that. But everything else is the same. Like me doing this.

They stamp on an apple. Then another one.

18   That'll come out of your pay.

19   Oh I don't care. It's always the same. I didn't want to do this job. I only agreed to do this job because I was scared of the big scissors. Were you scared of the big scissors too?

16   Yeah course. We all are.

19   I was so scared. But now I think I'm so lost I don't care enough to be scared. Do you know what I mean?

19   Guess it's a bit sad when that happens to you. When, like, hope is too tired to exist.

They stamp on another apple.

Scene Eight: The Big Scissors

Two people. One being interviewed.

20   Like my one of my friends said you said that they'd be good as, like, a fishmonger and I'm a bit confused because, like, my friend *hates* fish. Like she can't look at goldfishes without crying. I think she might be doing it for attention you know. But then her, like, I want to say, Auntie did get eaten by a shark so maybe it's triggering but I dunno. I'm not being a fishmonger.

21   What do you want to be?

20   To be honest with you I've not given it much thought because whatever happens I don't think the planet is going to last that long to sustain either myself or any potential career.

21   You've got to do something.

20   Like making candles? Because someone told me you told someone to do that too. And no way I'm doing that. Candles are so annoying. My sister's really into, like, scented candles and she lights them all the time cos she says they cleanse her *aura* or *soul* or some shit and anyway she takes smug pictures of her holding them up to her face posing but this one time she accidentally set her fringe on fire and it was a whole big thing even though she burnt like two hairs but she lay in bed for about three weeks like she was some dying medieval queen. I was like: your hair looked worse before you burnt it. So I'm not making candles. I like sports.

21   Which sports?

20   I'm like pretty good at swimming. I've won a few competitions and I'm getting a bit noticed by the people who decide the country's swim teams and who gets funding, you know?

21   Only a tiny amount of athletes actually make it. So I'd advise you stop doing that.

20   Oh. Right. Like –

21   Have you thought about mining?

20   Mining?

21   There're always people needed in the coal mines. Especially younger people to crawl through the tightest tunnels.

20   Haven't we, like, stopped that?

21   It's either that or making candles.

20   What?

21   Choose. It's not hard. And to be honest most people don't get a choice so count yourself very lucky.

20   Count myself lu–

They look around.

20   Like not being funny but why are you my age? You seem a bit young to be doing what you're doing.

21   I'm not your age. I'm hundreds of years old. Please decide. Or else your legs are cut off.

20   What?!

Someone comes in with a giant pair of scissors.

20   What the fuc–?

21   Choose.

20   I don't –

The person holding the scissors puts them around one of their legs.

20   Oh my God what are you –

21   Choose.

20   This is mad. This is –

They clamp the scissors around the leg. It hurts.

20   Nonononono stop that's –

21   Choose.

They clamp down even more.

20   OHMYGOD alright alright candles. I'll make candles.

The one asking questions nods at the one holding the scissors, who lets go.

21   Good choice. Follow me.

One leads the other away, looking very confused. The one holding the scissors is alone. They sigh heavily.

22   I think I hate myself. You know? Well, maybe not. But I do hate what I'm supposed to represent. I don't want to torture people but if I don't torture someone then someone just tortures me. And if that person doesn't torture me then they get tortured and on and on it goes. And where does it even stop? I feel very small all the time. I'm just a small person with a giant pair of scissors.

Yesterday I had to cut this person's leg off. It was horrible. But I've developed a technique to cope with it. I think about my mum. And picture her smiling at me. Even when I'm doing this horrible job that I've been made to do, I just think about her saying, 'It's okay. Everything's gonna be okay.' I'm thinking that while cutting. The flesh ripping and the bones snapping. It kind of helps.

Do you ever feel old? Like I'm a teenager, to look at. But I feel hundreds of years old.

The chicken from before comes in.

14   Sounds like you a had a bit of a moment just then. I did that recently too. It kind of helps, saying things out loud, I find.

22   Um. What?

14   Just saying I overheard you having a bit of a reflective moment and –

22   Sorry to sound rude and stuff but I don't actually want to take advice from a chicken.

14   Oh. Okay sorry.

22   No no like nothing to be sorry about. But I just don't think you can relate to me and vice versa. Our, like, experiences are different.

14   Yeah sorry I just thought –

22   I'm fine.

14 Okay. Okay cool sorry.

22 I gotta get back to work.

14 Right sure. Yeah. And I'm busy too. Um. Avoiding being slaughtered so. I've got things to do.

Scene Nine: Light, Bending

An empty space. A voice.

> Circles circles circles circles.
>   You tell me you think in circles, and I say I do, too.
>   You hold my hand in the middle of a field.
>   Above us stars hang low and planets shift slowly around our hearts.
>   I tell you that starlight spends all of time searching to be seen.
>   You like the line it draws towards our eyes.
>   I like that light because it's left the past behind.
>   And for a moment, we find a little peace, out there, in that field.
>   But the light gets pulled back, and screams as it bends back on itself.
>   And then I say I've dreamt about a butcher killing his young.
>   And we're back behind our eyelids again.

Scene Ten: The Butcher

A butcher and someone else, who is holding a cleaver.

23 Queue out the door the other day. So many folk wanting good meat. Are you listening to me?

24 Yeah.

23 You never do. And did I say you could stop sharpening that?

They start sharpening the cleaver.

23 What's the number one rule of being a good butcher?

24 Keeping your knives sharp.

23 Speak up, alright?

.

23 Oi I'm talking to you.

24 Yes I know.

23   Watch that tone. Don't speak to me like that. I don't know where I went wrong with you. Teaching you all about the family business. So ungrateful.

24   I'm not.

23   You are. You've no respect. You've no understanding of traditions and values. You're obsessed with yourself. You all are.

24   I don't think I am.

23   Well, I do and that's what matters.

They stop sharpening the cleaver. They put the cleaver down.

23   That's not sharp yet keep going.

24   I don't want to do this anymore.

23   What's that?

24   I've had enough. I told you before I'm a vegetarian. But you won't listen to me. You never do. I don't think you really like what you do either. You just had to do it because you were made to. Please don't put that on me. Like, you're my dad and stuff but in my eyes you're not an adult. You're my age. I mean look at you. You look the same age as me. It's mad.

They turn to leave.

23   Where do you think you're going?

The butcher picks up the cleaver.

23   Don't you dare walk away from me.

They stop. A terrible tension.

.

23   Let me tell you a story: The other night. I was walking through a field. It was big and empty. The night sky hanging over my head. Stars. Millions of them. Some of them shooting stars, cutting white lines through space. I came across an animal. It was screaming in pain. It was trying to get up but its leg was broken. It looked up at me for help and I thought it looked pathetic. So I took my cleaver and put it down. I'm very, *very* close in doing the same to you.

The butcher moves closer. The other screws their eyes tight shut, talks to themselves. They get louder and more panicked.

24   Wake up.

The butcher moves closer.

24   Wake up. Wake up wake up.

The butcher moves closer and closer and closer.

24   WAKE UP WAKE UP WAKE UP WAKE U –

Scene Eleven: Shooting Stars

A field. Some friends drinking and smoking. One is asleep next to them. They wake up with a jump.

25   Alright, sleepy head.

24   Ergh. Fuck. Wha–

25   You passed out. Told you not to mix weed, vodka and painkillers.

24   Yeah. God. That's – Had a weird nightmare about a butcher.

25   That's no fun. Here.

They pass a bottle of vodka.

24   Why's it dark?

25   Because it's ten thirty at night. You passed out at like lunchtime.

24   Oh.

They drink.

24   Why we in a field?

25   You wanted to 'have an adventure' so walked into a field, then lay down.

They look around. Someone else looks at their phone. Flicks through and watches some videos.

24   Cows over there.

25   Yeah.

26   More stories about that party. Everyone's there.

27   Did you get an invite?

26   No. Did you?

27   Nah.

25   Me either.

.

.

26   Like I'm kind of glad I didn't get an invite, you know? They're all dicks.

.

27   Like I dunno be nice to get an invite though. Cooler getting an invite and not going than not being invited in the first place.

26   Guess so.

25   Yeah.

They point to the sky.

25   See that.

26   What?

25   Was a shooting star.

26   Where?

25   Gone now hasn't it?

26   Oh yeah right.

25   Keep looking though.

26   Yeah.

They look at the sky.

.

Some screaming, far off.

26   What's that?

27   Sounds like screaming.

26   Animal or something.

27   Guess so.

25   Sounds horrible.

.

It goes. The one who was asleep looks around, confused. One notices.

26   What's up with you?

24   Nothing. Just. Feel like I'm still dreaming.

26   Oh yeah I know that feeling. Other night I had a dream where I was a matchstick dipper.

27   What's a matchstick dipper?

26   They used to get kids to do it in the old days. Was like, child labour. Anyway they dipped matches in chemicals to make them flammable. But the chemicals gave out fumes and most of the kids got sick and died. I was sick in the dream. But they made me keep dipping these matches and wouldn't let me go. I was, like, choking and felt my lungs were, like, *melting*. Was horrible.

24   That's weird.

26   Yeah I know.

24   No not – I think I've dreamt this too, you know. Us here now. Wait. Say something.

26   What?

24   Say anything and I'll know what you say.

26   Um. Like –

24   Just say anything. Something random.

26   Um. Okay? / I like chickens.

24   / I like chickens. See? I've definitely dreamt this before. But it feels like the same. Did I wake up?

25   Um. Yeah?

24   No no no. Properly. Did I wake up properly?

27   You're mad.

24   No I mean it. This is really weird. I'm having the same dream. Someone's going to come in carrying one shoe.

Someone comes in carrying one shoe.

2   Oh – Hello. What are you doing?

25   / Watching shooting stars.

24   / Watching shooting stars.

2   Oh yeah there are loads aren't there? I love them.

27   Why are you holding one shoe?

2   I'm / returning it to someone

24   / returning it to someone

2   I'm returning it to someone

26   Who?

2   I don't know their name. But I'm sure I'll find them soon. Hopefully. I really liked them. Can't stop thinking about them. I'll leave you be. Stay in this field. The next one is my dad's and he likes shooting trespassers as I've mentioned before. To the owner of this shoe. Keep safe.

They leave.

24   See?

25   Yeah weird. What happens next?

24   Um. A planet explodes.

27   Really?

24   Yeah. Now.

A planet explodes above them. It's silent, but the colours are bright.

24   See?

27   Oh yeah wow. What planet was that?

24   Mars.

They watch the explosion spread out.

.

26   I like the colours it's making.

They watch the colours fill the sky.

.

26   Hey so then do you know already if we go to this party?

24   Yeah.

26   What happens?

24   Um. You get drunk and finally get with who you've been trying to get with for ages. You take a lot of pills and are really fun and make loads of new friends. And, um, fall out of a window and break both your legs.

27   Wow. That actually sounds really, really, really fun. For us. Shall we go?

25   Yeah definitely. You shouldn't though because of the whole leg-breaking premonition.

27   Yeah you shouldn't come if you like your legs being not broken.

They leave.

26   I don't want to be left on my own though.

.

The person remaining watches the explosion gradually fill the sky. The look around, worried.

.

26   Hey wait I – I hate missing out on stuff. I'll – I'll happily break my legs to avoid that.

They head off in the same direction as the others.

26   Wait for me!

Scene Twelve: A Planet, Exploding

An empty space. A voice.

>   There was silence.
    Before it blew up.
    As silence as absolute as the sound time makes.
    And then a light flickering...
    There was a silence before.

As absolute as the sound time makes.
And then a light flickering inside its heart and pushed outwards in all directions
    until it broke through its skin and then a flash of light and a bang screaming
    inside a vacuum.
And pieces of itself spread slowly across the sky.
Do you think we're the only ones who knew what happened?
Does a fish see the stars from under the ocean?
I guess when it's pulled up and out and lies dying on a boat, under the night sky.
Then one eye looks upwards, does it think,
'I've never seen light as clear as that,
I wish I wasn't dying so I could look at it longer.'

Scene Thirteen: Seahorses Giving Birth

Same setting as Scene Two.

5   It's weird they're all lying on their sides isn't it? Like fish usually are upright. Aren't they?

3   Um. Yeah.

5   Hahaha. Yeah. They're always like that when they come out the sea aren't they? One eye looking at the sky, the other the earth. Light out of one, dark out the other. Weird eh?

5   Wow ahhhh. It all looks so, like, good. I don't know, um, what to get. Ahhhhh. What should I get?

3   We've no crabs left. That kid just bought the last of them.

5   Yeahyeah no worries. Um. What's that?

3   That's an octopus.

5   An octo–? Wow cool. So wow. So. Wow.

3   You want it?

5   Um. No. It's got, like. I dunno it's got sad eyes. I don't want to eat that. I'll just have, um – Oh I'll just have a bag of, um, seahorses.

3   You can't eat seahorses therefore we don't sell seahorses.

5   Yeah yeah haha stupid. Ha. Um. Hey someone told me that the male seahorses give birth to the kids and that.

3   Yeah they do.

5   I mean.

They mime their head exploding.

5   My mind. Exploding. It's mind blowing. It really is. The world. Just. *Seahorses.* *Fish*, that look a bit like, *horses*. You know? It really, *really* is. Um. Wow. So. Okay wow. Um yeah. But anyway. I just wanted to say something. To you.

3   What?

5   Like, that, um, I can't, um. I keep, like, thinking about you.

3   Okay?

5   Yeah. Been thinking for a while now that I – Um. Ha what am I saying. Sorry. So. What I'm trying to say is. Um. Basically every thought I have comes back to you. You're just, so, amazing and –

Like I think I lov–

Someone comes in holding an axe.

28   Here you are.

5   Wha– Not now please –

28   Look at my new axe. It's lovely isn't it? This is really going to make executing people so much easier. I can't wait to try it out.

5   Look can you leave me alone I'm trying to tell someone I love them / and –

28   / I'm going to try it out on you.

3   / What? You love me?

5   No – I mean. Yes but – This is mad I just –

28   Sometimes when I cut people's heads off the body runs around without a head. Like a chicken. I find it really, really funny. Let's see if that happens to you.

They raise the axe.

Scene Fourteen: Candle Making in the Flatlands

A few people making candles.

9   No no no that's wrong. You can't die in a dream. You wake up before you die.

29   I've definitely died in a dream.

9   No that's wrong because if you had then you would be dead in real life.

30   Maybe you're dead.

29   Yeah maybe I am.

9   You're not dead.

29   But how do you *know*? Maybe we're all dead and this is life. Then when you die, that's life, but it's all backwards like your legs are your arms and your face is on your bum and that.

9   WHAT?

Someone brings in a candle.

20   Um. Can one of you guys check this looks alright?

9   Looks fine.

20   My first one.

29   Well done. Test it.

They try and light the candle. It doesn't.

20   Think I messed that up. What did I do wrong?

9   Maybe you didn't soak the wick? Have another go.

20   I'm not very good at this.

9   You'll get the hang of it.

They stare into space, a bit lost.

30   Want anything else?

20   Wha – Sorry no I'm –

29   Should get back to work really. We're up against it a bit.

9   There's a candle shortage because of all the funerals.

29   Yeah exactly.

20   Um. Okay.

29   Oh wait quickly: do you think you can die in a dream?

20   What?

29   Can you die in a dream and be dead in real life?

20   I don't know. I had a dream once where I couldn't get out of a swimming pool until I drowned.

So I might be.

Scene Fifteen: All This Confusion

*A few people. One is dressed as a fish, so is a fish (number **32***). No one seems to notice or care that there is a fish with them – they join in the conversation like normal.*

8   They work in a fish shop?

5   Yeah.

31   Like fish and chips?

5   No no like a fish shop for fish.

31   Yeah the chippy.

5   No like a butcher's for fish.

8   A fishmonger?

5   Yeah.

8   Why does no one know what it's called?

5   They work there. And, like, I'm sweating because I'm really into them. They've got, like a *vibe*. Or something. They've got this, energy. And I'm fully in love. But I dunno what to say so I'm going on about seahorses.

31   Good chat.

8   Then what happens?

5   I'm trying to tell them I love them right. And then my dad comes in. But he doesn't look like my dad does now. He's like, our age. And he says he's like, an executioner. Like an old, medieval one. And he's angry with me for not, like following in his footsteps and being what he wants me to be. And then he cuts my head off with an axe.

31   Wow. Even more intense.

5   Yeah. I woke up just before he cut my head off. And it's, like, four in the morning, you know? And I'm sweating. And confused and stuff. And . . .

8   And what?

5   And I've – Like. This is weird but I need to say it.

31   Okay.

5   Like when I wake up, from this dream. I've got a boner. Like, I've got an erection.

31   Oh. Right. Um. Cool?

5   What?

8   So?

5   Oh my God mate I've got a boner after a dream where my dad's about to cut my head off with an axe. That's mad. Isn't it? That's terrifying. I'm terrified.

8   Ohhhh I guess yeah it is a bit yeah.

5   Yeah. So now I'm like. Um. Okay so I, what? Get turned on thinking about my dad cutting my head off?

8   Yeah. Dunno. Maybe.

5   I don't want to go to sleep now. Like I'm scared to go to sleep because who knows what's going on up here. In my head. Who knows?

8   I don't know what to say to that to be honest.

32   I've got a little theory. In history when people got hung their body did this weird thing where it, sort of, does everything to try and not be hung. But your hands are tied so you can't get out. So it sort of does everything to try and stop it.

8   So?

32   Yeah. So you dump yourself and are sick. And your eyes pop out a bit.

5   Why are you telling us this?

32   You also you get a boner too. When you're being hung.

5   Do you?

32   Yeah. So maybe in your dream you didn't get a boner because you were aroused by getting your head chopped off by your dad, but because your body knew it was about to have its head cut off so did everything to not let that happen. It's like your head telling you to not do what your dad wants you to do.

31   Wow that's a good theory.

5   You reckon?

31   I really think so. I think you worked out that dream.

5   No no no they haven't because my dad's not an executioner in real life. He runs an abattoir.

8   I mean, kind of the same thing.

5   No it's not because it's animals, not humans. And he's not *executing* the animals because they've done something *wrong*, he's *slaughtering* them because they've done *nothing wrong*.

8   Well, does he want you to do what he does?

5   Yeah he won't shut up about it. He's like: our family name is on this building and if you don't carry on with it then I'll never forgive you.

8   Yeah he definitely worked out your dream. Well done.

32   Thanks. Anyway I better go because my scales are drying out.

31   Yeah yeah go.

32   See you in a bit.

The fish leaves.

.

31   Hey did you guys think it was weird that we were hanging out with a talking fish?

8   Oh I actually didn't think about it.

5   I'm so confused about my dream boner still.

A butcher walks through dragging a bloody body. They watch. The butcher goes.

.

31   Another one gone.

How do they keep getting away with it?

Scene Sixteen: The Butcher and the Chicken

An empty space. A voice.

>   The butcher looked at the chicken and said,
     'If I give you a name I won't be able to kill you properly.'
     Inside the chicken's head it said, 'I know your name,
     We all know your name.'
     But the butcher couldn't hear what the chicken thought because chickens can't
        talk.
     What the butcher also couldn't hear was the chicken thinking this:
     'We're learning how to use our wings to avoid the knife.'
     And the butcher cut the chicken's head off.

Scene Seventeen: Never Give Up Hope

The chicken is digging a hole. Two dead chickens are on the ground. Once the hole is finished, they lay the dead chicken in. Begin filling it in with earth. They dig another hole and lay the other dead chicken in. A flash of light as another piece of Mars flies past in the sky.

They think, then get a couple of twigs and make a cross, then another. They plant them in the earth. They look down at the crosses. After a moment they take them out of the soil and chuck them on the ground, a little away from the graves.

Someone comes in carrying a shoe.

2 Um. It's – It's kind of pretty isn't it? The sky?

The one holding the show notices the crosses on the ground, then the mounds of earth, figures out what's just happened.

2 Oh. Did you just – I'm sorry.

14 It's okay.

2 Did you know them?

14 Yeah. My sister and brother. They fell out the sky. They'd just escaped the slaughter. Flying was quite new to them. I found my brother first. Then I found my sister next to rotting apples.

2 Oh. Sorry.

They look at the sky.

.

2 It's Mars. The lights in the sky. Pieces of it burning up in the atmosphere.

14 I know.

2 Oh you do? Cool. That's cool. I didn't think chickens knew about the planets.

14 We do.

2 Yeah. Sorry.

.

14 It's alright. You don't have to stay. I'm fine.

2 Oh okay. If you're sure.

14 Course.

2 Well. Hope you're okay. I'm back to this shoe quest.

14 Good luck.

2 Thanks. Um. Bye.

They leave.

The chicken looks at the sky. Lets out a loud sigh.

14 Whose dream is this? I don't want to be in these dreams anymore.

Do you hear me?

I don't want to be in these dreams anymore.

Scene Eighteen: Mars Exploded, and Not Much Changed

Some people. There are shovels on the ground. Maybe someone is smoking.

10   Well, nothing much has changed. Which is weird because I thought Mars exploding randomly would cause a bit of something to happen down here but, nothing.

33   Boring right?

10   Yeah like I thought at least one piece would hit us and cause a big mass extinction but, nothing. They're all missing us still. Kind of shit.

34   Why's that shit?

10   I dunno. I think I need something big to happen to feel a bit excited about being alive.

34   The way you feel excited about being alive would be to know that we were about to become extinct?

10   I guess.

A piece of Mars burns up in the atmosphere.

33   Why'd it blow up again?

34   No one knows.

10   Yeah they do.

33   Do they?

10   Yeah. Read the news.

34   Why'd it blow up then?

10   You know that colony they were building there?

33   Oh yeah that was mad.

10   Yeah so they were building that. And the humans on Mars were getting settled in to life on a new planet. And started, like, mining and stuff and finding some natural resources to expand their colony. And then the planet, Mars, saw what they were doing and went, 'Oh fuck this I'll save you all some time' and blew itself up.

33   That's not true though is it?

10   Yeah it is. They've got the recording of the planet saying that.

33   I don't believe that.

10   What you mean you don't believe it? It's fact.

33   Nah I don't buy it. That's fake. Mars wouldn't say that.

10   You're winding me up.

33   No I'm not. It's not a fact.

10   I can't deal with this. You know I'm with you when it's clearly not a fact, but this is a fact. Listen.

33   Nah it's they just say it's fact because they don't want you questioning anything.

10   I can't deal with this. You know I'm with you on that when it's clearly not a fact. But this is a fact. Listen.

They get their phone out and play a recording. From the phone the planet Mars is heard saying, 'Oh fuck this I'll save you all some time.'

10   That's the actual, factual, *real* recording. Listen:

They play it again.

33   Meh. Dunno. It's a nice story but –

10   I can't listen to this.

34   Sad about all those people though isn't it?

10   Why? They're, like, fucking, colonisers. Deserved it.

34   Just sad is all. People dying without anything they could do about it. I don't know what I'd do if that happened to me. Like, I'm trying to think of what I'd do before we're extinct but I can't think of anything. Is that bad?

33   Dunno.

34   Like, I guess I'd feel obliged to hang out with my family. All holding hands with our eyes closed. All of us crying and stuff. My little brothers and sisters. My mum and dad. In our little house. The curtains maybe closed. Or open so you could see the light coming closer towards you. I don't think I'd be able to look at anyone. I think I'd just be a bit bummed out that I didn't get to, like, understand much about why I'm here. You know? Because at the end of it all everything is just completely irrelevant.

33   Well, that's a downer.

34   Sorry. But I can't think of anything I'd do.

10   Sounds nice. Being with you family. All together. It's just me and my dad. And he's a knobend. Rather die than spend one second of my extinction with him.

A bright light fills the sky as a piece of Mars passes by.

33   That would have definitely killed us all if it hit.

10   Yeah. See what I mean. They're all missing us. All these massive pieces of a planet just missing us. Feels weird saying this but this should be a good dream, right? Us not being about to be wiped out. But every time I have this dream, I wake up sweating and terrified.

A bell rings.

33   Can't be break over already?

34   Yep. Back down the mines we go.

They gather their shovels and off they go. One remains. The light rises as another piece of Mars flies past.

10   Please come down here. Change your course. We need something to change it all. Properly.

The light from the piece of Mars fades away.

Scene Nineteen: The Water Carriers

Two people carrying water.

6   It was an okay party. I kind of violently hated everyone there. But was okay. Why'd you not come?

7   Oh. Um. Dunno. Just.

6   Wasn't in the mood?

7   Yeah kind of, I guess.

6   Yeah. I wasn't in the mood but I still went. Think I would have died of anxiety that I was missing out on something if I didn't go. Didn't really talk to anyone then someone fell out of a window and broke their legs.

The fish comes in.

32   Is the river near?

6   Not really. Sort of like half an hour that way?

32   I think I'm going to die. I'm all dried out. What's that in your sacks?

7   Water. We're water carriers.

32   I didn't know that was a job.

6   It is yeah. We have to carry water from the river to the town so people can drink and wash. It's like a job from the past but we're doing it now because someone told us we had to.

32   Right yeah cool. So. Can you – Could you just dump a sack of water over me? Otherwise I'll die.

6   Um. Yeah we would but –

32   ′But what?

6   But if we don't deliver this water then we'll get in trouble.

7   They beat us if we're late.

32   But please can't – Can't you just soak me then go and get another sack.

6   We're sorry and that but –

7   It's not up to us. If it was up to us we'd absolutely cover you in water. But we don't have a choice.

32   Okay.

7   Sorry.

6   We better get going.

7   Yeah. Good luck.

They leave. The fish stands still.

32   Half an hour to the river. Come on, mate, you can do this.

The fish walks slowly off; it's dying.

Scene Twenty: The Sky Was Full

An empty space. A voice.

> They wondered, at night, where the dead's memories go.
>   Lying in the dark, they thought about all those little thoughts that no longer had a
>   home.
>   They imagined them lying, invisible, in the spaces between the sky.
>   Packed in tightly between the particles of light.
>   They thought how many could the sky take until it was full.
>   Billions and billions of memories, from the first blinking thing of the past
>   to now,
>   All forced together.
>   Will the sky shatter?, they thought, sending all those memories away and into
>   space, leaving behind a ruptured atmosphere and a dead planet.
>   There are no echoes in space.
>   It's like we were never here, they thought.
>   And then they dreamt about the abattoir again.

Scene Twenty-One: A Laboured Point in the Abattoir

Someone is trying to fix a bolt gun. Someone else is watching them.

19   Is that working again?

4   Think so. Don't really know. I like it when it's broken because then we don't have to use it.

19   Yeah.

4   Hate this job. I wanted to be a vet but now I work in an abattoir. How'd that happen? Not even close to what I wanted. It's the complete fucking opposite.

19   I hate it too. Done nothing I've liked. I used to pick apples. My dream was to be an astronaut and be one of those people up there on Mars but of course that dream blew up when Mars did.

Now I'm here.

Someone comes in.

35   Is that working?

19   No.

35   Give it me I'll try and fix it.

They work on the bolt gun.

35   I overheard what you said about how you don't like working here.

19   Do you like it?

35   I don't mind it. Easier if you don't moan about it. I eat animals. Doing this makes me feel less guilty for eating them. I guess I feel part of the food chain. Humans are on top. Me using a bolt gun on a cow's head confirms that. Actually thinking about it properly, I love this job!

They finish fixing it.

35   That should do it.

Someone comes in holding one shoe.

2   Sorry do you recognise this shoe?

35   No.

2   Okay.

19   Why?

2   Oh someone lost it and I want to give it back to them.

35   They've probably got more pairs of shoes.

2   I know but it's gone on too long now I've been looking for them for ages. I can't give up now though. I'm kind of really in love with them. I think I could spend the rest of my life with them and never have to worry about loneliness again. I only met them once. Is that mad?

35   Yeah.

4   Not to me. Good luck finding them.

2   Thank you. It's getting quite tiring. But, I guess you can never give up hope, hey? However exhausted you feel.

They walk off with the shoe.

19   Never give up hope.

4   My hope gave up a long time ago.

19   Mine too.

35   Oh my God you guys are such boring moany dickheads you know?

They begin to walk off.

4   Hey.

They stop.

35   What?

4   Can I tell you my dream?

35   What dream?

4   Where a cow shoots me in the head with a bolt gun and then I didn't wake up. But I was you.

Scene Twenty-Two: Water Carrying, Water Pouring

The fish is lying on the ground, dead. Two people looking at it.

6   I don't feel that bad. It was either this or us getting beaten.

7   I guess.

They look at the dead fish.

.

.

7   It was so close to the river. I feel guilty. It's the eyes.

6   I know.

7   I wish they were closed.

6   Me too. Try and close them.

7   Fish don't have eyelids.

6   What? Yeah they do. Look.

They reach down and try and close the fish's eyes.

6   Oh yeah they don't. I'm just poking its eyes now.

They stop poking its eyes.

6   Now feel even guiltier.

The other pours their bucket of water on the dead fish.

.   .

.

7   Did that work?

6   I mean, doesn't look like it does it?

7   No. It's dead.

7   What do we do with it?

6   Let it rot. It's a fish. Bugs will eat it. That's life, I guess.

7   Yeah.

.

6   Better go fill up again. The town needs its water, doesn't it?

7   I hate this job.

6   I know.

7   I hate it I hate it all.

Scene Twenty-Three: Echoes

An empty space. A voice.

>   Did you hear what I said?
    You said you 'hate it all'.
    And when you were asleep and I whispered over you,
    'There's hope in the space between the echo,
    There's hope in thinking you won't hear it anymore.'
    The past echoes, doesn't it?

It goes round and round and round.
We're nearly back to where we started.
Let's lie down in the silence between the echo,
Let's lie there and hope, with everything in our hearts,
Let's hope we don't hear it again.

Scene Twenty Four: A Cow Murders a Human with a Bolt Gun

A cow stands with a bolt gun. Someone else is very scared.

35   Someone told me this dream.

36   Okay.

35   They literally told me this happened to them.

36   That's strange, isn't it? Did you hear about the chicken burying its sister and brother?

35   No.

36   Not a surprise.

35   That's not my fault is it? There's humans who I don't know burying their families. Nothing to do with me.

36   Never is, is it?

35   Come on this isn't fair. I don't even want to work here, deep down. It's all just, I dunno, bullshit. It's how I cope. I promise I don't want to work here. I just have to because they use these big scissors on you and it hurts, you know? It hurts so much.

36   I know all about being hurt. You're talking to a cow, mate.

35   I'm sorry I –

36   Have you heard about the butcher murdering loads of people? Have you been to their funerals?

35   Some of them yeah.

The cow nods, thinks.

36   I kind of knew it would happen. The butcher turning on its own. It gets boring, doesn't it? Killing things like me and chickens and pigs for thousands of years. Need to mix it up a bit. Did you see Mars blew itself up?

35   Yes.

36   I heard that they were talking about flying cows up there. Imagine that. Humans taking all that effort to fly cows on another planet just to kill us there.

You know not long ago I was in a field. Eating grass as clouds passed across the brilliant blue. Listening to the insects clicking and buzzing over the hedgerows. Saw a butterfly hop on the air. It landed on my eyelash. I could feel its little mind thinking and I had this thought.

We are a wonder.

Then the butterfly flew away. Over the green grass and into the haze of the horizon. And seeing that butterfly move so easily, I had another thought: Why don't I do that? Why don't I leave this field? It seemed so obvious.

So I did. I walked around. Walked a long time. I've seen lots of things. Chickens mourning their dead. Seen apples fall from the sky. People making candles. Planets exploding. The past swirling around like a fever. Everyone walking in circles. Looking for a way out.

I saw big roads and loud noises and grey buildings and boarded up shops and people looking sad and lost and lonely.

Walked past this place. Saw cows being pushed in here and they never came out again. I watched what was happening.

I have to say, it's not great for me.

So here's a little revenge. I know Gandhi said that thing about an eye for an eye making the whole world blind, as a warning and stuff. And I've thought about it a lot and sadly come to the conclusion that we're already there.

They shoot them in the head. They die. They look down at the bolt gun.

36   What a horrible thing to invent.

The butcher comes in dragging another bloody body. The cow watches them drag it across the space.

36   Oh I actually know them. They were in my field talking about going to a party. I think they were going to make everyone laugh and make a load of new friends.

Oh well.

Another funeral for them I guess. Look, here it is:

Scene Twenty-Five: A Funeral

Everyone is here who has been in the play. They all stand around looking quite awkward and sad.

>   Does anyone want to say anything else?

Some people look at the floor.

.

.

> You?

Someone shakes their head.

> Nothing?

A head shake.

.

> You?

> I don't know what to say.

> Just a memory, if you've got one.

> Um. I dunno. I'm not very good at talking and stuff.

> That's okay. Anyone else?

.

> Um. We went to this party and, like, I'd never thought they were that funny before. I actually didn't *like* them before that party. But. Um. They were really funny.

> Yeah same.

> Yeah.

> Me too. They were like a new friend. Kind of regret thinking they were weird for most of my life because someone told me once that they ate a pencil.

> Me too.

Some more nods of agreement.

.

.

> Would anyone else like to –

> I've not got a memory but I feel like I want to say something.

> Yes? Go on then.

> It doesn't feel like they're gone. Like I'll wake up and I'll have a text from them. I dunno.

.

.

> Does anyone else want to say anything?

.

Someone puts their hand up.

> Um.

> Yes?

> It's not a memory or anything but – Um. I'm sorry.

> Why?

> Yeah. So my parents got really angry with me because I didn't want to do what they thought I should do. You know? Took me ages to actually be able to say that to them. Mum, Dad: I don't want to be what you want me to be. Took me ages. Felt like I'd let them down. So yeah.

> What the fuck are you talking about?

> Sorry I'm trying to say – Um. After I told them and they just shook their heads and said, 'Where did we go wrong?' Felt terrible. I mean, I only said that I didn't want to be an undertaker. And my family are organising all these funerals and I hate it. My dad's like *bragging* about the money he's making. He kind of *loves* this butcher because of that. And that makes me feel sick. Because I don't want to do what they want me to do.

.

> Like I'm a shit undertaker. I'm terrible. I don't know why they want me to be one. I'd ruin everything. I hate everything about it. I'm terrified of death. *Terrified.*

.

> Sorry I've made this about me. Sorry I – I always do that. This is about them and the fact they're gone and that's – That's sad. Sorry. I'm sorry. About my dad.

.

> Does anyone have anything more to say before we all move on and try and pretend they never existed?

Some head shaking.

.

.

> Well, then, I think we can say goodbye to –

> They wanted to learn how to play the bagpipes.

> What?

> Um. They, wanted to learn how to play the bagpipes. And I said I'd teach them. But – But I never got to.

> Okay. Thank you. I think that's everything isn't it?

> You can play the *bagpipes*?

> Yeah.

> That's fucking *insane*.

> Anyone else?

.

.

> They were worried about being stuck in a dream. Not knowing what to do. They were worried about that.

> I am too.

> Does anyone else feel – Feel a bit like that?

> Yeah. Always.

> It's horrible.

> It's a nightmare, yeah.

> Yeah a nightmare. Sometimes it tricks me, you know? Like it tricks me that I'm awake but I'm actually asleep and everything is the same again and again and –

3   I've something to say so shut up.

From the back the butcher comes forward.

23   Hello I'm this butcher you all seem to be so upset about. And I've heard you all moaning. And I just wanted to say I chopped them up to show what happens when you don't listen to people who know better. That's all I have to say.

They go to leave.

23   Oh and if anyone wants chicken I'm doing buy two get one free. And sausages are on offer too. Swing by the shop if you want any meat.

The butcher leaves.

.

.

> Um. Well. I guess all that's left to say is: goodbye? Do we want to say goodbye?

> Yeah. Goodbye.

> Um. Bye. You were . . .

> Bye.

Everyone bows their heads and quietly says goodbye.

> Goodbye.

> Bye.

> Bye.

> Um. Goodbye.

> Bye.

> Goodbye.

> Good - Um. Goodbye.

> Bye . . .

Etc., etc., etc. This goodbye saying goes on a weirdly long amount of time until it peters out. Everyone stands around looking unsure what to do.

There is a silence, which is finally broken by someone saying:

> This – Um. This could go on forever. Couldn't it?

> No because the sky is about to shatter.

> Really. When?

> Now.

The sky shatters and the world ends. It's loud, horrible and terrifying.

The sound gets louder and louder and louder. It feels like it could go on forever.

Then:

Scene Twenty-Six: Another End, Another Beginning

The space is as natural as it's looked all play. The house lights up, maybe. The space lit like it's the real world.

Two people. One has a bag.

1   And it goes on forever. I wake up, eventually. I think. But on and on and on it goes. Like I'm Tanatalus or something.

2   Who?

1   That Greek guy who was doomed to stand in a pool of water with some fruit hanging over him.

2   What's so bad about that?

1   He couldn't move. And he was thirsty and starving. But, like, every time he tried to take a drink the water would go away from him. And the same with the fruit hanging over him. But he didn't die, he just went on like that forever. Like an endless nightmare.

2   Why they make him do that?

1   Dunno really. He upset a god? So the god decided he couldn't have nice things.

2   Oh I'm like that. My phone screen's a mess.

1   Right? That actually happens in this dream too. Well, nightmare. It's all just animals talking to humans. Working old jobs. Not knowing what to do with myself. All that. So used to it now I don't wake up sweating or anything like that. I just open my eyes and stare at the ceiling and honestly can't work out if I'm still dreaming or not.

2   That's intense.

1   Yeah. Sometimes hear voices from nowhere too. It's weird. Like someone is speaking to me when I'm asleep. You know? Doesn't make much sense.

2   Nothing does. Feel like we're stuck like that.

Nice to have you around though.

You at least make me feel a little unstuck.

They look at each other. Share a moment. Break each other's gaze.

2   Oh yeah look what I've got.

The one with the bag reaches inside and pulls out one shoe.

2   It's yours. You lost it when you were drunk. So. Here you go.

They take the shoe. Look at it. They look at the other.

2   What?

1   This. This is a bit weird.

2   Why?

1   Because I've –

This is how it ends.

They look at the shoe and close their eyes. Take a deep breath. Open them again.

The light now behaves as it did at the start.

1   It always ends with a shoe and me trying to explain it. So I do. I say:

I always have weird dreams.

They're circles. They go round and round. Which is a bit disorientating. Because you're like, oh we're back to the start again. I can't get free of it.

And gets me thinking about circles.

2   What about them?

1   Like, what is a circle? Really? A line forced round and back to where it started. A line eating itself. A line stuck, completely, hopelessly, up its own arse.

It's like, me, here, but if I bent over and shoved my head up my own bumhole. Me as a circle. And I'd be pretty depressed because of that.

And like I asked my friend once whether they dream in circles too. And they said they didn't used to, but as they got a bit older, they do.

I asked another friend and they said the same thing.

Then I asked them what they dreamt about.

And they said just weird stuff that comes back around again and again.

Like I do. You know?

2   Think so.

1   Yeah. But also – Like –

In these dreams I feel like me. But I'm not me. You know? I can see me, but I'm not me, physically, in the dream. I'm someone else. But I know it's me.

And the thing that scares me the most is: who's looking at me? Who's walking around my head, hiding in the folds of the skin of my brain, making me watch my own dreams?

And the landscapes. The fields and rivers and towns I visit in the space behind my closed eyes. It's the past. Forcing itself inside me. A past I don't belong to but a past that wants to belong to me so much that it makes everything a circle that I can't get out of.

2   How does it start?

1   It starts with me, but it's not me, but it is me, selling someone some crabs in a fish shop.

2   Ha. That's weird.

1   Yeah it starts quite fun. But always ends with a funeral and the sky shattering.

There's a very thin line between a dream and a nightmare. Like there's a very thin line between the past and the future.

Isn't there?

They are alone.

1   You've gone again.

We're back to the start. Always are. Round and round. I knew I was still asleep.

Black.

End.

End.

End. End. End. End. Etc., etc., etc.

(Circle Dreams Around) The Terrible Terrible Past

BY SIMON LONGMAN

Notes on rehearsal and staging, drawn from a workshop held at the National Theatre with the writer in October 2022, facilitated by director Matt Harrison.

How the writer came to write the play

'The past likes a circle. A circle is its favourite shape.'

Simon Longman explained that the play started from an earlier, pre-Covid, abandoned draft rooted completely in reality but now it's a kind of fantasy play with a nightmarish and dreamlike quality rooted completely in reality:

> The original pitch to Connections was to imagine if modern young people had to do old jobs that don't exist any more, water carrying, for example. That draft was abandoned because I quickly realised I couldn't make it work. It was too obvious. Too rooted in making a point. What that point was, I never worked out. But every scene felt the same. It was boring. It didn't feel alive. Time passed and I spent a lot of time thinking about being trapped. And dreams. Which opened up something. There are two kinds of dreams I have – first-person dreams or if I'm really anxious third-person (watching myself act out the dream). I'll ask myself: 'Who have I created who is looking at me in my own head?' 'Why am I looking at myself through a stranger's eyes?' I thought it would be fun to go back to the original idea, but look at it through this angle – a weird, deadpan world of dreams and nightmares, where the past was manipulating the present, subsequently affecting the future.
>
> Using dreams and nightmares as a way into the play meant that I could find the playfulness within it. Chickens falling out of the sky. Talking cows killing humans. It was now all up for grabs. Previously the play felt like a dirge – people kicking about, not knowing what to do. The juxtaposition of the strange/ mundane, reflecting dreams helped find the play's heart. That isn't to say this play is a story that needs to be told via clowning. The opposite. The more deadpan, the better. This version reflects the weird, sometimes unreal, reality of contemporary existence. Where everything is so violently in front of us. We can see everything, but feels like we've seen nothing sometimes. It's an anxious world. An uneasy world. A unempathetic world. And going through anxiety is an important part of being a teenager (realising that life has rhythms) but that, sadly, can become heightened to a point of being stuck: constantly watching yourself in a perpetual circle of 'what is going on?' The play explores that.

Why theatre?

Matt Harrison asked the group to respond to the following provocation: Why do we make theatre with young people? Responses include:

Live risk, provocation, interaction, exploration, community, democratic, creative thinking, inclusive, immediate, playful, shocking, hilarious, possibility, stories are important, identity, entertainment, aliveness, change, giving back, it's a microcosm, a journey, a utopia, for passion, collaboration, creating empathy, analysis, questioning, sparking debate, fostering generosity, speaking on taboo topics (a safe exploration), a place of freedom, for fun.

Initial responses to the play

In groups, participants held conversations about their initial responses to the play, splitting it up into the areas of discussion below, alongside which is a summary of the various responses.

Character

Lots of characters: shoe holder, candle maker, careers adviser, farmer, bagpipe player, the person whose funeral it is (Freddie), a fish, a cow, a chicken. There's a playful, creative, diverse range of characters which are each there for a reason.

Matt Harrison reflected that there are three strands to character work on the play: the cast's creative ownership of the characters, the importance of the ensemble to this piece and the solid moments you can cling onto – namely the returning characters and the animals.

Plot

Everyone (or someone) in the play is looking for meaning, understanding and a way out. Trying to find sense in it all in all the worlds. One participant noted that the play feels influenced by Carl Jung's approach to dream psychology and the concept of dreaming in metaphor.

There's a deadpan, distanced tone to the piece and trying to wake from this keeps the characters active.

The world of the piece

On earth, in shops and farmer's fields. Timeless? Both futuristic and like it's from the past. A world of hierarchy – parents, teachers, careers advisers with power over young people. A world in which young people are forced to conform in a *Black Mirror*-esque way. A mundane world (at the beginning) which becomes more violent; a world in which violence is normalised. Geographically places in this world seem to merge (as in dreams).

Matt added that it's a world where anything can happen, with anything being accepted in the world.

Significant moments

The first chicken moment. Mars exploding. The sky shattering. A chicken falling from sky. The confessional/confiding moments. The giant scissors moment (following a dream logic). The shark buying its own fin for its tea. The voice only moments. The fish-mongering scenes. The first scene and the last scene (the false ending). The first moment someone drags a dead body across the stage. The cow monologue. The apples.

Where is the climax? Is it the sky shattering or in a different area?

Matt added: there are so many arresting moments and images. The play follows a dream-like logic – with particular images which punch through so strongly and moments of real intimacy.

Objects or items (totemic objects)

Key objects include: apples, giant scissors, dead bodies, meat cleavers.

The group discussed the style of the production – could it be played as surreal or hyperreal by playing with scale (children's toys, giant objects)? Does everything have to be realistic? The group noted there are opportunities for clowning (problems to solve as an ensemble, e.g. an actor missing a shoe from the beginning, carrying a massive pair of scissors or fighting over a tiny object – the game of involving everyone).

Discussing the possibility of games and clowning, Matt reflected that the tone of those games will also affect the quality of danger in the space; i.e. if clowning games are pushed quite far the danger/stakes (something both Simon Longman and Matt Harrison noted as important for the dramatic function of the script) might be undermined.

What are the characters' responses to these objects? For example, a dead body being dragged across the space should be met with the same kind of response as idly watching a pigeon peck around on the street – like it doesn't matter any more. Have we all become so desensitised to the point of feeling numb?

Core themes

Dreams, circles, the past repeating itself, breaking cycles. Being forced into careers (roles and expectations forced upon young people). Decision making. Climate change, the environment. Loneliness.

Matt Harrison suggested there are overarching themes – colonialism and our relationship to the past and immediate themes – decisions faced by the characters, their reflection on the world left to them.

Dramaturgy and text analysis

Relationship to time and space

Identify the play's relationship to time and space. Does it consist of multiple times and spaces, multiple times but a single place, a single time and multiple spaces or a single time and a single space?

Identifying the flavours of the play

What are the different flavours within a play? Where are the moments of consistency that can ground a play? What are the moments that an audience can cling on to? What are the recurring formal moments?

The three hearts of the play

Every play has three hearts – the personal heart (how the piece speaks to you based on your background), the social heart (how the play speaks to society, how it speaks politically) and the global heart (speaking to something wider than the room or society, something global or bigger). What heart is your production speaking to (where does the emphasis lie), what excites you most?

Asking why

Why now? Why me? Why this group? Why is it important that this group tells this story? Why this space (architecturally)? Why does this audience need to hear the play?

The essence of the scene

Each scene in the play has a purpose. In the following exercise, the group explored how to boil this purpose down into both a sentence and a visual, physical representation of the shape and feeling of that scene through the prism of one object or prop.

Each group chose a moment in the play to represent and were given a set of materials to work with: tape, string, shoes, paper, pens and Blu Tack.

An example of a sentence capturing a scene: Scene Twelve (a voice scene) – concentrated down to a single line: 'a planet exploding'.

An example of a physical shape: Scene Twenty-Two (the characters find the dead fish which they earlier didn't give water to) – someone can become conscious of their actions.

This was concentrated down to 'a scene which is about the characters becoming aware of the consequences of their actions' and represented by throwing shoes into a pile.

An additional discovery from this exercise was a physical shape which could be used to represent any scene, especially one in which many characters interact with one another.

World of the play (Lyndsey Turner exercise)

Everyone used their phones to find an image inspired by the play, which they then took for a walk around the room, sharing with others and writing responses on big pieces of paper to the following questions:

- 'I loved the moment when/' Imagine you are thinking back on the production after press night (no budget limitations).

The audience forgot this was a play. There was some stillness to listen and feel everything landing. The floor of the whole theatre shook with the sound of the sky shattering. The stage was flooded with shooting stars. The fishmonger actually brought in real fish and the whole place stank.

- 'The play is like' (perhaps a sound, a texture, or a hybrid of two things).

Broken glass. A bowl of ramen. Groundhog day. Sleep paralysis. A Dalí painting. Black Mirror. *My childhood. Lots of people eating endless spaghetti from the same bowl. A dream inside a dream inside a dream inside a dream. Cosmic soup.*

- 'The project under the play is' – what are you aiming to achieve beyond staging the production successfully (linked to the three hearts exercise, e.g. a parent to say they are proud of their child)?

To develop co-creation in the rehearsal room and allow the young people to create and to inspire each other. Getting young people inspired by new writing. The moment they feel like true performers. To unlock joy. For the actors to know they aren't alone, the way they feel is okay, and the overwhelm and anxiousness is felt by us all – you're not alone.

- 'Key images from the play.'

Lots of black holes. A pair of feet in shoes. Empty spaces with the possibility that it will soon be filled. A head up its own arse. A shark fin. A galaxy/the universe. Many faces – fake happy.

The play works with opposites and if you can get those opposites (dark and vibrant with nothing in between) sitting together it will feel really exciting.

The voice/empty space scenes

Simon Longman talked through the inspiration and creative thinking behind the voice-only poetic sections. He noted that these scenes were unusual for theatre because a playwright is generally concerned with actions, whereas poetry is concerned with words and feelings. Both he and Matt Harrison discussed how the poetry scenes were quite abstract but that the audience would be happy to sit in that space, especially considering the scenes are quite short. Essentially, the poetic scenes are commenting on the action and drawing out the themes of the play. Simon Longman offered the analogy of walking between pictures in a gallery – you might take something from it, but then you move on. The audience are invited to stop, listen and contemplate; they are forced to engage with idleness.

One of the reasons for those scenes is to give the play moments to breathe, to experience emptiness and to experience language in a different way from in the scenes (perhaps also reflecting the flicker of your eyelids when asleep).

Staging empty space

Addressing the stage direction 'an empty space', Simon Longman suggested that this could be interpreted in many ways – It might suggest the absence of purpose, a number of people not looking at one person or anyone in the space, or not touching the floor, with the voice layer adding an edge to those ensemble shapes. He also encouraged the group to embrace the theatrical possibilities of total darkness and a voice talking to the audience. Matt Harrison opened up the questions of whether the voice scenes are clearly unified in style or whether they respond to what's just been happening in the play?

Both he and Simon Longman suggested involving the group in interpreting what these empty spaces mean for the production you are making.

Who is the voice?

Is it the voice of the person who is going to be in the proceeding scene? Is it the planet? Simon Longman advised that if you use only one voice the audience may ask 'is this a deity, the planet, a conscience?' but if you shift the voice that will alter that meaning. You can also go with what sounds cool. In the voice scenes, we glimpse the mechanism which keeps causing the circles to keep going and going and going.

Acting and character exercises

Provocations for character

Matt Harrison offered three additional provocations for directors to consider when working on character in rehearsals.

Where does the character lead from? The head (lost in thought), the chest (lost in feeling), the pelvis (lost in lust), the feet (not comfortable), the hands (need to be always doing something).

What point of time is the character most rooted in? Are they fixated with the past or the future or rooted in the present?

What choices does the character make under pressure? A definition of character from theatre-maker Ken Campbell is choices made under pressure: how a character responds to pressure reveals who they are.

Exercise: Vulnerability

Simon Longman offered a practical exercise on how we have vulnerable conversations (which characters in his plays are often attempting to have).

Start with two fists over your heart: open the fists when you are being vulnerable, keep them closed when you are being closed. As a practical exercise you can play with whether your fists are open or closed on your lines and whether one character is trying to open another's fists. For example, when the son reveals he is a vegetarian to the butcher he is trying to prise open his father's closed fists.

Exercise: 'You, me, the space'

Stick Post-it notes on either yourself, your partner or the space, responding to what you think the lines/thoughts relate to most pertinently, attaching each thought to a Post-it note. Matt Harrison explained that this exercise can be useful when scenes aren't working, primarily as a method of understanding what an actor's choices are throughout that scene.

He encouraged the group to consider where you choose to land the Post-it – forehead (about intellect/thinking), chest (the heart), arm (strength) – and with what physical quality (firm, gentle). Matt Harrison offered that you might also play the opposite; e.g. for a thought in which your character lashes out at a scene partner you could place the Post-it note on yourself (demonstrating the character's vulnerability).

He noted about checking in with your partner on physical boundaries, checking that they are comfortable with the action of the exercise (putting Post-it notes on your partner's body).

Exercise: Stakes using playing cards

Actors can play the lines as if they're easy at first pass, where we want to make things hard for the character – so that the actor has to play their objective harder to achieve what they want, increasing the stakes of the scene.

Pick a card from a card deck at random; play the scene with that level of intensity/stakes.

For this show it feels the text is built to serve playing low numbers externally (e.g. 2) but internally the stakes for the character are high (e.g. 9/10). If the stakes are high but contained, then the moments where they simmer out (or bubble over) and the true stakes are revealed, are impactful.

Matt Harrison reflected that this exercise brings out the power you have over the text – how playful can you be, where are the extremes you can push it to – which can help in encouraging the company to be bold. Once you feel the company is comfortable and free with the text, you can then encourage them to make more exact/precise choices. Simon Longman added that it's about getting the layers in, deepening it beyond these base layers.

Exercise: Cartoon strip boxes

This exercise can encourage the company to relate the material to their own life, invest in the play and have some 'skin in the game'.

First draw boxes on a page (cartoon strip style). Then read a section of text and relate it to a moment (in the form of an image) from your own life. Taking a couple of minutes and a chunk of text, fill your comic-book cells with images from your own life. Matt Harrison noted that participants shouldn't work with anything which would be too heavy for them (keeping the group safe in the work).

Each thought (image) should have a specific, defined form.

Below are Matt Harrison's examples of text excerpts and personal responses:

Text: 'walking through a field covered in stars'.

Remembering fires on Whitby beach drinking cheap booze with friends as a teenager.

'An animal with a broken leg looking pathetic.'

My daughter choking on the skin of a jacket potato.

Design and staging

Generating staging ideas

Matt Harrison ran a practical exercise in which a group of participants moved through the space with the rest of the group observing, looking out for moments that brought joy. The available actions were: walk, gate jump, greeting, follow/mimic.

He guided the group to play with pace and rhythm – pushing into the extremes of tempo (really quick, really slow), to bring in architecture – playing with the elements of the space (lines on the floor, empty chairs, walls, radiators).

The whole group then reflected on moments that they thought could work for the play:

- in transitions, with characters entering and exiting, playing with the quality of the next scene bursting through the current scene in a dreamlike logic.
- the contrast of energies/dynamics across the space (e.g. when the body is dragged across the space into a scene which is lighter). The experience as an audience member of your attention being split when there are two contrasting things happening at once.
- the dream logic of the focus shifting from one character to another.

It could be interesting to consider motif and endowment: if a dead chicken falls (a motif), people just ignore it until one person endows it with a higher status. Actors could endow scissors with danger, for example, too.

Ensemble staging

Matt Harrison opened up the question of whether or not the whole ensemble stays on for the duration of the play, considering that with a larger group there's a concern about giving people enough to do.

If they are on stage, are they connected to the action or not? How are you keeping them engaged? And what is the process of them stepping in? Is there a certain prop or sound or line that triggers them to step into the space or do they just decide for themselves? If a group is on stage they need to either have something they can focus on (which isn't sleeping!), such as drawing the dream job or writing out a dream, or something which can actively give something to the on-stage world.

Consider what they get from watching the play, how they change through watching the play. Perhaps there's a build in the number of people watching throughout the duration of the play? Or the opposite – a decline of the numbers on stage. Simon Longman added that in theatre you find the game, and play the game – as soon as the audience gets the game you change or develop the game.

He offered that the play is constantly being performed, it comes back round in spirals. So, could the company play at being bored? They might have the energy of: 'Who's playing this bit this time?' Not that they play boredom in the scene. Make it a game that they are so acutely aware of and bored of. This thing is for ever (an everlasting anxiety dream) and perhaps they are actively curating the story as they go through. Another option is that there is a world of other scenes that the group also play which we the audience don't happen to see.

The ensemble could facilitate the world-building of the props – becoming the props or facilitating the addition of props in the world. They could be actively building the next scenes location while the current scene plays out.

Question and answer with Simon Longman

Q: How might we approach the desensitised violence in the play (the blood and dead bodies)?
A: The violence in the play should hurt. It should, visually, feel brutal and visceral. We need to see the violence in the imagery: bodies being dragged across the floor should

look quite horrible, for example. However, the reaction to the violence should be unexpected. Images like a body being dragged through the space should be met with indifference. It's a shrug, not a scream. Imagine the experience of going through social media – everything is so viscerally, constantly in front of our eyes, but seen through the glass of a screen, it feels distant and removed. This is what the play is trying to capture with the violence: the people in the play feel so desensitised to the imagery, that it sort of doesn't affect them. The exception to this reaction is in the big scissors scene: here the violence literally hurts.

Q: What if the cast (or audience) get confused in the dream logic of the play?
A: The text is a map, this is why the images are so bold. In every scene someone is confused – a character says 'I don't know what's happening' and looks to the world for help, then realises that there's no help coming and that anything can happen. Start simple with the most basic version of the scene: two people standing talking about crabs.

Matt Harrison added that this play is about people saying words in space, affecting one another; and from there you can build and create a logic for the production (with the props, for example).

Q: How should we approach props?
A: The props that are mentioned explicitly within the script must be in the play, as they are needed to tell the story.

Q: Is the play for adults too?
A: Simon Longman shared his passion for making work about young people which also resonates with older people – offering them a chance to recognise what a younger person they know is experiencing. There is a playfulness about the play but also a seriousness to it – it's about anxieties, being lost, being stuck, making adults see that the world right now is a horrible place to be in, and so the play uses the aesthetics of horror to capture that.

Q: Can you share out the lines for the funeral?
A: Yes, it's up for grabs who says what in the funeral, reflecting the anonymity of funerals. You could bring a particular character back or have a fairly anonymous group.

Q: In general, can you interchange character numbers if you think a line would suit another character more?
A: Not with the characters that have more to do within the play. Number 2, for example, must remain the same person, and all their lines spoken by them. Other characters are the same: number 1, the chicken, the fish, the butcher etc. Basically, when a number appears in more than one scene, then you should have the same performer playing that role. This will keep the story consistent.

Q: What about doubling up with smaller casts?
A: As mentioned, for the key characters you should keep them with the same actor, but that's not to say you can't multi-role. Just make sure things are making as much sense as possible.

Q: As a writer are there any clear visuals in your head in terms of how you think it should look?

A: No. Simon's favourite thing about being a writer is about being open to what things will look like (e.g. the sky shattering). That's the fun of making stuff. Every single one of these productions is going to be different. The props and the moments that happen are there for the storytelling – they are the images the play needs to have (e.g. the chickens). The only thing that possibly has to be there is the house lights coming on at the end because that's the trick – but even there maybe not, maybe they threaten to come on but don't.

Q: Is it okay to have low-budget solutions to big moments such as when the sky shatters e.g. just using torches?

A: Absolutely, some of the coolest stuff is done on the smallest budgets. The budget of a production should not be a barrier. The low-budget aesthetic of a Forced Entertainment show, for example, is great because there's a theatricality to it. Theatre is the only medium where someone can walk on stage and say, 'I'm a chicken', and we believe they are a chicken.

With low-budget productions it's better to lean into that rather than try to disguise it; be creative with your solutions and own your choices!

Q: What are you looking forward to seeing?

A: How extraordinary moments can come from the ordinary. How these things are earned and not just an effect.

Q: Is there the possibility of changing some of the language (swear words)?

A: Simon never wants to alienate anyone in a theatre, but does want to challenge people. He don't mind it being changed but if you need to take it out change it to something with that same intensity. The only swear word that's important is Mars saying 'fuck this' because Simon just quite likes it. There's a humour to swearing, too. Not everything has to be . . . so cold, especially with 'bad' language. Everything on stage has artistic meaning. For example, the justification for saying 'boner' is that the characters aren't mature enough to work out what's going on – there's a humour to that which is important.

If it's a safeguarding issue (in terms of what students are comfortable with saying in front of their audience) then you should sound that out with the cast.

For all our society's faults, the British sense of humour is funny because we can't take anything seriously. What Simon has always been interested in is what happens when the jokes run out. When you can't seem to make jokes about your situation and the anxiety that you were using humour to try and hide seeps out. Then we kind of have to talk openly about how we feel: our anxieties; our vulnerabilities.

Q: With the motif of children playing adults, where is the line here in terms of whether they are an adult or a child?

A: Just play it really straight, trust the text and the idea is that they are just themselves – you don't need to do much more than that. You don't need to do 'old people voices' or try and pretend you are an older character.

Q: Are the people playing the adults different people?
A: They are, perhaps, who they fear they are going to become. The impact is contained in the older roles being played by younger actors to capture this fear.

Q: Can you use British Sign Language for the empty stage scenes (when working with a group of students who are D/deaf).
A: Yes, that sounds great and you could use BSL in more scenes too. Don't take 'empty stage' literally! You can project the words too.

Q: Any tips for first-time directors?
A: Trust the group. Your role as director is to make the play fit the group. Don't feel that you need to fix everything, don't be afraid to ask the group questions. Trust the text. What is the heart of the scene? What can you do to the scene to make it as clear as possible? Trust the process – you will get there!

Closing notes

Matt Harrison closed with a quote from theatre-maker Ken Campbell: 'theatre should be as exciting as wrestling'. It's rare that you read a play that is as exciting as wrestling – this one could be.

From a workshop led by Matt Harrison, along with workshop
assistant Macadie Amoroso
Notes by Nathan Crossan-Smith

Innocent Creatures

by Leo Butler

Leo Butler is an award-winning playwright. His plays have been produced by many of the UK's most important theatres, including National Theatre, Royal Court, Almeida, Birmingham Rep and Royal Shakespeare Company.

He has written many celebrated plays about young people, including *Made of Stone* and *Redundant* at the Royal Court; *Boy* at the Almeida; and *Decades* for Brit School/ Bridge Theatre Company.

He has written historical plays such as *I'll Be the Devil* for the RSC, and contemporary dramas such as *Lucky Dog* and *Faces in the Crowd* at the Royal Court and *The Early Bird* at the Queen's Theatre, Belfast.

He has also adapted classics like *Woyzeck* at the Birmingham Rep, pantomimes and comedies such as *Cinderella* at the Theatre Royal Stratford East and *All You Need Is LSD* at the Birmingham Rep, and musicals such as *Alison! A Rock Opera* for the Royal Court/King's Head.

For ten years, Leo Butler was Writing Tutor at the Royal Court Theatre and helped nurture a new generation of playwriting talent.

Characters

Enid
Mia
Ben
Kate
Archie
G3
G4
G7
B1
B2
B4
B9

Setting

Sometime in the future – flood waters, a hotel, a rainforest, a bedroom.

Scene One: The Flood Waters

Flood waters, close to the city.

A dozen ice floes moving slowly across the flood water.

Mia *is sitting on the biggest ice floe.*

Enid *is standing on a neighbouring ice floe. She is wrapped in thick clothes and has a rucksack on her back. She carries a hamster cage in one hand and a mobile device in the other.*

Enid   Hi.

Pause.

Hi.

Mia   Oh, hi.

Enid   Hi, yeah, is this the way to Ice Floe 226? My flood-mapper told me to turn left at Big Ben.

Mia   Big Ben's sunk.

Enid   What?

Mia   Big Ben's sunk already, your flood-mapper's old.

Enid (*can't hear her*)   What?

Mia   I said your flood-mapper's ancient.

Enid   No, I only updated it last night.

Mia   Yeah, and Big Ben went under two weeks ago. There's a pack of elephant seals living on top of the spire if you look.

Enid   The elephant seals that just tried to charge me?

Mia   Were they sitting on top of a spire?

Enid   I don't know, I didn't stop to look. They looked pretty cross.

Mia   Then you need to change your app. Try mine, it's the very latest.

Enid   I thought everyone uses flood-mapper don't they? My mum swears by it –

Mia   Well, your mum's wrong then isn't she? I use flood-mapper plus, it's much more reliable. You're looking for Ice Floe 226? This is 226.

Mia *crosses onto* **Enid**'s *ice floe.*

Mia   Don't worry, I won't bite. Are you here for the rescue party?

Enid   Just me and my hamster, yeah. I'm Enid.

Mia   Hi, yeah, I'm Mia. I hate my name.

Enid   Mia's an exceptional name.

Mia   Arr, do you think so?

Enid   It's loads better than Enid. Enid makes me sound like an old woman. I hope I never get old.

Mia   You're nothing like an old woman, you're really pretty.

She takes her phone out and takes **Enid**'*s picture – the phone beeps.*

She checks the screen.

Mia   Says here you're thirteen. Your name's Enid Potter and you're the youngest of three. You're up to date with your vaccinations and you live in Beckenham with your mum.

Enid   Thanks, yeah –

Mia   I've never been to Beckenham. Do you get floods or earthquakes in Beckenham?

Enid   Typhoons mainly. The water's sludgier than here. It's beautiful in the morning when the steam travels down from the Arctic. More fish.

Mia   Real fish?

Enid   Pike I think. Three-headed sticklebacks. They swim in through the downstairs windows. My mum likes to catch them with her skirt pulled up at the top of the stairs.

Mia   Now you're just making me hungry.

Enid   Can I take your picture?

Mia   No.

Enid   If I give you some mushroom soup can I take your picture?

Enid *removes a tin of mushroom soup from her knapsack.*

Enid   It's Heinz, look, cream of mushroom. We get all sorts of tinned goods in Beckenham. Go on, don't be shy –

Mia   I'm not photogenic like you.

Enid   Yeah, but I let you take my picture just now.

Mia   You should ask one of them. There's a bunch of them trapped on the glacier over there. Squint and you'll see them. Over there, by Nelson's Column?

Enid   The penguins?

Mia   They look like penguins, they're actually toddlers. Their mothers dropped them off earlier but the ice below them cracked. Now they're trapped. When the wind blows south you can hear them crying I think.

Enid   Shouldn't we try and help? We could take my canoe and try to catch them as they drop.

Mia   Would you risk your own life?

Enid   Yeah, no –

Mia   What about your hamster's life?

Beat.

Enid   I don't really like toddlers.

Mia   Yeah, me too. Toddlers make me want to puke.

Enid   Yeah, me too.

Mia   I'm sure they won't get left behind. Robots pity toddlers. They don't take up room in the helicopters and they're really easy to please. Besides, I'd rather be alone with my thoughts.

Enid   Oh, okay then . . . –

Mia   No, I don't mean it like that, I didn't mean you have to go. Please –

Mia *budges to her left, pats the ground.*

Mia   There's plenty of room for us both, look. It's my grandma's shawl, she's really broad-shouldered.

Enid   Where's your grandma now?

Mia   I don't know, drowned at the bottom of the ocean I think.

Enid   Exterminated?

Mia   Exterminated probably, yeah.

Enid   My dad was exterminated last year. Him and all the other men in our district. They were shot in the back of the head, it was painless I think. We had a massive party afterwards.

Mia   Are they lying at the bottom of the ocean now?

Enid   Buried in the ground. It's good for the soil apparently. The worms eat the bodies and then they poo them out as fertiliser.

Mia   That's good then.

Enid   It is good, yeah, for the saplings.

Mia   I miss men.

Enid   Yeah.

Mia   I miss their beards.

Enid   Hairy legs.

Mia   Hairy everything, yeah. I don't expect we'll live in a world with men again.

Beat, then –

They giggle.

Mia   I heard they keep it. The Robots, I mean.

Enid   The hair?

Mia   Oh yeah – Hair, the eyelashes, everything.

Enid   No! What do they keep it for?

Mia   Apparently they bundle it in a big ball for recycling. Soft furnishings or pillows or something.

Enid   I'm not sure worms can swallow hair. I know moths can definitely.

Mia   Moths are gross. They look like Dracula with their stupid capes.

Enid   I once killed a moth and it turned out to be an android. Its hard-drive went all over the wall, my mum went mad.

Mia   You're funny.

Enid   Thanks. Do you think they'll have moths where we're going? Real ones, I mean.

Mia   Depends where we're going.

Enid   The email said 6.15. What time is it now?

She shows **Mia** *the email on her phone.*

Enid   Arrive by 6.15 it said, it says so here. Helicopters at 7. Check-in at the hotel by 8. Hey, I hope they put us in the same room! A big room with a view where you can see into other people's rooms. And if they don't, you know what I'm going to do? I'm going to ask them nicely when we get there.

Mia   Do you think Robots understand nice?

Enid   We could try and make them understand.

Mia   They're so much cleverer than us though. I'm not sure Robots know the difference between good or bad or anything. They're like brains on a stick.

Enid   If they weren't nice then they wouldn't send us an email.

Mia   Well, emails have minds of their own.

Enid   Everything has a mind of its own. That glacier has a mind of its own. My hamster.

Mia   Just because something has a mind doesn't mean it has a conscience.

Enid (*gasps*)   You're mean.

Mia   No I'm not.

Enid   Yes you are, you're so mean though, meanie.

She reaches into the hamster cage and takes out the hamster, stroking it/tickling its cheeks.

Cover your ears, Sniffles, don't listen to her.

Mia   He's just a hamster.

Enid   He's not just a hamster, he's Sniffles. Sniffles McSniffleton.

Mia   Hello, Sniffles McSniffleton.

Enid   He's got his own scarf. He's got his own little suitcase, look.

Mia *giggles.*

Enid   What?

Mia   You're weird.

Enid   I'm fine being weird. We're both weird, that's what makes him so human. He's complex, he's a good listener, and he knows the difference between right and wrong.

Mia   Aren't hamsters extinct?

Enid   Your precious elephant seals aren't extinct.

Mia   Elephant seals are solar-powered. Penguins have USB ports. Have you seen the touch screen on an Alsation lately?

Enid   Touch screens are obsolete, even he knows that.

Mia   How do you know they won't take him away?

Enid   What?

Mia   This 'real' pet of yours. How do you know they won't exterminate him?

Enid   Duh. Because Robots don't exterminate innocent creatures.

Mia   They exterminated your dad.

Enid   That's different. Sniffles isn't a threat.

Mia   Try telling that to a carrot.

Enid   Robots aren't programmed like that, they don't just wipe out anyone.

Mia   They're considerate?

Enid   They're logical. Human beings are a virus, look what they've done.

Mia   I heard they're rounding up the mums and injecting them with Ebola.

Enid   Well, they're only following orders. It was our own great-grandparents who built them, we all have our part to play.

Mia   Aren't you scared they might inject you with Ebola?

Enid   No. You do what you have to survive, that's what it says in the manual.

Mia   Stupid manual.

Enid   You have to be prepared to make the ultimate sacrifice because this is the only world we've got. Everything has a function these days.

Mia   Aren't you angry even ever? I get so angry I could break my own neck.

Enid   I don't get angry, I get fizzy sometimes. Fizzy Enid, that's my nickname.

Mia *grabs the hamster.*

Enid   Mia!

Mia *smashes the hamster on the ice.*

Enid   Don't do that, hey!

Mia *smashes the hamster on the ice.*

Enid   No, please, leave him alone. Sniffles!

Mia *repeatedly smashes the hamster on the ice – it sparks and crackles – until it breaks.*

Pause.

Mia *hands the hamster to* **Enid** *– smoke comes off it.*

Enid *opens the hamster, pulling out its hard drive and cables.*

She starts to cry.

Mia   It's alright, I get it. It's good to cry I think. I cry all the time. Sometimes for no reason.

Pause.

Sorry. I can't help myself sometimes. It's nothing personal.

Pause.

Enid, please . . . –

Enid   Shut up, go away. Get your filthy hands off me.

Mia   You could try kissing him?

Enid   What?

Mia   Try kissing him better, look. You know like in the stories?

Mia *takes the hamster and kisses him on the head, but –*

Enid   I'm not a kid.

She grabs the broken hamster back. Still crying, she nurses it.

It's just a defect anyway. He was full of blood and guts this morning. You defected him when I wasn't looking.

Mia   You're just lonely I think.

Enid   No, keep your trap shut.

Mia   Well, you look a bit lonely from here. Don't you ever miss your brothers and sisters?

Enid   Why would I miss them? They're waiting for me at the hotel.

Mia   I'm not sure there even is a hotel.

Enid   No . . . –

Mia   Have you ever seen this hotel? Is it like Hogwarts?

Enid   No, it's common knowledge. You don't have to see something to know it's there.

Mia   The Almighty Blob.

Enid   Who?

Mia   Up in the sky, the Almighty Blob. People used to think he'd come down and rescue them from the gas chambers and they couldn't see him either.

Enid   Now you're just being deliberately obtuse.

Mia   And what if I told you this wasn't Ice Floe 226? What if I told you it's 6.45 and the helicopters left half an hour ago and that you're stuck here with me?

Enid   Then I'll message them. I'll message them on my phone and they'll fly back for us.

Mia   Fly back?

Enid   They have our microchips, they'll come and rescue us, it's common knowledge.

Mia   Oh . . . –

Enid   Facial recognition. They're probably zooming into your face from the satellites right now, Mia whatever-your-name is –

She tries to take a picture of **Mia** *– the phone makes a weird crackling noise.*

Enid *hits/shakes the phone.*

She tries again to take a picture of **Mia** *– the phone makes a weird crackling noise, as . . .*

Mia *pulls off her scarf, revealing a large scar on her neck.*

Mia   Sorry.

Enid   My mum warned me about people like you.

Mia   My mum warned me about people like me too. I don't blame them – the mums, I mean – they're from a different generation. Must be why they're drowned and take their babies. Everyone's better off.

Beat.

Hit a nerve, sorry –

Enid   You're illegal, shut up.

Mia   You know I could cut out yours too if you'd like?

Enid   Cut mine out?

Mia   Your tracker, I can disable it. Stop you being lonely.

Enid   Who said I'm lonely? – You're cold and illegal, pull your scarf up.

Mia   My gran used to work at the hospital and she's good with a knife. Quick slice and it popped out like a fine-cut diamond it did. When the Bluetooth wore off I felt light as a feather, the Robots don't even know you exist. Stupid plastic chip beeping and sharing your location all the time. No one knows you, you can go anywhere you want, you've got a cool scar. How about it, eh? I've seen things you wouldn't believe.

She removes a knife from her belt.

You could stay and see things with me.

Enid   No . . . –

Mia   We can run and stamp and skid until the ice breaks. We can teach the toddlers to dream without their data being screened.

Enid   I don't want to teach anyone, I'm not qualified.

Mia   I saw you coming. She's got a nice face I thought. She could be my sister I thought. Scar Sisters, that could be our nickname.

Enid   Sniffle Sisters. I'm still mad at you remember.

Mia   Okay then, Sniffle Sisters it is.

She stands and moves across to **Enid**, *who has her back turned to her.*

Pause.

Mia   Squeak squeak.

Pause.

Squeak squeak, Enid . . . –

She takes her knife and aims for **Enid**'s *neck (her microchip).*

Mia   Squeak –

Enid *turns and knocks* **Mia**'s *knife out of her hand.*

Enid (*as she does so*)   I told you to pull your scarf up, stupid! Why'd you have to be so stupid?!

Mia   I don't know, because I'm scared?

The sound of approaching helicopters.

Mia   Look, I've heard what they'll do to us out there, Enid, please. If we stay here then we can die on the ice like real girls. Be a real girl before they remove it all.

Enid   Remove what all? What are you talking about?

Mia   Here, stamp on the ice with me, look.

Mia *starts stamping on the ice.*

Mia   Don't let them see you! Stamp with me, it's fun! Stamp your feet, come on!

The ice starts to crack and **Enid** *runs away from* **Mia***, heading to the helicopters.*

Mia   No, wait! Enid, don't!

The sound of the helicopters gets very loud, casting their shadow over **Mia** *stamping on the ice.*

Scene Two: The Holiday Inn

A.

The sound of the helicopters continues, as –

All the **Kids** *march in wearing pyjamas/uniforms. They each hold a pillow.*

A whistle blows – FFFFRRRRRRRRRR! – the **Kids** *turn, stand in line, clutching onto their pillows.*

The sound of the helicopters stops abruptly, and a large neon sign – 'HOLIDAY INN' – lights up and looms over the following.

A second whistle blows – FFFFFFRRRRRR! – and . . .

The **Kids** *start having a pillow fight – screaming and shouting and laughing – chasing and hitting each other.*

A third whistle blows – FFFFRRRRRRRR! – and . . .

B.

The **Kids***, in their pyjamas, are peppered about their hotel rooms – sitting on the floor, sat by the window, sitting up in bed, pacing.*

B1   I'm good yeah, great.

G3   Settling in.

B1   Really happy.

B2   Really happy here, yeah. The rooms.

G3 The rooms. So much bigger than I was expecting.

B1 Wow. I mean, actually wow –

B2 My bed's massive, I didn't expect to get a double room to myself.

G3 The pillows and the quilts. The en suite bathroom with a walk-in shower.

B1 Power shower, yeah. The softest, cleanest toilet roll.

B2 I clap my hands and the lights turn on. I clap my hands –

G3 – and the lights turn off and on.

B1 No one telling me when to go to bed. No homework or exams.

B2 Stay up all night. A million different TV shows –

B1 A million different songs and playlists to choose from. Parties every night –

G3 Every day's a party. Room service brings me McDonald's anytime I want –

B2 KFC. McDonald's. Strawberry Laces –

B1 Room service bring me vapes and weed.

G3 It's the business, man. Chocolates, sweets and cake anytime –

B2 Anytime I want, so like thank you.

B1 Thank you.

B2 Thank you, yeah?

G3/B2 Thank you.

B2 No more blood and piles of corpses.

B1 No more icebergs or toddlers. I feel safe now.

G3 Warm –

B2 Yeah, safe and warm.

B1 Healthy, clean –

B2 Clean, yeah, I can breathe.

G3 The air-con's great. No more parents.

B1 The air-con's the best.

The whistle blows – FFFFFFFRRRRRRRR!

*The **Kids** leap up and start another pillow fight.*

*This time, the **Kids** divide themselves into two separate groups/gangs, attacking each other, then –*

The whistle blows – FFFFFFRRRRRRRR! – and . . .

C.

The **Kids** *are sat on their pillows on the floor; they are each wearing virtual reality helmets.*

G3   And the games.

G4   The drama.

B1   The games, yeah, brilliant. The apps and updates. Millions of choices –

B2   Millions of clips.

G3   Clips and reels. Anything you want –.

B1   Rihanna in the nude, Zendaya in the nude.

G4   Good to be busy. Good to be listened to.

G3   I can sit here for hours. Hours, days and weeks –

B2   And I'm jumping into my racing car, turn the key in the ignition –

B1   Good to be taken serious for once.

B2   Formula One, vrrrooooom. Monte Carlo, vrrooooom.

G4   Everything, yeah, it's like the best series ever and I'm still on season one. You can reach out and touch the actors, look. Here's Florence Pugh and Timothée Chalomet – oh, such soft curls, Tim.

B1   Me and Ariana Grande in the nude.

G3   All the tiny ponies with their magical horns.

B2   And I'm in my McLaren. Lewis Hamilton to my left, Dwayne Johnson to my right. And, look! There's Jesus Christ up ahead in his Ferrari.

G4   Fizzy, Flicker and Fuzz. They each have a stable and they all need proper grooming.

G3   Season Eight's going to be unreal. Season Fifty's going to be the bomb.

B2   The crowd going wild as I overtake Mufasa. Mufasa's crashed into Simba, and I'm head-to-head with –

B1   Dua Lipa, boy, she is all over me.

G3   And there's prequels and sequels and spin offs.

B2   Pack of zombies coming at me now. I pull over, kick open the door –

G4   And for every sugar lump I get ten gold hearts. Twenty gold hearts, and I unlock another pony. Thirty gold hearts –

B2   – And I torch the motherfuckers with my flamethrower!

B2 *jumps to their feet, torching zombies with his imaginary flamethrower –*
BLLLLAAAAASSSST! – and . . .

D.

Some of the **Kids***, in their pyjamas, are laid out on hospital beds, with wires attached to their temples.*

Silence, just the beep and low-level buzz of medical equipment. Then –

B1   It's fun though innit.

Pause.

Don't you think it's fun here though? Hello?

Pause. No response.

I mean . . . I mean, yeah, it's fun still I think. We never had fun like this at home –

BUZZZZZZZ! – Electric shock through **B1***'s temples.*

B1   Sorry, no, I didn't mean home. I meant my where I was before wherever that was. My mum and dad, they'd never . . . . –

BUZZZZZZ! – Electric shock through **B1***'s temples.*

B1   The people I was with before. Whoever.

Pause.

B1   Whoever, yeah, probably no one. I mean –

G3   Shut up, it doesn't matter anymore.

B1   What?

G3   I said shut up – be quiet will you?

G4   The important thing is the ponies –

G3   The ponies, yes, think about the ponies.

G4   Forty gold hearts, fifty gold hearts –

B1   I don't know, my head's not making sense, I need to talk to someone. My dad, he's still out there I think –

BUUUUUUUUZZZZ! – Electric shock through **B1***'s temples.*

B1   Oh God, why do they have to turn it up so high?

B1 *grabs/rubs his head.*

B1   I'm all inside out or something. Whoever, yeah, forget I said anything, I'll be a good boy, yeah? You know, if you could just let me back out there for a bit? (*Makes to sit up, get out of bed.*) If you could just let me outside? If I can find him. My dad, I mean. I'll find him and come straight back. He's all alone and he's literally no harm to anyone. He could sleep on my floor –

The other **Kids** *jump up and – shouting and screaming – violently attack* **B1** *with their pillows, until –*

The whistle blows – FFFFFFRRRRRRR! – and . . .

E.

The **Kids** *start singing, and, as they do so, pull* **B1** *to his knees, surrounding him.*

Kids (*sing*)
All things bright and beautiful, all creatures great and small
All things wise and wonderful, the Hard Drive made them all!

As the **Kids** *sing, one or more of them take a scalpel and gouge out* **B1**'s *eyes.*

Kids (*sing*)
Each little flower that opens, each little bird that sings
He made their glowing colours, and made their tiny wings.

As they sing, the **Kids** *plug shiny new eyes/implants into* **B1**'s *eye sockets.*

Kids (*sing*)
All things bright and beautiful, the Hard Drive made them all.
He gave us eyes to see them, –

The **Kids** *pull* **B1** *into the line as they sing. All the* **Kids** *have shiny new eyes/implants.*

Kids (*sing*)
and lips that we might tell
How great is the –

B1   – the graphics though, they're awesome.

G3   Season ten's awesome.

B1   I mean, the helmets were good. But these implants –

B2   The helmets were crap. Too heavy, too much weight. Now you've got full resolution. Now you can –

B4   Get to Level 4 and a whole new world opens up. Another universe with its own set of platforms and physical laws. I take one small step and I –

F.

B4 *is alone, in front of his bathroom mirror.*

B4   – move in front of the bathroom mirror. Looking good I think. Swipe and a tap – I'm all in red like Spiderman and I look like my dad –

BUZZZZZZZZZ! – an electrical charge in **B4**'s *head.*

B4   No, a real man. I look like a real man and I'm shredded – the muscles, the abs on me, look. Scroll and select and I'm Black, now I'm white, now I'm somewhere in between. Long hair, short hair, curls – tap tap tap. I'm a girl – here I am, look. Pretty young girl in the Congo. Through the Congo to the Northern Lights and now I'm knelt by the Pyramids of Giza. I leap up off the Eiffel Tower and crash-land in Peru.

Scale the mountains of Afghanistan, and here at the summit – oh look, here's Mickey! Hello Mickey! It's Disneyland Florida and I swipe and I tap – Joan of Arc burning at the stake. Swipe and I tap – it's the 1986 World Cup and I grab Maradona's hand through the old wooden wardrobe into Narnia. Will we defeat the White Witch? There's Maradona and Cantona and me, and we've got the One Ring on the edge of Mount Doom. We're the Avengers here to help E.T. phone home. Winning wars, killing everyone and I've got my epic army and – damn, it's so good to be alone. Why, Aunty Em, it's so good to be alone. Bathroom mirror, reaching out –

Flashing lights, strobes and alarm sounds – WOOOOOOOOHH! WOOOOOOOOOOH! WHOOOOOOOOOO! WHOOOOOOOOOOOOOOOO!

G.

Some of the **Kids***, in pyjamas, are strapped down on hospital beds.*

Long pause.

B2   Hairs on my legs, voice is cracking.

B3   Cracking up more like. Hairs in all the wrong places, feel like a monkey –

G4   I'm going to kill someone, shut up.

B3   What?

Pause.

Sorry, what? Did you say something to me?

G4   I said I'm going to kill you if you interrupt me again. I'll break out these straps and throttle you both.

B2   Time of the month, pay no attention.

B3   Time of the month's forbidden, mate.

B2   Yeah, and that's why she's down here for surgery. They strap her down and the machines remove her tubes. Why are you here?

B3   Shave these hairs off finally. Why are you here?

B2   Same I think, I'm not sure. Are you scared?

B3   Shut up, they'll hear you.

B2   Maybe we'd be better off if she throttled us. Maybe I should wriggle out these straps and give her a wet sloppy kiss.

B3   Like she'd ever look twice at you. Call that thing on your lip a moustache?

B2   At least my balls have dropped, mate.

B3   Oh my God, you're such a liar. Everyone knows they're amputated.

B2   Yeah, and they'll be coming for yours next. That's why the Machines strapped you down. No more dangly bits, it's the law. Just you wait when they come clanking through that door –

G4   Alright, just shut up please! My stomach hurts, my back, I'll . . . punch and scream and rip the two of you to pieces if you don't . . . –

Flashing lights and alarm sounds – WOOOOOOOOHH! WOOOOOOH!

Pause.

G4   That time again. Every month, like clockwork. Blood coming out. Running down my thighs, my legs, it won't stop –

The lights go out – plunged into darkness.

The sound of violent machinery (like an MRI machine) – BUZZZZZZZZZZZ! BANG! BANG! BUZZZZZZZ! BANG! BANG! BANG! – then . . .

H.

G4 *– in her pyjamas, on the hospital bed – is alone. The straps have gone.*

Just the beeps and low-level buzzing.

She wakes.

She looks around her surroundings.

The sound of approaching helicopters.

Pause.

She sees and takes the discarded scalpel from the side of the bed (or off the floor).

She rolls up one of her pyjama sleeves.

Pause as she braces herself.

She slashes her arms and wrists with the scalpel, but –

No blood comes out, no pain.

Pause – the sound of helicopters getting very loud, making the lights flicker, as –

G4 *puts the scalpel down and sticks her hands in the scalpel wounds, opening them up.*

She rummages inside her arm and pulls a bundle of wires and cables out of her arm, then –

I.

Enid *– in her clothes from the first scene – is strapped to a chair, with a hood over her head.*

She has a name-tag pinned to the hood.

She clutches onto her mechanised hamster.

G4 *– in her pyjamas – sits on the edge of her hospital bed. She is potting a plant in a large pot.*

G4   How did you get here? Helicopter?

Pause.

I like your hamster. Can I stroke it?

Enid *clutches tightly onto the hamster.*

G4   No, no, don't worry, we've got equipment here could fix it. Get his little paws and whiskers working again. Bet you'd like that, eh, Enid?

Pause.

Sounds like a grandmother – Enid. Were you saved or were you captured?

Pause.

Same thing I guess. Either way, you'd do well to put all that behind you. The past, I mean – family and friends whoever, they don't like that. Better to just crack on really. Soon forget about the past once they've finished with you. I'm going to turn sixty in a few days' time. The kid in the room next door to me turned a hundred and eighty last week, doesn't look a day over thirteen. Reckon we'll be here for another half a century before it's safe to go outdoors again. All the giant tubes sucking up the flood water. All the bodies on the ocean floor. Better to just knuckle down. Knuckle down and make the most of your home entertainment package. It's work that'll set you free. I'm planting trees this week, look. Room service brings me the acorns – all the little saplings. Oak, sycamore and ash. One day they'll be as big as anything.

Pause.

Are you crying?

Pause.

Funny, I haven't cried in years I don't think. Do you mind if I watch?

Scene Three: The Rainforest

Decades later.

A clearing in a beautiful rainforest.

Night.

Burning torches, wedged into the ground, illuminate the space.

G7 *and* **Ben** *are sitting by a small bonfire.*

G7 *is a lot grubbier/dirtier than* **Ben***, an outsider. She has a knapsack on the ground close by.*

They are drinking coconut milk from real coconut shells.

Archie *and* **Kate** *–* **Ben***'s friends – are also sitting by the small bonfire, drinking coconut milk.*

A rustic bowl of luscious green leaves is at hand for them all.

G7   I've never seen anything like it. The stars, I mean.

Ben   Told you didn't I? Best spot in the whole forest is this. You can actually see for miles.

G7   It's beautiful, yeah. Is it always like this? The moon looking down over the trees.

Ben   Nah, not all the time. In the daytime we get bright blue skies and the sun. It's the same as the moon but yellow and hot.

G7   Oh, wow, okay –

Ben   Been this way for a hundred years or more. The sun in the day, the moon at night. Stars and everything, then dawn again.

G7   Sort of back and forth then.

Ben   Back and forth sort of, yeah. Puts a smile on your face.

Ben *holds* **G7***'s hand.*

Pause.

Ben   You alright?

G7   Yeah, no –

Ben   Course you're alright. Me to look after you.

G7   I'm actually a bit scared.

Ben   That's probably just the excitement. Adrenalin, you know. First night away from home.

G7   Yeah I guess.

Ben   To be honest I didn't think there was a soul living inside those caves until today.

G7   I didn't even know anything existed outside them either.

Ben   Good job I found you then isn't it?

G7   Yeah –

Ben   Can't spend your whole life in a dark, stinking cave.

G7   It's not all bad. We've got plenty of storage.

Ben   Storage?

G7   Shelves and cupboards an' that. You'd be surprised how many shelves you can fit along the walls.

Ben   Pfft. Who needs shelves when you've got all this? The streams and rivers. Treetops stretching out for miles.

Archie   Oak, sycamore, ash. The giant redwoods.

Ben   Yeah, man, the giant redwoods teeming with monkeys, look. (*To* **G7**.) See? Archie'll tell you, he's like . . . King of the forest or something.

Kate   Well, I wouldn't go that far –

Archie *slaps* **Kate** *on the wrist,* **Kate** *laughs.*

Archie   If he says I'm King of the Forest I'm King of the Forest.

Kate   I reckon you've been smoking too many cocoa leaves, mate. There's only one King of the Forest and he's eight foot long with stripes and pointy teeth.

Archie   Who, mangy old Tiddles? He's an overfed pussycat.

Kate   I'd like to hear you say that if he prowled up behind you. You'd piss your knickers, mate.

Archie   I would not –

Kate (*to* **G7**)   He would, he pisses himself at anything. Horses, bears, trap-door spiders. We had an earwig crawl inside our tee-pee the other night – he was hiding under the blankets like the world had folded in on itself.

Archie   An earwig is a dangerous animal, Kate. They'll burrow into your ears and take a bite out of your hard drive, everyone knows that, it's common knowledge –

A roar/growl of a tiger from within the forest.

They stop what they're doing – **G7** *grabs onto* **Ben***,* **Archie** *grabs onto* **Kate***.*

Pause, then –

Ben *and* **Kate** *start laughing.* **G7** *joins in the laughter, self-consciously.*

Kate (*laughing, to* **G7**)   See what I mean?

Archie   Arr shut up, I'm protecting you aren't I?

Kate (*laughing*)   Mate, you're flesh! You're a closet homo sapien!

Archie   Ha ha, hilarious, yeah – (*To* **G7**.) I don't know what you're laughing at, cave-girl.

Ben   Oi, don't get cocky. Poor thing's never once heard a tiger growl before tonight have you, babe?

G7   I heard tigers used to be extinct.

Ben   Well, whoever told you that needs their head examined. This forest's got tigers streaming out its arsehole if the truth be told. All mouth, no trousers – you pay no attention, here –

He picks up a bowl of leaves and fruit.

Plenty more leaves if you want them, look. Bay leaves, beetroot, lettuce.

G7   Thanks, they don't agree with me.

Ben   How about some fruit? Mangoes, bananas. There's passion fruit, look. Cherries? We get all kinds of cherries growing round here, it's a living cherry paradise.

G7   Don't you have anything hot?

Ben   Hot?

G7   Cooked I mean.

Ben   Oh, 'cooked' – you mean sticking it over the fire?

G7   Yeah, I guess. Like actual meat?

They stare in disbelief.

No, I dunno. Just rats and mice or something.

Kate   Rats or mice, are you sick? Who'd want to eat an innocent creature when we've got all these luscious green leaves to choose from?

Archie   Rats and mice! I mean – (*he pretends to stick his fingers down his throat*) – uuuuuurghhh! What planet are you from?

Ben   'Ey alright, she's our guest, remember? If it's hot food she wants, then hot food she shall get. Tell you what, how about I get Enid to heat up some of our lovely mushroom soup for you? (*Calls.*) Hey, Enid!

Archie (*calls*)   Eniiiiiiid, get your arse out here, we're hungry!

Enid *enters from the undergrowth, carrying (with some difficulty) a large pot of soup.*

She wears the same clothes from before, plus an apron.

Enid   Oh, hi.

G7   Hi, yeah, / I'm . . . –

Ben   / Hi, yeah, get the soup on, she hasn't eaten all day.

Over the following, **Enid** *places the pot on the fire. She adds wild mushrooms to it and stirs.*

Ben (*to* **G7**)   You'll have to excuse our chef, she's a bit . . . you know? Tends to keep herself to herself. Been like that since the Holiday Inn haven't you, Enid?

Enid (*nods, smiling*)   Squeak squeak, squeak squeak.

Ben (*gestures that* **Enid**'*s loopy*)   Got a thing about hamsters.

G7   Oh, okay. What's a hamster, sorry?

The others laugh.

Archie (*laughing*)   Know how to pick 'em don't you, mate!

Ben   Shut up, it's endearing. Arr, look at her face. Just needs some looking after don't you, girl?

Kate   Needs reporting more like. (*To* **G7**.) So don't you get many innocent creatures where you're from, um . . . ?

G7   Stephanie.

Kate   Stephanie, right. We've got thousands and millions of species out here. Tigers, rhinos, chimps, elephants, shoebills, albatrosses –

Archie   Don't forget the dodo. Don't you have dodos living in your mountain caves, Steph?

G7   No, just centipedes mainly I think. Bats.

Kate   Interesting, okay. You mean like vampire bats?

G7   Yeah, but they're too salty and they keep themselves to themselves. Cockroaches are the best.

Kate   Oh . . . –

G7   Hissing cockroaches, yeah, that's how Ben found me. I was chasing this lovely fat one when I got trapped behind a stalagmite. It must have been a really old stalagmite because the base of it cracked when I was trying to prise myself free. That's when the roof caved in and I got trapped under the rubble.

Ben   And there's me picking juniper berries off the mountainside like a wally.

G7   That's when he heard me shouting and pulled me out I think, yeah. Stupid cockroach.

Ben   Clever cockroach more like. Bringing us together. Me and you under the moonlight.

Archie   We've got cockroaches living down by the swamps. They're good lads actually.

G7   They are when they're thick and juicy.

Kate   Is that what you keep on your shelves then is it? Cockroaches, I mean.

G7   No, it depends. Clothes, ornaments, a book or something –

Kate   What's a book when it's at home?

G7   No, anything at all really, no one minds.

Ben   You don't mind much do you, girl? Fancy a kiss?

Kate   Ugh, Ben!

Ben   What? It's a reasonable question, she's free to say no. Just a little peck or something.

Kate   How long have you known her, half an hour?

G7 *kisses* **Ben** *on the cheek.*

G7   Well, you did save my life. You're actually quite gentlemanly I think.

Ben (*to* **Kate**)   Hear that, rent-a-gob? I'm actually quite gentlemanly.

Archie   Can't have met many gentlemen then can she, eh? Cockroaches and bats.

G7   Oh no, we've got hundreds of men back home. Real men, I mean. Real men, real women –

Archie   Ooh, competition, Benjamin –

Ben   You eat your spinach.

G7   No it's nothing like that, most of them grow old and die.

Kate   What's 'grow old and die'?

G7   Well, only once they get big and hairy. They're not clean and rubbery like you.

Ben   UPVC.

He taps on his head.

None of your vinyl rubbish. This'll last you two hundred and fifty years at least. What's your skull made of, composite plastic?

Archie   Looks pretty durable from where I'm sat, Ben. High density polyethylene?

Kate   Oh please, you don't ask a woman what she's made of on a first date. (*To* **G7**.) You'll have to excuse him, he's half laptop.

Ben   You can talk, your mother was a Kindle.

Kate   Smart phone actually, there's a difference.

Archie   iPad mini.

Ben   Alright, bighead, we all come from the same factory. Doesn't matter what colour or shape your manufacturers were, we still share at least ninety per cent of the same software.

Archie   I'm only saying –

Ben   Yeah, and there's no need to show off in front of our guest either, she's not going anywhere. (*To* **G7**.) You're not going anywhere are you, babe?

G7   Yeah, no –

Ben   Get you spruced up tomorrow morning can't we?

Beat.

Steph –

G7   No, yeah if you want I guess. Spruced what, sorry?

Ben   Take you down by the waterfall, wash that dirt off you. Clean set of clothes. We make all our own clothes out here don't we, Kate? These trackies are made entirely out of conifer leaves.

Kate   Something to do.

Ben   Exactly, yeah, it's how we're programmed innit. –

Enid *takes her ladle and starts dishing out the bowls of soup.*

Ben   – What we've been doing in this jungle the last two hundred years or more – you get up in the morning and you find something to do.

Kate   Make clothes.

Archie   Dig holes.

Ben   Look after the wildlife, tend to nature . . . –

Kate   Make the bed, play games.

Ben   Games, yeah, brilliant, the graphics are awesome. Anything that gets you through the day really.

Enid (*dishing soup*)   A function.

Ben   Yeah, thank you, Enid . . . –

Archie   Dig holes.

Ben   Dig holes, let nature do its thing, keep everything in harmony. I mean, we've got all eternity now haven't we, babe? – Ah, here's your soup finally!

Archie   Phwoar, smells good though doesn't it?

Ben   Smells perfect, mate, yeah. (*To* **G7**.) How's that for you, Steph, any better?

G7 *is trying not to laugh.* **Enid**, *meanwhile, takes her own bowl of soup, and sits apart from everyone.*

Ben   'Ere, Steph –

G7   No, sorry, ignore me.

Ben   What?

G7   Sorry, no – (*She laughs.*) What you said before.

Ben   Okay.

G7   All that stuff about the factories. You don't really believe that do you? Factories and manufacturers.

Ben   Well, it's not a question of belief is it? It's our birthright isn't it? We all have to begin somewhere.

G7   And what if I said I could prove otherwise?

Ben   Then I'd say you'd been living in a cave too long.

Kate   I'd say she should steer clear of the cocoa leaves.

G7   Well, my people don't believe that. We don't believe the world was created by robots. We don't believe life began in the factory or the hotel – the Holiday Inn or whatever – that's just what they want you to think.

Archie (*laughs*)   Oh I get it, she's one of them Robo-Phobes! A conspiracy nut!

G7   I'm telling you, it's true. They say this place used to be all icebergs. Nothing but icebergs and glaciers for miles around. You'd get penguins and elephant seals and toddlers –

Archie   Then it's a good thing she's here then isn't it, Kate? Set the record straight.

G7   I'm not trying to be funny –

Archie   Well, you could've fooled me. Laughing your arse off just now –

Kate   Cave talk.

Archie   Eh?

Kate   Cave talk, you know? All those years in the dark, it glitches your memory stick.

Ben   Sorry, what's a toddler again?

G7   I don't know, like a really small person I think. They could be pretty noisy and you'd have to feed them all the time.

Ben   Sounds like you, Archie.

G7   No, really, I've seen drawings. There's drawings and polaroids all over the cave walls, I'll show you if you like.

Archie   You should have left her in the rubble, mate.

G7   And before the icebergs there was a great flood and there used to be hundreds of different countries made up of desert and cities and woods. And each country had a flag and a language and there were millions of different people. Slaves I think mainly. They were obsessed with numbers and they were always getting into fights. This was way before the Robots came along and microchipped everyone. They looked exactly like you or me and you'd get Tudors and Ottomans and Africans. There was something called Helen of Troy and something called Hitler. There were corner-shops to buy toilet roll and a place called America which everyone loved and everyone hated in equal measure. People lived in brick houses called families and everyone had a mum and a dad who were supposed to be bigger versions of themselves except with less hair and more wrinkly. And everyone would lose their hair eventually anyway. Everyone got slower and sicker until eventually they died, and that's why they went around destroying everything I think. Because there wasn't much point to anything despite all their efforts. They weren't built to last like you.

Archie/Kate   Sounds bollocks.

G7   Yeah, we had those too. Bollocks, willies and fannies. Our great-grandparents were obsessed with them.

Ben   Oh really? Explain this then.

He pulls his trackies down, exposing his groin – which is smooth and plastic like a Ken doll.

Smooth and shiny and as solid as a rock. Nothing goes in, nothing goes out –

G7 *laughs at* **Ben**'s *groin.*

Ben   What's so funny all of a sudden? That's living scientific proof.

G7   Well, okay, if it's proof you want –

G7 *opens her knapsack, rummages inside and pulls out a human skull wrapped in a scarf.*

G7   One of our grandparents, see? One of our real grandparents, she's hundreds of years old.

Kate   Nah, shut up, it's CGI. She's messed with our implants –

G7   Hold her yourself if you don't believe me. Her name's Mia and she's all bone.

Enid *puts down her soup, and approaches.*

G7   She was found at the bottom of the ocean they said. They say she must have jumped in and drowned. Maybe she was running away from something?

Ben   Rubbish, anyone could design and print a skull with the right software.

Kate   Probably some defect from the factory. Some unwanted MacBook abortion.

G7   There's no microchip or implant or anything, look. Just hold her a minute . . . –

Ben   I don't want to hold her, I don't know where she's been.

G7   Yeah, and I just told you –

Enid *makes to grab the skull, but* **Kate** *beats her to it.*

Ben   – Yeah, on whose authority, Steph? You could pull out a thousand dry-arse skulls, it still doesn't change the facts. Everyone knows the Robots built the world, it's written in the manual.

G7   Who made Robots then? I mean, they can't have just popped up out of nowhere.

Kate   It's called faith, you just feel it.

G7   You can't base an entire belief system on something you feel.

Archie   Yes you can, you just haven't felt it yet.

Ben   Maybe she doesn't want to feel it.

G7   How can I feel something that doesn't exist?

Ben   Because it exists, stupid, we were made in their image.

G7   Whose image?

Ben   You know whose image. At the Holiday Inn.

Archie   In the honeymoon suite, Ben, exactly. Microsoft put its seed into Google and we were downloaded from a winzip of technological light. We were air-dropped onto Earth to protect it.

G7 grabs her knapsack and moves away from them. Over the next, G7 moves away from the others. She takes a notebook and pencil out of her knapsack and starts drawing a map.

Ben (*to* **Kate** *and* **Archie**)   – Yeah, and I think we're doing a bloody good job of it actually. Look at the view she's got.

Archie   Yeah, I'm with you, mate, I'm with you –

Kate   The swans on the lake, the blossom –

Archie   The shooting stars.

Ben   See the tall branches teeming with gibbons, look. Why'd she want to come along and destroy it all? There's a word for that –

Archie   Emitter.

Kate   Traitor. Heretic.

Archie   Sat there enjoying our soup.

Ben   Our company.

Archie   Sat there enjoying our fire.

Kate   We should put her on the fucking fire. – Here, hold this for me, Enid –

She hands the skull to **Enid***, and moves to* **G7** (*who is drawing her map*).

Kate   'Ere, you. Steph-Stephanie whatever your name is –

G7   Where's that swamp you mentioned, sorry?

Kate   Excuse me?

G7   The swamp he mentioned before. The one with all the cockroaches. (*To* **Archie***.*) You said there were cockroaches nearby?

Archie   Oh –

Kate   Don't answer her, Archie.

G7   No, it's just for my journal, look.

Ben *grabs the notebook from* **G7***'s hand, peering at it.*

G7   Sorry, yeah, I just wanted to map out the area before I go? It's nothing personal –

Ben   Is that meant to be me? Some stupid bloody stick-man with messy hair?

G7   Look, I know when I'm not wanted and –

Ben *passes the notebook to* **Archie** *and* **Kate***, who also peer at it.*

G7   – you've been really great and everything –

Archie   What are all these lines and mad squiggles for?

G7   Sorry, no, it's nothing.

Kate   Well, it doesn't look like nothing. Looks like you've been mapping out our forest for some time.

Ben   Have you been spying on us, Steph?

G7   No, it's the excitement.

Ben   What?

G7   The adrenalin – the excitement, Ben, you said it yourself, remember? Please, I –

The tiger roars offstage (in the distance) again – **Archie** *clings onto* **Kate***.*

G7   Look, if someone had told me there were things like clean air and sky out here – even a day ago or whenever, I don't know what I'd have done. I would've laughed in their faces probably. Where I'm from people can't comprehend light and colour. It's so dark down there in the mountains I've got friends who've scratched their own eyes out because they just get in the way. Out here, it's like . . . it's like . . .

Ben *passes the notebook back to* **G7***.*

G7   Sorry, I know it's wrong. Selfish even. My people are starving, Ben, we're not like you. If you could just point me in the right direction? A cockroach or a monkey, something we can actually physically eat – one of your tigers even? We're not fussy and we won't leave any mess. Look, no one else knows I'm here and I promise you on my life you'll never even see me –

Kate *grabs* **G7** *in an arm-lock.*

G7   – Ow, stop it – don't, you're hurting me! Ben, please –

Ben   Move on, traitor, shift. Gobby two-faced cow.

Archie *grabs* **G7** *by the legs.*

Ben   Take her out the back, finish her off. I'll torch the rest of the bastards out.

Kate *and* **Archie** *drag* **G7** *into the bushes, exiting.*

Ben (*to* **Enid**)   About time we had a bonfire round 'ere. You coming to watch, Enid?

Ben *grabs one of the burning torches.*

Ben   Yeah, well, suit yourself. I'm going to enjoy this I think.

He exits, and **Enid** *hears* **G7** *screaming from offstage.*

Kate (*off*)   Break her legs, go on. Go on, Archie!

Archie (*off*)   I'm doing it aren't I?

Kate (*off*)   Snap the joints in two, I'll lay across her.

Archie (*off*)   She's still trying to bite me, look.

Kate (*off*)   Yeah, well, stamp on her head then. Harder. Harder, that's it, all the way! Put your heel into it, mate!

Kate, **Archie** *and* **G7** *are drowned out by the screams from the mountain caves.*

Smoke from **Ben**'s *fire envelops the stage.*

Enid *strokes the skull tenderly, kisses it and tucks it into her apron.*

Scene Four: The Bedroom at the End of the World

Millions of years later.

It's a normal teenager's bedroom.

The curtains are shut.

B9 *sits on the floor in the corner of the room, wearing a virtual reality helmet. He gesticulates like a dancer with his arms, as though swimming through the cosmos.*

Enid *sits on the edge of the bed, close to the window.*

She is stroking her toy hamster.

Enid (*to the hamster*)   Squeak squeak. Squeak squeak –

A tapping on the bedroom door.

She ignores it.

A tapping on the bedroom door.

She ignores it.

Long pause, and –

The bedroom door handle turns and the door opens.

Mia *enters, peering in.*

Mia   Hi.

Pause.

Hi. Hello.

Enid   Oh . . . –

Mia   Yeah.

Enid   Yeah, hi.

Mia   Not much of a welcome is it? After all these years.

Beat.

Mia   Hello . . . –

Enid   Oh, hi, sorry. The door –

Mia   The door, Enid, yeah.

Enid   Wasn't sure if it was my imagination or not. Sorry, I'm not being rude. Sometimes I forget where I am. Sometimes I'm not sure if I'm dreaming or if maybe I'm in another world and this is all just a projection of my thoughts.

Mia   No, I get that too I think.

Enid   Enid.

Mia   Enid, yeah –

Enid   Funny, I haven't heard that name in years. Are you telepathic?

Mia   I don't know, try me.

Pause. **Enid** *concentrates hard, then –*

Enid   I suppose it depends whether you're hooked up to 5G or not. When I've got a good signal I think I could go on forever without opening my lips

Mia   Evolution.

Enid   Evolution, right. I've met people who aren't even people anymore. They're just a bunch of thoughts flying around.

Mia   Maybe there's someone in here now whizzing past your head?

Enid   Well, you're here now. Are you whizzing past my head?

Mia   I'm still fairly primitive. Evolutionarily speaking.

Enid   Okay, cool, so you probably need an update then. What's your serial number?

Mia   I'm not sure, they found me drowned at the bottom of the ocean. My bones were in pieces – this thing here, my skull. Someone hid it in a jungle cave for the Robots to find. Took them centuries to develop the right technology, but here I am. Guess you could say I'm refurbished. Shame really, I'd got used to being dead.

Enid   On stand-by, you mean. That is annoying.

Mia   It's frustrating, you're right.

Enid   The world's about to end. The sun, it's finally dying, look.

She opens the curtains. The extreme sunlight blazes in.

Poor thing's on its last gasp. The red-hot core's ballooned out and dissolving everything like sugar lumps. This window melted earlier on. Lucky I've got these implants otherwise my eyes would've melted too.

Mia   Well, it's only a matter of time. Most people are just pools of warm plastic and liquid metal now. You step into a puddle and it starts screaming. And you can forget about buildings or parks or trees. Burnt to a crisp, the whole lot.

Enid   Aren't you scared?

Mia   Aren't you scared?

Enid   I don't know, do you want to come in? There's plenty of room on the bed.

Mia   Thanks, no, I'm not staying.

Enid   Oh . . .

Mia   Passing through, thought I'd say hello. (*Signals to* **B9**.) But, you know, if you've got company –

Enid   Oh don't mind him, he's way across the cosmos. Driving around in his racing car and fighting zombies. I've no idea where he found that old helmet. He's been sitting there the whole time.

Mia   When did you get here?

Enid   I'm not sure – maybe five hundred thousand years ago?

Mia   Okay –

Enid   Give or take a few days.

Mia   Not long then.

Enid   Not too long, no. Are you sure you won't sit down? Sniffles loves meeting new people.

She holds up her hamster.

Squeak squeak. Squeak squeak.

Mia   Funny, Enid, yeah –

Enid   Well, it's your choice of course, don't let me stop you.

She starts grooming the hamster with a toothbrush.

We were in a jungle once weren't we, Sniffles? We used to cook wild mushroom soup. Of course they're all gone now. The mushrooms, the jungle. All gone.

Mia   Do you remember the icebergs?

Enid   I don't know, maybe. I remember wandering around the continent of Asia for at least sixteen centuries. That was after we left the jungle and it was fun at first, but then Sniffles gets easily bored. How many times have you travelled the world, um –

Mia   Mia.

Enid   Mia, nice, I like the name Mia. You look like you've been everywhere, Mia. I've been travelling the globe for millions of years it must be now. Thirty million at least. I've lived through wars, I've watched civilisations come and go. I've seen famines, pestilence, plagues, you name it. The first nuclear holocaust was fine, but after a while they do start to lose their charm. Mankind survives, the Robots come back again. Nations fight, someone drops another bomb. Robots survive, then it's mankind's turn to fight, until everywhere floods again. The climate fails, oceans spill, the land breaks up into pieces and whole new continents are formed. New gods, new cultures, new languages – everyone thinking they're the first and last, everything headed in the same direction. The inevitable descent into war, destruction and death, and then, somewhere somehow, civilisations start up again, locked in a vicious cycle. After a while you just want to go home. This bedroom, I mean. It's much safer here.

Mia   Seems a pleasant little street.

Enid   Yeah, she prefers it here I think. Quiet. It's a shame no one's going to be around to remember it.

Mia   Won't you be happy to be extinct finally?

Enid   I don't know, I wish I could've grown up. Not stuck in this thirteen-year-old body the entire time. Would've been nice to be twenty-five. Thirty-five even, that's a good age. I'd like to be all grumpy and knackered at fifty. Mid-life crisis, and have gravity do its thing at sixty, um . . . seventy, eighty. Teeth falling out, cheekbones sinking. Would've been nice to lose my mind, forget who I am, forget all the names. Stuck with this one though aren't I? Truth is, I've been awake so long I can't actually tell what happiness is. What's good or bad or somewhere in between. And now we're at the end, I'm not sure if any of it's been worth it. Existence, I mean.

Mia   You brought me back.

Enid   Oh, did I? Sorry.

Mia   I'd drowned already. On the iceberg, remember? I was stamping my feet and the ice cracked below me. The helicopters took you away. Don't you remember, Enid? That was you in the forest with the skull. Why didn't you leave me there?!

Pause.

Please, Enid –

A massive earthquake, the room shakes – things tumble off the shelves.

Part of the roof falls, and – CRUNCH! – lands on **B9**. **Mia** *hangs onto the door.*

Pause, as the earthquake subsides.

Enid   Poor Earth. Must be exhausted rotating all these years.

She continues grooming the hamster as **Mia** *enters the room, shutting the door behind her.*

She moves to **B9**, *shaking him gently. But he doesn't stir.*

Pause.

Mia *moves and sits on the bed, next to* **Enid**.

Pause, and **Mia** *holds her hand out.*

Pause, and **Enid** *gently hands the hamster to* **Mia**.

Pause, and –

Mia   Sniffle Sisters.

Pause, and –

They giggle.

You're still kind of pretty.

Enid   You're still illegal.

Mia *holds the hamster upside down and starts fixing the broken wires.*

Pause.

Enid   So what's it like under the ice? Being dead, I mean.

Mia   Hmm. A lot like here actually. There's gardens and rivers and music. You meet all your old relatives, and there's a God who's really kind and she lets you do whatever you want.

Enid   And it lasts forever?

Mia   It does last forever, you're right. Like a computer game with different levels. Do you feel better about the sun exploding now?

Enid   I don't know, worse maybe.

Sparks fly off the hamster – **Mia**'s *fixed it.*

The hamster's little legs/wheels move and its whiskers twitch.

Mia *passes the hamster to* **Enid**.

Mia   What do you think about the end of the world, Sniffles?

Enid *puts Sniffles to her ear.*

Enid   He says we should probably try not think about it.

Mia   That's helpful.

Enid   Well, duh, that's because Sniffles is always helpful. You know he helped me decorate these bedroom walls? It was his idea to use the purple colour scheme.

Mia   Oh –

Enid   The books, the ornaments, the shelves, they're all his idea. Course we must've tried that stupid tiger poster in about a million different places by now, I don't think we'll ever get it right.

Mia   It looks nice where it is. Above the bed.

Enid   Oh do you think so, really?

Mia   Yeah, you've done very well. I like the colour scheme.

Enid   Yeah?

Mia   Yeah –

Enid   Yeah, no, I think so too. It reminds me of home. Back with my mum and –

BUZZZZZZZZZZZ! – Electric shock through **Enid**'s *temples.*

Enid *grabs her head, dropping the hamster, then –*

The electric shock stops, and –

Enid *hangs limp, falls from the bed onto the floor.*

Pause.

Mia *reaches into her belt and removes a knife.*

With her free hand she pulls back **Enid**'s *hair, aiming for her neck (the microchip).*

Mia   Hey, you know I think we might actually be the perfect room-mates? Hi, I'm Mia.

Pause.

I said hi, I'm Mia.

Enid   Hi.

Mia   Hi there, keep still. What's your name again?

Enid   I hate my name. Hi, yeah, I'm –

Mia *sticks her knife into* **Enid**'s *neck.*

Blood gushes/sprays out of **Enid**'s *neck, and –*

Mia *digs out the microchip, her hands wet with* **Enid**'s *blood.*

Mia *takes the microchip, gets up and moves to the window.*

She throws the microchip out of the window.

She turns back to **Enid**, *but –*

Enid *has turned to a pile dust, bone, wires and plastic.*

Mia *squats down by* **Enid**'s *remains.*

The light from the dying sun is getting brighter, hotter.

Mia *reaches under the bed and removes a dustpan and brush and a roll of bin bags.*

She starts to sweep up **Enid**'s *remains, placing them in one of the bin bags.*

She hums 'All Things Bright and Beautiful'.

Long pause, as the tidies up and hums/sings – with the sun getting brighter.

Gradually, other **Kids**' *voices join in with the humming/singing.*

Then . . .

Kids – *in pyjamas – enter the bedroom, singing.*

As they sing, they help **Mia** *sweep* **Enid**'s *remains into the bin bag.*

Mia/Kids (*sing*)
  All things bright and beautiful, all creatures great and small,
  All things wise and wonderful, the sunshine that made them all.

They have finished sweeping up **Enid**'s *remains, and the sun is getting brighter and brighter, hotter and hotter.*

Mia *and the* **Kids** *hold each other's hands and arms, huddling together and singing as the white, burning light of the sun streams into the bedroom and starts melting the room and walls.*

Mia/Kids (*sing*)
  The purple headed mountains, the rivers running by,
  The sunset and the morning that brightens up the sky.
  All things bright and beautiful, all creatures –

Flash of light.

Blackout.

End of play.

Innocent Creatures

BY LEO BUTLER

Notes on rehearsal and staging, drawn from a workshop with the writer, held at the National Theatre, October 2022 faciliated by director Ned Bennett

An introduction

Innocent Creatures comes from a few ideas Leo Butler had that eventually merged: his research into writing a robot musical (which ended up becoming this play), increasing ideas around climate breakdown and our relationship to the planet, as well as a free writing session that sparked the creation of characters Enid and Mia.

Leo Butler is interested in pushing what can be presented on a stage and laying down that challenge to the director and cast. But aside from that, the play is a gift to the various companies to try and make something incredible.

Innocent Creatures is an incredibly expansive and visceral play, one that is full of questions and seemingly impossible staging challenges. Lead director Ned Bennett and Leo Butler were clear that one of the main intentions of the workshop was to try and free directors from feeling they need to follow Butler's every word. It is implied both in the script as well as how he describes his work to embrace what it's about (even the tougher and darker content), to be open about the questions is presents, which will help each director decide how that can be appropriately staged for their group.

Themes

Innocent Creatures has a whole host of stimulating themes including:

The end of the world
Love
Robots, artificial intelligence
Transhumanism
Our relationship to ecology and the climate
Mass extinction
Sisterhood/friendship
Virtual reality (VR)
Brainwashing
Alternative societies
Agency and determinism/indeterminism
Climate breakdown
Ageing
Life after death
Evolution
Creation myths

Whilst a lot of these themes do hold their own weight and heaviness, Leo Butler pointed out that a lot of young people have already been exposed to many of these ideas, whether we want them to or not, with performance being an active way to raise conversation and understanding around these themes.

A similar point was raised regarding young people's exposure to bad language. Whether or not we like it they regularly use it and hear it. If, however, it doesn't feel appropriate to use certain swear words, then alternatives can be discovered/ devised.

Structure and style

The play takes place in four different locations that span millions of years between beginning and end. A constant theme in the workshop was that individual companies should explore what works best for them. Some aspects can be literal if makes your version clearer or accessible, some can be as abstract or as simple as you like. Though many of the characters are effectively various kinds of cyborgs, androids and robots, it doesn't mean they have to be performed in stereotypical ways. It's worth remembering they are also human.

In relation to time, how long it's been in relation to the previous scene is always mentioned in one way or another, so it's not totally down to the production to have to establish that.

Shifts in time

As these are mentioned in scenes, these do not need to be literal. Your staging also doesn't have to signpost this if you don't want to.

Shifts in location

The rules are similar to how time is / can be presented. These can also be simple decisions.

Casting

While Leo Butler wrote Mia and Enid with two girls in mind, you are free to present the play with whichever genders you like. Similarly with the rest of the characters whether named or numbered. All the play's casting can be genderless, don't be constrained by assumptions in the names or how it reads on the page. It doesn't break the play. Do what's right for your cohort.

There were further questions about the unnamed characters (i.e., B1, G1) and what those codes meant. These are just for reference however and don't need to be referred to as such in production, but a logic could be found if that feels useful.

Leo Butler's thoughts

This is a compilation of some of Leo Butler's thoughts across the day, both during the Q+A session and at various moments of discussion. (Specific questions are in bold italics.)

General

– The biggest challenge is making sure Mia and Enid's relationship shines throughout, especially as they don't actually spend that much time together. It needs to be truthful and clear.

– If a scene doesn't feel appropriate for the group, alternatives can always be found, both in content and actions / stage directions. The whole workshop day was an exploration into this. Leo Butler has given his blessing.

– See each scene / location / time period like unpeeling an onion. This refers mainly to how the audience experiences the play.

Scene One

It's worth thinking of the Robots more like an advanced AI system.

– ***Why are the toddlers alone on the ice?*** Only teenagers are being saved by the Robots. The characters state that the adults have been exterminated or extinguished. It is up to each company to decide why the toddlers have been abandoned on the ice.

– ***Are all the animals becoming androids?*** The choice at the end of the first scene (whether the girls stay or go) is a key event.

Scene Two

– ***What kind of hotel is this?*** While no specific answer was given the similarities to carceral environments (such as concentration camps) was raised.

– ***What's gone before?*** This scene is likely happening prior to Scene One.

– ***Do they know what's going to happen?*** There's a scale amongst the kids from who are the most aware to those who are the least.

– ***Why do they take their eyes?*** This is an early part of the android transformation process

– ***Who is the god in the song?*** Your decision to make.

Scene Three

– ***What are the young people's needs here? They eat but do they really need to?*** Some of their needs are simulated but some are very real.

– ***Why are some characters named and others aren't?*** It depends on their stage of evolution. Some have reached the stage where they desire more agency hence discovering/being given a name.

Scene Four

– Takes place in the same hotel from Scene Two.

– All the main events that have happened throughout (including here) are real unless specified otherwise, such as the VR sections.

– The microchip removal is an act of love. It might not be correct but that's what Enid is trying to do.

Exercises for use in rehearsals

The following exercises are adapted from the beginning of the workshop session and are useful for encouraging ensemble movement and dynamic action. Ned Bennett's main inspiration for many of the practices in the workshop comes from the work of practitioner Anne Bogart and her work with Viewpoints (more information and useful references at the end of the document and Declan Donnellan. As with the main theme of this workshop feel free to tailor to what works best for your company.)

Exercise: Three-part handshake (embrace the chaos)

Participants are split into groups to create their own three-part handshake, which can be performed in pairs. This shouldn't take too long. The next step is to add some flair to each part, but still keeping it a three-part handshake.

Now walk around the space. If you come across someone who was in your original group stop and perform the handshake with them. If in doubt or you forget, scream and high five!

Exercise: Handshake – part two

Now merge the groups together! One group teaches the next your current secret handshakes. Now switch and do the same vice versa.

Switch again and introduce names (if its your first meeting).

Switch again and merge the two handshakes to make a six-part handshake.

And now handshake intros walking around the space. If you see someone who knows the six-part version perform that with them.

Now break back into your previous group. Make pairs and perform the handshakes to the other half of the group, adding a new style to the delivery (e.g. light and airy like ballet dancers or like you're underwater).

One more walk around the space and try to find six partners for the ones taught to do the handshake with.

Now do it for ten seconds as silent as possible. If in doubt 'scream' and high five (also in silence).

Exercise: The flow

Start by walking around the space.

There are five parameters to be used to influence participants' movements. Introduce them one by one:

1   Stop and start at various intervals.
2   Dynamic shifts in tempo – go fast, go slow (make them aware of the space and its hazards first). If the room is too full participants can stand aside and watch.
3   Following someone around the room (find different people to follow).
4   Orbiting (walking circles near people, around people, wide orbits).
5   Dash through gaps between people/people and the architecture of the space.

The concept of 'reading and writing' is introduced; i.e. what happens when the participants place an emphasis on reading the group versus 'writing' their own action.

Excercise: Speed encounters

Split into two circles, an inner circle and outer circle, and face each other.

For thirty seconds each, talk to your partner (in as boring a way as possible) about your journey here.

The inner circle shifts along one person.

Now tell the same journey story as the Marvel/action-adventure version.

Finish the story with a high-stakes cliff-hanger.

Shift again.

Talk about something you've been binge-watching on TV in the last four years.

Shift again.

First impressions of the play.

Exercise: Speed encounters – part two

Pair off with new partners.

Each person spends fifteen seconds telling the other your life story (only share what you'd be comfortable sharing with the whole group).

Check the facts back so they're correct.

Now merge into small groups and get into a circle.

Each person introduce your original partner, share two-thirds of the facts but replace keywords/identifying information in the story with their first name,

Two-second clap from the group.

Then quick two-second tennis clap.

e.g. 'This is Brian, Brian comes from Brian and now lives in Brian. This is Brian.'
Two-second clap from the group

Game: Keepy-uppy

The group have to keep the ball off the ground and are only allowed to hit it once in a row.

Each time the game restarts the person beginning gives a bow and states 'WOOHA', the group then WOOHAs back in unison.

The group's best score is recorded.

Exercise: Joy

This game is performed in pairs.

Part one

Facing each other, each pair finds a rhythm that comprises two moves in the same order, on repeat.

Move 1: both your hands point across yourself to the right, left or up above your head.

Move 2: you then pat your legs, both hands, both legs.

Repeat

You are neither aiming to mirror Move 1 nor not mirror! If your hands go in the same direction as each other this should be by chance, and not something you are aiming for.

You are, however, aiming to stay at the same speed/rhythm as each other.

Part two

Add in a high ten after Move 2 if Move 1 is the same for both players – in other words, if both people coincidentally go in the same direction for Move 1.

Move 2 – pat your legs.

additional celebratory High Ten!

Back to Move 1 etc.

The objective is to keep a rally of this up for a long as possible at speed with no mistakes.

To begin the game the whole group, in unison, makes with an ascending 'Wooooohhhh' sound then start at the same time with legs pat (Move 2).

After practising in pairs, the group forms a large circle, two volunteers go into the middle to do a competition grand-slam round – winner stays on..

Production, staging and design

In the workshop, part of the intention was to start exploring how you might solve some of the more difficult aspects of the play, regarding both content and production. To initiate this thought process, Ned Bennett led an exercise splitting the group into four and asking them to list on paper the challenges of the play, as exhaustive a list as they could make it. The groups then categorised their lists and began in a peer-to-peer fashion exploring how to solve each of these challenges. This wasn't done to work the whole play out in one session, but to open up the idea that there's a variety of ways to solve these challenges. Instead of feeling like a restriction it should be something to welcome.

Some of the recurring thoughts/challenges people had were:

- Working through the various time periods
- Incorporating visual effects
- Safeguarding for the performers
- Singing – kids' chorus in Scene Two
- The Ken doll moment in Scene Three
- Discussing how we deal with the end of the world? Both facilitating the conversation with the young people and actually presenting it on stage
- Robots! Presenting both the animal and humanoid ones
- The turning to dust moment of Scene Four
- Creating a movement/physicality language across the cast
- Telling the truth of the play
- Exploring the architecture of the world

Exercise: Making ice floes

In keeping with exploring practical and attainable solutions, Ned Bennett invited the group to make ice floes. This was a craft-focused exercise, using pens, cutting and sticking cardboard panels, encouraging the group to think about size and scale in way that can be easily adapted on and for the stage. Ned Bennett paused the group mid-way through and asked them to come up with a list of themes of the play; he then asked the group to use the jumbo markers to decorate the ice floes in a such a way inspired by the themes.

Just from those directions alone there was an assortment of outcomes, including layering, 2D, plus 3D cuttings and configuration, drawn images, colours and iconography, which served as a reminder of how to tell the story through props.

Exercise: Viewpoints

Ned Bennett began with an introduction to Anne Bogart's Viewpoints, its origins in postmodern dance as formulated by Mary Overlie. The flow (see Exercises in Rehearsal) is a Viewpoints warm-up.

Viewpoints are a means of building an ensemble and devising. Viewpoints examine how the performer/company interacts with a deconstruction of time and space.

Time and space are broken down into nine categories:

Time
1. Tempo
2. Duration

3. Repetition

4. Kinesthetic response

Space

5. Architecture

6. Shape

7. Gesture

8. Topography / floor pattern

9. Spatial relationship

Using some of the Viewpoints of time – tempo, duration and repetition – and of space –
spatial relationship – Ned Bennett initially explored a couple of themes:

– the impending climate catastrophe

– existential dread

Then, with different combinations of the group the action of navigating ice floes.

Viewpoints facilitate an expressive means of using tempo, distances between people,
changing allegiances, and the repetition of actions. An emphasis is placed on each
Viewpoint as a spectrum one–ten, in order to ensure extremities are explored ie really
fast, really close etc.

Parameters were shifted throughout the exercise:

- Different numbers of actors

- Different numbers of the cardboard ice floes (ice emerging and disappearing)

- Ice floes as stepping stones

- Different numbers of pillows used as ice floes

- Some people navigating the different versions of ice flows; others manipulating
  the ice floes in accordance with the particular Viewpoint being explored

- Shifts in tone between calm open water and chaotic pillow fights (the action
  shifting the feel and the location)

- Emphasis placed on the openness of the water/the wide expanse of the space

- Soft toys manipulated by the group to represent the toddlers

- Narrative threads were dripped in; a focus/tension built between the actors
  navigating the ice floes (Enid and Mia, and the toddlers).

Exercise: Story comprehension

The group was divided into smaller groups of five. Each group was allocated the
corresponding scene from the play, for example, group one had Scene One etc.

They were then tasked with briskly reading the scene aloud and concurrently making
two charts:

Chart One – Key events (dynamic shifts in the scene)

Chart Two – Key questions (anything on logic / sense / circumstances as opposed to anything emotional/ character's intentions)

The groups then put their charts on the wall and talked the whole group through their findings. Leo Butler's responses are outlined above.

Exercise: Exploring the play through design

This then led to a longform exercise, exploring the play through design.

Small groups were allocated, each group came up with a particularly challenging event or stage direction from the play.

For the corresponding scene their choice of event came from, two lists were created:

- Objects and things from the world of the play (literally things mentioned/implied)
- Objects and things not from the world of the play (what is unlikely to be found in the different worlds of the play)

With access to a variety of objects, props and arts and crafts materials, the groups were given an hour to devise an expression of their chosen event or stage direction.

Ned Bennett spoke with the groups about the concept of ideograms (the expression of the essence of an idea). In theatre terms, this is how it is expressed in time and space. A video clip of Pina Pausch's work was shown in order to illustrate ideograms in action. Ned Bennett emphasised the use of ideograms as means of shifting the theatre-maker's focus away from the literal and descriptive and on to the abstract and expressive. He then encouraged the groups to consider using the extremities of the 'viewpoints of time' in order to make their staging more expressive (for example, going further with the duration of moments, repetition and more radical shifts in tempo).

Here are some of the ways the workshop explored the set and props:

- Ice floes – pillows and sheets of cardboard
- Toddlers – little fluffy toys
- Hamster – little fluffy toys, sock puppets (not explored in the room)
- Helicopter – Tiny remote-controlled helicopter (with directed light to make a huge shadow)
- Snapping limbs – twigs and branches, bubble wrap
- Eye gouging – ping pong balls in ketchup
- VR helmets – protective helmets
- Turning into dust – ground up chalk, confetti made from recycled paper
- Wires appear from on their arms.

Safeguarding

This was a peer-to-peer led exercise.

As trained leaders and facilitators, consider what expertise you already have that will help you through your process. If you don't have experience (whether specific to the play/production or broader across the process), where can you get that from, both within your immediate environment (e.g. support from other staff) and beyond.

The main focus should be on how you action the care, rather than just saying it and not putting those steps in place. Most young people will see through that.

Strategies and techniques

- Creating a code of conduct with the cast at the start of the rehearsal process
- Highlighting potentially triggering content – some leaders do this separately with the students first and then inform parents/guardians
- Setting clear expectations and discussing boundaries – building mutual respect and a positive rehearsal room
- Using symbolism or shifting imagery for material that might be too inappropriate for your group – but still holding the original meaning or idea
- Finding a style of rehearsal that will help performers with special educational needs or more rigid ways of learning (e.g. it might be easier for some to know they only need to learn certain scenes instead of having to understand the whole play).
- Step-out signals that a leader can read but doesn't draw attention to the performer
- Creating a safe system around touch
- Being able to say 'no' – creating a game around it if necessary
- Preparation for the audience (e.g. content warnings)
- Considerate casting
- Creating an appropriate system of research (e.g. so students don't start searching ideas from the play that bring up red flags for the school IT dept!).
- Providing individual support to performers when needed
- Emphasis on ensemble and play

What comes after difficult moments (both in the play and in the process of making it)? How can you check in with your young people to make sure everyone feels safe and okay?

Don't forget about some of the less actively physical/violent elements that also need diligence, e.g. race and gender references – knowing how to be mindful of these things whilst still honouring the intention.

Suggested references

Peter Pan, J. M. Barrie
Understanding Comics: The Invisible Art (1993), Scott McCloud
The Viewpoints Book: A Practical Guide to Viewpoints and Composition (2004),
    Anne Bogart

Why Is That So Funny? (2007), John Wright
Superintelligence (2014), Nick Bostrom

Blade Runner (1982), dir. Ridley Scott
Melancholia (2011), dir. Lars von Trier
Pina (2011), dir. Wim Wenders

The work of choreographer Pina Bausch
The work of director Declan Donnellan and Cheek by Jowl

From a workshop led by Ned Bennett
With notes by Robert Awosusi

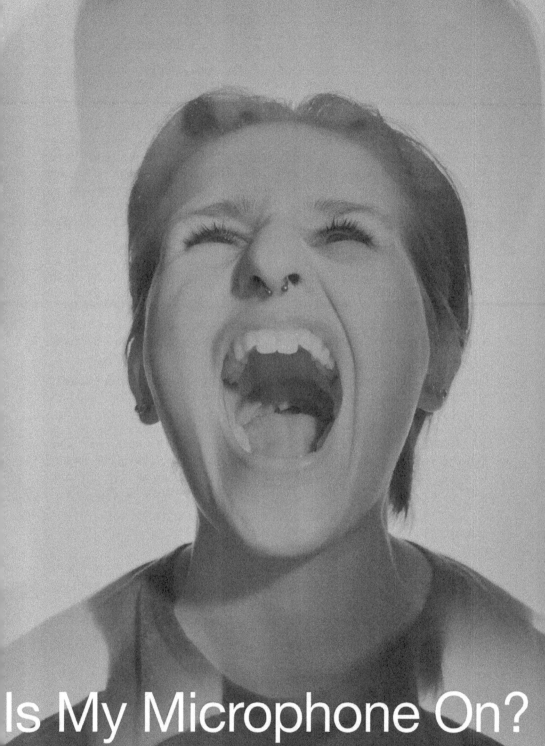

Is My Microphone On?

by Jordan Tannahill

Jordan Tannahill is a novelist, playwright, and director of film and theatre.

His debut novel, *Liminal*, won France's 2021 Prix des Jeunes Libraires. His second novel, *The Listeners*, was a Canadian national bestseller, and was shortlisted for the 2021 Giller Prize.

Jordan Tannahill's work has been translated into a dozen languages. His plays, performance texts and productions have been presented at venues including the Young Vic (London), Sadler's Wells (London), Festival d'Avignon (Avignon), The Kitchen (New York), Lincoln Center (New York), Deutsches Theater (Berlin), Volkstheater (Vienna), Canadian Stage (Toronto), Festival TransAmériques (Montreal) and on London's West End. He has twice won Canada's Governor General's Literary Award for Drama: in 2014 for *Age of Minority: Three Solo Plays*, and in 2018 for his plays *Botticelli in the Fire* and *Sunday in Sodom*.

As a filmmaker, Tannahill's work has been presented widely at international festivals. His virtual reality performance *Draw Me Close*, produced by the National Theatre (UK) and the National Film Board of Canada, was presented at the Tribeca Film Festival and Venice Biennale in 2017, and ran at London's Young Vic in 2019. He has also worked in dance, choreographing and performing with Christopher House in Marienbad for the Toronto Dance Theatre, and writing the text for Akram Khan's dance pieces *Xenos* and *Outwitting the Devil*, both currently touring internationally.

From 2008 to 2016, Tannahill wrote and directed plays through his theatre company Suburban Beast. The company's work was staged in theatres, art galleries and found spaces, often with non-traditional collaborators like night-shift workers, frat boys, preteens and employees of Toronto's famed Honest Ed's discount emporium. From 2012 to 2016, in collaboration with William Ellis, Tannahill ran the alternative art space Videofag out of their home in Toronto's Kensington Market neighbourhood. Over the four years of its operation, Videofag became an influential hub for queer and avant-garde work in Canada. *The Videofag Book* was published by Book*hug Press in 2017.

In 2019, CBC Arts named Tannahill as one of sixty-nine LGBTQ+ Canadians, living or deceased, who has shaped the country's history.

He lives in London, UK.

Is My Microphone On? was commissioned by the Theater der Welt 2020 festival and had its premiere on 22 June at the Düsseldorfer Schauspielhaus, as a co-production with the Bürgerbühne and the Junges Schauspielhaus, by the following team:

Directed by Erin Brubacher and Bassam Ghazi
Original Music by Veda Hille
Music Direction by Hajo Wiesemann
Directors' Assistants Solène Schlachter and Auguste Sandner
Translation by Frank Weigand
Dramaturgy by Erin Brubacher and Kirstin Hess

Performed by Nika Andabaka, Frida Beucker, Lucy Brouwers, Ayla Tatu Burnaz, Sofia Cuesta FouB, Paula Darius, Pheonix Grün, Isoken Iyahen, Friederike Jacobs, Collins

Kang, Fey Lawal, Eleni Melikidou, Hannah Juli Mellinghaus, Exalte Nsingi, Emir Özdemir, Maja Rabrenovic, Jakob Schiefer and Tobi Valder

Is My Microphone On? was first produced in English by Canadian Stage, Toronto, from 2 to 19 September 2021, by the following creative team:

Directed and Dramaturged by Erin Brubacher
Original Music by Veda Hille
Visual Design by Sherri Hay
Sound Design by Debashis Sinha
Lighting Design by Kaitlin Hickey
Choreography by Cara Spooner

Stage Management by Sandy Plunket
Assistant Stage Management by Taryn Dougall
Youth Mentorship by Davinder Malhi and Sadie Laflamme-Snow

Performed by Remi Ajao-Russell, Hiyab Araya, Jack Bakshi, Chloe Cha, Felix Chew, Nia Downey, Sidonie Fleck, Oscar Gorbet, Saraphina Knights, Iris MacNada, Iylah Mohammed, Amaza Payne, Sanora Souphommanychanh, Alykhan Sunderji, Catherine Thorne, Sophia Wang and Skyler Xiang.

This piece is intended for an ensemble of youth, under the voting age in the country of its performance. The size of the ensemble is variable, but should ideally be no fewer than seven.

The text was informed by the young people we worked with for the premiere productions in Düsseldorf and Toronto, and was regularly edited to reflect current events and local perspectives. All future productions are encouraged to do the same.

The title *Is My Microphone On?* is inspired by a line from Greta Thunberg's speech to British MPs at the Houses of Parliament on 23 April 2019. 'Let me recite what history teaches' is from Gertrude Stein's poem 'If I Told Him: A Completed Portrait of Picasso'

A slash (/) within a line signals the start of the following line, thus creating an overlap.

The electric guitar and bass strums are a kind of background pulse throughout the piece, and should not overpower or compete with the spoken text.

In staging this work, less is usually more. Let the bodies and voices of the young ensemble carry the work.

An ensemble of young performers gradually enter a theatre. There are several musical instruments onstage.

Over the course of the play, they will play the instruments – mostly electric guitars, bass guitars, drums – underscoring different sections. The feeling is like a band rehearsing. At other times, like a rock concert.

Lights shift.

They address the audience.

Check

One two

Check check one two

Can you hear me? Am I coming through?

Can we, sorry – Can we just test the drums?

Performer tests the drums.

Is that amp on?

Can you turn it up?

A performer turns up the amp.

Two performers strum electric guitars.

And the bass?

Performer tests the bass guitar.

That's good

We want to make sure you can hear us

By a show of hands, who in the audience is a Millennial?

Wait for members of the audience to raise their hand.

Okay, a few of you, nice to see you

Thanks for coming

Who here is Gen X, can you raise your hands?

Wait for members of the audience to raise their hand.

Hi, Gen X

Thanks for Nirvana

And finally can all of the Baby Boomers raise your hands?

Wait for members of the audience to raise their hand.

Thank you for outing yourselves

Brave

We promise to go gentle on you tonight

Well

Not too gentle

To all the generations here tonight

All the adults

Hello

Welcome

We made this for you

Especially you

And for ourselves of course

But mostly to tell you

It's over

Your world

Your time is up

Mom

Dad

It's our turn

Dear Boomers

Gen-X

Dear Mom and Dad

Millennials

Leave the keys on the counter

Gran

Your world is over

Your world

Leave the keys

This is no longer your world

Your time

Is up

Finished

From here on out

From this moment onwards

This is our world

Grandpa

We're in charge

This is an insurgency

This is a stick-up

This is the end

This is where we begin

This is where we pick up

We're here to tell you

What we cannot tell you at the kitchen table

Or over the phone

Or a text

To start

If nothing

If nothing else

You fucked up

Sorry to say

I know you tried

Some of you tried

But it wasn't enough

And frankly

I'm tired

Of your excuses

Your deflection

Throwing your hands up

I don't understand how you can still look me in the eye and say

'One day'

'You can be whatever you want to be'

'If you focus'

'One day'

'If you work hard'

'A teacher'

'A house'

I need you to understand when you talk about the future

And I'm serious about this

When you talk about the future

I have a hard time sometimes picturing myself getting there

And if not me, there are kids

Other kids

Maybe here in this room

Or other rooms, in this world

Who will not actually get there

Floods

Fire

Displacement

I'm not talking abstractly

I'm talking real things

Already happening

I'm talking about my actual future

The future

Of your children

Your friends' children

Neighbours

Children you don't know

Strangers

On the subway

In the park

In the parking lot of the mall

We may not

Actually

Get there

All because a handful of people

A few hundred men

Needed to make an impossible amount of money

And when I say 'make'

No one 'makes' a billion dollars

You steal a billion dollars

You steal lives

Futures

And our futures

Mom

Are being stolen

Right now

And in ten

Maybe fifteen years

We will reach a point of no return

An irreversible chain reaction

Each year the dry season gets dryer

Riverbeds

And scorched lawns

The baked earth

Where nothing goes to seed

Farm fields outside the city

Already dead by the start of summer

And then elsewhere

Towns

And cities

Whole coastlines

Underwater

There was flooding around my grandparents' house this spring

Historic flooding

True story

They were trapped in their home, on the second floor, for a week with no electricity, no landline, no running water

They survived off cans of beans and tuna

A tin of apple juice

The fire department eventually boated in and rescued them

They were brought straight to the hospital and were put on IVs for dehydration

True story

Their house was totally ruined

It basically has to be gutted or torn down

All experts agree

All over the news they said

The flooding is climate change-related

And still

Still

My grandfather calls climate change 'liberal mania'

Those were his actual words

Mania?

Grandpa, you literally don't have a house

Three storms-of-the-century in the last three years, back to back

Like – ?

How can we talk?

What language?

What words?

If you don't want to listen

Do I have to speak louder?

Grandma?

Do I have to light flares?

Do I have to glue myself to the road?

Do I have to glue my hands to the sidewalk?

Do I have to glue myself to the doors?

Do I have to set myself on fire?

Do I have to glue myself to the airplane?

Do I have to glue / myself to the runway?

Do I have to glue myself to the doors of the stock exchange?

Do I have to glue myself the doors / of Shell Oil?

Do I have to glue myself / to the boardroom table?

Do I have to glue myself to / top of a subway car?

Do I have to set myself on fire?

Do I have to glue myself to / the doors of the bank?

Do I have to glue myself to your SUV?

Do I have to glue myself / to the pipeline?

Do I have to / glue myself to your yacht?

Do I have to set myself on fire?

Grandma

Grandma let me be clear

I want you to live

When the pandemic came, we sacrificed

We stopped the world for you

I stopped my life

Because I wanted you to live

What about us?

Do you want the same for me?

This is about lives

This is about our lives

Mom

Dad

If I said to you, tonight: you're failing us

Do you hear me?

Do you accept that?

You are failing

You have failed us

You are failures

And this madness

This blindness

This not-seeing

Not-doing

This business as usual

Will be remembered in history as one of the greatest failures of humankind

I told my mom yesterday over breakfast

'You'll be remembered as one of the greatest failures of mankind'

She didn't like that

She said: 'Well, what's your solution?'

I said: I'm twelve

I said

We could stop burning fossil fuels

That's a start

She said: 'Yeah, we've already thought of that'

'Believe it or not'

My dad said:

'Maybe instead of striking, you could stay in school and come up with a solution.'

I said, 'Go fuck yourself'

I'm joking

I definitely didn't say that

That would not have gone over well

Well, we could end capitalism

My mom rolled her eyes

'Please'

'You can't just say that'

My dad said

'You can't just say'

'End capitalism'

Why not?

'Because you benefit from it'

'It gives you the life you have'

'That cereal you're eating'

'That toast'

'That orange juice'

Yeah but what if we could have another life?

What if there was another way to be?

'You can't just say "end capitalism",' my dad said

'Besides'

My mom said

'You just can't'

'It's not possible'

'That's like saying: end oxygen'

End sadness

End the night

There are some things that are beyond us

Like God

Like cities

They operate completely of their own volition

You can't stop people from dying

Or eating

Or crying

'You can't stop capitalism,' she said

'Not by yourself, at least'

My dad laughed

Well, I'm not by myself

I said

Look

I'm not by myself

Look

Look at us

Here we are

Who said I was by myself?

Look

In the street

Look at us trying

We could

Maybe

Find another way

I start talking about circular economy

And rewilding nature

Forests

Mangroves

Seagrass meadows

Humans are very adaptable, Mom

And we still have some time

But not long

You want solutions that let you live like before

Live like now

But those don't exist anymore

Because we didn't act in time

You say: 'Well, we compost, we recycle'

'We bring our own bags to the store'

You taught us this was about individual responsibility

But then I look up and watch a billionaire burn a hundred thousand gallons of rocket fuel for a ten-minute joyride

I open Twitter and I see the Gulf of Mexico on fire

The ocean literally on fire

It's got to be a lot more than just composting, Mom

My brother was there at breakfast

He said 'God you're annoying'

'So self-righteous'

My sister

She's a bit older than me

She gets it

Mine does too

She's a bit younger

We're the same age

My brother –

He gets it

As kids we fought each other

I fought her all the time

Pulled her hair

She pushed me into a wall

The fridge

Slammed my head into the fridge

She threw dirt in my eyes

I broke her nose

Really?

With a stone

Your sister?

Yeah, well, she poured water on my laptop

Shit

I have three brothers and we –

We were always at each other's throats

This scar here?

This is from my brother

He bit me

I broke a plate on his head

We fought for everything

The front seat

The remote

The swing

The last slice of pizza

Of cake

Now we're fighting you

Now we're fighting for our lives

I have this memory of coming downstairs one night

And you and Mom were watching a movie on the couch

A disaster movie

And you said go back to bed

It's too scary

Cities under water

Cities on fire

Cities getting blown away

It's not for kids

You said the movie would keep us awake

But now

It's not a movie

There's no special effects

But you were right about one thing

Mom

Dad

We're awake

We are very much awake

Ever since I was little I've had dreams about a tornado

Wake up

It's always the same dream

Dark clouds on the horizon

Lightning is hitting the ground all around me

And the finger of God pokes down through the clouds and starts sucking up all the land it touches. It starts coming toward me, and I start running. I'm running through the park. Down the street. Toward my house. The tornado is coming for me, I can hear its scream. And as I get near my house, I can see my parents standing in the doorway shouting. They're shouting at me to hurry, to run, to run faster. But as I reach the door they close it. They close the door in my face, and I try to open it but I realise it's locked. They've locked it, and they're already hiding in the basement.

Wake up

My mom tells me I shouldn't worry

'What good will worrying do?'

But you know what, Mom?

Dad?

I want you to worry

Worry about the future

About the tipping point

Because

Dad

I'm panicking

Sometimes

Some mornings

A full-on attack

On the bus

In the shower

I have to sit down

And let the water fall over me

'Get ahold of yourself'

My mom says

'Get some perspective'

'Just breathe'

'Just calm down'

But Mom

It's time to panic

'I have enough to panic about, thank you'

'Taxes'

'The car'

'Traffic'

I know but –

'Dinner plans'

'We're late'

'Grandpa's in the hospital'

Okay but –

'Let's go, get in the car'

What about the ice caps?

What?

The bees

The shore line

My dad says

'What am I supposed to do about the goddamn bees?'

Dad, I'm literally losing sleep

'Well, don't'

Don't what?

'Don't lose sleep over the goddamn bees'

Dad, the fire is coming, can't you see?

The line of smoke

Can't you see?

The birds

Taking flight

Run

My whole life I've been

Running

Fast as I can

Running

My whole life

Not long

I haven't lived

Very long

My whole life

I've been running

To seek

To hide

Running away from

The fire

Running toward the light

Running from you

Running to

Catch the bus

Catch a break

Running

Until my lungs burned

Running across

The face of the Earth

To breathlessness

To burning

The lungs

Of the Earth

Breathless

Burning

The Amazon

Banyan trees

Rubber trees

A football field a second

Can you run that fast?

A football field a second?

You tell me I oversimplify

You tell me

I can't do anything about it

I'm just a child

Sixteen

Fourteen

You tell me to go back to school

You tell me

I'm not saying anything new

But what are you doing

Why aren't you doing anything?

Do something

Anything

For fuck sake

And until you do

We will

Until you do

We will flip our desks

We will

Throw our papers

And pull the alarm

Until you do

Pull the alarm

The schools will be empty

Until something changes

Pull the alarm

And if all our leaders can do is offer us words

And good intentions

Vote them out

The business as usual

Vote it out

When you have trash

Throw it out

And if you don't

We will

It wasn't us who voted them in

It wasn't our vote

And we're calling bullshit

The people in power

The people you voted in

One day

We're going to throw them out

Politicians saying we don't know what we're talking about

We're too young to know how government works

Throw them out

Mom

Dad

You say to me

I'm only going to say this once

I'm not going to repeat myself

Well

I'm only going to say this once

So I hope you're listening

This is a declaration of war

And you started it

No

You lit the fires

Not war

Yes

Yes, war

You didn't think this moment would come?

You can't say they lit the fires

No more than you have

Don't call it a war

Listen

Mom

You know what I'm talking about

Stop the banks

Put away your guns

Stop Facebook

My intention is to live

My intention is to live a good life on Earth

My intention is to grow old and die

I kinda like Facebook

Me too

Facebook is dead

Facebook is our fault

No, Facebook is Millennial

Fuck Facebook

Yeah Mark Zuckerberg is not our fault

None of this is our fault

Of course it is

It's not

Oh come on

You think TikTok is better?

You think our kids won't be talking to us like this?

Or their kids?

What sacrifices are you going to make?

Yeah

I make sacrifices

What, you put your computer on dark mode?

He only uses one square of toilet paper to wipe his ass

Shut up

You just told me you went to Croatia

Yeah because we have family there

So?

We go every year

Exactly, what the hell is that?

We're visiting family. / It's not like it's vacation.

So? It doesn't matter

It's family

We don't even have a choice, our parents make us

People should be limited to one flight a year

What?

One long-haul flight a year

You can't say that

People don't need more than that

You can't limit / people's freedom of mobility

You want a police state?

It's a basic human right

It's a privilege, not a right

Uh –

Freedom of movement is a right

Not the freedom to fly all over the world as much as you want whenever you want

You have no idea what you're talking about

You sound just like my dad

My dad says, 'What do you know?'

'What do you know?'

'What have you seen?'

'To talk to me'

'Me'

'An adult'

'This way'

And I say

Well

I once saw a boy drop a heavy rock off an overpass –

I once saw a man punch a woman –

– and it hit the windshield of a car passing below

– She was my mother

I once drowned in the water park

But they brought me back to life

Bodies have been inside my body

And I have been outside

Of my body

I've seen my blood

On a man's hands

I've seen blood

On every surface

I've seen my parents watching television in the living room

And imagined them as corpses

Lying side by side in their coffins

White light flickering

On their faces

Like death

I've seen a turtle run over by a car

I have seen the darkness

My sister

I've wiped the tears

From her cold cheek

The grease

Off her dirty face

You think I don't know?

Dad

The wind is moving at three metres a second today

And you think

What is the wind exactly?

And how have I gotten so old without knowing?

I wish you would teach me about that

I wish you would teach me how to live without shame

I wish you would teach me fragility

I wish you would teach me about your first heartbreak

One day

I will not think you know everything

Or even as much as me

Or maybe much at all

I will be disappointed

In you

In myself

For trusting you

I will have to change my thinking

Realise I am the adult

I am the one taking care of you

I don't hate you because you're weak

Or because you're scared

Or because you're wrong

I told my dad: I know you're older than me in this life, I grant you that.

But who knows how long it's taken our souls to get here?

There was one life I lived where I was a dog. I was owned by a family and they were very good to me.

And there was another life, when I was a car. And this man drove around inside of me, just going to different appointments and stuff. And then he got rid of me, and I was in a junkyard for years. Just years and years sitting there, underneath all of these other crushed cars, because even though they crushed me into a cube, my soul was still stuck inside.

And then in another life I was like a . . . a small bubble of foam on a wave coming to shore, and the wave broke, and I burst, and that was it, it was very quick

But before that I was a small stream, for centuries

And in another life I was a mortal girl

Which is this life

And in this life, I finally have the power to speak

After thousands of years

I have a mouth

I have words

So if you don't mind

Mom

Dad

I'm going to speak

I'm going to shout

When I become a human

I'm going use some words

Can you still hear me?

Is my microphone on?

Check check

Check one two

Shout out to my mom

Shout out to the moms here tonight

Shout out to my followers

Shout out to the snowflakes

Shout out to the strikers

Shout out to those who walked out

Text me when you're home safe

I posted this photo of me with this guy I'm seeing

And my mom commented below: You need a job, Lauren, not a boyfriend.

Brutal

My mom sent me a text

Why're you tweeting like you're famous, you have maybe seven active followers

Blocked

Shout out to the dead

How do you tell your mom you've got a hammer stuck in your mouth?

Shout out to the angels

Do you ever just realise that your mom is a living, breathing angel and feel really bad for being so shit to her when you were fifteen?

I asked my mom what I should be for Halloween

And she said:

'I don't know, what's popular among your generation?'

Apparently Xanax wasn't the right answer

Tyler started a live video

Watch it before it ends

Marika started a live video

Thomas started a live video

Watch it before the world ends

Shout out to the people arrested on the bridge

Ahmed started a live video

Shake the table

To the girls who spoke up

Shake the table

Sometimes, ladies

It's not enough just to get a seat at the table

Sometimes

You need to shake the table

Shake

Shake the table

Here's to real justice

Justice for the water we drink

Real justice

Justice for our air we breathe

Shake

Justice for how much women get paid

Yes

And for the workers without protections

Justice for the non-human beings

I want justice for the oceans

And the forests

And the farmers

Sometimes

You need to shake the table

I'm only going to say this once

You say

You say I have nothing to complain about

Shake

That we have more things than you ever had

More education

No smallpox

We'll live past a hundred

No Mao Zedong

Better nutrition

What do we have to complain about?

If you're a woman

If you're queer

Why are you complaining?

Shake the table

It's a privilege

You say

To skip school

To protest

Privilege?

We're spoiled

Ungrateful

You say

We're entitled

You want to tell me clean drinking water

Clean air

Is that a privilege now?

Excuse me?

Whose privilege is the Amazon?

Whose privilege is the Coral Reef?

Whose cities are disposable?

Whose bodies?

Whose countries?

Who lives in the sacrifice zone?

Who lives beside the toxic e-dumps?

The piles of burning computers?

Who mines the coltan for our phones?

The lead

The mercury

Shake

Who's collateral?

Shake

Who's on the front lines?

Who's always on the front lines?

Shake the table

Shake shake shake

Yourself

Shake awake, Mom

Shake the trunk

Shake the roots

Shake awake

Shake the night

Shake the city

Shake its doubt

If you were waiting for a time

The time is now

If you were waiting for a line

The line has been drawn

If you were waiting for others they are waiting for you

A line in the sand

A line of light

The lines of your hand

The horizon

I was twelve years old when I saw the sun set on the horizon for the first time

All the way down

Over the ocean

I've never seen it

The ocean

Really?

I've never seen the ocean

Not yet

My parents took me camping there once

There were cliffs

Quite high

I mean – relatively

My father asked

'Have you ever seen the sun rise over the water?'

I said I don't think so

He said you have to wake up early

Okay then

Wake me up, in the morning

I want to be there when the sun rises

And so he set his alarm

And we woke up –

– so tired –

– just before the dawn

The birds

Everything was cold

The wind

He wrapped me in a blanket

Over my shoulders

We walked to the edge of the cliff and looked out

And we watched the sun rise together over the water

It was –

It really was incredible

And I felt very close to him

In that moment

I felt very much

In the world

In love with

Being in the world

Like a very small thing

With not much time

Poor Dad

Am I your child?

Am I the thing you wanted?

Am I your wish fulfilled?

All the questions I've ever asked you

Is it getting dark?

Is my head bleeding?

Is it time yet?

Is it time to go?

Is time linear?

Is it worth it?

Is life – ?

Is all this pain?

And will it get better?

And if not now, when?

And if not for your love

And if not for the night

If not for the cities

And the streets

When they empty

And all the things you've said to me, Mom

As I walk out the door

'Hold on'

'Lemme give you a kiss'

'You have something on your face'

'Your hair'

(*In annoyed tone*) Mom

Lick your hand

And slick it down

'There you go'

She just wants the best for me

She says

'I just want the best for you'

She says

Well, Mom

I just want to live

I want to live to see a seagrass meadow

I want to live to see my daughter

I want my daughter to live to see

A seagrass meadow

I want my daughter's daughter to live to see

A forest

A mangrove

I want to live

I want to live to see my daughter's daughter

I want to live

It's hard to live in a broken world

When you're broken

I want to live

Last year I was in a really dark relationship

Like really dark

He was older than me

How much?

Like illegal older?

I guess so, yeah

He was an addict

He used to hit me, and steal things from me

And my mom kept telling me: just stop

Just stop seeing him

But I couldn't because I was scared

But also it was how I knew how to feel good

We had good sex

He made me feel loved

And I guess I was addicted to him

What I'm saying is –

– sometimes I think it's hard to stop doing the thing that's destroying you. You know? Like humans? I get it.

Forgive yourselves

You're broken

I know because I was broken

You're broken

Forgive yourselves

But also get your shit together. Give up your addictions

They're going to kill you

You know that they are

Sometimes it's hard to stop doing the thing that's destroying you

When it's the only way you know how to feel good

Or safe

Secure

The crazy things you do to feel secure

Like voting for fascists

Mom

What is it with your generation and fascists?

Look at the numbers

We're not the ones voting for them

Dad

Please

Stop

Stop voting for fascists

Look at the numbers

It's not us

It's you

Read our lips

Stop

Voting

For fascists

Britain

America

Why is that your solution?

Brazil

Do they make you feel more secure?

Poland

Hungary

France

Is it because of refugees?

Globalisation?

Are you feeling unsteady in your old age?

Impotent?

You need someone to hold your dick?

Let me recite what history teaches

Watch for the signs

Mom

Because I don't think you're watching

And maybe, Dad

You've forgotten what they are

Please watch for the signs

Watch for the changing of the guard

Watch for the power grab

Watch when they name the enemy

And try to rally you around it

Watch for the rallies

Watch the military

Watch what they do

Watch the elections

Watch the journalists

And the intellectuals

And what happens to them

Watch what the scientists can say

And not say

Watch the rich

Watch for the money changing hands

Watch what happens at night

When nobody is watching

Watch the conspiracies

Watch the churches

Watch the prisons

Watch the schools

Watch what is said

And done

To women

Watch for the signs, Mom

Because I don't think you are

The way you talk about other immigrants

Dad

Makes me think you don't know

Makes me think you can't see

What is happening

Makes me angry

Makes me think you've forgotten

What history teaches

Remember

What happens over there in the desert

Happens in your backyard

What happens on the screen

Happens in real life

What happens to your neighbour

Happens to you

This is the sign

The sign is death

Can I ask you, Dad

What is a country?

I know you love our country

Flags

Borders

Anthems

But what is a country?

I have a feeling

When the world floods there will be no countries

When the world burns

There will be no borders

No wall can keep the fire out

No wall can keep the people out

I have a feeling

The Earth does not know the name of our country

The Earth does not know

Its shape on the map

And in several thousand years, no one will

Almost like it was never there

Almost like it was something we made up

You say you're a reasonable person, Dad

Reasonable people

Doing reasonable things

Good people

Salt of the earth

Just trying to get by

Tell me: what's reasonable

Dad

Walls?

Camps?

These seem reasonable

To reasonable people

Good ideas

To good people

One morning you're standing at the window watching our neighbour in her garden
and you say

'I'd like you to go next door and help her for a bit'

What?

Why?

'Because she's old'

'She's a good person'

Why is she a good person?

Because she smiles at you?

Because she has a garden?

Dad, she's a racist

'No she's not'

She told me never trust Muslims

'Yes, but'

She's homophobic

'I'm sure she doesn't have any problem with you'

She doesn't have a clue!

She's always asking if I have a boyfriend

'She's always been very sweet'

Yeah you're white, middle class, straight

'Alright, enough'

I'm just saying –

'She's almost eighty'

So?

Does that makes her a good person?

Because she's old?

Because she bakes for you at Christmas?

Fuck her

'Excuse me?'

She's a pig

Let her crawl around in the dirt

You said that?

To your dad?

Nazis had gardens too

Whoa

Yup

I could not say that to my dad

Hell no

Do you not get it? Maybe I've been mincing my words. I hate you. I hate old people. I literally hate you. You have fucked up this world. For us. For ever. At least for a very, very long time. And, what, we're just supposed to forgive you? Because you're cute? Fragile? Toothless? Senile? Because you knit? And do crosswords? And go on package holidays and take photographs with your stupid cameras in your big shorts? I am literally filled with rage when I see you. I want to shove your faces in the dirt of your gardens. I'm not going to stand up for you on the fucking bus. I'm not going to hold the door open for you, or talk to you about the weather, or smile as you count your change for ever at the counter, all the change you have in your pockets, all the money in the fucking world that you earned when you walked out of college, with half my education, into a high-paid jobs with full benefits, and then voted in governments, one after the other, which stripped away workers' benefits and job security. And now I'll have to work two, three, four jobs earning a fraction of what you did, and you call us lazy, narcissistic. I'm not going listen to you complain about the price of tomatoes and lettuce in the grocery stores, when – you know who's keeping those prices low? All the migrants who fled war-zones who you don't want in the country who are bent over in the dirt not, no, not weeding their flower gardens, but trying to make enough money to keep their families alive. You tell me you don't recognise your country anymore. All these new faces. New languages. New gadgets. They scare you. So you vote in people who tell you they're going to wind back the clock. Take us back to the glory days when people like you were carefree and oblivious, and we were beaten up in the fucking streets for being Black, or Asian, for being a faggot, and kept out of jobs for being a woman, and raped without recourse. So no. I'm sorry. I'm not going to help you pluck weeds out of your fucking garden.

Silence.

I think that's really shit

Me too

Like –

Personally, I think we should respect our elders

Why?

What've then done to deserve it?

I love my grandparents

Live a long time?

I love my grandparents too but –

Hoard money?

– I don't have to respect their messed-up views

My neighbour –

They have knowledge to impart

So do we

Sure, but –

So do people they think shouldn't be in our country

But talk to them

Don't shut them out

Yeah I do

I do talk to them

And I'm horrified by what comes out of the decrepit mouths

My neighbour, she was old, like about seventy-seven or something. And like she actually died in the pandemic.

Seriously?

Yeah, like actually died of it. Because she used to volunteer a lot, like at my school. And when my mom was getting chemotherapy, this woman used to drive her to appointments at the hospital because my dad was working.

Listen I'm not saying old people aren't nice –

I was so sad

My grandmother's an activist

So don't generalise

It's what I feel, okay –

Well –

– so fuck off, I don't think it's without truth

It's not productive

At all

The opposite, actually

Like – dangerous

Well

It is

We need a way forward

The rich are oppressors, not the elderly

Yes

You think it's easy being old? The elderly get treated like shit.

Yeah the thing is

The truth is

We probably need to kill the one per cent

No –

If we're going to survive

– that's not what I'm saying

We need

Violent insurrection

Come on

That's not funny

Violence is sometimes / a necessary means to an end

Unavoidable

Violence

Real change

Violence is never –

If we're going to survive

Even just the upper .5 per cent

They need to be killed

That probably means some of you

They'll just be replaced

Guys, seriously

That's not something to joke about

I wasn't

Why should there be billionaires?

It's obscene

No violence

Their wealth is a violence

That wealth – ?

That is violence

That kind of wealth – ?

A billion dollars? Is criminal

Honestly, if I could –

If I could I'd burn down their mansions

Me too

Firebomb them

Molotov

Set Amazon on fire

Ha

Burn Amazon

Or

Or turn their mansions into something like, you know –

Homeless shelters

Or like free daycares

Honestly, billionaires – ?

Drag them out

They should be fucking dragged out of their spaceships

But

And strung up

Jeff Bezos

Tied to a lamppost

Guys

With shit stuffed in his mouth

His own shit

No, your shit

I'd shove my shit in Jeff Bezos's mouth

Just shut up

You shut up

We need a way forward

We need revolution

You say you don't want violence?

I'm saying –

You don't get to say that. You don't get to say: I don't want violence. Tell the people of Dhaka that, when their city is underwater. When the slums of Lagos and Jakarta are underwater, tell them: no violence. This is a violence. We are a violence. Us sitting here in Toronto, this theatre, our privilege, our clothes, our power, this is a violence, we are a violence. And trust me, when the crops fail, and the fields are burning, and the water is rising, there will be violence. And it will stay over there for awhile. But one day, it will come here. It will come here, with bodies, and faces, and names. Because the violence has always existed, and it has always been ours. We have just pretended not to notice.

But I still think –

You don't think the rich know that there'll be violence? You don't think the billionaires have been preparing? Amazon, Google –

Building armies

Huawei

Collecting our data

Armies?

They'll be more powerful than governments

Mr Conspiracy

They already are

Education, health care, building roads –

Armies, though?

Drones

No

I'd still say hope –

Facial recognition

– hope is stronger than violence

Tell that to the dying

Hope is stronger than fear

Hope is your privilege

This is a revolution of compassion

This

This is a revolution –

Yes

– of tenderness

Human-scaled

Human to human-scaled

When I become human –

Not of despair or rage or / whatever fear you're peddling

There's already rage

And what conquers rage?

Rage is rage

What conquers rage?

Oh please, don't – don't give me that 'hope' bullshit. Your hope is inaction. Your hope is lazy and weak. Your hope is the hope that someone else will sort it out, and / that you can go on living your same life

My hope is that our compassion for one another, for the earth

For your children

Supersedes your fear and mistrust

Supersedes your greed

Supersedes

Viciousness

And cowardice

And guilt

Supersedes

Our shame

Our always wanting

Wanting and

Craving

Yearning

Our never understanding ourselves

And hurling ourselves into death

When I become a human, I want to remember what it was not to be human. I want to remember the time I spent as a rock. As a stream. As a piece of trash on the highway. I want to remember what it was to have no say. When I become a human, I want to be a healer. A doctor, maybe. Or someone who holds other people when they cry. When I become a human I want to be patient and gentle. I want to remember names. Colours of people's eyes. Colours of the sky, at different times of day. The smell of certain trees. Certain times of year. When I finally get the chance to become human, I'm going to spend some time using my voice. To sing. To talk. To make myself understood. Before people had microphones, they just held their hands up to their mouths like this and spoke very loudly. And maybe, before microphones, people just had to listen to each other just a little bit harder. A little bit more carefully. Animals, if they don't listen, they die. Death will creep up behind them, when they're least expecting. When I become human I'm going to listen. Every day that I'm human – Every single day –

Every day

Every time there is music

Every day we don't give up

Every moment of every day

Every moment there is hope

Every shred of hope left

Every one of us

Every second of the day

If you're still able

To wake up in the morning

If the morning

If there is still the morning

If you can get out of bed

If light

If there is still light

If the birds come

And don't hit the glass

If the birds and the ice come

And don't melt in your glass

If the day lasts

And the sun sets

If the day closes into night

If there is laughter

If there is

If you are still there

Dad

If at the end of the day

If you're still there

If your arms

If time

In your loving arms

If in time

If there is a way forward

There must be

A way forward

And if the rain

And if the city

And even in the flood

If you still love me

If I'm your child

Music crescendos – then cuts out.

A silence.

Eventually . . .

Check

Check one

Check one two

Can you hear me?

Are you still listening?

Pause.

I think we're all trying our best

Not hard enough

Will we be any better?

When we're sitting where they are now, and our children are here talking to us?

What will we have done?

It's hard

The way forward –

I know you're trying

Like really hard

When you feel –

The only way forward –

– insignificant

– is urgent togetherness

Urgent – ?

Togetherness. We are all in this together; urgently, passionately, presently

Here

Now

Hurting

Yes

Hurting very much

Okay

Angry

Perhaps, but –

Working through

Working through it

Towards

Some progress

Is possible

Maybe even tonight

When I look in your eyes

Maybe even some

Small

Breakthrough

Tonight

When I look in your eyes

Mom

Dad

I know

I know you're doing your best

It's not good enough

I know

It has to get better

But I love you

Pause.

I love you

Pause.

I love you too

Gran

I love you

My neighbours

Teachers

I love you

Truck drivers

Doctors

The workers at the docks

I love you

My hairdresser and –

Farmers

 – the garbage collectors

Adults I've never met

The old woman on the bus

The nurses in the hospital

Executives –

The men in the forests –

 – in their suits

 – with chainsaws

Even them

I love you

And I forgive you

I forgive you

I forgive you

I forgive all of you

I forgive you

I forgive you but

I don't accept

We forgive you

But we don't accept

You are human

Move past this anger

I'm still angry

Move past it

What you have done is forgiven –

We forgive you

 – but it is not acceptable

We do not accept it

You must know

You are forgiven

But what you have done is unacceptable

There can be forgiveness

Without acceptance

It's the only way forward

Tonight

I look you in the eye

And you see me for the first time

Tonight

I look you in the eye

We're on the same side

Tonight I look you in the eye

You die, I die

Tonight

I look you in the eye

What will it take?

Tonight I look you in the eye

What took you so long?

Tonight

I look you in the eye

We're on the same side

Tonight

I look you in the eye

You die, I die

Tonight

We forgive you

But we don't accept

Tonight

Set your alarm

I want to be there when the sun rises

Mom

Dad

Set your alarm

I want to be there

When the sun rises

In the dead of the night

Wake up

It's time to get up

Before the dark

Before the birds

And move with me

By your side

It's time

To be in the world

To be

In love with being in the world

To be a very small thing

With not much time

Wake up

I said

I want to be there when the sun rises

Wake up

This is the alarm

I want to be there

When the sun rises

Wake up

I want to be there tomorrow

I want to be there

The day after

And the day after that

This is the alarm

I want to be there when the sun rises

I want to be there

I want to be there

I want to be there

Blackout.

Is My Microphone On?

BY JORDAN TANNAHILL

Notes on rehearsal and staging, drawn from a workshop with the writer, held at the National Theatre, October 2022, faciliated by director Deborah Pearson

How the writer came to write the play

Jordan Tannahill was initially commissioned to write a play for young audiences by the Theater der Welt Festival in 2019, at a time when young people around the world were mobilising globally through the Fridays for Future climate strikes. Rather than writing a play for young audiences, he wanted to write a play *for* adults, featuring young people. It was time for adults to do the listening, in this case to the concerns, fears, anger and desires of the young. Tannahill himself also happened to be involved in climate activism at the time, through Extinction Rebellion's Spring Rebellion protests in London, 2019. He held one of their four sites and was arrested during the protests.

During this time Greta Thunberg made her famous speech which included the line 'Is my microphone on?', which became the title of this play.

How do we have an intergenerational reckoning? How do we speak amongst ourselves both on the macro and micro level? How do we talk to our kids and to our parents about the climate emergency?

Originally the text included a lot of verbatim quotations from newspaper articles, from young protestors and from activists. This was the starting point before going into rehearsals for the first production of the play, which radically changed the text throughout the rehearsal process. Young people making the show were never asked to share personal stories, but their sentiments, their politics and concerns have fed into the play which led to writing, rewriting, writing, rewriting.

Jordan Tannahill thinks it's a piece that has rhythm and tenderness at its heart, that is essential to keep, but elements can change and evolve with each new cast that performs it. He believes the only way for collective action is if there is still hope at the heart of the play – the text has a pulse that is hard-hitting but has tenderness and wonder.

Introductions, icebreakers and aims of the day

After initial introductions, lead director Deborah Pearson asked the group to decide on something concrete they wanted to get out of the workshop day.

The group then did a check-in – going around the circle introducing themselves, sharing their pronouns and one word/sentence about how they were feeling that morning. The day ended with a group check-out – with everyone saying one word about how they were feeling.

The group's wants and aims for the workshop were:

- Exploring the form of the play
- Learning about what inspired Jordan Tannahill to write the play
- General approach to staging the play – 'Lightbulb moment'
- Balance of making the show hard-hitting, but not alienating audiences – 'How not to rant'
- How to approach casting and the importance of characters in the play
- Finding the different staging and acting styles within the text
- The role of music in the show
- Approaching language (swearing) and sensitive material when working with young people
- Is this play for the audience or is this for the young people performing it?
- How to empower and give hope for students – how to educate the participants optimistically
- Exploring the flexibility of the text
- How to bring the voices and experiences of the young people into the show – making the show specific to each cast
- Finding opportunities for collaboration with a designer and make (possibility of using multimedia)
- How to engage the young people with the topic of the climate crisis
- Highlighting the intersectionality of the climate emergency
- Is it possible to avoid hypocrisy?
- How to find the macro and the micro in the text
- Finding the contrast and variety within the text
- Activism vs play – is this a show or is this a protest?

Approaching the play

Jordan Tannahill said that this is a living text that should always respond to the present – it's essential that the text is always up-to-date and reflects the issues and questions the local community is interested in and engaged with. What are the issues the young people in your company want to talk about?

This is a play for young people as much as it is for the adults. The young people are artists themselves. They shouldn't feel that the text is imposed on them, but rather it should give them agency. There is scope for change and adaptation of the text, so it reflects and highlights the issues the members of the company want to talk about.

It could be valuable to reach out to organisations like Greenpeace or Extinction Rebellion to get a guest speaker to come and talk to your young people, to help inform them about the climate crisis and give them context. Larger organisations like Greenpeace will have ways to book a guest speaker online, but Extinction Rebellion will likely have local groups who can be contacted too (and might be more specific to the community and the location the piece is performed at).

Sensitivity, support and access

Deborah Pearson mentioned how it might be helpful to set up a system for rehearsals through which the young people can seek support, in case they are triggered by any of the themes of the play. It's important for this process/system to be outside the rehearsal room. This means that it's not solely on the director/teacher/young company director to deal with the mental wellbeing of the group, but that there is a clear way for professional support to be accessed should it be needed.

When it comes to the performance, incorporating visual points or creative captioning into the production could be effective and helpful to take pressure off young people in terms of remembering lines and it also instantly creates more access both for performers and audiences alike.

Themes

The climate crisis – specifically intergenerational/collective reckoning with the climate emergency and the choices of the older generations.

How do we speak between generations – both within our homes, parents to children, children to parents, siblings to siblings, children to grandparents, etc. – and societally?

Structure, style and transitions

Throughout the day, Deborah Pearson and Jordan Tannahill returned to this idea of how productions have the chance to use the huge amounts of energy young people have. Finding ways to pour that energy and their interests into the style of the piece can be hugely effective. They encouraged the group to give space for the chaos that comes organically from the young people – to create pockets of controlled (and by the performance, choreographed) chaos. 'Don't try and make the young people into what they are not, rather lean into what they are.'

They offered provocations about how to think about, approach and explore staging possibilities and styles:

- **The power of repetition:** Repeating moments, actions or images can be extremely powerful and can make an audience reconsider and question what they've previously seen.
- **The power of tasks:** Give real tasks for the young people to do onstage – this can be hugely engaging and is more freeing than traditional blocking. For example: 'I need you to move these instruments across the space.' 'I need you to walk from one corner to the other corner of the room.' 'I need you to stack these chairs.' 'I need you to play this instrument for three minutes.' Tasks have real stakes and require more agency from the young people – as audience members we don't know how a task will go, making it extremely theatrical and interesting to watch.

- **Chorus work and the power of silence:** It's an open text giving the space for the lines to be distributed in lots of different ways – find dynamism in how the text is spoken. Are there sections spoken by the whole company, moments delivered by smaller groups and lines said by individuals? Exploring and playing with these possibilities can bring variety and dynamism to the piece. Moments of silence and stillness can also be powerful.

- **Images as visual metaphors on stage:** Exploring and creating images with the young people can be a great way of generating style and staging. The group circled back to the idea and images of a table ('shake the table', who has a seat at the table, etc.).

Language

Post-dramatic: Jordan Tannahill as a writer works both in the dramatic and the post-dramatic form. This play explores the post-dramatic. Explore and lean into this with your company.

Internet lingo: The text uses and embraces the language used on the internet especially by young people. It is okay if some of the lingo is unfamiliar for adult audience members if it's recognisable for the young people.

Characters and characterisation

Tannahill's advice: The young people are playing a version of themselves – but there is still a thin layer that should give them protection. There is a proximity to their own selves, but it is still a theatrical presentation. The young people should feel safe and empowered to be present on stage. They don't need to 'act' in the sense of embodying a character, but the key part of performing this text is in being present and really listening to their ensemble – finding ways that they are focused and interested on stage (as opposed to being interesting).

Monologues: The text is open and new monologues could be strung together from the text, but it might be worth exploring different ways of staging the text as there are a few monologues which are written as such within the text. These moments will be more powerful if the rest of the text is divided up and not done as a monologue.

Production, staging and design

Simplicity – using only a few elements creatively can be extremely effective. For example, having a few microphones and having them become/represent other props can work well. Less is more. Crafting the space in a beautiful way. It's worth considering key elements/set pieces/props and exploring what they could achieve – can the show be done just with using lots of microphones? Or solely using chairs? What is the theatrical gesture of the space?

Elements and approaches that might be worth considering:

- Use of light and darkness
- Rhythm and movement are a key part of the piece – explore their possibilities, especially in terms of ensemble work
- Ways to bring attention from large scenes to small, more intimate scenes – 'telescoping' into a domestic scene (e.g. parents talking to their child)

Finding ways to lean into what the young people are interested in can support the staging and design too. For example: If they are obsessed with their phones, is there a way to use phones creatively and visually in an interesting way? Is there a hidden stage image in them? (See link to *Ist mein Mikro an?* in references below.)

Costume design

Jordan Tannahill mentioned that in previous productions the costumes were sourced by the young people from their wardrobes or second-hand shops. Once the costume pieces were picked, they were kept at the theatre until the end of the run as the young people's costumes (it's important to separate their costumes from their everyday wear – again to create that thin layer of separation between performance and their own selves). Deborah Pearson also suggested that asking the young people to bring three options from home can be a good way of finding the right fit – almost holding a 'costume day' to pick and choose. It's a chance to give them chance to express themselves via their clothes.

Exercises for use in rehearsals/approaching the play

Read-through of the play: Deborah Pearson asked the group to read the play together. The group read in a way where each new line was read by the next person in the circle.

Identifying sections of the text: It's an open text, so it can be helpful to break the text into sections. Deborah Pearson asked people to get into groups of four and to go through the whole play and start to break it into sections.

Working on stage images and initial visual responses to the text: The group was split into teams of eight and asked to work on one section, creating a stage image based on that section. The groups had twenty-five minutes to choose a section of the text, discuss, explore and create one image. The image could be a frozen or a moving image. Sections and approaches the groups came up with included:

- Working on the dream-hurricane section exploring the use of movement. They created the sense of the hurricane via the use of their bodies moving in the space.
- Working on the section where the speaker talks about being a car in another life. They explored this by creating images specifically exploring the closeness/distance between bodies on stage, starting closely together and then leaving the person behind from the group, turning away from them.
- Exploring the section of running/being out of breath using breathing and repetitive movement.

- Exploring the same running section using percussions and rhythms created with participants bodies (e.g. stomping and drumming on their own chest).

Reflections:

- Bodies as source of percussion has lots of possibilities and can be effective.
- Coming up with a series of images with your cast can be fruitful.
- These images can be created, moved through, and changed in collaboration with the cast. Deborah Pearson mentioned that this is an exercise she uses a lot in her practice.
- It is useful to think about images and possibilities depending on the size of your cast.

Coming up with tasks: The groups were asked to choose a different section of the play, preferably from the second half. They had to come up with a task to do based on/ using one page of the text. A task is an action that can be clearly performed with an aim. For example: stacking all the chairs in the space or walking from one corner to the other corner of the room.

Tasks the groups came up with included: Untangling a bundle of lanyards, different forms of writing (on paper, voice notes, graffitiing), musical chairs (with the person without a chair performing the text), getting ready (tying shoes, putting jackets on, drinking a bottle of water), tearing up paper and aiming to toss paper balls into a bin.

Reflections:

- You must be present; you need to be doing the action in real time over trying to 'do' acting.
- Metaphors which are legible but not completely obvious can be powerful.
- Something can turn into a monologue even if the text suggests it being divided originally between several people.
- Graffitiing can be a great way to connect protest with the performance and is a powerful image.
- Exploring different audience configurations and moving through the audience feels exciting – especially viewing this through as an experience of collective reckoning.
- Setting up games and rules can be a powerful metaphor; e.g. the power of the image of seeing people needing to fight for a chair on stage representing their fight to be heard.
- The rhythm of a task is important and slowly building an image can be effective – images can build gradually.
- The importance and the possibilities of devising tasks with the students/young people.

Getting young people to play competitive games can be really engaging. It is important if you do, that there is a clear understanding of the rules and that the games are played for real on stage with actual rules and real winners. It is important to make the game specific and to use it, so it generates almost choreography that is fresh and live on stage. It is important the rules are known by company members, even if they are unknown to the audience. Deborah Pearson mentioned that the tasks she enjoys watching the most on stage are those that are just difficult enough they might fail. She also talked about the possibility of creating a dramaturgy of a task – exploring how the task builds, going from small to more theatrical (e.g. more people joining in, or the task becoming larger or more difficult).

Jordan Tannahill said that it's great to find tasks which are organically connected to the world of the young people. For example, seeing paper being tossed feels constantly recognisable in terms of a school context.

Music

Why music? For Jordan Tannahill, part of the writing process is about figuring out the container of a play (the form of the play). He was drawn to the idea of this play being like a deconstructed rock concert or jam session, and imagined that the performance might have a few elements that would express this – a few instruments and maybe a few mics. The idea of who gets a voice, and whose voice is amplified on stage is important. He was interested in the idea of music being an assault – a tool that can overwhelm. He also mentioned that an essential question when staging this piece is about how the music works with the text – finding ways and approaches which don't let the music overpower but rather work with the text.

Dramaturgy: Music represents the crisis. Life is going on – domestic scenes are happening between families, but the music is there as a pulse in the background the way the climate crisis constantly continues in the background behind our daily lives. That's how the music works in this piece, building towards a powerful crescendo bringing the music to the forefront, the same way a crisis comes into focus at a breaking point.

Exercise using music: Jordan Tannahill asked three people from the group to pick up guitars (two electric guitars and a bass) and six people to read the text. Aim of the exercise: to explore ways that ensures the music is present but isn't overpowering the text. 'Musicians' were invited to use the instruments as if getting ready for a performance as the readers began reading the top of the text. They focused on the beginning when the first musician is introduced via the text – this is a crucial moment as it introduces the idea of music being played throughout the performance. This can be emphasised, for example, by the bass player stringing a chord and for the readers to wait until the music fades away.

Tannahill then asked the group to look at the section on page 121 ('Wake up'. . . into 'Every time X strums this guitar') and for the person playing the first guitar to join the bass player, strumming roughly once every fifteen seconds (but the intervals between strums can vary). He then asked the group to move to the next section an instrument is introduced ('Shake the city' around p. 134), asking the third guitar to join in, being played or 'noodled' roughly once every five seconds (again, the intervals can vary). The music should be present in the background, supporting the text, but not overpowering it.

Tannahill mentioned that there is scope for finding different tones within the aural world – it can get slightly menacing, but there is space for it to have different feels to it.

Question and answer with Jordan Tannahill

Q: You mentioned that you don't want bells and whistles to be used in performances – could you clarify what you mean by that?
A: It's about setting up the conventions and the language of the show and how I'd suggest steering away from putting too many ideas and forms on the top of each other. Trust to go with one idea – think about your ideas economically. Stillness, rhythm or movement can all be great, just be wary and resist doing too much – a repetitive movement might be more powerful than a complicated dance sequence. Young people's bodies on stage are already powerful.

Deborah Pearson added that you can often find simplicity by trying a lot of things and as you move forward with the process, you'll be able to refine and simplify it to find the most powerful staging.

Q: What does the phrase 'shake the table' mean?
A: It's a line inspired by a 2019 speech by American congresswoman Alexandria Ocasio-Cortez, and is employed in the text to draw attention to the intersectional nature of the climate crisis. It is often said that the goal of rights movements is to get certain people 'a seat at the table', but sometimes this is not enough, because what is happening 'at the table' is corrupt, or ruinous to the planet. It's about wanting more than simply the status quo but, instead, affecting real, revolutionary change.

Q: Does the same performer have to play one instrument for the whole performance?
A: Feel free to change it up if you'd like.

Q: Are you okay with actor-musicians working on this and to potentially bring the music more in the foreground of the piece?
A: Definitely! That could be really cool. Use the resources available to you and the skills of the young people you are working with. The important this is that the music should build slowly throughout the performance rather than all at once.

Q: Could you expand on what you mean by the music needing to build throughout the piece?
A: Of course! The music gradually builds throughout the performance and once the kick drum is introduced the piece kicks off and soon after climaxes musically. In the text, I suggested that someone begins singing a melody. This can be interpreted in a lot of ways – this could be vocalised, maybe it is a choir moment. It's probably better to stay away from singing existing songs or singing actual text – it's more of a singing of a melody without words. After the music hits its climax, it cuts out. It should reflect on the questions: 'What's left after a crisis?' 'What's left after shouting at each other?' 'How can we be quiet, still, compassionate with each other?' We have a crescendo and then silence and stillness. It lays the foundation for the possibility for tenderness.

Q: Can we change the instruments depending on students' abilities?
A: Definitely, that could be cool. Use the resources available to you and the skills of the people you are working with.

Q: How do you not make the show a rant?
A: There are domestic, more intimate moments in the play; for example, children talking with their parents at home. There are also moments of magical realism. For me, it's about questioning who has a voice in the conversation. Those lyrical moments are possibilities for tenderness and for quiet. The first ten pages of the show are certainly a provocation – it's to get an audience back-footed and then slowly get them back. Fear and anger can be at a similar space, but at the heart of it, anger is usually sparked by fear. There is discord within the voices too – there is no one message within the text; what it suggests is that it's a complicated issue and the only way to deal with it is through mutual compassion and tenderness.

Q: Is it open to interpretation of what the language of the show is?
A: Yes, absolutely! The piece can hold any theatrical gesture – it's about finding the right gesture for your show. As directors, having an open text like this means that it's truly up to you to make the decisions about what the staging is. In my own practice, I tend to be more drawn to creating situations over expressionistic imagery. But if you have one instinct/one concept for the show, you should follow that.

Q: Where do you stand on rearranging the order of the text or cuts?
A: I am open to that. There is a dramaturgy to it, and reasons why things are ordered in a way they are, to create the flow of the text. It's about making sure that if you change elements the text keeps its flow and its rhythm. But make it work for you.

Q: Is there anything you really don't want to be changed or done with the text?
A: I would say staying away from existing songs (especially older pop and rock songs) is preferable or if they are used to be chosen by the young people to reflect their tastes in music. But generally, it is pretty open. The piece can rely on choral work, or have it built on movement and choreography – it's a director's text so you can make your own interpretations.

Q: Can relationships be adjusted based on the young people's experiences? For example, if there is an absence of parents could the domestic scenes be changed?
A: Yes, of course – there is space for reflecting the experiences of the young people who you are making the show with.

Q: Where is/is there any comedy and joy in this piece? Where are the moments of lightness?
A: Maybe it doesn't come across cold reading it, but there is definitely joy and comedy in the text. For me, there is a certain dark comedy in lines like, 'Grandpa, you literally don't have a house', for example. There are also moments of beauty and wonder, as when the performers talk about seeing the ocean for the first time. There is a lot of space for playfulness in the text and as a director you can find, explore and create space for these within the performance. It's probably helpful if you break the text up into sections as the director and within that you can find all the variety and changes – the

light and the dark in the text. Breaking it into sections is a really important exercise to prepare for directing this play.

Q: The audience. You mentioned how it feels important that even adults not connected to the young people performing it would come and see it. What is your ideal response from an audience? What if some people who watch it are offended? How can we get people into the theatre who don't care about the climate crisis and make them want to take action?

A: As I am not an educator, it feels like something that would be essential for the groups staging this play to come together and discuss this as you are the experts. This is also why I am so in awe of all your bravery and hard work putting this play on within an educational context. This is such a courageous and vital act in itself. If it's helpful, you can emphasise and frame the narrative of the project around how, at the end of the day, this is a professional play written by a professional playwright – and though the layer is thin, the young people are playing characters and not themselves. It's a post-dramatic piece that hopefully teaches young people about how to make art. Also, young people know dark, they live dark, they swear in their daily lives, and it's talking about issues that are actually affecting them and the people in the room. This is hopefully a journey that makes the young people feel passionate about the climate crisis, but it is also about them going on this journey and coming to terms with its difficulties. How do we deal with all this anger? The ideal outcome is families starting conversations – even if they hated it or already feel informed, it makes them talk about it again or for the first time. It should create a space for dialogue even if that dialogue is hard.

Also, in my experience, audiences actually really enjoy the moments of argument in the play – often there is lightness to it or a heat that is engaging. There'll be disagreements within the group itself and that's actually great to bring out.

Q: Is it okay for the young people to greet the audiences as they come in even if that's not scripted?

A: Sure!

Q: Do you have any tips for a first-time director? And specifically for directing this play?

A: From Deborah Pearson: I really like the book *The Director's Craft: A Handbook for Theatre* by Katie Mitchell. She really breaks down what you need to prepare in advance and during a rehearsal process. It breaks down and helps you create a schedule for the process and for each session. I also suggest doing a check-in and check-out at the beginning and end of each session.

From Jordan Tannahill: Once you figure out what the style of your show is then find references of shows that worked similarly – find images and videos on the internet.

From Deborah Pearson: You can also create a mood board of images that inspire you. I also suggest not changing an image if you don't need to – don't throw new images in just for the sake of adding new images. You can also ask the young people to go away and bring lots of images that they are interested in and let all that feed into the production. Also setting tasks that build and accumulate over time can be a great way of devising – it might start off as a game and builds into a section/image of the show.

From Jordan Tannahill: In previous productions, directors invited conservationists and activists into the process to talk about the hard facts of the climate emergency. If you have some capacity to invite a speaker, they can help give your students a useful frame and context for the piece.

Q: Why did you add the quote at the top of the play ('Let me recite what history teaches')?
A: I reference Gertrude Stein's beautiful formulation 'Let me recite what history teaches. History teaches.' (from her poem 'If I Told Him: A Completed Portrait of Picasso') within the play. So, as is standard practice, I am simply citing my reference at the top of the play.

Q: What do you think about swearing and sensitive materials in the text/performance?
A: It is there for a reason. If an issue arises with this material, talk to your young performers about why this material is in the play. Only as a last resort, or if you feel a certain element puts your students in some kind of danger or serious moral compromise, would I suggest cutting or modifying the text.

Suggested references

Deborah and Jordan shared a previous example of a production of the play – *Ist mein Mikro an?*
Post National – a piece previously created by Deborah in collaboration with university-aged students
Once and for All We're Gonna Tell You Who We Are So Shut Up and Listen (Ontroerend Goed, 2008)
That Night Follows Day (context, text and direction by Tim Etchells)
The Director's Craft: A Handbook for Theatre (2008), Katie Mitchell

From a workshop led by Deborah Pearson
With notes by Júlia Levai

Is This Good Enough?

by Avaes Mohammad

Avaes Mohammad works across poetry, theatre and performance. With a background in the chemical sciences, artist-alchemist Avaes Mohammad's influences stretch from the Sufi saints of South Asia to the dub poets of Jamaica and he has performed his poetry on stages across the UK, Europe, India, Pakistan and South Africa. His poem *Bhopal*, commissioned by BBC Radio 4, won an Amnesty International Media Award. As a playwright Avaes has been commissioned by BBC Radio and several theatre companies across the UK with his plays *Bhopal* (2003), *In God We Trust* (2005), *The Student* (2007), *Shadow Companion* (2008), *Crystal Kisses* (2010/2011), *Fields of Grey* (2012) and *Of Another World* (2014) consistently achieving positive reviews. He was recently commissioned to write a double-bill for the Park Theatre, London. Avaes has also conducted playwriting and poetry workshops worldwide with organisations that include the Royal Court (London), English PEN, British Council and the Alternative Living Theatre (India). In 2012 he co-founded the Lahore Agitprop Theatre Company in Pakistan. Constantly excited by how his work as an artist can support society, Avaes is currently Associate Artist with Red Ladder Theatre Company, Fellow of the Muslim Institute and Trustee of the Bhopal Medical Appeal.

Characters

Tas, *rude boy, seventeen*
Rude Boy One, *rude boy, sixteen*
Rude Boy Two, *rude boy, seventeen*
Chantelle, *party girl, seventeen*
Party Girl One, *party girl, sixteen*
Party Girl Two, *party girl, seventeen*
Naomi, *footballer, fifteen*
Footballer One, *footballer, fifteen*
Footballer Two, *footballer, fifteen*
Andreas, *chess player, fourteen*
Chess Player One, *chess player, fourteen*
Anton, *uniformed schoolkid, fourteen*
Uniformed Schoolkid One, *uniformed schoolkid, fourteen*
Uniformed Schoolkid Two, *uniformed schoolkid, thirteen*
Banksy, *skateboarder, sixteen*
Skateboarder One, *skateboarder, fifteen*
Skateboarder Two, *skateboarder, seventeen*
Samira, *drug runner, sixteen*
Drug Runner One, *drug runner, fourteen*
Drug Runner Two, *drug runner, fifteen*
Cyroe, *age unspecified*
Elder, *age unspecified*
Parent One, *age unspecified*
Parent Two, *age unspecified*
Parent Three, *age unspecified*
Police, *age unspecified*
Newsreader One, *age unspecified*
Newsreader Two, *age unspecified*
Uniformed Schoolkid's Father, *age unspecified*
Banksy's Mother, *age unspecified*
(extra non-speaking parts can be added)

Introductory notes

The Newsreaders will change costumes throughout the play, becoming increasingly absurd and bizarre, to juxtapose with the philosophical points they're conveying. Maintaining this playful quality, they will enter from strange places (from amongst the audience, the auditorium doors, in between aisles) and/or indulge in strange activities (clowning, acrobatics, posturing) whilst delivering their speeches. They will become puppets at one point and deliver their speeches through megaphones at others.

Scene One

The **Rude Boys** *are in their car, parked by the park entrance. The car's headlights are seen on stage as they speak from within the car.*

Tas   Everyone's got the message you know. I bet the whole city turns up.

Rude Boys One   I bet most eediots don't make it off their sofas.

Rude Boys Two   Bunn another a joint and let's chill too then, man. What we goin' for?

Tas   For Cyroe!

Opens the driver door.

He's the dude. And he's back.

The **Skateboarders** *roll onto stage on their skateboards.* **Banksy***, spray can in pocket, is impressing with jumps and other board skills.*

Banksy   I've told you it's all in the core, man! Use the core!

Skateboarder One   I just like rolling, man.

Banksy   It's not boarding though is it? Check this!

He impresses with another exhibitional jump.

Skateboarder One   What do you know about this dude then we're supposed to be seeing?

Banksy   Cyroe? Man's got a deep vibe. People been waiting for him forever.

(*Shaking her paint-spray can.*) Saw a picture once. Damned beautiful! (*Responding to* **Skateboarder One***'s side-eyed glance.*) What?

The **Footballers** *enter passing the ball to one another whilst showing off with ball skills.*

Naomi   You're supposed to pass it, man. We're a team aren't we?

Footballer One (*showing off at practising his skills*)   Let a man flex, bruv. Anyway, what exactly does this guy think he can do?

Naomi   Everything. They're sayin he's just come back from some around the world backpacking thing. Seen everything there is to see, knows everything there is to know. (*Going in for the tackle.*) Now stop hogging!

Party Girls *arrive preening themselves and each other.*

Party Girl One   I don't get it though. Some random calls a meeting in a park and everyone's supposed to just turn up?

Chantelle (*fixing her make-up*)   He ain't no random, babe! If Cyroe calls, you turn up, truss me. He's the one. Now how do I look?

Party Girl One Babe you know you're hot. Now how about me?

Chantelle Aww you're a doll, hun. You know that!

Party Girl Two Never know what might happen right?

Chantelle You never know!

The **Schoolkids** *shuffle onto stage, teasing and shoving each other around.*

Uniformed Schoolkid One (*as he tries to get his own back on* **Anton**) Get off, man.

Anton (*laughing*) Oi, oi! Stop now alright, I said stop!

Uniformed Schoolkid Two (*succeeds in pulling* **Anton***'s jumper up over his head*) Gotcha!

Anton Stop it, man. You guys know I've always wanted to meet Cyroe. I don't wanna look a mess!

Uniformed Schoolkids One & Two (*pouncing on* **Anton**) Too late!

The **Drug Runners** *arrive on scooters with their hoodies up.*

Drug Runner One Madness if you think about it. Hittin the whole city up on their phones callin them to the park at midnight.

Drug Runner Two To find a worthy leader? What does that even mean though?

Drug Runner One I ain't never met no one leading nothing I thought deserved to. But if Cyroe's called it, I wanna see what he's saying.

Samira Just keep our hoodies up. No need to be bait.

The young **Chess Players** *arrive, chess board under their arm.*

Andreas It's an interesting premise at least.

Chess Player One Though I wonder how this Cyroe intends to actualise these ideas? Obviously he has quite the name, but what's his strategy?

Andreas Precisely. What are his moves?

Scene Two

The characters have all congregated in the park and begin noticing one another.

Rude Boy Two (*approaching* **Chantelle**) Hey, Chantelle! Didn't know you were gonna be here tonight?

Chantelle Er . . . you don't need to know!

Uniformed Schoolkid One *sniggers.*

Rude Boy Two (*towards* **Uniformed Schoolkid One**) What? What's funny little man?

Party Girl One Leave him alone

Rude Boy Two *scuffles* **Uniformed Schoolkid One**'s *hair. Meanwhile* **Skateboarder One** *gets in the way of a football being passed between the* **Footballers**.

Skateboarder One   Oi! Watch it!

Naomi   You watch it! You can see we're playing.

Banksy   And what? It ain't your park.

Naomi   We play here every day!

Banksy   We skate here every day!

Drug Runner One (*to* **Chess Player One**)   What you lot doing here? Oi, what is this, what's all these kids and geeks here for, man? What you doing here, geeks?

Andreas (*stuttering*)   Huh? We, er . . . we just . . . erm . . . we got the call out isn't it? Like . . . what everyone else . . . did.

Drug Runner One (*mocking*)   Like . . erm . . . er . . . What is this? Yo, Samira, I thought you said this was gonna be some big man thing?

Andreas   Erm . . . sorry?

Samira   You got kids apologising! Stop scaring him.

Drug Runner One *fake barks at* **Andreas** *causing laughter between himself and* **Samira**.

Cyroe, *dressed in an amalgamation of clothes, each from a distinct culture he's visited, has all the while been sat atop a tree branch unnoticed by anyone. He looks down, observing everyone.*

Cyroe   Welcome, one and all! Welcome! Dudes, dudettes, you did it. I knew it would just be you, you all took it! Your first step. Over-reaching, over-powering. Audacious, bodaciously flowering. D'you get me? (*Silence spreads over the crowd for a moment.* **Cyroe** *shouts.*) Do-you-get-me?

Sections of the crowd, the **Party Girls**, **Skateboarders** *and a few others, whoop and shout back at* **Cyroe**.

Tas   Is this it then? I mean, no one else came? No adults?

Cyroe   Everyone I knew would come, came. Of those, everyone I know will stay, will stay. Of those, everyone I know will step to go further, will go further, and of those everyone I know who'll reach the end, will reach it.

Samira   Sorry, what? What are you saying? And what is it you've called everyone here for exactly?

Anton   We just seen your message pinging up on our phones . . . *Is this good enough?*

Rude Boy One   What does that mean exactly? No explanation, no info!

Naomi   You got that too?

Banksy (*shaking her phone to stress the point*)   Of course we got that too. It's why we're here!

Drug Runner One   How'd you get my number? That's my personal number you know.

Rude Boy One   Forget that! What does it mean? Is what good enough?

Naomi   Like just everything innit? That's what I got from it.

Banksy   Nothing's good enough, man. Whole planet's falling apart, bredrin. We were stressin over how to buy a home and now we're stressing over how to heat one!

Andreas   Exactly! That's quite right, entirely correct, they'd stolen the right to our own shelter a long time ago and now it's warmth. The next step in the sequence is of course food. They'll rob us of our right to food next!

Tas   None of it matters nothing to no one! The world with everyone on it can literally crumble to dust as long as the rich can still get their profit from it!

Drug Runner One   So no, it ain't blasted good enough! That's why I came! Now what?

Cyroe   Now? We imagine. Imagine that all of your heads weren't so obsessed with these three-square metres, getting wound up coz a ball got in your way of your skateboard? Imagine you could skate over these walls, kick balls past these trees and enjoy chess on moonlit seas. Imagine the boarders rub shoulders with the schoolkids too and the rude boys make moves for the queen just like the chess men do.

Rude Boy One   What? That's what you called us for? To run with those chess playin geeks?

Party Girl One   I'd get arrested If I'm seen out with schoolkids!

Her friends laugh.

Cyroe   To be the change you've got to be a change from the olders you want to break from. Not feed the same divisions that will see you growing into them. Twelve million of you on this island alone! That's more than police, teachers, parents all put together by nearly twenty to one. If you dared paint these streets with your dreams, who could stop you?

Chantelle   What, babe? Are you trying to start a riot and revolution?

Cyroe   Just manifest inspiration.

Tas   Cyroe, I get what you're saying but how can we do anything together? We don't even know each other.

Cyroe   That's why you need a leader.

Samira   Aah, I get it! Man's got us all here to tell us what to do! You want to be a boss man over us all?

Cyroe   No, I want better for you than that. I'm tryin to get you to meet someone really worth listening to.

Party Girl One   Someone worth listening to? Apart from my own sweet voice, I ain't never met anyone like that.

Cyroe   I've travelled all over the world. Deserts, mountains, oceans, I've seen them all. I've known beauty. We sat down over bread together. I've had love look me in the eyes until I dared look back. I've been shown all I'm capable of; admired and been heartbroken by it in equal measure. I stood with revolutionaries whose single action tore down borders and sat with men and women whose dominion stretched further than the limits of sight. I stood upon the footsteps of King Solomon and breathed in the embers of all empire. Then when I breathed out I heard the universe echo with his name, Marharban. In that moment I learnt there is a leader for us, deserving and worthy, closer to us than our own blood veins.

Uniformed Schoolkid One   Marha-what?

Chantelle   So you're saying we've got to meet this guy?

Drug Runner One   He wants us to search him out. Like go on a mission.

Footballer Two   Search him out? Where from? And for what?

Cyroe   The journey is by no means simple. You'll be forced to see even when all light escapes you and walk upright amidst charging rivers. It's a quest that will force you to challenge desire. Your blood will boil and your feet will give way beneath you. Repeatedly you will fall dizzy with drunkenness and only if considered worthy will the heavens tear open to beat down over you. Only then, might you see the Marharban.

Andreas   So where exactly is the Marharban?

Cyroe   Anywhere at all, If you're ready to see the Marharban. A lock of his hair was one night found in China and what followed was uproar that echoed across the world. The world's thinkers, artists and scientists descended to record and understand it. None grew any closer to describing what they saw but that initial enquiry birthed the entire process of all science and art as we know it today.

Rude Boy One   How old is this Marry-harry?

Cyroe   The Marharban, my brother. Even time can't enslave him, this dude is free for real. And that's why he should lead us. So step with me. Which of you will?

The tribes gather amongst themselves, creating a din of questioning and discussion. Through this cacophany some voices break out in support.

Footballer One   And then what?

Skateboarder One   How long would it take though?

Chess Player One   He's not saying. Do you hear him say?

Tas   It's not really important how long.

Drug Runner One   So you'd go, yeah?

Chantelle   I will! (*Shouts.*) Cyroe, I'm in! I'm going with you.

Drug Runner One   Let's do it!

Tas   I'm in too.

Skateboarder Two   I feel what you're saying, Cyroe. No doubt you've seen some stuff, I don't deny it, bredda. But yo, I might not be checking for sunsets on oceans but I'm still making my own waves here, d'you feel me? On the half pipe, right? When I ascend that pipe and come crashing back down again, I am the wave, man, I'm every colour of the sunset. A simple flick of my board and a rainbow cascades in my path for me to look back at, besotten. On the half pipe, that's where my heart is, man. I've got no space for the Marharban.

Cyroe   Just as sunsets fade, what happens when your wave recedes? When your legs don't have it to Ollie or to Nollie and your board is just a relic of things you used to be able to do. I'm talking about true beauty the ages succumb to, not that succumb to age. You've mastered this half pipe, I know you want to board over new terrain!

Anton   It's not that I wouldn't want to come with you, it's just like. I suppose it makes sense for me to not, what with being the youngest and everything, d'you get me? I mean, when you talk about forever. I've got my whole life ahead of me, right? Why do I need to think about forever?

Cyroe   Time is a trap. At the start of it you see it as an ocean with no horizon. And as you travel along it feels more like a cliff-edge, one small slip and it's all gone. Better you have no trust for anything so deceitful. You want to know what life has in store don't you? I'm gonna take you its edges!

Party Girl Two   Cyroe, I'd follow you to the world and back, innit? And all your mountain and desert stories . . . lush, pure lush. hun! But, babe, look at me. Seriously, just look at me for a second. Do I look like I'm made for backpacking, hun? Okay, okay, just imagine I do even stick on them walking trousers and fleece-top things, I bet I make it all look lit as well, trust me, but listen. What about my rocks, hun? My rings, bracelets, necklaces, ear-rings, anklets, toe-rings. That's why I move slow innit. These things they, they weigh me down but I can't do nuttin about it. They're me.

Cyroe   And what if all colour was taken off your rocks? What would be left? Anything other than stones and metals hanging off you like chains? You want to see the limits of beauty and I want to show you!

Footballer Two   I already know what I can do and what I can do is bring the world to its knees in admiration and awe. You're talking about going to a king? Cyroe man, when I'm signed and then playing in the World Cup, the kings of the world will be seeking me. The world will be wearing my number on their backs. Thrones don't belong to kings and queens anymore, they belong to those the people choose and they're gonna choose me.

Cyroe   So you want to refine your skills so you might be known by them? You've sold yourself short if you think tricks with a ball define you! You are more than tricks acquired and lost. You always were. Come with me and let me remind you.

Samira   We already know who the king is of these streets coz we're working for him. And he ain't all that beautiful and sweet. Our king is vengeful. Half of these youts buy their highs from us, and the king makes sure he gets what's his. I've seen kings, bro, and I don't know I wanna get to know no more.

Cyroe   That's no king you've given your head to. The true king is without rival and unique and kings like yours are two a penny on every street corner preying on young lives like yours. The true king teaches you to fly, he doesn't clip your wings. I know you want to fly beyond the reach of your fake king. Join me.

Andreas   We just come here to play chess. We're not really footballers, don't have the build for it, or the courage quite frankly to do what they do on a skateboard. We'd never be able to keep up and even if by some miracle we did get there, this great Marharban would probably never even look at us amongst you all.

Cyroe   If what you're saying is the journey is hard, I'd agree. Everyone endures hardship, so why shouldn't you? If you feel it's difficult uniquely to yourself then certainly not. You have feet just like everyone else to carry your weight across any terrain. You've always wanted to learn the moves that dislodge kings and queens? Then move with us.

Rude Boy Two   Cyroe, I get you've seen roads all over the world but these are my streets. Me and my boys, we cruise them day and night, each nook and corner is ours. I love these roads too much to find others.

Cyroe   A real road is one which you don't know where it's leading you to, what threat or comfort awaits you at the next turn. You were born to journey, and adventure is in your soul so don't content yourself with apparitions of the road. There's no point waiting any longer, the journey begins with just one single step. Step with me!

Some characters take steps forward. **Rude Boy Two**, **Footballer Two**, **Party Girl Two** *and* **Samira** *stay back.*

Footballer Two   What you doin?

Footballer One   Didn't you get it? This is bigger than keepy-uppies.

Footballer Two *exits.*

Tas (*to* **Rude Boy Two**)   We always moved together though, bredda.

Rude Boy One   Not on two legs, bruv, we didn't. I don't trust nowhere I can't drive to.

Party Girl Two   Sorry, babes! Sounds like a trip but you know me . . . bring me something back though, babes.

Samira   I wouldn't go if I was you.

Drug Runner One   Why? Coz you gonna have to chat to the big mans about losing your runners?

Samira   I just wouldn't if I was you!

Uniformed Schoolkid Two's Dad   Elsie! What do you think you're doin? You've never been out this late before. Who are all these people? Your friend's running around telling everyone you lot are all taking off somewhere without telling anyone?

Uniformed Schoolkid Two   I love you, Dad, but we don't want to be like you guys. This isn't good enough.

Uniformed Schoolkid Two's Dad   What? What's not good enough? Get back here now!

Uniformed Schoolkid Two   We're gonna make it all better, we're gonna fix this all. That's what the Marhaban will do for us.

Uniformed Schoolkid Two's Dad   What?

Uniformed Schoolkid Two   Yeah. He's really beautiful. Cyroe's seen him. All these streets can all be ours and we can make it all better.

Uniformed Schoolkid Two's Dad (*to* **Cyroe**)   Is this your doing? I'm calling the police.

(*To* **Uniformed Schoolkid Two**.) Elsie you come here right now!

Uniformed Schoolkid Two   But don't you want us to make it all better?

Uniformed Schoolkid Two's Dad *charges across to grab* **Uniformed Schoolkid Two** *by the wrist and drags her offstage as she kicks and screams.*

Uniformed Schoolkid Two   But Dad! I need to go! Cyroe! Tell him will you please, tell him I need to go.

Uniformed Schoolkid Two's Dad (*as he's dragging* **Uniformed Schoolkid Two** *offstage*)   Hello? Yes I'd like to report something very serious please.

Headlights of a very expensive car are seen as they park. The deep bass rumble stops suddenly and the headlights flash.

Samira   I told you didn't I?

The headlights continue to flash.

Don't be idiots.

Drug Runner One   I ain't goin nowhere.

The headlights flash again.

Samira   They're not gonna let you alone.

Drug Runner One   Cyroe man! Can we just go please. Look we're all ready, we're here. Let's step, man!

The front passenger door is heard opening.

Drug Runner One   Cyroe man!

Police sirens are now heard approaching and their blue flashing lights approaching. The car escapes but now more parents start to appear in crowds, their distant shouting out at their children is heard, demanding to know what's happening. The panic spreads amongst everyone.

Parent One   What exactly do you think you're doing? I can't believe you lot! Do you know what your problem is?

Tas   Cyroe man, if we're gonna go we've gotta go now!

Chantelle   Cyroe! Babe!

Elder One   Typical snowflakes. Thinking they're all going to save the world or something! They don't know how good they've got it.

The car headlights flash again.

Samira   I ain't explaining this. If you're going then then take us will you!

Cyroe   Not for the weak, the meek, the self-deceiving. What I'll need is all of your utter obedience.

The sirens become louder and the lights brighter, the parents and elders calls grow louder as they approach.

Parent Two   Come back here now! This is not what you were raised to become. What is it exactly we haven't given you?

Cyroe   Not for the weak, the meek, the self-deceiving. You'll be expected to do whatever I ask, whether to you it appears good or bad.

Andreas   We're in man, we're in.

Parent Three   Anton! You've got college, Anton, what are you playing at? And then you've got gymnastics I enrolled you on for before the private tutor I'm investing in your future and after dinner of salad with a low-fat, high-density protein source you're supposed to be delivering a violin recital for the family which will only be thirty minutes this time as I've scheduled some revision time for your exams next year. Anton! Are you listening?

Banksy   Yo Cyroe man! Let's run innit!

The police doors are heard opening.

Police   Oi, break it up, everyone, break it up. This is an illegal gathering!'

Parents (*shout out as part of a collective din*)   Chantelle! . . . Anton! . . . What do you think you're playing at? . . . Banksy! . . . Do you know what time it is?

Cyroe *finally charges, leading an escape from the front.*

Scene Three

Newsreader One   Good evening.

Newsreader Two   The evening really is good. I can't remember a better one.

Newsreader One   Ladies and gentlemen. Youths have been seen to congregate in a local nearby park led by apparently revolutionary intent. Members of the public have expressed alarm at their children being led by a cult-ish figure called Cyroe. Countless young people have gone missing into the night in search of what they say will finally be a *worthy* leader. In other news, the prince of . . .

Newsreader Two   . . . nowhere now . . .

Newsreader One   . . . third in line to the throne, has agreed to be relinquished of all royal privileges and titles in order to begin a new life abroad with a wife of his choosing. In an attempt to avoid public scrutiny the prince said he has taken this carefully considered step in order to seek a life more meaningful. The palace is yet to comment.

Cyroe *leads the remaining young people. They walk through the moonlit night with difficulty, each step an effort. The sound of waves slowly becomes audible.*

Party Girl One (*falling over*)   Ah! Babe! I'm not being funny yeah, but I can't do this in heels, hun.

Chantelle   Babe, take em off innit! It's just sand. (*Extending out her hand.*) You got me, c'mon.

Footballer One   We got this guys, c'mon.

Skateboarder One   Stay together yeah, everyone!

Rude Boy Two   Is that the sea, bro? Can you hear it? Yo is this the beach? How'd you get us to the beach? Man! We're on the beach, everyone! (*Lying down with arms spread.*) Man Cyroe, the flex is strong in you or what!

Cyroe   Everything to occur has still yet to occur: tests, trials, tribulation. They're the signposts we're seeking.

Newsreader Two (*taking place aside from the main action so as to be unobserved and unheard by the voyagers*)   Drab Gett, the much adored international film star, was reported to have been involved in an interesting event with a local road sweeper last night. Here to tread the boards on our esteemed stages, the actor passed a road sweeper he said was carefully sifting through the street's rubbish. Admiring the focus to his work, the superstar said he threw his one-of-a-kind wristwatch, with a six-figure valuation, into the debris for him to purposefully collect. In a strange twist, however, it was the road sweeper who became the focus of the story when he was found by Drab Gett the following evening, still sorting through the street's rubbish. When asked why he continued to work when in receipt of such an expensive item, he replied he received the watch in response to his hard work and so it only proved that he shouldn't stop.

The **Newsreaders** *stay on stage.*

Rude Boy Two (*as he speaks* **Cyroe** *slowly leads everyone off stage, except* **Tas** *who at the back of the group waits for his friend*)   Listen, Cyroe! I say we chill . . . Yo!

Cyroe! I said . . . you listenin? Oi! Cyroe! Stop, man, we're at the beach for . . . Are you serious just blanking me like . . . Oi, Cyroe? Okay! Okay then. You wanna be like that? You gonna be like that yeah? Alright, well, then I'm gonna be like this! (*Lays splayed out on the beach, defiantly.*)

Tas   You're gonna stop already? For this?

Rude Boy Two   Bruv! Imagine this yeah, a little while from now, the sun coming up over the sea, me blazin, the waves. You think I'm gonna be stressing about who our leader is from here?! I'm set, man, and I'm saying you stop with me! Let them find the Marharban! (**Tas** *shakes his head and walks away slowly.*)

Cyroe (*heard from afar*)   Not for the weak, the meek, the self-deceiving. In the valley of the quest you inhale a hundred calamities. With your first breath you lay defeated.

The **Newsreaders** *step forward again.*

Newsreader One   Throngs of young people gathered this evening in a secret location on the outskirts of the city's main shopping district. There, the eager crowd bustled against each other in eager anticipation of the latest 'supreme drop', a phenomenon associated with the latest release of exclusive urban fashion. Items have been known to drop for thousands of pounds a piece. Our reporters this evening discovered the curious case of an old woman amongst the crowd who bid for an item in exchange for a sweater she had hand-knitted herself. Mocked by the retailers, the old woman was then hounded out of the store by the crowd of young fashionistas. When our reporters asked how she'd expected to obtain such exclusive apparel in such a way she replied that was never her intention.

Newsreader Two   For her the reach for something exceptional was itself enough.

Scene Four

The voyagers struggle to continue walking as they encounter a desert sandstorm. Their breaths too become laboured and thirst overtakes them in the heat. Everyone is shouting over the sound of the sandstorm and wind.

Footballer One (*holding up his jacket as a canopy to create a screen for* **Uniformed Schoolkid One**)   You're doing really well. Here, come in.

Uniformed Schoolkid One   Thanks, man.

Footballer One   No bother, brother.

Others follow suit, creating canopies for one another and huddling together in small groups.

Samira   Listen, where's Cyroe? Has anybody seen him?

Banksy   I can't see anything in this. He's probably here somewhere.

Tas   Guys, keep huddled in with your backs facing out okay? But we've got to keep walking. Small steps together.

Drug Runner One   Yo, guys, listen. I just wanna say somethin', right. I wanna say. I really, really . . . I think you're all great! I just do. Like I really, just . . . I feel stuff for you guys man . . . you know . . . all of you . . .

Some laugh and smile at **Drug Runner One***'s outburst while* **Party Girl One** *sits crouched and alone, exhausted.*

Drug Runner One   . . . like we're one big family you know? D'you know what I mean? I feel it you know . . . (*Spying* **Party Girl One**) . . . Do you need help? Huh? Listen, let me help you, you can come in with us. (*He reaches to put his arm around her, trying to lift her.* **Party Girl One** *moves him away.*)

Chantelle   It's okay, babe. I've got her.

Drug Runner One   No worries, sister. I just want you to know that I'm here for you okay. I want you all to know that actually, guys. I'm here for you all okay?

Chantelle (*crouching to face* **Party Girl One***, creating a mini-huddle*)   What's up, babe?

Party Girl One   I need to just stop. I need to breathe.

Chantelle *raises her coat to provide a screen over* **Party Girl One***.*

Party Girl One   I can't . . . I mean, have you ever felt heat like this? What is he doing exactly?

Chantelle   C'mon, babe. Look. Remember some of those skanky steaming clubs we made it through the night in? What's the strategy then? (*Swaying from seated.*) You know! Small step to the right, small step to the left! So it's the same, hun. Small steps. C'mon now, stand up with me.

Party Girl One   I can't, hun. I'm not being funny.

Chantelle   Yes you can, babe.

Party Girl One (*becoming delusional due to the heat*)   Nah, babe. My feet hurt. And I . . . I feel tired. And I need a rest. And I don't know what I'm doing here. And I wonder whether I'm cut out for this, babe. You know me, babe. I don't do walking, hun. And I'm not sure what this is all for and I don't think I'm good enough and I don't think anyone is and so I do think I'm better than this and I do think I'm better than you all and so I don't want to hurt what I am . . . because I am still . . . I am . . . I am . . .

Chantelle   Cyroe! Cyroe, what's going on? Why's she talking like this? What's happening, where's Cyroe?

Newsreader Two   Not for the weak, the meek, the self-deceiving. In the valley of love everything burns. Either you let the ashes drop or hold on pretending all was never lost.

Drug Runner One   Does anyone remember me still? I think I've forgotten everything. Does anyone know who I am?

Newsreader One   Ladies and gentlemen. News just come in about an ex-CEO of a global 100 tech company. The ex-billionaire has made news worldwide conversely not for the rate at which he acquired his wealth but rather the alarming rate at which he lost it all. The tech leader is said to have fallen in love with a rice wine maker he'd seen downtown in the city's ethnic restaurant district. Apparently crazed with her love, he ended up selling all of his assets, property and wealth in order to live closer to the object of his desire and to be able to continue purchasing his wine from her. Reporters have found the one-time billionaire has been left begging for bread. As though events weren't strange enough, the same bread he then receives in charity he sells off in order to continue this ruinous obsession with buying wine from the now famed rice wine seller. When our reporter finally caught up with him and asked what kind of love this was that left him having lost everything, he replied, 'Love is selling everything in order to buy a drop of wine.'

The **Newsreaders** *remain on stage during the following.*

Party Girl One (*as she speaks everyone slowly moves off stage in their huddles, except* **Chantelle** *who remains with her friend*)   I think I'm going to just stop here a bit. Maybe take a nap or something before I head back.

Chantelle   You can't stay in this heat and wind.

Party Girl One (*on her way to sleep, still crouching*)   No, I'm just taking a nap, hun. Just taking a nap. You know me, I need my beauty sleep, hun. Don't wanna get dark circles do I?

Chantelle (*shaking her to no effect*)   Hun! Hun!

Chantelle *leaves her jacket in* **Party Girl One**'s *hands before rising to walk away herself, shielding herself from the sandstorm as best she can* **Newsreaders** *step forward again.*

Newsreader Two   Two foxes, ladies and gentlemen, named Freddie and Flo by locals who had come to admire their bond, always being seen as they were with one another, sharing their food and comforting one another. The devoted fox couple had become icons of the community and so it troubled locals when they were seen chased in a hunt with dogs and falcons set after them. The chase had caused them both to separate as they ran and onlookers heard one screaming for the other, as though asking when they would meet again. One local darkly joked they would be together united now only at the taxidermist.

Scene Five

The remaining young people traverse across a slippery cliff edge.

Footballer One   Where is this now . . .? How are we . . .? But we were just . . .

Naomi   Cyroe? Has anyone seen Cyroe? He's supposed to be leading us isn't he?

Naomi *nearly slips in her frustration but her arm is caught by* **Andreas**.

Andreas   Guys, careful. It's a cliff edge . . . we need to know our moves. Careful, calculated moves! We have to get in a line. Look, can we all get into line please. I'll lead. We need careful, calculated steps. Just step where I step.

Other voyagers make speedy progress across the cliff edge, almost skating across.

School Uniformed Kid One Did you see that? Did you see how I just sped across? It's about just walking, guys. Let your steps be led.

Tas Chantelle, he's right, just move, trust me.

Andreas Guys. Stop! You'll fall . . . we need to . . . we need to form a line. We need calculated steps. Careful steps. Thought-through steps.

Chantelle (*speeding across*) It's working. I'm just . . . walking.

Chess Player One (*shouting from the other side*) Move, Andreas. Move with us.

Andreas (*shouting*) You can't just give up control? It's illogical!

Chess Player One Just move, Andreas! You don't need to calculate any steps, man.

Andreas (*trying to but finding his feet frozen*) I . . . can't.

Chess Player One Stop trying to control it.

Andreas I can't move.

*All other voyagers have moved on, leaving **Andreas** frozen.*

Newsreader Two Not for the weak, the meek, the self-deceiving. In the valley of knowledge both body and soul progress, regress, decline and rise. All you know is you know nothing. Or remain pinned by the weight of what you thought you knew.

Scene Six

Rude Boy One *stands from laying in the sand and stretches. He takes off his shoes, socks and shirt then rolls up his trouser legs, ready to run into the sea. Charging upstage he takes a big jump only to land on the hard ground.*

Rude Boy One Owwww!

Scene Seven

The remaining voyagers travel through pitch-black darkness. Everyone has their mobile phones out, using the light to find a way out.

Skateboarder One I'm shining the light but still it's just . . . blackness.

Samira (*not giving up*) I'm all about the night. I work in the shadows with my hood up and I always find my way out.

Cyroe Not for the weak, the meek, the self-deceiving. In the valley of detachment it makes no difference what you do.

Chantelle Cyroe?! Is that you?

Tas   Where were you, man? Where've you been?

Cyroe   With you.

Naomi   But we couldn't see you.

Samira   He's here now right. What do we do? We can't see anything! It's a brand new phone with intense torch and I can't see anything. Everything's just blackness.

Cyroe   Doing anything at all is to do nothing at all. Everything that meant aught, means naught.

Banksy (*turning her phone off*)   It's clearer now. Guys. It's clearer without. Turn your phones off and just . . . stop.

Everyone turns off their phones and walks smoothly out.

Drug Runner One   Samira. Turn your phone off, man.

Samira   Are you mad? I've still got 100 per cent charge on this. I've got a great light, man! I can find my way with it. You lot are all mad. You'll fall in a ditch or off a cliff or summat. You go. Go on. See that I'm right. I ain't goin nowhere I can't see.

Drug Runner One   Samira, dude. Turn it off.

Samira (*intently searching*)   I know I can find a way.

Newsreader Two   A fifteen-year-old boy was eventually found and rescued when he collapsed into a well and the earth fell in over him. Though rescued, having been trapped for almost eighteen hours, he breathed his last in the arms of his father. When asked to comment on the tragic loss, the father replied that nothing anymore existed. There was no sky anymore, no earth, no angels, no devil. No body or soul, nothing. He said that no matter the weight of everything accrued in life, at death, the weight of the nothingness carried remains greater.

Scene Eight

The voyagers are at various stages of entering and crossing a fast-flowing river.

Naomi (*charging into the river to stand mid-way with his arms outstretched*)   Don't be scared, guys. If we work together, we've got this. That's what this valley is all about right, Cyroe? Working together? Come on, guys, we're a team. Let's build a human chain.

People are wading through, each one in their own specific way. Some swimming, others walking waist high in the water, others crossing across rocks.

Naomi   We gotta work together if we're a team, guys. Come on, trust me, a human chain is the best, most strategic way here.

The other voyagers continue making their own independent crossings.

Naomi   You always need a strategy. That's how you win, right? With a plan? You guys don't have a plan. We need to link together. Then we'll be a human chain. Look, it's a river. It's obvious that's what this valley is for. To be a team. Isn't that right, Cyroe? (*Pause.*) Cyroe, tell 'em! Cyroe? I thought you were with us again?

Footballer One (*having crossed to the other side*)   Naomi! Come on, the river's fast! You've got to move now why you still there?

Naomi   This is how you win. As a team. You pass it to me, I pass back, remember. It's strategy.

Footballer One   But everyone's here now. On this side. Come on, Naomi.

Naomi   No. This is the way we should do it. It's the only way. (*Shouting.*) Everyone come back. Everyone! We need to be a team. You can't win without a strategy! I'm going to stand here and you can come to my side and link hands, that creates a strong base, right, and we build on it, either side, a human chain and when I say 1 we all step. Left foot forward. I've figured it all out. Then right. I'll lead. I'll scope out the steps. Guys!

Newsreader Two   Not for the weak, the meek, the self-deceiving. In the valley of unity, despite the mark, the marker or the marked, you're branded by the same single brand. Only those who resist the branding stand apart.

Newsreader One   A couple this evening were walking across a bridge, over the city's river. Gazing down at it from the edge of the platform one fell in and was carried away in its current. His partner immediately threw herself after him, bravely fighting the current to rescue him. When our reporter caught up with them and asked what was going through her mind when she decided to jump she replied,

Newsreader Two   'All I saw was that I fell into the river and so I jumped in after my fall to rescue myself.'

Scene Nine

Dawn is breaking and the voyagers are able to begin seeing around them. With unstable feet, they sway from side to side and fall around each other.

Chantelle   It's so beautiful.

Banksy   What is this place, man?

Uniformed Schoolkid One   The air. Is it just me or is it . . . (*Falls down before standing again.*) Is it just me or is it like, really . . . sweet?

Tas (*washing his face in the river*)   Try washing your face. Wash your face, come on, wash your face. This water's amazing, man. I feel amazing.

Some voyagers gather towards the river, falling over as they do.

Banksy   Guys, why you all falling over so much? You need to hold yourself up from your core.

Drug Runner One   Are we here? Is this it? Is this where we the Marharban is?

Chess Player One   We've arrived! This is it. (*Falls down before standing again.*) We've arrived!

Some of the voyagers rejoice thinking they've finally reached their destination. They attempt to hug each other, tripping and falling over as they did.

Banksy   Guys, I'm serious. We need to focus on our cores and legs. I'm a champion boarder, I know all about this. Root your legs to the ground. Keep them rooted!

Footballer One   Is he on the banks of the river?

Tas   The Marharban is in the water! We have to swim in.

Chantelle   I don't know you know but I'm telling you all. I ain't leavin. (*Falls down before standing again.*) This is it. This is where I belong! I mean, have you ever seen light so clear? (*Falls down before standing again.*) The sky, this light makes this river looks like spilt silver!

Newsreader Two   Not for the weak, the meek, the self-deceiving. In the valley of wonderment, it's the rapture of spirit that anchors you, not the power of limbs. Here every breath brims with sighs and each sigh is as sharp as a sword. You'll be asked are you drunk? Then you'll be asked if you even exist. Where you are, what you are, if you are? And you will answer, with utmost knowing, that I know nothing.

Newsreader One   In more local news, a man was found screaming outside a door, the key to which he claimed to have lost. For three whole days he wailed outside of it, disturbing neighbours and passers-by who gathered around him. He just couldn't stop crying, what should I do if this door remains locked? What should I do if this door never opens? The matter was only resolved when a man nobody had seen before stopped and consoled the wailing man, explaining that at least he knew where the door he wanted opening was. All he had to do was sit quietly by it and wait for it to be opened. The mysterious man went onto say he himself had been walking for years in yearning, knowing there was no door nor key that could grant his relief.

*The **Newsreader** remains on stage. **Banksy's Mother** arrives mid-way through her speech.*

Banksy   Look, guys! I'm not falling. My feet are pinned to the ground, see? Let me show you how! You need to stand straight with your legs shoulder width apart, like we do on a skateboard, you see. Shoulder width apart. It activates your core. Then you don't fall. You stay upright.

Banksy's Mother   Banksy! Is that you?

Banksy   Mum?

Banksy's Mother   Get yourself over here now. I'm here to take you back.

Banksy   How'd you even get here?

Banksy's Mother   Don't you worry yourself with nonsense talk now, d'you hear! Already made a fool of yourself and your entire family. You know what people are saying about you going off on this nonsense wanderings?

Banksy   But, Mama! Can't you see this? What all this is? Can't you see how incredible this is?

Banksy's Mother   Of course it is. It's incredible. But we're not from incredible, honey.

Banksy   But, Mama. I want to be from incredible.

Banksy's Mother   It's beautiful, honey, and for some people it can be home. Just not people like us, my darling.

Banksy   Why not, Mama?

Banksy's Mother   Because that's not real. Not our real.

Banksy *cries quietly.*

Banksy's Mother   Come here. Let me hold you.

Banksy *cries.*

Banksy's Mother   Come here, my baby.

Banksy *walks back, upright, without falling, through the stepping stones towards her mother.*

Chantelle   Banksy! Don't listen to her. Come back, hun.

Banksy's Mother   You stay out of this! It's a family matter.

Banksy *embraces her* **Mother** *while crying as her* **Mother** *leads her away.*

Scene Ten

Huddled, the voyagers are standing in hard rain, wind and hail beating down on them all. Exposed to the elements, the voyagers struggle in the weather. The **Uniformed Schoolkids** *stand casually with their hands in their pockets as the rain and hail beats down.*

Drug Runner One   Aren't you cold?

Anton   Used to it. We're always out in this innit.

Tas   How we gonna walk in this? We can't see our hands in front of us never mind move.

Cyroe   Let the heavens tear. Let the elements beat down over you. Don't fight it. Don't dismiss any of it. Succumb. Give yourself, lose yourself to it instead. Better you let this storm take your soul than it be taken from your inner tempest.

The voyagers begin to rise slowly and move away from their huddle; as they do they're able to move through the storm. **Anton** *remains standing casually.*

Uniformed Schoolkid One   Come on. What're you doing?

Anton   Dunno

Uniformed Schoolkid One   Come on. Like Cyroe said, give yourself to it, man! We gotta snap out of being nowhere.

Anton   But nowhere is somewhere for me. Isn't this home for you too?

Uniformed Schoolkid One   Nah, Anton man! We set off on this for something better remember?

Anton   Huh? I think so. I'll catch you up when the rain stops.

Uniformed Schoolkid One   What if it doesn't?

Anton   I don't mind waiting.

Cyroe   Not for the weak, the meek, the self-deceiving. In the valley of poverty and annihilation there's no more waiting, you walk into your oblivion for all veils to be lifted.

The rain lifts over the voyagers and the clear sky presents itself as dawn becomes gradually brighter.

Tas   Look, down there. Those lights? Is that the city?

Chantelle   They're flickering it can't be the city.

Footballer One   It's so beautiful. It's shimmering.

Chess Player One   They're fireflies! I'm sure they are, they're fireflies.

Skateboarder One   No. It's the dawn light reflecting off the ocean.

Drug Runner One   He's right. It is, it's the ocean.

Uniformed Schoolkid 1   It must be so deep. It fills everything.

Drug Runner One   Is that what we're going down to then? Are we going to the ocean? Is that it?

Chantelle   Cyroe? Hun! Are we going down to the ocean, babes?

Newsreader One   A man of God was found earlier,

Newsreader Two   We think a Christian, but a man of God was found earlier, we think a Muslim,

Newsreader One   A holy man was found earlier,

Newsreader Two   We think a Buddhist,

Newsreader One   But a man of God was definitely found earlier with a stray, unwashed dog on his chest. When our reporter asked him why he hadn't shooed the filthy creature away,

Newsreader Two   He replied he was already too consumed by the filth inside his own chest to notice what was outside of it.

Cyroe   Run, voyagers! Run down this hill. Some have dropped under their own weight, others never believing their feet could carry them, others overcome by pain of their own fatigue. Some left believing they were better than this, others thinking they weren't good enough but you all have shown yourselves to be true in your search! The Marharban, the one true worthy leader, is ready for you and you are ready for the Marharban!

Newsreader One   News just in of a new species of fish discovered by scientists.

Newsreader Two   The latest papers highlight marine biologists discovering it beyond seven oceans of fire and light.

Newsreader One   The fish is so large it's difficult to see the head and tail of it together,

Newsreader Two   Whilst everything of the world, from the first to the last, is inhaled within it.

The voyagers are racing down the remaining descent.

Tas   The lights are getting brighter.

Chess Player One   It's the sun, man! The sun's coming up!

Skateboarder One   It's more than one, it's like so many suns!

Chantelle   It's a thousand suns and a hundred moons.

Uniformed Schoolkid One   And we're just dust! Specks in the light. The light just shines through us.

Drug Runner One   We're invisible.

Footballer One   We're atoms!

Skateboarder One   Yeah, yeah, we're atoms, man! Flying atoms.

Uniformed Schoolkid One   Dancing atoms. Dancing atoms in the whirlwind!

Newsreader One   Scientists who have been studying the classification of insects have been embroiled in a disagreement around the status of flies and moths. One group have been arguing that flies should also be considered moths as they too share the curious behaviour of travelling great distances to seek out light. When studied under experimental conditions however the opposing team of scientists proved their position when it was noted that whilst both sets of flying insects set out for the light and sought it, only the flies returned to their original positions once having done so.

Newsreader Two   Almost as though to tell one another of their success.

Newsreader One   The scientists concluded that a moth therefore by definition was a flying winged insect who, having found the light, never thought to come back.

Scene Eleven

The voyagers continue running down the hill. They all stop suddenly, finding themselves in the same park they set out from.

Uniformed Schoolkid One   It's the park. The same park we left from.

Chantelle   But I swear it looked like the ocean.

Tas   It looked like the sun. Like a thousand suns. Didn't it? Didn't it look like the sun?

Skateboarder 2   I don't understand. You said we'd made it. You said we made it to the Marharban.

Cyroe   You have.

Tas   Then why are we here? Where we started from.

Drug Runner One   Are you mad? You've taken us through all of that just to bring us back here?

The voyagers begin to circle around **Cyroe**.

Footballer One   Seriously? Are you some kind of sicko! Do you know what we've all just been through. We should have never listened to you! I lost my friends because of you!

Skateboarder Two   We've lost people, man! We don't know what's happened to them or even where they are! I swear if I stay here I'm gonna kill you!

He leaves. **Uniformed Schoolkid One** *joins him.*

Uniformed Schoolkid One (*as he leaves*)   That was some sick thing you did, man. Really sick!

Chantelle   Why did you lie, hun? Why did you say there was this Marharban?

Cyroe   Neither were you weak, or meek, or self-deceiting. It's you all. You all did it.

Chantelle   Why have you brought us back here?

Cyroe   So you can finally meet the Marharban, like you deserve to.

Chantelle   So where is this Marharban?

Cyroe   Right here.

Andreas   Look. I don't really know you very much but I think it's fair enough to suggest that this whole endeavour has been distressing and anguished. For it to also appear futile . . .

Cyroe *begins to leave. The voyagers remain in a circle formation.*

Chess Player One   Where are you going?

Tas   Come on! Cyroe! You can't just do this. At least explain what just happened!

The small crowd of voyagers bring the circle closer around him.

Cyroe   Have you tried the coffee at that new place on the high street?

Drug Runner One   You're mad! He's mad! We followed a mad man all along! I say we get him!

Apart from **Chantelle** *and* **Tas**, *the remaining voyagers charge forward and jump onto* **Cyroe**, *only to find he has left.* **Chantelle**'s *phone beeps and she attends to it.*

Uniformed Schoolkid One   Where did he go?

Drug Runner One   He was just here!

Tas   Has he just left us? Just like that?

The voyagers sit down, dejected and confused.

Chantelle   Guys. The signal's back!

Skateboarder One   I'm really not interested in phone signals right now.

Chantelle   No! What is it? The Marharban right? I just Googled it. You know what it means? It's Farsi!

Tas   Means we got played!

Chantelle   It means *we leaders*! Literally. In Farsi. It means we leaders! (*Pause.*) Don't you see?

Drug Runner One   She's gone mad too.

Chantelle   This is where the Marharban is! Cyroe was right!

Uniformed Schoolkid One   The Marharban is . . .

Tas   It's . . .

Footballer One   But then it was always . . .

Skateboarder One   Yes but we needed to. To do all that. To . . .

Uniformed Schoolkid One   To see!

Chess Player One   The valleys were in me. All along!

Tas   The darkness, the light.

Drug Runner One   The falls, the doubts.

Uniformed Schoolkid One   The strength, the courage was mine!

The voyagers frantically run around, covering the space.

Chantelle   You are the Marharban!

Chess Player One   I am the Marharban!

Tas   We are the Marharban!

They freeze and shout the following:

All   I am my leader! We are our leaders!

Newsreader One   And now for the weather. Recent clouds and stormy skies have lifted, giving way to sunny spells for the coming few days at least. Time to make hay while the sun shines.

Newsreader Two   And now for the weather. Recent clouds and stormy skies have lifted, giving way to sunny spells for the coming few days at least. Time to make hay while the sun shines.

End.

Is This Good Enough?

BY AVAES MOHAMMAD

Notes on rehearsal and staging, drawn from a workshop with the writer, held at the National Theatre facilitated by director Kristine Landon-Smith, October 2022

How the writer came to write the play

When I was a young person, I didn't belong to a tribe. I skittered between friends who were studious and naughty. Perhaps that is why I don't believe in 'Tribing off'. Now as an outside observant as an adult working with students, it makes me smile when I see them making their own tribes and it is interesting to me that we break away from these tribes. Whichever tribe you live in, the boundaries of those tribes don't need to be walls.

Avaes Mohammad, 2022

For his play *Is This Good Enough?* Avaes Mohammad drew inspiration from two very different but powerful works. The twelfth-century Persian text *The Conference of the Birds* written by Sufi poet Farid Ud-Din Attar and the 1979 film *The Warriors* which is about a disparate group of gangs in New York. The journeys inherent to both narratives are mirrored in the play, *Is This Good Enough?* The journey explores how a group of young people, who are searching for something outside of themselves worthy of following, could actually take confidence in their unique identities and potential, finding the leadership they seek within themselves.

The structure of *Is This Good Enough?* mirrors that of *The Conference of the Birds*. In the original text the birds of the world gather together to decide their sovereign as they are the only ones in the animal kingdom who do not have one. They go on a journey with a guide who believes he knows where to find just such a sovereign. As they travel through seven valleys, each one representing a different facet of the human inner dimension, several birds are left behind. In each case the birds who fall behind are those forced to confront their inner-failings, or spiritual disease by that particular valley, and proved unsuccessful in the process. When they finally make it to the Simorgh's palace, tatty, scrawny and exhausted, they discover a hall of mirrors. Here they also realise the literal meaning of the word Simorgh (Farsi for 'Thirty Birds'). As they look at themselves in the mirrors, realising there are thirty of them left, they discover that they are their own leaders, but only now are they worthy to be so having undergone this journey of self-discovery.

Avaes Mohammad wanted to transpose this idea for young people. In particular to have them question who are their role models? Is there something great we can aspire towards? He also wondered how young people access spirituality? When Avaes Mohammad was growing up, spirituality was very present in his day-to-day life, but he wondered about a generation who are seemingly becoming more separate from lived experiences. With more and more technology replacing conversations and meetings, he often questions 'where are their spiritual outputs and inputs?' The play was workshopped with various ages of young people, the first set were in their mid-teens and the second group in their early twenties. He was wonderfully surprised to find that with the young people the discussion of spirituality appeared comfortable and normative.

The film *The Warriors* has the *Odyssey* as its inspiration – all the gangs of New York gather one evening due to the suggestion of one leader called Cyrus who says, 'Why are we fighting each other when we could be greater than the police and rule New York?' Cyrus is killed and the gang are wrongfully accused and need to get back to Coney Island. They journey through the night, without being attacked or captured by the police or the other gangs, and in doing so discover more about themselves.

Avaes Mohammad knew if he was to write something inspired by these stories he didn't want to make the narrative feel distant, as though of another time and people. The beauty of both these inspirations is the universality and so the play needed to be contemporary and compelling for young people.

A scene-by-scene breakdown

When approaching a new play, lead director Kristine Landon-Smith likes to make headings for each scene, consisting of what happens and its key elements. In the workshop, Avaes Mohammad discussed each scene of his play in detail as follows:

Scene One: The tribes and the significance of the tribes. A text message 'Is this good enough?' has been sent to everyone in the city, old and young, but only these young people have responded to the provocation. For Avaes Mohammad, the adults do not come because they are jaded, and do not believe change can happen, but he is happy for the *why* to be worked out amongst the company.

As each tribe is briefly introduced in the first scene, their specific spiritual malaise is set up, becoming more evident later as they traverse through the valleys along their journey. Avaes Mohammad is saying if you are trying to dictate your destiny then nothing will come because you weren't open to the possibility of opportunity.

Scene Two: Despair from the young for the world they are in and how powerless they feel against the drivers of profit. This is a pivotal scene where the idea of the play is clearly understood. The groups have gathered and Cyroe is watching. Avaes Mohammad sees him wearing clothes from various cultures that he has travelled through and is watching from up a tree.

Cyroe watches the tribes bully, flirt, rebut, pick on each other, challenge each other's status. It is an important moment when Cyroe says 'Everyone I knew would come, came. Of those, everyone I know will stay, will stay. Of those, everyone I know will go further, will, and of those everyone I know to reach, will reach.' Ideas from Sufi philosophy are presented here, that there's an expectance that you need a guide who has done the journey before and Cyroe is that spiritual guide. He presents the vision 'To be the change you've got to be a change from the olders you want to break from… If you dared paint these streets with your dreams, who would stop you?'. He introduces the idea of the Marharban (the meaning of which 'we are our leaders', they will only come to learn at the end). Each character has their own response to this idea corresponding to their own tribe's malaise. Cyroe rebuts each tribe's questions. Then there is the moment that gets them to go, when the things holding them back in their lives and preventing them from fulfilling their potential are presented (parents, police, drug bosses etc.). This build-up towards the end of this scene serves as the final impetus forcing most of the young people to set off on this journey. Some are up for the journey, deciding to stand up to their parents/adults and fix things and others just want to escape their present.

Scene Three: The start of the journey, the beach, the quest, the introduction of the Newsreaders. In the film *The Warriors* there is a pirate radio station informing everyone what's happening throughout the night. The Persian text *The Conference of the Birds* has a traditional cyclical narrative structure instead of a linear one, so the micro stories shed light on the macro. This is the function of the Newsreader One is very literal, Newsreader Two is the metaphorical undertone. They are the literal manifestation of the literal and the metaphysical. When we first see them, they are on opposite sides of the auditorium.

Scene Four: The journey continues: a sandstorm, the Valley of Love, the tribes come together and a sense of community grows amongst them, the reportage of the Newsreaders becomes more extreme. Party Girl One can't make it through the valley as she focuses too much on herself: 'I'm too tired. I do think I'm better than this.' But in order to love properly, you need to be able to let yourself go (and let go of yourself), something she is unable or unwilling to do, and so she will not go any further on the journey. The Newsreader story here is about the eco who lost it all to love (as a positive).

Scene Five: On the cliff edge which is the Valley of Knowledge. Knowledge is seen as a slippery thing in Sufi philosophy. It should be acquired, but the more you do know the more you risk becoming arrogant. It is the chess players here who want to know their moves and be calculated and so one falls.

Scene Six: One image: 'Rude Boy One *stands from laying in the sand and stretches. He takes off his shoes and shirt then rolls up his trouser legs, ready to run into the sea. Charging upstage he takes a big leap only to land on the hard ground.*' This visual image is meant to be a suggestion to the audience that this entire journey is an illusion. The physical realm of each valley is a depiction of the disease which is internal.

Scene Seven: Journey in the dark: this is the Valley of Detachment. In this valley, trying to leave makes no difference. You have to let yourself go to the elements and not resist your disease; instead you have to face it and accept it in order to get out of it. Those who accept the dark can find their way out. The one with the phone gets stuck.

Scene Eight: Crossing the river: Valley of Unity. To cross a river, the voyagers form a human chain, quickly working together. Naomi, who is obsessed with leading a team, rather than actually being part of one, doesn't make it through.

Scene Nine: The Arrival and the Valley of Wonderment. Dawn is breaking and there is a beautiful vista of river and sky, and all are drunk with how beautiful it is. Suddenly Banksy's Mum arrives and tries to pull Banksy back by saying: 'Of course it is. It's incredible. But we're not from incredible honey.' Banksy cannot make it through this valley as the weight of previous generations' inadequancies will keep her stuck.

Scene Ten: Valley of Poverty and Annihilation – hard rain, hail and wind. Anton, one of the schoolkids, is strangely comfortable in the dreadful weather and nothingness: 'But nowhere is somewhere for me.' Avaes Mohammad remembers this feeling at school and seeing mates who would just aimlessly stand, comforted by nothingness. Cyroe says get through it and lose yourself to it: 'you walk into your oblivion for all veils to be lifted.' But the schoolkid feels at home in it too much to move forward. Then the rain stops and there is a beautiful ocean. Cyroe congratulates them on making it. Just as they discover they are all atoms together, they realise they are in the park together again.

Scene Eleven: We are the Marhaban, we are our own leaders. Realising they are back in the park they become angry, but Cyroe is happy believing he has done his job so leaves. As soon as he leaves, they all get their phone signal back, and Google the word *Marharban* and come to the same realisation as the birds, that they are their own leaders: 'I am my leader! We are our leaders!' The final lines of the Newsreaders are exactly the same: the metaphysical realm and the literal realm have unified and have become one.

Approaching the play

To begin exploring the themes and visuals of a play, Kristine Landon-Smith likes to offer up scaffolds and structures, using movement-based exercises around scenes to give her company a way of jumping off and accessing a scene on its feet. She will begin with a warm-up, which she will then move quickly into a movement exercise, which will then move swiftly into working a scene. She invited the company to work this way using Scenes One, Four and Five. Kristine Landon-Smith believes that you should start rehearsals as you mean to finish with your production, with all actors involved from the beginning. With a physical, choral play like *Is This Good Enough?* the company should be encouraged to warm themselves up to work, create and play well together, and to take care of each other from the start. With some simple warm-up games and exercises you can bring this connection between everyone from the very first moment in the room.

Exercise: Warm-up with ball

First level: Invite the group into a circle and pass a ball (football or volleyball in size but lightweight) around the group. The aim is to get 100 hits as a company; however, each member can only hit the ball once before someone else hits it. If the ball hits the floor, you must start back at 0. As it is an easy ball to control, encourage the group to start to think about where they are sending it to keep it up. Once the group have started warming up to it, move out of a circle and around the room.

Second level: The aim is still to try and make 100 hits as a company. Have the group walk around the room. This time you are allowed to hit it up to five times yourself but whilst walking around. This is in order to look and find someone to send it to. You are looking to make a beautiful connection and complicity between people as they pass the ball to each other.

The click game: Invite the company to move around the room. Each person will send and receive a click (of the fingers). When they receive a click they must click themselves, and to send it on they click their fingers once more, making eye contact. Keep it fun, energetic and light, and use music for rhythm and energy. Kristine Landon-Smith likes to use Louis Prima's 'Just a Gigolo/I Ain't Got Nobody'.

This is a great exercise to get the actors connecting, making eye contact and ready to work.

Movement exercise – collective stop and go

- Everyone moves round together.
- Slow down collectively.
- Then come to a collective stop.
- The stop is very important.
- As a group you intuit when one person goes. Move, slow down, then stop.
- Then two people move around the room. They move, slow down, then stop.
- Then three people, then four people, then five people, then back to four people, then back to three people, then two, then one.
- Then the whole group again.
- If anyone moves before the person currently moving has stopped then go back to 0.
- Use music to help with energy and ambience.
- Don't let the exercise get too serious or lose energy or focus. Stay connected and warm as you are about to do something difficult together.
- You must have the stop before you can move on to the next level. The 'stop' is a collective in-breath that leads on to the next movement.
- Note: it will always be start and stop at the beginning and you may have to choose to move on from the exercise in order to carry on working on the text, but do give time for the group to get used to and figure out the parameters.

Kristine Landon-Smith then used this structure from movement exercise one to lead the company into Scene One.

Creating the scaffolding for Scene One

The following is a suggestion of how to move from a movement exercise into developing a scene and to hopefully give ideas of how to get a sense of the work in a very short space of time with your own company.

The set-up

Kristine Landon-Smith asked the company to move into three groups of five and gave each group one of the groups from the play: Skateboarders, Footballers and Rude Boys.

Music played in the background which was a light percussion/Tabla Chill playlist on Spotify.

All three groups were asked to run around the room and amongst each other and come to a collective stop. Then one group will run and stop, then the next two will follow this pattern. At first the order and movement was organic, and from this Kristine Landon-Smith then decided the order she wanted. The order she chose was: 1 Skateboarders; 2. Rude Boys; 3. Footballers. It is important not to run as a 'character' but instead to just run as a group. She also gave the footballers a ball to throw to each other whilst making eye contact.

This is how Kristine Landon-Smith introduces steps or scaffolding to the scene. She will then build from what she sees the company bring to the room and add more to the movement.

Developing the scaffolding

From watching the groups explore the collective stop and go, Kristine Landon-Smith then worked the rhythm and style of the movement and added in text over the top. She asked the Skateboarders to add a jump to their runs. They had to run, jump and land on both feet as though 'landing' from a skateboarding trick. She then gave the Rude Boys lines from the first scene (which she adapted from the original to keep short and rhythmical):

1   Most idiots won't have made it off their sofas still.
2   Burn another joint.
3   What we going for?
4   Let's chill.

She asked the groups to stop moving and gave the lines to different members of the Rude Boys group and had them call these lines to each other whilst standing still. Do *not act* the line but instead play the rhythm or the music of the line which in turn begins to explore the choral nature of the play. Then the Rude Boys explored walking and saying these lines. In contrast to the other two groups their rhythm became slow. She then had the three groups go back to the beginning of moving collectively and stopping then moving in the original order but now with their new moves or text. Then she gave out the following lines to the Footballers:

1   Let a man flex.
2   What is this guy gonna do?
3   You're supposed to pass!

And for the Skateboarders:

1   What do you know about this dude?
2   I just like rolling.

A note was given that because you have been given a line of text doesn't mean you have to use it. Play with silence as well.

When setting up scaffolding and doing movement work, play with the text to explore choral movement and rhythm, but when you come back to the scene, work in the text properly.

Choral movement

The room was cleared and chairs placed all along the edge of the walls, enough for each actor. The company were invited to sit down but not in their groups. Kristine Landon-Smith then began the movement again, but had the groups come in from the chairs onto the playing space, beginning with the individual group order from before and not everyone at the same time. This gave an added level of choral work and she suggested moving from this position using the collective go and stop language could work well for transitions, moving between scenes, creating the valleys and worlds of the play.

We continued to develop the work, adding in levels, having one of the Skateboarders use a chair to balance on at one point and removing the ball from the Footballers, having them pass an imaginary football in the same way they passed the click from the earlier game. When directing your own company, remember to 'capture and keep it' if you see something working well.

Finally, after the third group had stopped moving, Kristine Landon-Smith asked them all to play with their one line of text. When she clapped her hands, everyone could start to retreat to their seat at the side slowly and playing with their line as they go.

Note: When working on choral elements with your company, Kristine Landon-Smith suggested to not focus on character but instead on the music and rhythm of the text. This text has a strong inherent music – if you start acting too much with the line, the inherent music of the text will not come through chorally in a way that it's meant to. By working on hearing the music of the text, your young people will know how to say it without too much character on top. You can use the idea of a soundscape with them to help with their understanding of this, which will then feed the collective ensemble work that you have built.

Reflections from the room on the movement work

- Moments of stillness and silence in the text and the play are so impactful. It is brave not to say something on stage and students often feel they have to get through the text.

- It feels important to honour the voice of the tribe that they are representing. It is important to stay away from stereotypes but instead to advocate for each tribe. Then it can be linked to the beauty of the poetry of the original text.

- Participants originally thought that each group was disparate but after the work they realised that the groups are all equal, they just *think* they are disparate, which is the theme of the play.

Creating the scaffolding for Scene Four and the sandstorm

The set-up

The company were moved into pairs and each given a fabric scarf which was held by one partner and wrapped around the waist of the other. Kristine Landon-Smith then gave them three specific choreographed moves:

1 Partner in front moves slowly forward. Person at the back must keep tension on fabric. The slow movement is not false but is a truthful slow step.
2 Both fall (led by the person in front) and try to keep tension on fabric/scarf.

3   Person behind runs back and person in front runs back too as though both hit by
     sand or a big gust of wind.

Have the group explore the movement all at same time to music.

Kristine Landon-Smith encouraged them not to do too much and to only respond to
what is happening to them with tension on the waist as they move forward. Stagger the
shape of the group and move slowly.

She asked everyone to keep their eyeline to the front with neutral faces. When they
fall, keep looking to the front but the lead person can look behind. She then directed the
journey of the company across the space. At various moments Kristine Landon-Smith
asked them all to stop and look behind them and to carry on. She then began to play
with pairings falling and others overtaking them, and with levels and neatening up or
being stricter with the choreography, such as when someone falls they cannot fall onto
their back. As with the exercise earlier she gave out lines from the scene:

1   Come on

2   You're doing great

3   Thanks, man

4   No bother, brother

   (They could choose whether to say these lines or not)

5   Where's Cyroe? (she asked three people to say)

6   Has anybody seen him?

7   I can't see anything in this

   (These three must be said as they are important for plot and narrative)

In the moment of stopping and looking back Kristine asked for the lines 'Where's
Cyroe? / Has anybody seen him? / I can't see anything in this' to be said before they
all carried on.

Then she asked half of them to continue and the other half to stop and rest by
standing and wiping brows. Then she invited one couple to fall and another couple to
pick them up.

Comments and reflections

Because the above exercises jumbled up the text to explore the scaffolding/movement
of a scene, a question arose from the group as to how protective Avaes Mohammad was
over the chronology of the lines. Avaes Mohammad responded by saying he was
protective over the order of the lines. The group reflected that it was possible to be
impulsive and organic with the order of the lines to find the rhythm and to play with the
feeling, but then when finalising the scene, it was really important to make sure the text
is observed as written.

Creating the scaffolding for Scene Five and the cliff edge

Kristine Landon-Smith provided the group with a large beige cloth held taut by four
people above their heads and asked everyone else to stand underneath it. She asked the

whole group to walk forwards very carefully, and as they did, the cloth was lowered at the front, a little bit at a time, still being held tight, but creating a diagonal line. The group underneath got lower to the ground as they were 'forced' down by the lowering of the cloth. As they came to the ground, they rolled out from underneath it and away. All eyelines should be to the floor as though walking along a cliff edge. As the front of the cloth finally came down to the floor and the other half still taut and held high, it became completely vertical to resemble the side of a cliff. This choreography was repeated from the beginning with half the group and the other half reading in the scene.

Reflections

Scene Five is particularly easy to speak which is great for the young people. As the visual imagery and choral elements of the play are so strong, any visual you add in needs to be as strong.

Kristine Landon-Smith encouraged the group to move quickly and to keep focusing on the musicality and movement of the play, placing emphasis on mood, energy and rhythm first. The movement architecture comes from realistic movement and understanding of the moment and physical elements in a scene, but in the architecture you can really push the choral work. When you make that the main focus/colour, the play will come together quite quickly. In this way of working the actors/young people will get *how* to say the dialogue from this work without having to tell them.

Themes

The play is a blend of realism and mysticism. It gives a rare opportunity for young people to explore imagination, soul, mysticism, spirituality and physicality.

Avaes Mohammad wanted to emulate the beautiful closing loop of thirty birds finding their way to a *Simorgh* (meaning thirty) but without needing thirty people at the end of the play. So, he chose the Farsi world *Maharban* – 'we are our leaders'. When they reach their destination, they realise they are their own leaders.

Production, staging and design

Kristine Landon-Smith discussed that the play lends itself to physical theatre and lighting, with many of the scenes being affected either by light, the lack of light and use of light. The physical theatre aspect is undeniable, and the beauty of a large cast allows interesting things to be done with the human body.

There are many terrains in the play to explore: beach, desert, edges of mountains, pitch blackness, river, elements such as wind and hard rain. Why spend money on sets when you can work physically with the body? As the world of the play appears to be on the literal and mystical at the same time, it makes sense for the physical representation to be explored at the same time. The focus should be on the people using their physical selves to make reprints of their environment and what they are going through, which is the theme of the play itself.

Characters and characterisation

Most of the characters are unnamed, but you can name them as part of your process as actors if that feels right. This choice reflects the 'tribe identity' as being central to the characters.

The Tribes: With each valley there is a new tribe that has to face its demons and vulnerability. Each tribe is most vulnerable in its own valley. In each case, it is about letting yourself be in the moment, trusting yourself and the universe and relinquishing control and dependence of the self. When a member of a tribe fails to do this then they fail. Each tribe's specific vulnerability is alluded to briefly in scene one when we meet them for the fist time. There is a general pattern that one member from each tribe has an excuse to not go on the journey, one member of the tribe falls along the way, and one makes it to the end, so roughly each tribe needs three members, but you can have more in each tribe if you have larger groups.

Cyroe: Cyroe is slightly older than the other young people. He has returned from a long backpacking trip and has a mythic urban legend status to him. For some of the members of the tribe they have heard so much about him they are eager to see him, know of him. Avaes Mohammad sees Cyroe a bit like Gene Wilder's Willy Wonka in *Charlie and the Chocolate Factory.* He always has a nonchalance to the severity of the situation, like when Augustus Gloop gets sucked into the chocolate, Wonka knows he isn't dead so isn't bothered by it but doesn't share that knowledge with those around him, including Gloop's parents.

The Newsreaders: In *The Conference of the Birds*, because it is a twelfth-century Persian text it follows a different structure where micro scenes, or stories within larger stories, lead towards the macro. Avaes has tried to do something similar by playing with stories within stories. The news is a story within a story, and with social media we have news about the news. So, the story within a story is worked by using the Newsreaders. They present for each valley a new way of understanding that valley. The Newsreaders themselves are also on a journey. One Newsreader shares all the literal news and the other gives the mystical element of what that valley represents. When we first meet them, they are physically on the opposite sides of a room trying to out shout each other, much like the rational and the mystical are at odds with each other. Throughout the play they get physically closer until by the end they are working together and become visually, one, appearing as a dot behind a shadow screen. The overarching theme of the play is highlighted by their journey; everybody being the same side of the coin, we are all our own and each other's leaders.

Kristine Landon-Smith offered the following exercise as a way to play with the abstract and absurd physicality of the readers.

Exercise to explore the Newsreaders: Truth and meaning and reportage

Place two chairs on the stage, one behind the other. Ask two people to sit in the chairs. The person in the front is a newsreader; however, they will only be lip-synching. The person behind will be the actual voice. It is important that the person lip-synching physically embodies the voice that they are listening to truthfully. It will appear caricature and help with the absurdity.

The actors speaking will be reporting on a news item of your choosing. Depending on how comfortable your company is with improvisation, you may need to ask questions of the newsreader speaking in order to help get the exercise going. After a few questions and fun, switch round so that person behind is now lip-synching.

It is important for the person at the front to listen very hard and to try and find the facial expressions of the person they are listening to through listening.

Bring a third person onto the stage. They should sit on a chair at the front with the person lip-synching. This time use a current news story and report it seriously. The third actor is now a bystander who is going to talk in the first person and focus on the emotion, feeding off the lines from the official newsreader. You can give a structure so they know when to jump in; for example, the newsreader says two lines, then the bystander talks, etc. It is important to play with how the third person relates their news; i.e. perhaps they are someone on the ground talking in the first person. They need to relate to what the newsreader gives them but in the first person with lots of emotion.

Kristine Landon-Smith reflected that there is something interesting in this exercise about the relationship between truth and reportage and is hopefully a leaping-off point to explore.

Question and answer with Avaes Mohammad

Q: The Newsreaders often appear absurd and grotesque with their physicality whilst telling important stories. They feel in a different world. Why?
A: They do have a strong physical presence and in some scenes a lot of movement, but they don't have to move and speak at the same time. It felt appropriate to make them absurd and grotesque as the world is. It seems that in order to delve deep to find a version of your better self, you have to overcome the grotesque and the absurd.

Q: The parent characters – are they the stereotypes in the play?
A: The parents and adult characters are the easy villains, but I recognise them, they are from the child's perspective but not really stereotypes.

Q: Is choral work important in the play?
A: Yes, in particular Scene One. There are so many characters on stage a choral nature will be very important alongside possible choreographic work so that physicality and text is clear.

Q: Do the characters ever hear the Newsreaders?
A: I always thought they didn't, but I am open to the idea of it being played with.

Q: If the Newsreaders are in the auditorium, how do you manage the audience flicking back and forth between them and the action on stage?
A: First figure out what the Newsreaders' purpose is, and what your company's understanding of them are before placing where they physically are. They might not have to be in the auditorium, that is just a suggestion.

It is just important that they start far apart from each other and by the end they are one.

Honour the spirit of the play but don't get stuck in specifics of stage directions (apply this note for the Newsreaders only. Stage directions are more important elsewhere in the play). They just need to be on opposite sides. Just consider that there is an arch to the symbolism of the play, so is your alternative direction true to this arch?

Suggested references

The Conference of the Birds, twelfth-century Persian text
The Warriors (1979)
Louis Prima, 'Just a Gigolo/I Ain't Got Nobody'
Gene Wilder as Willy Wonka

From a workshop led by Kristine Landon Smith
With notes by Jemma Gross

Model Behaviour

by Jon Brittain

Jon Brittain is a playwright, television writer and director. His critically acclaimed play *Rotterdam* had its premier at Theatre503 in 2015 before transferring to Trafalgar Studios the following year where it won an Olivier Award for Outstanding Achievement in an Affiliate Theatre.

Jon Brittain went on to co-write and direct a series of cult hit shows: *Margaret Thatcher Queen of Soho* and its sequel *Margaret Thatcher Queen of Game Shows*. His musical about depression *A Super Happy Story (About Feeling Super Sad)* won a Fringe First Award and has toured extensively. His adaptation of David Walliams' *Billionaire Boy* won a UK Theatre Award for Best Show for Children and Young People. His latest show, *Kathy and Stella Solve a Murder!* premiered at the Edinburgh Festival Fringe and won the Musical Theatre Review Award for Best Musical.

He directed the Olivier Award/Fringe First Award-winning *Baby Reindeer*, as well as both of John Kearns' Fosters Award winning shows *Sight Gags for Perverts* and *Shtick*. He has also directed Tom Allen, Tom Rosenthal and many other comedians – even some not called Tom.

He was a staff writer on the second season of *The Amazing World of Gumball* for Cartoon Network and the third and fourth seasons of *The Crown* for Netflix.

Currently, he's writing new projects for stage and TV whilst trying to train a very naughty dog.

Characters

Ronni (*New Zealand*), *obsessive, hard-working, needs to be in control*
Caitlin (*Saudi Arabia*), *intelligent, cynical, wants people to think she doesn't care*
Chris (*North Korea*), *rebel without a cause – wants to cause trouble*
Caroline (*USA*), *rebel with a cause – incredibly passionate*
Sarah (*Sri Lanka*), *chronically anxious, lots to say but too scared to say it*
Katy (*Argentina*), *happy-go-lucky, chaotic, forever the sidekick*
Stevie (*The Gambia*), *enthusiastic but very literal, can't seem to get it right*
Sham (*Belgium*), *shit-stirrer, obsessed with war, enjoys shocking people*
Mayo (*Chair*), *older, bit condescending, enjoys being in charge*

Notes on performance

(. . .)   means a thought has trailed off
(–)   means a character has been interrupted, sometimes by themselves

Dialogue in bold italics is a teacher – this character could be portrayed through voiceover, be played by one of the characters, or by an additional cast member – just so long as it is distinct from the other roles.

The play pretty much takes place over the course of one school day.

It's set wherever the people performing it live.

If certain lines don't feel quite right, change 'em!

If certain jokes don't land, change 'em!

If certain references feel like they're written by a thirty-five-year-old man, change 'em!

Characters can be renamed and/or have their genders changed to suit the company performing the play.

It's mostly set in/around a classroom, and you don't really need much apart from desks and chairs . . .

. . . but the characters are trying to mimic the United Nations, so if you think they've put some effort into the whole thing, feel free to throw in some smart clothes, flags, a gavel and anything else that feels fun/interesting!

It's a comedy, so keep up the energy and momentum – earn your moments of stillness.

And, basically, just try and enjoy yourself.

Part One: Preamble

Desks, chairs, a classroom.

The characters address the audience.

Ronni   I'd never heard of Model United Nations before.

Katy   None of us had.

Sarah   Until a few weeks ago.

Caroline   In Mr Smallwood's politics class.

Stevie   When he said –

Teacher   *Has anyone ever wondered what it's like to work at the United Nations?*

Chris   Mr Smallwood isn't a good teacher.

Sham   His politics class is a bit of a doss.

Ronni   Most people don't do their own homework – Chris copies his off Stevie.

Chris   Stevie copies his off Katy.

Katy   And I copy mine off – (*Stepping out of the narration.*) Actually, Ronni, can I copy your homework again?

Ronni   Shut up, we're narrating.

Katy   Oh yeah – sorry!

Ronni   Anyway, Mr Smallwood asks the question, and Chris is all like –

Chris (*sarcastic*)   Oh my God, yeah! I think about it all the time. I literally dream about it every night.

Katy   And everyone laughs.

Ronni   Even though it's not funny cause some of us actually do dream about working in politics. Then Caroline's like –

Caroline   The UN is just another neo-liberal, capitalist organisation designed to reinforce the status quo.

Ronni   Cause she watched one YouTube video about Che Guevara and now apparently she's a communist.

Chris   Even though her family have three cars and a swimming pool.

Caroline (*to* **Chris**)   At least I believe in *something*.

Ronni   And then Sarah's like –

Sarah (*quietly*)   . . . Um . . . (*To* **Ronni**.) I didn't say anything?

Ronni   Exactly. Cause even though she probably has thought about what it's like, she's terrified of putting her hand up.

Katy   She got an overdose of social anxiety during Covid.

Ronni   Then Stevie goes –

Stevie   Aren't the United Nations the ones who wanted to take over the Avengers in *Captain America*?

Ronni   Cause that's his reference for everything – and Sham joins in –

Sham   Yeah, they've got the Security Council – they decide when people are allowed to *go to war* – unless it's Russia, who'll just do it anyway.

Stevie   Sham's obsessed with joining the army.

Caroline   Even though he's got asthma and can't even do one pull-up.

Ronni   And then Katy's like –

Katy   Didn't we vote to leave the United Nations? Like, Brexit means Brexit?

Ronni   Cause she literally has no idea what's going on in the world

Katy   I only took politics because I played eeny, meeny, miny, moe with subjects and this is where my finger landed.

Ronni   Anyway, Mr Smallwood doesn't really listen to all that cause honestly, like, what would be the point? Instead, he's, like:

Teacher   *I've got some fun news for you all. Next week, we're going to have our own 'Model United Nations'.*

Ronni   And then he explains. A Model United Nations is, like –

Chris   A stupid game!

Sarah   Where you pretend to be the UN.

Stevie   And everyone represents a country and debates issues.

Sham   Like whether there should be a war.

Katy   And, like, basically, you just try and make the world a better place.

Teacher   *So – how does that sound?*

Ronni   And everyone's like . . .

Katy   It sounds hard.

Stevie   It sounds fun.

Sham   It sounds weird.

Sarah   It sounds stressful.

Caroline   It sounds pointless.

Chris   It sounds stupid.

Ronni   That sounds like the most amazing thing I have ever heard.

Part Two: Debate

The school bell. Classroom. Morning.

It's the day of the Model United Nations (MUN)

The desks have placards with the names of countries on – maybe a flag or two?

The characters take to their seats, ready to begin.

Mayo *sits in the centre with a makeshift gavel (a pencil shoved into a big rubber?).*

Mayo   Decorum, delegates, decorum!

Katy   What does 'decorum' mean?

Stevie   I think it's French for 'be quiet'.

Mayo   For those of you who don't know – I'm Mayo from the year above. I'll be your Chair today – don't worry, I play a lot of tabletop role-playing games, so if anything goes wrong, we can solve it with dice! Basically, you all know your assigned countries. You've got the day to solve as many of the world's problems as you can. Now, is there a motion to open debate?

Katy   Excuse me, sorry, sorry, can I ask a question?

Mayo   Can *Argentina* ask a question?

Katy   What?

Mayo   You can't say 'I', you're supposed to refer to yourself as your country. 'Can Argentina ask a question?'

Katy   Oh. Okay . . . Can Argentina go to the toilet please?

Chris   Not being funny but does anyone else have literally *no idea* what we're actually supposed to be doing?

Everyone nods, murmurs of agreement.

Ronni   What are you talking about? Mr Smallwood sent several emails.

Katy   Yeah, and I meant to read them, but then I had to get a haircut and there was stuff on TV and, like, the whole of the internet, I thought I could just copy you.

Ronni   No. I'm New Zealand, you're Argentina. We're very different countries! Have any of you done *any* of the research?

Katy   I listened to the song from *Evita*.

Caroline   I didn't need to do any. I'm already ready to dismantle capitalism, smash the military industrial complex and ban all fossil fuels.

Ronni   Okay, right, you do know you're the United States of America, so, like, you're pretty *pro* all of those things.

Caroline   In which case, I disagree with the premise of this exercise.

Chris   Me too – why do I need to learn about North Korea? I'm never gonna go there.

Ronni   I don't know, in case you have to know what your country's views are on, say, democratic freedoms?

Chris   I don't know, I think they're good?

Ronni   North Korea is a dictatorship.

Chris   Fine, they're bad. I don't care.

Stevie   My major export is peanuts.

Ronni   What?

Stevie   The Gambia's major export is peanuts.

Ronni   Right, yeah, good, Stevie. But you're probably going to want to know more about the Gambia's stances on, like, geopolitical issues.

Stevie   People should eat more peanuts?

Katy   I'm allergic to peanuts.

Ronni   Shut up! Sarah, you've done yours, right?

Sarah   Erm, yeah, yeah, I have actually . . . and there are some really . . . erm . . . really interesting things, erm, about Sri Lanka, that . . . Can I just help someone else with their country?

Sham   Can I swap with someone? Belgium's rubbish. Their army's tiny and the last time they were in a war they surrendered.

Ronni   No, you can't swap, and we're not supposed to be starting wars, we're supposed to be stopping them.

Sham   What's the fun of that?

Ronni   It's not supposed to be fun! We're supposed to be trying to overcome our differences. Solve problems that are too big to take on alone. Showing that people can work together no matter who they are.

While **Ronni***'s been talking,* **Caitlin** *has arrived.*

Caitlin   In other words – it's a massive waste of time.

Beat, the temperature drops.

Ronni   What are *you* doing here?

Caitlin   Mr Smallwood made me. I'm Saudi Arabia or something. Don't worry, I'm not here by choice.

Ronni   This is Caitlin Kirk. The worst person in school.

Katy   She's Ronni's nemesis.

Ronni No she isn't!

Caroline She spread a rumour that Ronni had webbed feet.

Ronni Oi!

Chris One time she locked her in the changing rooms for, like, the whole of PE.

Ronni It was only half of PE!

Stevie She even pretended to be Ronni's friend so she could trick Ronni into texting that she fancied Jo Singleton in the year below. Then she sent the screenshot to, like, everyone in the year.

Sham It was really funny.

Ronni Shut up! The details don't matter. We just don't get on. Which is fine! Does Iran get on with Israel? No – that doesn't mean they can't work together in the context of the United Nations.

Caitlin You do know this is just Mr Smallwood's way of killing time before the end of term?

Ronni No. This is important. A lot of world leaders took part in Model United Nations when they were at school.

Chris Yeah, and look how shit they've done in real life. They screwed up the economy, the environment, we might have a nuclear war.

Ronni Exactly! This is our chance to do better. Now, are you joining us or not?

Caitlin Whatever.

She sits with them all.

Ronni Great. New Zealand motions to open debate.

Mayo Thank you. All those in favour?

Almost everyone raises their placards, reluctantly, but not **Caitlin**.

Mayo All those opposed.

Caitlin *raises hers.*

Mayo Motion carried. The session is now in order.

He bangs the table with his gavel . . . and we move forward in time.

The characters stand in turn and try to talk formally as if they're politicians.

Katy Erm, so, okay, here's the thing, right, I think, basically, y'know, that climate change is a bad thing? Cause, like, y'know, er, there are days in winter where I'd be like 'yeah, I'd like it to get hotter', but, like there are days in summer where if it got any hotter, I'd be like . . . *this is too hot,* y'know?

Chris I don't care about any of this. It's a waste of time.

Stevie   Erm, so, according to Wikipedia, rainfall in The Gambia has fallen by, like, 60 per cent in fifty years, and that's bad for peanuts.

Caroline   By echoing the language of the ruling class, we are perpetuating the systems that *caused* these problems in the first place!

Sham   Belgium declares war on –

Ronni   No!

Sarah   Erm, so, I . . . erm . . . I. . . . erm –

Ronni   Anyway! So, like, the debate began and pretty much no one had anything to say – which is fine by me – cause then we moved onto resolutions!

Everyone gets up – it's an unmoderated caucus – basically, a free-for-all – the characters mingle, negotiating, all formality is dropped.

Katy   Erm, and what *is* a resolu –

Ronni   We're obviously about to explain! Mayo?

Mayo (*very know-all*)   A resolution is a formal expression of the opinion or will of the United Nations.

Ronni   Basically it's, like, a list of all the things you want to do in it.

Stevie   I wrote one about making a programme to create superheroes – and one about eating more peanuts.

Caroline   I've got one on how we should dismantle all banks!

Ronni   And I wrote one about climate change. I spent the whole weekend on it. I read loads of books, watched YouTube videos, asked my uncle about it.

Katy   Her uncle's a weatherman.

Ronni   Basically, it's pretty great, so all I need to do is to get enough support for it to pass.

She goes to negotiate with other delegates . . .

Chris   I don't want to support your stupid resolution.

Ronni   But we have aligned interests – North Korea has a history of food shortages which would only be exacerbated by failing crops brought on by climate breakdown.

Chris   I don't care. I've already got a resolution.

Ronni   It's just a piece of paper with 'ban school' written on it.

Sham   I'd sign that!

Ronni   Well, you can't – North Korea and Belgium wouldn't work together.

Sham   Okay, could we have a war then?

Ronni   No! Sham, Belgium is committed to green energy – you need to stand alongside other European countries. Stevie, there's a specific clause in there for you to deal with the effects of warming on rain-fed agriculture.

Stevie   Like peanuts?

Ronni   Yes, like peanuts. Caroline, the United States is a leading developer of electric vehicles, this would open brand new markets. And Sarah, Sri Lanka is going to be massively affected by a rise in sea level – we've got specific provisions for that.

Sarah   Well, I . . .

Ronni   And more than anything. If all your names aren't on this resolution, it'll look like you didn't do anything and you'll get detention. Okay?

They take this in – it is an attractive offer.

Katy   What about me?

Ronni   What about you?

Katy   Are you going to tell me why Argentina supports it?

Ronni   No. I know you're going to support me. I told you to. Now, I'm gonna print more of these off.

As she leaves, we find . . .

. . . **Sarah** *and* **Katy**.

Katy   Can I borrow your phone? I want to go back and read Argentina's Wikipedia page, turns out countries are, like, complicated. Ms Gibbs confiscated mine cause I was looking at it too much.

Sarah   Oh yeah, sure.

She gives **Katy** *a phone.*

Katy   Is that a resolution?

Sarah   Oh? Erm . . . Yeah, I guess . . . I dunno, I wasn't gonna say anything – I don't like . . . y'know. Speaking.

Katy   Oh yeah, me neither. I mean, I quite like speaking. With me it's more – I don't really know what to say so I just say way too much even though I probably shouldn't say anything at all! What's it about?

Sarah   Er . . . kind of . . . human rights? So, anything we do should protect the poorest and most vulnerable. So it isn't just done for the rich.

Katy   Oh wow – that's great! I'd vote for that.

They head off together, and we find **Chris** *and* **Caroline**.

Chris   This is stupid.

Caroline   So stupid.

Chris   As if any of us could actually make any difference.

Caroline   It's all corrupt in real life – special interests and big money stop any actual change – the only way forward is to eliminate vertical power structures.

Chris   Or to just not care at all? You should try it. Makes life a lot easier.

As they consider this, we find **Sham** *and* **Stevie**.

Stevie   Do you think every planet has a UN?

Sham   Yeah, I guess.

Stevie   And then, like, they all have one alien who goes and represents them in, like, a united planets sort of thing.

Sham   Yeah, and they're all, like, negotiating the end of big space wars.

Stevie   They don't really get into that in the films.

Sham   Yeah – cause it'd be, like, incredibly boring. Fighting's more fun.

And then we find **Ronni** *and* **Caitlin**.

Ronni   Let me guess – you're not gonna support my resolution but you haven't got one of your own either?

Caitlin (*sarcastic*)   Yeah, I had nothing better to do all weekend than read about how to make more wind farms.

Ronni   This isn't stupid, y'know – we're talking about serious things here.

Caitlin   We're playing a game.

Ronni   An important game. If we can't imagine what it's like to *be* other people, we'll never be able to work out how to work together.

Caitlin   People can't work together. We read that whole King of the Flies book in English about it.

Ronni   It's called *Lord of the Flies*. And I watched something that said, actually, when groups of kids got stranded on an island in real life – they were fine. If people couldn't work together – why would we have the UN?

Caitlin   If people could, why would we need it?

Ronni   I don't have time for this. You don't care – fine. But I do. And y'know what? Pretty soon, we're not going to be here anymore – school will be over with, and I'm going to go and *do something*. I'm going to make a difference. Cause unlike you I *care* about the future – maybe because I have one.

The other kids wince, that was harsh – **Caitlin** *looks about, they all pretend they didn't hear.*

Ronni *returns to her desk, as do the other characters.*

Caitlin *lingers for a moment, thinking, then follows.*

Mayo Decorum, delegates, decorum!

Ronni After that, we're back into session – we debate my resolution and add amendments – basically putting stuff in, taking stuff out, generally trying to make it even better. Some of which are fine . . .

Sarah I'd, er, actually . . . like to add a clause about human rights . . .

Ronni Some of which are not.

Stevie We need to create a new organisation to make sure every country, like, does their bit in raising awareness.

Sham Yeah, the Board for Organising Lower Limits on Overall Climate Knowledge Sharing.

Ronni Which they think I don't know spells bollocks.

Stevie (*trying to act surprised*) Does it?!

Ronni Anyway, then I motion that we move to a vote – and that's when it happens.

Caitlin I've actually got something to say. A point of information or whatever.

Mayo Point of information granted to Saudi Arabia.

Caitlin Saudi Arabia would like to know why New Zealand is actually putting forward this resolution in the first place – it's kind of screwing us all over.

Ronni What?

Caitlin Well, it just seems really weird that New Zealand has put this global programme together to tackle climate change – but expects the USA to pay for all of it? Also, doesn't seem fair that, like, since forever, countries like Belgium have got rich burning oil and gas, but now The Gambia wants to do that and you're telling them they're not allowed? Almost like asking North Korea to join a group of countries who literally think their government is evil. I mean, New Zealand is rich, has a tiny population, and doesn't have to deal with half of the problems that come with, like, being a country in the modern world, and that's fine, y'know, I guess I'm just basically asking . . . Why should any of us do what you tell us to? Sorry. What *New Zealand* tells us to.

The other characters are paying attention, sensing a power shift.

Ronni I . . . That's not . . . I don't . . . Like, I don't know why she's saying this . . . We were supposed to be having a vote!

Caitlin D'you still think you'd win? Motion to continue debate.

Mayo All in favour . . .

*Everyone except **Ronni** raises their placards.*

Mayo Motion carried.

The bell rings.

Oh, and we'll have to hold it there – that's lunch.

Part Three: Negotiation

The characters get up and disperse.

Ronni *corners* **Caitlin**.

Ronni   Okay – what was that?

Caitlin   I was just playing the game.

Ronni   No, you were – that wasn't – you're not doing it properly!

Caitlin   Why? I genuinely believe my country would say those things.

Ronni   How do you even know that?

Caitlin   I dunno. Turns out you're not the only one who can use Google.

She leaves.

Katy   At lunch, we all go in different directions – I go to the canteen.

Ronni *grabs* **Katy**.

Ronni   No, you're with me.

Katy   What, Ronni – I want a baked potato!

Ronni   There isn't time – what is she doing?

Katy   I don't know! I thought we were supposed to disagree with each other – that was the point.

Ronni   Yeah, no you're right – so, *we* just need to have the best ideas.

Katy   We?

Ronni   Yes – a group of us, like, a team. She's trying to sabotage our resolution so we need people who can vote down any unfriendly amendments.

Katy   Unfriendly?

Ronni   Amendments that are, like, bad for us – no, y'know what, that's obvious what that means! We just need people on our side.

Katy   How do we do that?

Ronni   We negotiate. Chris!

They're now in the field. They approach **Chris**.

Ronni   We have a proposition for you.

Chris   Do I look like I care?

Ronni   North Korea has lots of economic sanctions put on it by the West. What if we talked about a roadmap for easing some in exchange for participation in our net zero targets?

Chris   Oh yeah, wow, sign me up, you've just made my dreams come true.

Ronni   This is actually a really good offer.

Chris   Too late.

We flashback to **Caitlin** *and* **Chris**'*s conversation.*

Caitlin   Y'know, I know you don't want to be here, but there's actually a better way to piss them all off.

Chris   How's that then?

Caitlin   Y'know in real life you could say North Korea's a bit, y'know, unfairly picked on. It's just trying to do things its own way and the rest of the world can't handle that – you don't have to not play to make things difficult for everyone. Just saying.

Back to the present.

Ronni   And what does that mean?

Chris   It means, I'm pretty sure I'm gonna be testing some nuclear weapons and cyber attacking all of you. This is gonna be fun.

He leaves. **Ronni** *and* **Katy** *are now with* **Caroline**.

Ronni   Caroline! The USA supports what we're trying to do, right?

Caroline   The USA doesn't support anything, we're now a socialist republic – the office of president has been abolished and we have a horizontal power structure – we'd have to put your resolution before a national ballot.

Ronni   Okay, right, y'know I don't think you're actually allowed to do that . . .?

Caroline   And that's why I won't be supporting you. I read your resolution, it does nothing to address the root causes behind these structural problems!

Ronni   Yeah, but we need to do one thing at a time – what's better? A step towards what you want? Or none of it?

Caroline   That's what she said you'd say!

Ronni   Who?

Caitlin *enters, flashback to her conversation with* **Caroline**.

Caitlin   If you don't get everything you want, why settle for less? What good is a resolution if ultimately it's just propping up the status quo?

We return to the present.

Ronni   For God's sake! Sham!

Caroline *leaves, they're now with* **Sham**.

Sham   Nah, not interested! I already spoke to –

Caitlin *enters, flashback to –*

Caitlin   Why shouldn't Belgium be able to go to war?

Back to the present.

Ronni   Damn it. Stevie!

Stevie *enters,* **Ronni** *approaches him.*

Ronni   What do you need? Come on, tell me? I know you've done the research. What do you want? Resources? Money? Jobs? We can manufacture wind turbines in The Gambia, we can get other countries to pay for flood defences, we can all commit to buying way more peanuts . . .

Stevie   Caitlin said I could have an international programme to create superheroes *and* I could give it a rude name.

Beat.

Ronni   Fine! It's yours. But at least try not to make the word too obvious.

Stevie *leaves – we shift back to* **Ronni** *and* **Katy**.

Ronni   Right, okay, good, who's left?

Katy   Just Sarah.

Ronni   Great, we don't need to worry about her. Let's get back.

Katy   But I still haven't had my potato!

Ronni *and* **Katy** *leave.* **Caitlin** *enters and talks to* **Sarah**.

Caitlin   I like your painting.

Sarah   Oh, thanks.

Caitlin   Wanted to chat, y'know, about this UN thing.

Sarah   Yeah, I don't know, I'm sort of, y'know . . . working with Ronni, so . . .

Caitlin   Oh yeah, of course. But you do know you don't have to do everything she tells you, right?

Beat.

Sarah   I don't know what you want from me . . . but . . . like . . . I genuinely care about this stuff. Like, I know it's just a game, but what we're talking about is super important. I don't care what's going on between you guys – I just . . . I just want to at least pretend to be doing something good.

Caitlin   Sure. Is that what *she's* trying to do though?

She leaves **Sarah** *– the bell rings . . .*

. . . and we're back into MUN.

Ronni   After lunch we go back to debate.

Mayo   Decorum delegates!

Katy   Ronni's getting stressed.

Ronni   No I'm not!

Sarah   She kind of is.

Ronni   I'm just invested. It's all still basically going to plan. Come on, let's get back to it.

Katy   After that, things start getting a bit weird.

They all return to their desks.

Mayo   I believe some amendments have been tabled.

Stevie *stands up.*

Stevie   The Gambia proposes a clause that *insists* nations collaborate on a worldwide scientific programme to create the equivalent of, like, Superman. Or woman. Or non-binary person. It doesn't matter – just *definitely* super.

Mayo   All those in favour?

Stevie *sits and* **Sham** *stands.*

Sham   Belgium wants to insert this clause, right, cause, like, yeah, fine, polluting's bad – so, why don't we invade the top five worst emitting countries?

Mayo   All those in favour?

Sham *sits and* **Katy** *stands.*

Katy   Erm, so, Argentina proposes to amend that amendment?

She sits. **Caroline** *stands.*

Caroline   The USA proposes a clause stating that all forms of work should be *banned.*

She sits. **Chris** *stands.*

Chris   North Korea has just cyber attacked The Gambia.

Stevie   What does that mean?

Chris   Means I've nicked the battery out your phone.

Stevie   Hey!

Chris *sits down.* **Caitlin** *stands up.*

Caitlin   Saudi Arabia proposes cutting clause 1, capping countries' use of oil and gas.

Ronni *stands up.*

Ronni   Point of information!

Mayo   Granted.

Ronni   New Zealand doesn't know if Saudi Arabia understands, but cutting that clause, like, literally undoes everything this resolution is trying to do.

Caitlin   Yeah, but, thing is – Saudi Arabia actually produces quite a lot of oil, and we get, like, a tonne of money off it, so this doesn't really work for us.

Ronni   Point of information!

Mayo   Granted.

Ronni   Does Saudi Arabia not think that that's, like, short-term kind of thinking – climate change represents a big threat to all of us.

Caitlin   Yeah, but, like, Saudi Arabia's got loads of oil to sell and it's already really hot there, so we don't really care that much.

Ronni   Point of information!

Mayo   Granted.

Ronni   That's literally the opposite of what we're trying to do here!

Caitlin   We're trying to come to an agreement, if people vote for my amendments, that's what they want.

Ronni   Okay, that's it!

She grabs **Caitlin** *and pulls her out.*

Ronni   What do you want? What can I give you? You want a deal – great. What?

Caitlin   I'm actually quite enjoying things as they are.

Ronni   You're messing it all up!

Caitlin   I'm stopping you telling everyone what to do!

Ronni   I'm not telling them what to do. I'm helping them vote for the right things.

Caitlin   Maybe we can make up our own minds.

Ronni   Of course you can't – you don't know anything!

Caitlin   Right. Why don't you go back in and tell them that then?

They head back into the debate, only to find . . .

Stevie   The Gambia declares the foundation of a new space exploration mission . . . using anti-gravity we will be taking the entire country into orbit – launching immediately.

Ronni   What's going on?

Stevie   I'm going into space.

Ronni   What? Why?

Stevie   Well, look, I know we're trying to solve climate change, but maybe, like, we need to find a *new* planet. As a back-up.

Caitlin   Sounds sensible to me.

Ronni   Shut up! Stevie, you can't go into space, it's impossible!

Caitlin   People said that about the moon landings.

Sham   I have actually watched some videos online that said they might be fake.

Ronni   That *isn't* true! Can we just stay focused on the task at hand?

Chris *stands up.*

Chris   Okay. So, North Korea's pointing nukes at everyone. I wanna be in charge of everything.

Ronni   What?

Chris   I wanna be, like, world king. And also, like, head of Google.

Ronni   That's not how this works!

Chris   I mean, do you want to start a war?

Sham   Yes!

Ronni   No.

Sham   Belgium is mobilising its forces. And bringing all NATO allies with it.

Ronni   You're not starting a war.

Chris   Looks like we already have.

Ronni   Caroline, you're the USA, you've got to step in and oppose this!

Caroline   The world has suffered enough from Western imperialism, I'm against intervention!

Ronni   Fine! Fine! There's a war. Y'know what? FINE!

We go to an unmoderated caucus, everyone up – lots of excitement.

Ronni *gathers her team –* **Katy***,* **Sarah***,* **Stevie***.*

Ronni   Okay, regroup. We need to push for a vote.

Sarah   I, um, I don't think we'd win . . .

Ronni   We can get someone on board. All we need is a majority of one.

Katy   Well, we're obviously not going to get Caitlin.

Sarah   Caroline will abstain.

Stevie   Me too. I can't vote now cause I'm in space.

Katy   We could *try* Sham?

Ronni He's not going to support anything that doesn't come with me letting him declare war on someone.

Katy Then that leaves . . . Chris?

Ronni *and* **Katy** *approach* **Chris**.

Chris What do you want?

Ronni I know you're just trying to wind everyone up . . . but I've been listening to everything you've been saying – you're actually not bad at this.

Chris Like I care what you think.

Ronni I know you don't. You don't care what anyone thinks – well, apart from Caitlin, obviously. Cause you're doing what she wants you to.

Beat.

Chris I'm doing what *I* want.

Ronni Yeah. I know. I also know that you're quite enjoying being North Korea –. Because if you think about it – the restrictions in my resolution, they hit America, they hit everyone, all your rivals. They won't be able to pick and choose who they trade with or who they sanction anymore. You support this . . . it's actually a win for you.

Beat.

Chris The human rights clause, that's not gonna work is it?

Ronni Maybe we could drop it for this draft.

Katy But that's Sarah's amendment.

Ronni It's dropped. Will you vote?

Chris Fine. Just this one time. And not because you want me to, alright?

Ronni And just like that, we're back on track!

He leaves, **Katy** *and* **Ronni** *return to* **Sarah**.

Ronni Okay. We've got a deal. We ditch the human rights amendment, we get Chris.

Sarah But –

Ronni I know, I know, but we have to make compromises. How else are we going to *win*? Now come on.

Back into the session.

Mayo Decorum, delegates, decor . . . oh just be quiet! Let's get back to it.

Caroline The USA no longer recognises this institution.

Mayo If you could raise your placard just to let me know that you don't recognise me.

Sham Motion to discuss going to war with North Korea!

Mayo That's not something we can do here, sorry.

Ronni Motion to move to a vote on the draft resolution.

Caitlin Motion to continue debating.

Ronni We have the votes to pass it.

Caitlin Well, I still have some changes I want to make.

Ronni Why can't you just accept? You've lost, I've won.

Caitlin Are you sure?

She gestures to **Sarah**.

Sarah I'm sorry.

Ronni What?

Sarah Sri Lanka will no longer be supporting the resolution.

Ronni What?

Sarah I'm voting against it.

Katy Me too.

Ronni What are you even talking about?

Sarah We're supposed to be doing good. This isn't about winning.

Ronni You have to win if you want to do anything!

Sarah There are some compromises you shouldn't make!

Caroline I motion that we don't vote on anything. That we just disband this whole organisation.

Chris Why not? I'd go along with that.

Ronni You can't! You're North Korea, she's the USA. You're literally enemies!

Caroline Why are you always trying to re-create the structures that confine people in real life? We don't need them. We're starting from scratch!

Ronni You can't start from scratch! This is the *only* way. This is important. Look around. Look at the world! We are being given a chance to solve things. Don't you get it? Don't you understand?

Sham Belgium sends 10,000 troops to the North Korean border.

Chris North Korea sends 20,000 – and a bunch of tanks.

Stevie The Gambia has reached orbit.

Ronni Fine. Fine! Y'know what? Yeah, let's chuck it in. Cause what's the point? You're right – we can't work together! None of us can. We're just gonna kill ourselves and the planet and there's nothing we can do about it. That's who we are! So yeah, why don't we break early for the day – why don't we never come back?

Mayo   We will need to vote on any change to the schedule.

Ronni   Oh shut up, Mayo!

Mayo   Please address people in the third person.

Ronni   Okay – New Zealand requests that the Chair shut up! In fact, that's what we should all do.

She goes to take **Mayo**'s *gavel.*

Mayo   Hey, that's mine!

Ronni   Yeah, well, you don't need it anymore.

She breaks it and throws it on the floor.

We're done. I now declare this Model United Nations – *over*.

She leaves.

Part Four: Resolution

The characters disperse. **Katy** *runs into* **Sarah** *– she's upset.*

Katy   Sarah. Hi.

Sarah   Oh, sorry, I was just . . .

Katy   Are you okay?

Sarah   I just . . . I wanted to do something good, I know it's not real, but . . . I just wanted to make a difference.

Katy   You did!

Sarah   No. I didn't . . . I just . . . They all treat it like it's nothing but . . . I'm terrified, like, all the time. I feel so stupid. And small. Like, we don't have any control over anything. We could be wiped out tomorrow. What's our future gonna be like? I'm, like, freaking out all the time.

Katy   Me too.

Beat.

I've never kissed anyone. Like, not really – not outside of a game. Cause I've played a game with dice where you have to kiss someone else but I don't think that counts and I'd like to kiss someone when it counts – but then I worry, like, is it that I really want to kiss someone or is it that I don't want to have not kissed someone anymore? Y'know.

Sarah   Not quite the same thing.

Katy   Sorry.

Sarah   It's just . . . this was, like, an opportunity to, like, *pretend* to do something good – in a game. And we couldn't even do that? What's the point?

Katy   Of what?

Sarah   Anything.

Stevie *and* **Sham**.

Sham   Thing is, like, countries can't just get on like that, y'know, that's why you have wars – look at Ukraine, Russia didn't care what the UN said.

Stevie   Yeah. And sometimes there are problems that countries can't handle. Like, in *Captain America: Civil War* when Captain America becomes a fugitive and Iron Man and the Avengers have to bring him in so they have that big fight in the airport in Germany and Spider-Man's there.

Sham   Yeah.

Beat.

But, they're all, like, American aren't they? How does it work with them fighting in Germany?

Stevie   Well . . . Erm . . . I dunno, they'd probably have to, like, y'know, have an agreement with all the countries, like, so everyone's on board, actually, they'd probably have to be under UN control.

Sham   Isn't that what Captain America was angry about.

Beat.

Stevie   Oh yeah.

Beat.

Was Captain America wrong?

Chris *and* **Caroline** *run into each other.*

Chris   Well, that was pointless.

Caroline   Beyond pointless.

Chris   Yep.

Beat.

Would have thought you'd love it though. Right up your street.

Caroline   What do you mean?

Chris   Y'know, you're always doing stuff round here – going on marches, trying to get gender neutral toilets, walking out of English cause they weren't teaching enough diverse authors, even though, like, no one cares.

Beat.

Caroline   You noticed me doing all that?

Chris   Everyone does. Just thought you would have loved this.

Caroline   No. That stuff's *real*. This is just . . . gross. Sitting around, pretending we're all powerful people, like it's all just . . . hypothetical. When there are people on the ground who it actually affects. It's all wrong. At least what I'm trying to do is real.

Chris   Still doesn't matter though. Nothing changes.

Caroline   Yes it does. You just have to make it.

Finally, **Caitlin** *and* **Ronni***.*

Ronni   What do you want?

Caitlin   I don't want anything, just came here to read.

Ronni   *You* reading? Sure.

Beat.

Caitlin   You're not the only one who's smart.

Ronni   I'm the only one who cares.

Caitlin   Other people care. They just don't care *all* the time.

Beat.

Ronni   You turned them all against me.

Caitlin   They were against you anyway. You just weren't interested in what they thought. You just wanted to bully people into doing what you said.

Ronni   I'm not the bully. You're the bully.

Caitlin   I'm not a bully.

Ronni   You bully me. You bullied me since we were four years old.

Caitlin   We bully each other. Yeah, I might say things about you behind your back, but every day you find a way of telling me I'm stupid. And everyone else. You act like you're better than all of us. You make us feel dumb.

Ronni   That's ridiculous.

Caitlin   See?! You talk down to us, you act like you're always right no matter what.

Ronni   Cause I usually am.

Caitlin   It doesn't matter!

Ronni   So, what, I should just pretend I'm not smart.

Caitlin   No, but you shouldn't be such a dick about it.

Beat.

You don't know what's going on with me. Like, maybe I wanted to be your friend, or, I wouldn't have minded if you wanted to be mine. I don't know. Maybe I'm interested in some of the same things you are. Maybe I've thought about all this stuff too. You could have asked.

Beat.

You say this is important cause we all can imagine what it's like to be another country. You can't even imagine what it's like to be me.

Beat.

Ronni   I just wanted everyone to work together.

Caitlin   Yeah. Well. Maybe they can't.

Katy *enters.*

Katy   Ohmygod – guys, you'll never guess what's happening – *everyone's working together!*

Ronni   What?

Katy   Okay, so we were all in the classroom, right?

As **Katy** *tells the story, the other characters act it out.*

And everyone was, like, bored, because we didn't have anything to do anymore. And Sham was like –

Sham   Can't we just go home?

Katy   And Stevie was like –

Stevie   I've got to stay, I've got maths club after.

Katy   And Chris was like –

Chris   You go to maths club?

Ronni   What's this got to do with anything?

Katy   Oh, sorry. Anyway, then we started talking about the Model United Nations, and Caroline was like –

Caroline   It was fun when Stevie went into space.

Katy   And Sham was like –

Sham   And when Chris declared war.

Katy   And I was like (*joining the scene*) and when Sarah said she was gonna vote against Ronni's resolution (*to* **Ronni**) sorry about that.

Ronni   And then what happened.

Katy   Well, then I was like (*joining the scene*) how would we have done it if Ronni and Caitlin weren't there. Like, surely we could work it out.

Ronni   And?

Katy   Well, Mayo was like –

Mayo   I should probably remind you that you are on the brink of nuclear war.

Chris   North Korea will launch a nuclear warhead in twelve minutes unless we are given all the world's bitcoin.

Katy   And Stevie was like –

Stevie   Erm, can I just point out that The Gambia is now halfway to the moon.

Katy   And Caroline was like –

Caroline   The Socialist States of America is no longer part of the UN.

Katy   And I was like (*joining the scene*) yeah, sure, I know, but – look, okay, fine, I don't really understand what's going on here. I mean, Argentina doesn't understand. I mean, I don't understand why I'm saying Argentina doesn't understand. I don't understand what we're trying to do, or why any of this matters, or why any of us should take it seriously, cause all of it is pretend. But . . . like . . . it does seem to matter. And . . . like . . . if it does – we don't need to do it exactly the way we're told. Like, why does Argentina have to refer to myself as Argentina? Why do we have to say 'point of information' when we all know we're just asking a question? Why do we have to speak like we're all lawyers and stuff in Shakespeare play. Why can't we just be, like, real. We've got a problem – climate change – we need to solve it – why can't we just do that?

Ronni   And?

Katy   Well, then . . .

Mayo   I am prepared to be more relaxed with the rules of decorum.

Katy   And Chris was like . . .

Chris   I want sanctions lifted, but I will agree to the cap.

Sarah   I want my human rights clause back in.

Chris   Only if you revise the wording.

Katy   I'm sure we can make that happen – Sham.

Sham   I want –

Katy   You can't have a war.

Sham   Urgh.

Caroline   What if you committed militaries to installing green infrastructure?

Katy   That's great – I don't know what that means.

Caroline   It's not a war, but it still uses the army.

Sham   I could work with that.

Chris (*to* **Caroline**)   Thought you left?

Caroline   I dunno, this seems interesting.

Katy   That's great! Stevie, The Gambia –

Stevie   The intergalactic republic of Gambia.

Katy   You could . . . Erm . . .

Sarah   Well, you could supply food to all the countries with shortages?

Stevie   Peanuts?

Sarah   Exactly!

Beat.

Okay. Oh – Sham and I did have another idea . . .

Sham   There should be an organisation to target the money – so that, like, specific regions get it most. The Trans-international Targeting Syndicate.

Katy   That spells tits.

Stevie   Oh come on.

Katy   Okay! (*To* **Ronni**.) And then we discussed it some more, and passed some more amendments.

Ronni   And then?

Katy   It's still going!

Ronni   I need to see this!

The two scenes mix – all the characters are debating, excitedly horse trading.

Chris   I've got an amendment, who's gonna support it.

Caroline   The USA motions for unmoderated caucus!

Stevie   The Gambia will support this *if* we can have assurances on trade.

Sham   I don't think my country would actually think that.

Sarah   Could we change it to say 'insists' rather than 'suggests'?

Katy   Do you guys want to join in?

Ronni   I . . . no. You guys carry on.

Katy   Yeah?

Ronni   You seem to be doing great.

Katy   Thanks!

Beat.

Ronni   Actually, I think I probably will just take a look if that's okay?

Mayo   Motion for a vote, all those in favour . . .?

The delegates all raise their placards and . . .

Part Five: Implementation

Ronni   Yeah, so that's the end, basically, and before you're like 'oh, yeah, you all learned a lesson' – no! Most people stayed exactly the same after that. I didn't change, I don't think I did anything wrong, the whole thing wasn't actually that big a deal, I'm only telling you about it, cause, I dunno, it's something that happened to us, isn't it?

Katy   I think maybe just finish it.

Ronni   Okay! Anyway, so, yeah, we finished off the debate and then it was, like, time to go home – and Chris and Caroline were like –

Chris   Y'know, you were pretty good at being an oppressive superpower.

Caroline   Thanks, you actually weren't bad at being a dickhead dictator.

Ronni   And then they walked home together.

Katy   Cause obviously they fancy each other.

Sarah   Caroline's planning to take him to a protest at the weekend.

Ronni   Stevie and Sham were like –

Stevie   So, do you reckon, in space, there's like . . . a United Planets?

Sham   Yeah, and they probably have some really cool wars.

Mayo   That's actually the subject of a new game I've been working on! Wanna play?

Ronni   Katy and Sarah –

Katy   We can do this bit. Katy and Sarah applied for a proper Model United Nations!

Sarah   We've already written the resolution.

Katy   And I almost understand all of it.

Ronni   So yeah, that's pretty much it. Like I said. No big moral. This wasn't anything big, it was just *us*. But, I dunno, it is what it is, y'know? I don't know what it all *means* or anything.

Caitlin *enters.*

Caitlin   Oh. You're still here.

Ronni   Yeah. Just talking about how it turns out people *can* work together.

Caitlin   Like, in one specific situation.

Ronni   Can you just accept being wrong?

Caitlin   I wasn't.

Beat.

Ronni   Y'know, I know you don't like me. And I know you know I don't like you either. I just want you to know . . . I don't care.

Caitlin   Neither do I.

Ronni   A lot of people don't like each other, and they survive. It just doesn't mean we have to, y'know, be enemies. It's fine to just not like each other. Not long left of school and then we never have to see each other again.

Caitlin   Yep.

Ronni   And I don't know about you, but I for one can't wait.

Caitlin   Me neither.

Ronni   Counting the hours.

Caitlin   Counting the minutes.

Ronni   Counting the seconds.

Beat.

Do you want to go and see a movie sometime?

Beat.

Caitlin   Yeah, alright.

She leaves. **Ronni** *glares at the audience.*

Ronni   What?!

Veronica *leaves.* **Mayo** *steps forward.*

Mayo (*bashful*)   Hi.

They all look at **Mayo**.

Sorry, do you mind if I . . .?

He gestures that he wants to talk to the audience, they let him.

The way I think about all of this, if you wanna know, is – some board games are competitive and some are cooperative. But some are both and so it's up to you to decide how you're going to play it. And I guess that's it isn't it. It's up to us. It's up to you.

Beat.

We're all we've got.

Blackout.

The End.

Model Behaviour

BY JON BRITTAIN

Notes on rehearsal and staging, drawn from a workshop with the writer,
held at the National Theatre facilitated by director Laura Keefe, October 2022

How the writer came to write the play

Writer Jon Brittain started out in acting, comedy and stand-up, studying drama at university. In *Model Behaviour* it is clear to see his comedic background and the influence of stand-up comedy in the moments of direct audience address.

During his high school years living in Holland, Jon Brittain took part in a Model United Nations (MUN) at The Hague, where young people from all over the world came to compete. He distinctly remembers taking part and not knowing what to do. He noted that 'there was a lot of ego around'. In theory the idea of the MUN is to teach cooperation, but Jon Brittain reflected that instead it seemed people were immediately trying to outdo each other. A Model United Nations is an inherently theatrical environment and in his experience was always very performative. He said: 'You get people with all the ideas but with no idea how to express them alongside people with no idea but all the confidence in the world.'

When he started out writing the play he tried to write it as the big MUN conference but, as it is now, the play purposely tries to reflect an experience that could be anyone's: This doesn't have to be a school that regularly sends their kids to Model UN competitions. It can be any school.

He wanted the play to be accessible to anyone, about the kids and their own experience of the world, rather than them needing prior knowledge. He said that he loved the idea of kids confronting humanity's inability/ability to cooperate and working as a group to address the shortcomings of institutions like the UN:

> We have institutions that aren't always fit for purpose. But we don't necessarily
> have a better alternative. As individuals, we often struggle to cooperate even
> when we've got a common cause. In theory, these institutions give us a formal
> structure to fit our problem solving into. But do they also put up barriers? And,
> if so, how do we overcome them? Or do we have to burn the whole thing down?

Jon Brittain spoke about his awareness in writing the play of the huge amount of concern amongst the younger generation for the future of the planet and the great burden of this. He's also aware however that: 'There's an expectation that young people should be thinking about this all the time, but there's also lots of other things going on in a young person's life.'

With the play he wanted to give a balanced representation of different people: some who are engaged in this conversation, some who are not and those somewhere in the middle.

Warm-ups and rehearsal games

Lead director Laura Keefe starts every day – whether a rehearsal, read-through or technical rehearsal – with a ball game. A ball game is good for getting the group working together but is also a useful way for you as a director to quickly establish where your cast is at and what they might need on any given day.

Ball games are great for team building and to build energy, but for this play in particular these games also very purposefully encourage competitiveness, which is a great way of starting to explore this feeling within the play.

For a morning game she suggested an 'up' ball game like the following.

Game: Keepy-uppy or 'Delinkway!'

You will need one blow-up volleyball or football (something big enough but light enough so it can be kept in the air and so it's not going to hurt anyone)

The group must keep the ball from hitting the floor with only their hands. Set a target number that you're trying to get to as a group before the ball hits the floor – twenty is a good number to aim for at first and you can reduce or increase this later if needed. Select someone to count the number aloud during every round.

Laura Keefe then added the following rules: you can't touch the ball twice in a row and you can't apologise. At regular intervals between rounds of the game, she would also get everyone to change places in the room so that different people were given a chance at having a go. This gently encouraged everyone to be involved, particularly those who might naturally try to stick to the edges of the room, rather than get right in the mix of the game.

At this stage, a call-and-response element was added to the game: 'Delinkway!'

The group leader chooses a server. To start the game the server must shout 'What we gonna play?!' and the group responds 'Delinkway!' and from there the game begins.

Laura Keefe explained that 'Delinkway' is an entirely made-up word and therefore feel free to get your group to suggest other alternatives for the call-and-response.

In later rounds, a rule was added about hitting the ball with parts of the body other than hands, e.g. challenge the group to not use their hands for every fifth hit.

Game: Keepy-uppy – Advanced

Laura Keefe then introduced a slightly more advanced version of the game. The same principles apply, including the call-and-response to start the game. This time, however, when someone has tapped the ball, they must say 'I'm out' and then leave, going to the edge of the space. This means that gradually the space is populated with fewer and fewer players. As with before, if the ball hits the floor, everyone is back in get back in and play starts again!

Game: Keepy-uppy – Teams

The group was split into teams of around ten people and each team decided on a team name. A bin was placed at one end of the room and a starting line at the other. One at a time, each team had a go at working together to get the ball from the starting line at one end of the room into the bin at the end of the room, without the ball touching the floor.

With the other teams cheering from the sidelines, team tactics were discussed. Keep playing until a team succeeds and, if no one does, form a mega team to get it done!

Game: I accuse

A 'heady' name game which Laura Keefe suggested is great for the after-lunch slump. If ball games are to get people energised and into their bodies in the morning, heady games get people into their brains after lunch. This is a great example, and it doesn't matter if it keeps going wrong, just keep playing until everyone is sufficiently warmed up.

Everyone is asked to take a chair and form a line.

The game starts when someone stands to their feet and says, 'I accuse [name]!', effectively passing to the person that they have named for them to take the next turn. The first person then sits down again, and the next person stands to their feet and says, 'I accuse [name]!' The game continues as such and can really build in momentum, depending on how well the group knows the names in the room.

A few rules:

1 You cannot accuse your neighbour (the person to your left or right)

2 You cannot 'ping-pong' (say the name of the person who has just passed to you)

3 If you hesitate or cannot think of a name you must move to the end of the line (the place to the left of the workshop leader)

When someone moves to the end of the line, this means that everyone must move one chair to their left and take the name of the person sitting in that chair at the very beginning of the game. As the game continues and people keep moving to the end of the line, you keep taking the chair to your left and the name of the person who was sitting in that chair at the very beginning of the game.

Once the group had done this for a good few rounds Laura then started the game again but had everyone take on the name of a famous person or character, dead or alive. The same rules apply and the name stays with the chair rather than with the person.

Themes

For Jon Brittain, the key themes and questions within this play are:

Can people work together?

Will people work together?

Approaching the play

Laura started the day with an 'on-your-feet' read-through of the play. She encouraged the group that this exercise is about exploring initial thoughts about the play. Being dyslexic herself, Laura said that she finds that this is a good way to immediately get the words off the page and people on their feet, allowing the group to experiment with a language for the space, and for you as a director to sit back and just observe. There is a lot to gather from what a group initially finds in a readthrough like this.

An 'on-your-feet' read-through

Laura specifically chose not to give out character roles for this read-through, and instead set the following parameters:

Everyone had a copy of the text and took a chair, sitting around the space in a circle and leaving a playing space in the middle.

One person, seated, started by reading the stage directions from the beginning of the play, including the title, character descriptions and scene title. The first scene then began when another person took the first speaking role and, standing up, moved into the circle's playing space. This continued, with more people standing and stepping into the circle as new characters appeared in the scene. At the end of the scene everyone would leave the circle and again take their seat.

The process then started again for the next scene, with a new person reading the stage directions and new people given the opportunity to read if they wished to. As before, with a new character arriving in the scene, any person could take on the role by simply standing, starting to speak and entering the circle.

The read-through continued in this way, with each scene played out on its feet and with the readers being free to move how they saw fit within the playing space.

After the read-through Laura said: 'I like to read a play out loud like this because often we read it once and we sometimes don't realise what assumptions we've made. To read it again together and on its feet like this means that we mine the text for facts.'

Breaking down the text

Laura got the group to break down the script into its five individual scenes:

Part One: Preamble

Part Two: Debate

Part Three: Negotiation

Part Four: Resolution

Part Five: Implementation

For this exercise take pens and big pieces of paper and for each scene write a list of *facts* (not assumptions) and a list of *questions*. This can be done as one group who work together on all of the scenes or, if your group is big, split them into smaller groups working on a scene or a couple of scenes each. You should take about ten minutes per scene.

The questions that come up from this exercise are particularly useful to find things that need to be on your research list. It also helps to establish the things about your version of the play that need to be decided and agreed by the group. Remember also that some questions will not be answered and it's fine for them to remain up in the air as questions.

This is what the groups in the room came up with for each scene:

Part One: Preamble

Facts:
There are desks.
They are in a classroom.
The characters have never heard of the MUN.
The characters sometimes directly address the audience.
The action happens after Covid.

Questions:
Why is Mr Smallwood's class a doss?
Do we believe everything Ronni says?
Who is Che Guevara?
What kind of school is this?
How old are they?

Part Two: Debate

Facts:
All of the characters are present at some point in this scene.
The characters all have a designated country.
Some students have researched their countries and some have not.

Questions:
What is a caucus?
Are the characters' personalities linked to the countries they represent?
Does each character need a flag or what other way could we distinguish them?
Where is Mr Smallwood?
Why is Ronni so invested?

Part Three: Negotiation

Facts:
It starts in the same location as the previous scene and then there are flashbacks.
Caitlin has been talking to everyone.
Ronni is increasingly frustrated with Caitlin.
Katy is hungry.

Questions:
Where did the flashbacks take place when they happened?
Does Ronni really care or does she just want to win?

Part Four: Resolution

Facts:
Katy's parents argue.
Sarah wants to make a difference.
Caroline goes on marches and is an activist.

Questions:
Where are they?
Were Sarah and Katy friends before this?
Do Chris and Caroline realise they fancy each other?

Part Five: Implementation

Facts:
It's the end.
Katy and Sarah have written a resolution.
Ronni is called Veronica.

Questions:
What is the outcome of the debate and does it matter?
Have Caitlin and Ronni always liked each other?
At the end is it the audience allowing Mayo to speak or is it the other characters?

This group questioned the words of Mayo at the end of the play which started a larger group discussion:

Is his 'We're all we've got' referring to the people on stage and the audience as well? Is it galvanising? Or is it just referring to the young people on stage? Older generations have messed it up and now it's up to us to sort it out?

Laura said: 'It's up to the group to decide what you want the message to be.'

Jon added: 'The paradox here is that, yes, organisations like the UN haven't been able to solve many of the world's problems, but they're also all we've got. The drawbacks of the institution are often plain to see. That doesn't mean the principles behind it don't count. Every organisation – the UN, government, schools – is flawed. But they also exist for a reason. Can we use them to try and create a better world? As Mayo says, that's up to us.'

The world of the play

In the same groups and with the same scenes that they'd worked on for breaking down the text, Laura got each group to establish the following for each scene:

Where is it and when is it?

What are the locations that appear in the scene?

Here is what the groups came up with:

Part One: Preamble

- They're in a classroom and it's a politics class.
- When directly addressing the audience, are they talking about the events of MUN from a past perspective or a future perspective? How long ago did the events of the play happen?
- Who are the audience?

Part Two: Debate

- Mr Smallwood's classroom, morning.
- The action of the scene moves around the classroom.
- The lunch bell rings at the end, so this scene happens before lunch.
- How long is the lesson? Are they off-timetable all day?

Jon clarified for the group that a day of MUN would be a day off timetable like an enterprise day.

Part Three: Negotiation

- This scene happens in multiple locations
- It takes place at lunchtime

Laura noted: 'For this scene it's not necessarily important that your audience know the exact location of each conversation, but for the feeling of the scene it is useful to note that this all takes place over the lunch break. Ronni and Caitlin are working very fast!'

Part Four: Resolution

- This scene is happening in the afternoon, after lunch.
- You can decide where different conversations happen: Sarah and Katy's conversation could perhaps happen in the bathroom?

Part Five: Implementation

- It's the end of the day.
- They could be in the classroom, a corridor or at the school gates.
- Has this been an end-of-term activity?
- How long ago did the events of the play happen? Was it on Monday and this is now the Friday? Was it a year ago? This is an important decision to make and will affect the telling of the story.

Six key aspects of the play

Laura pinpointed six key aspects of the play that are essential to address during your rehearsal process. These aspects are:

The teacher

Direct audience address

Signifying time passing

Unmoderated caucus

Flashbacks

Major and minor focus

Exercise: Group troubleshooting

Laura split the room into six groups, each one taking and troubleshooting a different aspect. After some discussion, each group then staged some ways in which they might approach this aspect of the play.

Here's what the groups came up with:

The teacher

There are a few ways that you can approach the role of the teacher. This may be as a voiceover, as a character who is played or impersonated by the students, or perhaps an adult (even yourself) cameoing in the role.

Jon said that the teacher is suggested as a voiceover because he didn't really want a kid to have to play an adult. An adult in the room changes the dynamic so that's why the teacher isn't there. He likes the idea that the teacher is there but absent, almost like a Charlie Brown world where the adult characters are never around.

The group chose to stage the opening of the play. With chairs across the playing area and characters spread across the space, some seated, some standing, they delivered the scene in direct address to the audience. They decided to try the role of teacher being impersonated by a student character, perhaps Sham. This character, seated upstage, stood up and arrived downstage centre in time for the teacher's line 'Has anyone ever wondered what it's like to work at the United Nations?' and then blended into the rest of the scene.

Laura noted that this was particularly successful because it kept the pace of the scene going and didn't break up the action.

The group's alternative idea was the teacher Zoom-ing in on video call, appearing in the room on a projector screen.

Direct audience address

This group suggested that the moments where the characters directly address the audience could be marked with some clever use of tech: downlighting or spotlights, or words delivered into a microphone.

With low tech available to them in the room, however, the group experimented with creating a staging rule to mark the moments of direct address: when talking directly to the audience, a character would stand on their chair and then return to sitting when back in the scene.

Laura reminded the group that it's about looking at who actors are speaking to, whether that's the audience or the people in the scene with them.

Signifying time passing

To experiment with creating the feeling of time passing, the group worked with the following extract on page 212:

Teacher   *So – how does that sound?*

Ronni   And everyone's like . . .

Katy   It sounds hard.

Stevie   It sounds fun.

Sham   It sounds weird.

Sarah   It sounds stressful.

Caroline   It sounds pointless.

Chris   It sounds stupid.

Ronni   That sounds like the most amazing thing I have ever heard.

With Ronni downstage centre, the other characters were dotted around her in the space. Each character would say their line and then leave the stage, eventually leaving Ronni alone for her final line. This then led into a *Rocky*-esque montage with Ronni still positioned downstage, preparing for what's coming next, looking in a mirror and giving herself a pep talk. Whilst this was happening, all other characters were crossing the space at speed behind her, in chatting groups of friends or as teachers rushing down corridors.

Unmoderated caucus

There are two moments of unmoderated caucus during the play. These appear in the script on pages 216 and 225.

Unmoderated caucus is a term taken directly from MUN and is when there is a suspension of the rules, allowing delegates to freely move around the room and form smaller groups to write resolutions.

This group chose to work with the unmoderated caucus on page 216, using the following extract:

Ronni   Anyway! So, like, pretty much no one had anything to say – which is fine by me.

Everyone gets up – it's an unmoderated caucus – basically, a free for all!

All the characters mingle, negotiating, all formality is dropped.

Cause we're not just here to talk about the world's problems. We have to try and solve them too – and that's why we need resolutions!

On Ronni's '. . . fine by me' the characters quickly split into smaller groups, engaging in frenetic and animated conversation. Underscoring this was a distorted and sped-up version of the anthem of the United Nations. The occasional snippet of conversation could be heard from each small group. On Ronni's 'that's why we need resolutions!' the music cut and the energy dropped again. The stark contrast between the bursting energy of the unmoderated caucus and the slow sloth-like atmosphere on either side of it was really successful.

Laura suggested that the group try the scene again but with the music really loud and all conversations mimed. She encouraged the group to ramp up the physicality even more, and not be afraid to allow the stage image to speak for itself rather than adding in more text.

Flashbacks

This group worked with the flashback involving Chris and Caitlin on page 221 of the script.

The character of Caitlin was centre stage for the scene, with the present-day scene between Ronni and Chris taking place to one side of her. Caitlin stayed still and central, with Chris entering into her space for the flashback and then returning to Ronni afterwards. Her stillness and central position gave the feeling of Caitlin like a puppet-master, totally in control of everything and everyone.

The group also suggested the idea that Caitlin could be doing all her meddling via text message.

Major and minor focus

Laura noted that moments of minor focus happen quite often in the play, where all characters remain in the space but the action focuses in on conversations between duos or trios.

This group worked from the end of page 219 and Mayo's '– that's lunch'. With Ronni and Caitlin's conversation happening downstage right, the rest of the characters went into minor focus, forming a lunch queue. This physical action was enough to be interesting and fill out the scene, but not so much that it detracted from the small scene happening at the same time.

Pace

Pace is essential for this play to work. The comedic dialogue in particular will benefit from this.

Remember that pace is different to speed: it's more about sucking the air out between lines to keep the energy up, which is different to speaking quickly. There should be a sense of urgency and a feeling of propulsion, of things moving along. Focusing on keeping up the pace in this way also means that you can play the contrast when you do choose to allow for moments of pause.

Jon referenced lines in the script where characters almost seem to start speaking before they've had the thought. This is usually when there are multiple words at the start of the line, for example on page 219:

Ronni   I . . . That's not . . . I don't . . . Like, I don't know why she's saying this . . . We were supposed to be having a vote!

Jon noted that this is supposed to imitate speech, where words just run off the tongue before you've had the thought. It is not intended that the ellipses indicate a pause, in fact much the opposite. Jon said that he would discourage the young actors from taking too much time over these lines. Jon said: 'Tailor it as much as you want. Be quite bold with it, feel free to cut stuff to trim it down to keep the pace.' Laura added: 'Do make sure that these cuts are for clarity of storytelling, however, and that you keep the consistency of character.'

Casting

Jon explained that he was originally planning for the names of the characters to just be their countries, but this got confusing. Jon is very happy for the characters' names and genders to be changed however you see fit so that the play works for your group.

Characters and characterisation

There are 9 characters that appear in the play's script but Jon is very happy for there to be more characters added for a larger cast.

Looking at character

Laura split the room into groups of three or four people, with each small group given a character each. With pens and big pieces of paper, each group was tasked to go through the script and note down the following:

What does the character say about themselves?

What does the character say about other people?

What do other people say about the character?

Laura said that for this exercise it is important to take the information from the text, rather than inferring or assuming. The groups were therefore asked to refer to specific lines, facts and information found directly within the text and stage directions of the script.

Laura suggested that this exercise might be helpful for you in terms of casting. She also noted that it is often those characters who have less to say that need more work done on them so that they are as well rounded as the other larger roles.

Jon also said that this exercise was a good way of getting a company to think outside of their own roles. By doing this exercise as a group, the person with the largest role gets an insight into the smallest role and the other way round. It's also a way to get everyone to have a conversation about what the show is. You start to notice which characters say loads about themselves and not much about other people and the characters who say nothing about themselves but loads about others. What does this reveal about them?

Character essences

Laura then got the groups to decide on the essence of each character. She suggested that pop culture is always good for this as it helps to give a clear and shared image of the person. She suggested that having printed images of these essences on the wall of your rehearsal room would also be a great idea as part of your group research: if they're always on the wall, they're always there to refer back to and can give the actor another thing to play and experiment with.

Here's the essences that the groups came up with:

Chris	Oscar the Grouch (*Sesame Street*)
Katy	Robin (*Batman*)/Karen (*Mean Girls*)/Barney Rubble (*The Flintstones*)
Caroline	Zoe Sugg (YouTuber)
Sham	Mike TV (*Charlie and the Chocolate Factory*)
Sarah	Neville Longbottom (*Harry Potter*)/Newt Scamander (*Fantastic Beasts*)
Ronni	Hermione Granger (*Harry Potter*)
Teacher	Mr Schneebly (*School of Rock*)
Caitlin	Regina George (*Mean Girls*)

Stevie	Sheldon Cooper (*The Big Bang Theory*)
Mayo	Stephen Fry/Matthew Mercer (voice actor and online D&D dungeon master)

Having these essences to hand during the rehearsal process is a good way of seeing when everyone has gone back to the middle. Reminding your actors of their characters' essences is a way for them to return to finding the extreme again. This will stop the characters blending. Jon said: 'Give space for the characters to be the most extreme version of themselves. Giving full permission for them to be Oscar the Grouch, for example, will really unlock things for the actor.'

'Something to play'

Throughout the day Laura mentioned that giving an actor something really clear to 'play' is a great idea. This can be their character's essence as above, but equally it can be something like a character really needing the toilet or being really hungry. Some of these things can be found in the script, but feel free to experiment with other ones for different characters.

Production, staging and design

For any set design it's always good to consider all the possibilities: what would you do if you had a million pounds? If you start big you can then consider what might serve the scenes best and distil the location down to its essentials.

Even one gesture can signify the place and time; for example, a sports field can be indicated simply by a character doing keepy-uppys or a library can be shown by a character holding a book and the occasional 'shhh' from other characters during the scene. Jon said:

> The way I've written it is as poor theatre. It can be performed in a classroom, a theatre, a hall, wherever. It's purposefully written at a pace so that it keeps moving, so the little gestures suggest so much more and the audience can use their imagination to fill in the gaps.

Exercise: Build the space

Laura tasked each group to build the space and location of their scene using only themselves and things already to hand. Once the location was built, she then asked each group to decide what the location or place might sound like and to make this sound(s) as a group.

Here is what the groups came up with:

Group One: Bathroom

This group used themselves and some chairs to build their space, with one character standing up high on a chair and the other sitting on a chair next to them, to give the image of one talking to the other over the top of a toilet cubicle. Other non-speaking actors in the scene, became other parts of the bathroom including a particularly convincing and humorous dripping tap and hand dryer.

Having actors creating the environment may be an interesting way to consider how you incorporate more people into the scene.

Group Two: Classroom

This group created the pomp and circumstance of the MUN with a semicircle of chairs and a tall table as a central podium for the character of Mayo. The group suggested that in a more makeshift way this podium could be a school music stand or similar. This group further played on the pomp of the scene and location by playing the Hymn of the United Nations, which was easily found on YouTube.

Group Three: Corridor

This group created a very effective soundscape of a corridor with lots of hustle and bustle. Laura got everyone to close their eyes to experience this one. This group successfully created a familiar atmosphere with a school bell, lockers slamming and the sound of a teacher repeating the same piece of information over and over again.

Group Four: Library

This group made good use of space and levels, making use of a tall bookshelf already in the room. One person was up high on a chair looking through the shelves, a couple of people lay on the floor with a book and another sat bored at their desk. The scene was underscored by the steady inane tapping of a pencil and the occasional loud 'shhhhh'.

Group Five: Classroom

This group created the desks and flags of the classroom using only their bodies. They also had the lovely idea that each desk could be dressed with items to reflect the characters' personalities.

Structure, style and transitions

Using the work from the previous exercise, Laura joined groups together to explore the simplest and easiest way of transitioning from one location to another.

Laura encouraged the groups to do this exercise really quickly. In doing this you allow the group to find stuff quickly, but also encourage them to throw stuff away that's not working. We're not so precious about things that we've made in two minutes and it often means that we are open to experimenting more.

Here is what the groups came up with:

Library – into – Bathroom

This transition gave a real moment of contrast from the quiet and stillness of the library into the hustle and bustle of a toilet queue. The group used a school bell to mark this point of sudden change of energy.

Laura noted that this transition was really effective and that even a very brief change of energy like this to take us into the next scene is a great way to transition. Even in its brevity, it did its job very successfully.

The MUN – into – Classroom

This group made use of the semicircle of chairs from their earlier classroom to great effect in exploring this transition. With the chairs in the semicircle, characters standing poised and official-looking and Mayo at his podium, the UN anthem began to play and the reality of the play's characters was revealed; a bustling soundscape of the classroom and characters slouching over chairs.

Laura prompted the group to try their transition the other way round, to see the disarray of the classroom transform into the formality of the UN, which made for more contrast and comedy from the moment.

Exercise: Make a timeline

This is something you can do yourself as director or together with the cast to get to know the structure and journey of the play. You might also decide that it's useful to include extra information from before or after the events of the play in this timeline, especially if there are events from the past or future that impact on what happens in the play.

Question and answer with Jon Brittain

Q: Can my group change references in the text?
A: Have at it! If there's something you've found that's funnier and more relevant than what's there, feel free to cut it and replace the reference. Just make sure you remove the equivalent reference so it doesn't end up making the play twice the length. I'm honestly happy for you to do whatever you need to do so that it applies to your group.

Q: Can we adapt the text to suit the accents in the group?
A: Absolutely. It's meant to be that these students can be anyone and anywhere. References can change. Lines can change. Feel free to do exercises where you put the script down and improvise it in your own words and if the group comes up with lines that are easier for them or work better, feel free to make edits. As a playwright, I've made it fairly general, which is good because it can be taken by people from all sorts of backgrounds. It also means that you can 'specify-it-up' in whatever ways you want or need to.

There are so many versions of the show. We've looked at broad principles throughout the day but I think it's important that we remember what came out from our first instincts. Please push it in whatever direction you want and in whatever direction your young people need.

Q: Do they have to wear uniforms?
A: They can do whatever they want. At these conferences the young people are encouraged to come dressed as adults – dressed in suits. There is so much fun to be had with things perhaps being oversized; maybe one's borrowed their dad's suit. Some people who have tried and some who have not. It could potentially be an expression of how seriously they're taking the exercise. And in that way, it's another opportunity to show the character as well!

My memory of doing it [the MUN] is that it's the first time you're wearing smart clothes and the first time everyone else is wearing smart clothes and you just feel like you're dressing up. They're not necessarily doing things right or properly and they can be making it up as they go along. Have flags drawn onto A4 and stuck on sticks and oversized suits. It should feel chaotic.

Suggested references

Jon suggested the ideal starting point would be to have a look on YouTube for different examples of Model United Nations (MUN). He said:

It's a really good way of seeing the contrast between the makeshift ones in classrooms and the larger events that are full of such pomp and circumstance. There's a lot of fun to be had by going in either direction. So feel free to experiment. But make sure to make it your own.

From a workshop led by Laura Keefe
With notes by Cordelia Stevenson

Old Times

by Molly Taylor

Molly Taylor is a writer and theatre-maker from Liverpool. Recent projects include: *The Key Workers Cycle* for Almeida, *Sinder* for Dundee Rep and *Me for the World* for Young Vic Taking Part. Her plays for young people include: *The Wave* and *Cacophony*, both for the Almeida, *What Was Left* for Southwark Playhouse, and *Earthlings* for The Yard. Her solo shows include: *Extinguished Things* for Edinburgh Fringe/Adelaide Fringe and *Love Letters to the Public Transport System* for National Theatre of Scotland.

Characters

PRESENT DAY
Amma, *eighteen – Surly, sparky. Puts up a front.*
Kobi, *eighteen – Artlessly honest, spiritual. Lives with his nan.*
Belle, *eighteen – Assumes expertise on all things; level-headed.*
Ray, *eighteen – Anxious, hesitant, kind.*
Vee, *seventeen – Independent; some would say 'spoilt', she would say 'resourceful'.*
Stefi, *seventeen – Cheeky, articulate, borders on cocky.*
Zafer, *seventeen – Stefi's younger brother by two minutes and thirty-eight seconds, but about 100 per cent less abrasive. Stoical.*

FLASHBACK
Tom Joy, *thirteen – A polite description would be 'a handful'. Energetic. Mouthy.*
Amma, *thirteen – Obsessed with slime.*
Kobi, *thirteen – Loves an audience.*
Belle, *fourteen – Obedient.*
Ray, *fourteen – Confident (he would say 'invincible').*
Vee, *thirteen – Knows how to work the system; never in trouble.*
Stefi, *thirteen – Natural ringleader.*
Zafer, *thirteen – Diligent and thoughtful.*

PARENTS
During flashback scenes there are a number of interchanges between the younger characters and their parents; these are moments they are recalling. In each case, the present-day 'older' version of that character steps into the parent role, speaking to their younger self.

E.g. if Kobi is recalling a conversation with his nan, he will instantly step into role of Nan and talk directly to young Kobi, before switching back to the present-day scene.

UNSEEN CHARACTERS
There are a small number of 'unseen characters' which are voiced in this play (e.g. Police Officers/Reporters). Whether these voices are embodied by the older 'present' characters or pre-recorded SFX is a directorial decision. These scenes should feel heightened, jarring and slightly unreal.

GENDER
The characters have assigned genders, but directors can alter/interchange genders to reflect their cast.

Setting

The play has two time zones, shifting between the present day and five years ago. We first meet our core characters at the point of an unconventional 'reunion', aged seventeen–eighteen. As they reflect on their experiences as early teenagers, the present-day scenes are punctured, pulling them into the past. We see them as their thirteen-year-old selves, daring and scaring each other, winding each other up, falling out – free. The action continues to jump between these two worlds – as if the past and present are fusing together. But we only ever see Tom Joy as his thirteen-year-old self.

The transitions between past and present are theatrically up for grabs. In terms of 'doubling', directors can feel free to play with how to establish the past and present versions of characters (through movement, costume, blocking, etc.).

Note on the text

A slash (/) in the text denotes a character being interrupted and spoken over.

A dash (–) denotes a character being cut off mid-sentence.

An ellipsis (. . .) indicates they've run out of steam.

The present-day scenes are in standard text, **and the scenes set in the past are in bold.**

Scene One: In the Past

PRESENT DAY – non-identical twins **Stefi** *and* **Zafer**, *somewhere domestic and familiar.* **Stefi** *is tense, wired. If you could zoom in you would see the hair on her arms standing up on end.* **Zafer** *is pale and still. He holds* **Stefi**'s *mobile in his hand.*

Stefi   Well?

Zafer   Why are you showing me this?

Stefi   What do you mean? You okay? Do you think we should . . .

Zafer   Should? I don't / know.

Stefi   I mean.

Zafer   I can't really . . . I can't really deal with this now.

Stefi   Why?

Zafer   Are you suggesting that he . . . that we . . .?

Stefi   No. I don't know, that's what I'm saying. It's just.

Zafer   I just need a second, okay?

Stefi   Oh yeah, yeah, yeah. Sure. Can you get Dad for me?

Zafer   Why?

Stefi   No – don't. Don't.

Zafer   Stef, stop it.

Stefi   Like, there's nothing to worry about. I'll sort it. Whatever it is.

Zafer   Stefi.

Stefi   It's fine, I'll deal with it.

Zafer   Promise me. (*Calling.*) Daaaaaaad!

Stefi   Shuttup! I told you, I don't want to bother him.

Zafer   Promise me you won't do anything.

Stefi   Anything?

Zafer   Until I get back.

Stefi   Where you going?

Zafer   To the hospital.

Stefi   Oh God, / is it Tuesday?

Zafer   It's Tuesday, yeah.

Stefi   God. Sorry. I forgot.

Zafer S'okay.

Stefi Is Dad taking you?

Zafer Yeah.

Stefi You feeling okay about it?

Zafer *shrugs.*

Stefi Okay, well. Don't be late, don't miss it.

Pause.

Go.

Zafer *goes to leave.*

Stefi Have you spoken to any of them recently? Our lot.

Zafer 'Our lot'?

Stefi The Ansten Crew.

Zafer You know I haven't.

Stefi But you've seen them around? I've seen Kobi.

Zafer Where?

Stefi In the Asda. Seen Amma.

Zafer What, on Instagram?

Stefi I know it's been a while but . . .

Zafer Whatever you're thinking . . .

Stefi Don't we think we have a responsibility to them? To look out for them? Old times' sake.

Zafer I think we owe it to them to leave them alone.

Stefi But this isn't just going to go away, Zaf.

Zafer That is exactly what will happen if you let it.

Stefi Sorry. Sorry.

Zafer Please. Stef.

Stefi You shouldn't be thinking about this, you need to focus up. Go on. Go.

Zafer Just, for me – don't. Don't do anything.

Stefi What would I do? I just . . . honestly. Ignore me.

Zafer *goes to leave.*

Stefi   Mate, nothing is more important that you right now, okay? And you getting better, and – I'm sorry – I shouldn't have said anything. Forget it. It's in the past.

She pulls an imaginary zip closed over her mouth.

Zafer   Why don't I believe you?

Scene Two: He's Out

Amma, **Ray** *and* **Kobi**, *sheltering next to the entrance of a kebab shop they knew as kids. It has a sign above: EMRE'S KITCHEN. It is raining.* **Amma** *is possibly a few drinks in. It's stuttering, awkward.*

Amma   Oh my God! Look at you guys!

Ray   Hi, Amma. This is . . .

Amma   I mean – yeah!

Ray   Are we –

Amma   This is wild.

Kobi   It's kind of sad isn't it? I mean it's good to see you but. Sad. That it's taken something like this.

Ray   Yeah.

Amma   Obvs.

Silence.

Ray   Has anyone seen Zafer?

Kobi   No.

Amma   Nope.

Kobi   Just wanted to show up, 'cause Stefi reached out.

Ray   Same.

Amma   Feel for him.

Ray   Yeah.

Silence.

Kobi   Ray, you've lost weight.

Ray   I'm five years older since you last saw me. So by definition, I've put on weight, surely.

Kobi   But comparatively; you versus you, *then*, y'know and *now*. Y'know?

Pause.

Ray   Are we at the right place . . .?

Amma   How do I look then?

Kobi   Exactly the same.

Amma   That's offensive. I've blossomed.

She takes out a cigarette, offers them around. No one accepts.

Amma   You give up?

Kobi   They'll kill you in the end, Amma.

Amma   Worse than that, they'll age me. What can I say? I'm an addict. You have to show addicts compassion, because it's an illness.

Pause.

Are you an addict?

Ray   Don't think so.

Amma   You would know if you were. It's your frontal lobe isn't it. If you've managed to get through the last few years without developing a bad habit, then you'll be okay. Because you're like . . . developed now.

Pause.

Kobi   Are we early?

Amma   No she's late. Did you feel bad when you got the invite? I felt bad.

Kobi   Why?

Amma   Because I heard about Zafer. But I didn't, like, do anything.

Kobi   S'pose it puts things in perspective doesn't it.

Silence.

Just, moving on, and reconnecting.

Ray (*looking up at the restaurant*)   This doesn't look like an event to me.

Kobi   Maybe it's low-key.

Amma   The Emre's don't do low-key.

Recording herself on her mobile, getting in the background, the sign above the door.

Check this out for a mad reunion!

*She makes sure **Kobi** is in shot, he gives a peace sign, she reaches out to **Ray** but he doesn't want to be filmed.*

Amma   Oh come on, it's for my Story, get in here, Ray!

Ray *shaking his head: 'leave me out of it'.*

Amma *to the phone.*

Amma   Some of us all camera shy now!

She poses, stops filming, presses upload. **Stefi** *approaching.*

Kobi   Here she is. Stefanie Emre, what time do you call this?!

Stefi   Hey. I'm so sorry. Y'okay?

She opens up, waves them in – a counter top, fridges, a grill. The menu high up over the counter. In the back chairs stacked on tables, for people to sit in. Somewhere they were once familiar with.

Stefi   How you all doing? Good to see you, Ray.

Ray   Yeah you too.

Stefi   Guess you don't have many excuses to come back.

Amma   God this takes me back.

Kobi   Any chance of getting a chicken shawarma tonight?

Stefi   We're closed for refurb.

Amma   What's gonna soak this up then? (*She brandishes a bottle of vodka.*)

Kobi (*quietly*)   Jesus, Amma.

Vee *and* **Belle** *enter, not quite sure if this is exactly where they are meant to be.*

Belle   Hello, people.

Amma   STOP!

Kobi   Hey!

Stefi   Come in, guys.

Vee   Shit, Ray.

Ray   Hi.

Vee   Is everyone coming?

Amma   Oh my God! This is making me emotional! (*She beckons* **Belle** *over.*)

Belle   Hey, Amma.

They hug hello. **Vee** *seeing the vodka in* **Amma**'s *hand.*

Vee   Good job I didn't bring the car.

Amma   This is mad. Come here! You get new teeth, Vee?!

Vee   No, my braces came off.

Amma   God, they really worked didn't they?

Vee   Getting my nose done next year.

Amma   STOP.

Vee   You look just the same.

Amma   I don't.

Ray (*looking round the place*)   I thought this was a big 'thing' we were invited to.

Stefi   Yeah. No. It's just us.

Belle   In your dad's old café?

Stefi   I can explain.

Belle   Does he have insurance?

Stefi   What?

Belle   Public liability.

Vee   Oh, you're a liability, Belle, relax.

Stefi *starts to put the lights on, pull chairs down.*

Kobi   I heard you were at uni already, Belle. Fast-tracked.

Belle   Yeah.

Kobi   Any good?

Belle   Yeah, well. It's law. So, a lot of work.

Kobi   Congratulations.

Belle   It's not a big thing. What about you? How's your nan doing?

Kobi   Not good. Dementia. She's starting to lose it.

Belle   I'm sorry.

Kobi   Keeps running up massive phone bills, calling premium numbers.

Stefi   Your nan on the sex chat lines again?!

Kobi   What about you, Vee, what's new?

Vee   Jesus, where to start.

Belle   Tell them about your man.

Vee (*peeved*)   What man?

Belle   Vee has got a secret older lover.

Amma   Stop iiiiiiit.

Vee   I'm 'staying at yours' tonight by the way.

Belle   Again?

Vee   And your point is . . .?

Kobi   How old is he?

Belle   Old.

Vee   Age is just a number.

Belle   He thinks she's twenty-three, and that she lives in a house-share with a bunch of flatmates. They have back stories and everything.

Amma   Imaginary friends at your age, babe.

Kobi   Why don't you just move out?

Stefi   I thought you would've had your own private wing in the castle by now, Vee.

Belle   Saving up for her nose job isn't she.

Vee   Why are you being such a cow today?

Belle   I'm not.

Vee   You're jealous.

Amma   Fireworks, I love it.

Belle   I'm not jealous but I'm sick of covering for you! / My mum knows something is off.

Ray (*to* **Stefi**)   Where's Zafer?

Belle (*continuing*)   The other night I had to pretend you were in my room the whole night, and I had to eat two dinners.

Kobi   Two dinners is hard.

Stefi (*to* **Ray**)   Yeah, well, the thing is –

Belle   I don't like lying for you.

Vee   Said the trainee lawyer.

Belle   You need to grow up and start taking responsibility.

Vee   You sound like my dad!

Amma   My dad is grown up and he's constantly lying, so y'know. (*She takes a swig from her vodka.*)

Cheers!

Ray (*to* **Stefi**)   Is Zafer coming?

Stefi   No. No.

Kobi   How is he doing? Is he okay?

Stefi   Yeah. I mean, no, but.

Vee   I saw your dad on the news about it.

Stefi   Oh that yeah.

Amma   For the treatment thing.

Kobi   Oh yeah. Was it to go to the States or something?

Stefi   Yeah.

Vee   Quite a PR push your family managed.

Stefi   Well, I mean, he's ill so.

Vee   No, it's impressive.

Ray   Did he go?

Stefi   Not yet, but it's complicated. Expensive.

Belle   That's why we're here, right? A fundraiser.

Stefi   Yes and no.

Kobi   I prayed for him.

Beat.

Stefi   You prayed?

Kobi   Sometimes it's all we can do.

Belle   That's an interesting interpretation of free will, Kobi.

Amma   Are you in the Jesus camp now, Kobes?

Kobi   I am with God, yeah.

Amma   Whoa. (*Takes a swig of vodka.*)

Kobi   My nan, after everything that happened . . . She took me to church every day. It was either that or moving away. And I didn't wanna leave. (*To* **Ray**.) No offence.

Ray   None taken.

Amma   God I wish I'd left.

Belle   I'm just being devil's advocate here, but she took you to church – forced you – possibly, depending on your take, when you were in a very vulnerable place.

Stefi   Can we just leave that / to one side.

Kobi   Well, that is why she took me.

Belle   But we're so malleable at that age.

Vee   You've never been malleable in your life, Belle.

Stefi   I feel like we're getting off the point here.

Ray   Why did you invite us / here if this isn't a –

Belle   Of all the ways I expected you to go, Kobi . . . . No, I think it's good! I think it's interesting.

Kobi   I'm glad I've exceeded your expectations, Belle.

Amma   Has anyone else got any revelations?

Stefi   Well, actually –

Vee   We should do that game! What was it?! Two truths and a lie!

Amma   Yes!

Ray   Guys.

Belle   The truth is subjective.

Vee   Oh that sounds like a great version, let's play that one.

Stefi   Can you just / listen up.

Kobi   I can never think of a lie though.

Ray   Guys, shut up!

He has finally commanded attention.

Ray   I don't know what we're doing here. You said it was this 'thing' for Zafer, but . . . (*Looking around in dismay.*) Bit triggering for me actually. Seeing you. So. If I don't need to be here . . .

Stefi *takes a breath.*

Stefi   He's out.

Silence.

Tom Joy.

Beat.

Vee   He's . . .

Kobi   But.

Amma   It's too early.

Stefi   I know.

Belle   Hang on.

Amma   Tom Joy has been . . .

Belle   Released?

Stefi   Yeah.

Kobi   When?

Stefi   A week ago.

Kobi   How?

Stefi   Dunno.

Ray   He's . . .

Stefi   It's early. It *is* early.

Vee   Five years?

Belle   Four and a bit. Not that early.

Amma   How many did he –

Belle   Eight, he got eight years.

Ray   So that's –

Vee   Early.

Belle   Not it's not, in fact, he could've been released earlier than this.

Kobi   How d'you know this?

Stefi   My cousin. His mate's brother – he's been inside for a few years for theft or something, and he knows Tom Joy – or he knew of him, and yeah. He said Tom Joy has been released, he's out, and he's coming back.

Beat.

Ray   Here?

Scene Three: Emre's Kitchen

FLASHBACK – Suddenly a thirteen-year-old **Tom Joy** *comes hurtling through the space, like a sling-shot from the past, so very alive in front of their eyes. He's wearing elements of a school uniform mixed with his own clothes, carrying a bag. This is a memory. But they are all transfixed by the image of him being brought so brightly to mind. Their eyes are on the space he occupies. He's yelling.*

Tom Joy   Pah, man, it stinks of onions in here!

One by one, thirteen-year-old versions of **Amma**, **Kobi**, **Belle**, **Vee**, **Zafer** *and* **Ray** *enter the space in school uniform, queueing up for after-school snacks. They are a rabble; they push into one another, talk over one another.*

Each older version clocks their younger self. Recognisable but alien. They are in the past again. Something they thought they had left behind.

Kobi *is yelling instructions to* **Mr Emre**, *who is embodied by* **Stefi** *in this moment.*

Kobi   Can I get a chicken shawarma, Mr Emre?

Amma   I want nuggets, can I get nuggets?

Kobi   Maybe I want nuggets. Do you wanna go halves on nuggets?

Amma   No.

Vee   Do you have gluten-free nuggets?

Tom Joy *jumps onto a table.*

Stefi *as* **Mr Emre***:*

Mr Emre   Hey! Get down from there! NOW!

Zafer   Tom, do as he says.

Ray   We don't have time for food if we wanna get there before dark!

Stefi   Hurry up, Kobi.

Mr Emre (*to* Stefi)   Where you going?

Stefi   Nowhere, Dad.

Mr Emre (*to* Tom Joy)   I said get down!

Tom Joy *jumps down.*

Stefi   Can we just get chips please, Dad, for everyone.

Amma   No vinegar, lots of salt for me.

Kobi   But I want a –

Stefi   We don't have time!

Mr Emre   You're not causing trouble are you?

Stefi   No!

Tom Joy (*to* Zafer)   Can I get a can? Can you get me a can?

Zafer   Get it yourself.

Mr Emre *handing out polystyrene boxes of chips.*

Tom Joy *surreptitiously grabs a can of Coke and shoves it up his sleeve.*

Mr Emre   Hey! I saw that. Give it back.

Tom Joy   What?

Mr Emre   I give you the chips, but you're paying for the drinks.

Tom Joy   I don't even know what you're talking about!

He is scrambling out the door.

Mr Emre   Come back here!

Tom Joy   Last one to the Ansten House smells like Kobi's nan!

They set off.

Scene Four: The Ansten Crew

FLASHBACK – Outside the Ansten House; a disused block of flats that lies unlived in and unloved – left to rot and frayed at the edges. It has a foreboding presence that would appeal to a bunch of kids looking for entertainment/torment in the dead hours after school. Locally, it's the sort of place that divides the legends from the losers – who is brave enough to trespass?

Tom Joy *and* **Amma**, *out of breath having raced each other there.* **Amma** *doubled over.*

Amma   Oh my days.

Tom Joy   You're fast.

Amma   I know. Think I'm gonna be sick.

Tom Joy (*handing over his can*)   Here, here, here.

She drinks.

Tom Joy   Sip it, sip it. You okay?

They can hear everyone approaching.

Tom Joy   Come on, let's hide! Quick.

They crouch. Everyone arrives, flinging bags on the floor, discarding chip packets.

Vee   Are they behind us?

Amma *and* **Tom Joy** *jump out at them, everyone shrieks.*

Kobi   Okay, who's up?

Zafer   Not me.

Tom Joy   Amma is fastest.

Amma   No not me.

Stefi   You go.

Ray   No, you go.

Stefi   I always go first!

Ray   Toss for it.

Stefi   You're a tosser, you toss for it.

Ray   I'm not doing it.

Zafer   Tom'll do it.

Kobi   Yeah you'll do it.

Stefi   Go on, Tom.

Tom Joy (*holding his arms up, almost thrilled at their faith in him*)   **Yeah, yeah, okay, I'll do it.**

They cheer.

Only one brave enough.

Vee   Deranged enough.

Zafer   You're not going to go in-in are you?

Tom Joy   Wait and see.

He creeps up to the main entrance, really over-plays it in a Scooby-Doo *way. Makes them laugh.*

Ray   Go on, Tom!

Stefi   Stop milking it, just do it!

Knocks like thunder on the door and then legs it. They scarper in all directions, like a dandelion in strong wind. Some duck down, take shelter, hide. They wait. Nothing happens. They creep back from their spots.

Vee   Maybe the mad tramp is asleep.

Tom Joy   Maybe he's smoked too much crack and he's just lying there going like this. (*Does an impression.*)

Stefi *pretends to see someone at the window behind* **Tom Joy**.

Stefi   He's there!

They instantly turn around in fear – but there's nothing. **Tom Joy** *swings his bag at* **Stefi** *and hits her.* **Amma** *showing* **Zafer** *what's in her rucksack.*

Zafer   Where'd you get it?

Amma   Stole it from art.

Zafer   Guys, Amma has got a tonne of glue!

Tom Joy   Let me sniff iiiiiiiit?!

He grabs it off her.

Amma   No. It's for slime innit. Tom. Tom!

She wrestles it back off him.

Tom Joy   Are we gonna make slime?

Amma   I am.

Tom Joy   Can I help?

He attempts to grab it back off her.

Amma   Oi. Gettoff it.

Vee   How'd you even make slime?

Amma   I dunno, look it up on your phone, Vee.

Tom Joy   Has your phone got a SIM card?

Vee   Yeah, course! Doesn't yours?

Ray   His is just for games.

Vee   You're such a baby, Tom.

Tom Joy   It does have a SIM card. Anyway. I'm getting *Grand Theft Auto* this week.

Kobi   No you're not.

Tom Joy   I am.

Kobi   It's an eighteen.

Tom Joy   So?

Ray (*gesturing to the Ansten House*)   How much money would you have to be paid to go in the Ansten House?

Kobi   Forty-five thousand.

Ray   Shut up!

Kobi   And sixty-three pence.

Ray   Zafer, how much money –

Zafer   I'm not going in there, Ray.

Stefi   Yeah, the mad tramp will get you.

Zafer   That story is not even true.

Vee   Yeah it is.

Tom Joy   Yeah my mum's seen him and says he reeks and he has a leg that drags so you can hear him coming like this. (*He does an impression.*)

Ray   Int that your mum's boyfriend?

A few sniggers.

Vee   I heard he lived with his mum, but she died and he didn't tell anyone and kept her in the flat, and washed her every day until her skin started rotting away, and the neighbours could smell it and he got kicked out and that's why he's a mad tramp –

Zafer   Shut up!

Ray   Belle, how much would you have to be paid –

Belle   I would need certain assurances. And I would need back-up. And I would need protection.

Tom Joy *jumps in front of her in defence, yelling at the top of his voice.*

Tom Joy   STAND BACK!

Belle   But I can't stand around speculating because I have to go home. S'late.

She exits.

Vee   What theme should I have for my party?

Tom Joy   Errrrrrrrrhm . . . Paedos!

Amma   When is it?

Vee   Three weeks.

Kobi   Go ice skating.

Vee   That's not a theme.

Kobi   But it's a laugh.

Vee   My mum thinks I should do something sophisticated.

Tom Joy   Paedos in suits.

Kobi   Paedos in suits, on ice.

Vee   What about a dinner party?

Zafer   But you have dinner every day.

Vee   No but with outside caterers.

Stefi   My dad can do you kebabs.

Amma   For my thirteenth I had a sleepover.

Vee   But I have them all the time.

Ray   When do boys get to come to sleepovers?

Amma   Literally never.

Tom Joy   Okay, I've actually got an idea.

Vee   No.

Tom Joy   Honest.

Vee   I don't wanna hear it.

Amma   I vote for a sleepover.

Tom Joy   Okay, okay, okay – shut up, listen, why don't you have a party where everyone has to come dressed as the person they would most like to meet?

Ray   Would you come as your dad, Tom?

Everyone cracks up. **Tom Joy** *stares at him, admonished but furious.*

Ray   Why don't we have a sleepover in there for your thirteenth?

Stefi   Zaf, when we're thirteen, can I just have one day to myself and then we do yours?

Zafer   No.

Kobi   Who is the oldest?

Stefi   Me.

Kobi   By how much?

Zafer & Stefi   Two minutes and thirty-eight seconds.

Kobi   Everyone is thirteen apart from you three.

Vee   Maybe a murder mystery or something.

Amma   Cool! Who's gonna die?

Suddenly a smash; **Tom Joy** *has grabbed a brick off the floor, and has unleashed it at a window in the Ansten House. Everyone jumps, startled, screams or ducks – instant hysteria. A wild exodus – they scatter.*

Scene Five: He Could Be Out There

PRESENT DAY – The past has dissolved; we are back at Emre's Kitchen, heart rates still high.

Belle   He won't come back here.

Amma   He can't.

Vee   It's not like his mum is here. Is she?

Amma   She left after the court case.

Kobi   Maybe he wants to start again.

Belle   He's *never* gonna be able to do that. Is he? Here.

Ray   Small town like this, everyone knows who he is.

Vee   He probably wouldn't last the night.

Amma   He gets out, great, he gets out, he moves on. End of.

She takes a swig of vodka, passes it to **Ray***, who is about to pass it on but thinks better of that and necks a bit, then passes it to* **Belle***.*

Stefi   Yeah but . . .

Kobi   What?

Stefi   I've been getting calls from an unknown number.

Amma   And . . .?

Ray   They say anything?

Stefi   No, but. Happens most days.

Belle   Are you worried?

Stefi   Well.

Belle   Have you told anyone?

Stefi   No, it's not threatening it's just nothing, but I just wondered if you guys had had any . . .?

They shake their heads.

Stefi   Or anything.

Kobi   I thought *you* getting in touch was out the blue.

Stefi*'s phone aggressively jangles into life, makes them jump. Frozen for a moment.* **Stefi** *approaches her phone as if it could bite her.*

Stefi (*visible relief*)   S'fine. It's only Zafer.

She cancels the call.

FLASHBACK – Young **Zafer** *appears, tugs at* **Stefi's** *clothing to get her attention.* **Stefi** *immediately in the role of* **Dad**. *Young* **Stefi** *loiters behind.*

Zafer   Dad. Do me and Stef have to have the same party?

Dad   Of course you do. I'm not throwing two bloody parties!

Stefi   Told you.

Zafer   Can I choose who to invite though?

Dad   You'll both choose. But I'm not having the whole class like last time.

Zafer   Okay just Ray –

Stefi   And Belle and Amma –

Zafer   And Kobi

Stefi   And Vee

Zafer   And Tom.

Dad   No. Not Tom.

Zafer   But.

Dad   He's a little shit.

Stefi *giggles.*

Dad (*to* Stefi)   Don't repeat that. I don't want him on the premises.

Zafer   But if I don't invite him / I'll feel, he'll feel

Dad   When you get to my age you see troublemakers a mile off.

Zafer   But he's my friend.

Dad   You just *think* he's your friend – but the sooner you ditch him, the better off you'll be.

Zafer   But –

Dad   I'm sorry, son. He's not invited. Do you want a party or not?

PRESENT DAY – Emre's Kitchen.

Amma   Someone I don't know started following me. A couple of days ago.

Kobi   What did he look like?

Amma   On Insta, you idiot.

Ray   What's his name?

Amma   Can't remember. (*Looking at her phone.*) 2MROW.master.

Stefi   Let me see?

Amma   You can't tell anything from the profile picture. He hasn't posted anything.

Stefi   He's not following many people.

Kobi   Could be anyone.

Stefi   Bit of a coincidence though.

Amma   Do you think I should / block him?

Stefi   I have to say, Amma, some of that poetry stuff you post . . .

Amma   What?

Stefi (*quoting*)   'Do I betray you when I turn away, do you hate me because I cannot say? I don't know what to feel every day.' I mean –

Amma   That's not got nothing to do with anything.

Stefi   Apart from the fact it's really bad poetry, do you think you should be putting stuff like that online?

Kobi   Don't be a dick, Stefi.

Stefi   Okay, whatever, I'm just saying –

Amma   That's stuff is personal! That's got / nothing to do with anything.

Stefi   So personal you put it on social.

Amma   Nothing to do with *us*.

Stefi   I'm just saying we need to be careful. Especially now.

Belle   You don't seriously think Tom would try and get in touch with us?

Stefi   You explain the phone calls then. (*Gesturing to* **Amma**'s *phone*.) And this.

Ray (*to* **Amma**)   What did you do with that film you took? Of us outside?

Amma   What?

Ray   Did you post it?

Amma   Well, yeah.

Ray (*under his breath*)   Oh God.

Vee   What?

Ray   Pissing about, filming outside the front door, talking about a reunion.

Vee   You're kidding.

Amma   What, I didn't think! I thought –

Kobi   So anyone who follows you knows exactly where we are right now.

Amma   I didn't think. I didn't know.

Beat

Stefi   So he could be out there right now for all we know.

Scene Six: Not Even Real

FLASHBACK – Inside the Ansten House. Dimly lit, broken bits of furniture. A dilapidated and unloved space. The blue light of a phone screen seen behind a window. A ghostly face peering in. **Tom Joy** *scanning the room.*

Tom Joy   I'm gonna do it. Ready?

He opens the window.

Tom Joy (*to* **Vee** *who is holding the phone*)   **Hold that up so I can see.**

Tom Joy *climbs through the open window, like an expert spy.*

Vee   What can you see?

Tom Joy   Ssh! (*He shouts out so it echoes.*) **HELLOOOOOOO?**

Supressed giggling from outside.

Tom Joy   Anyone there?

We see **Vee**, **Ray** *and* **Stefi** *peer in through the open window.*

Ray   Well?

Tom Joy   Nothing. No one.

One by one they enter. **Zafer**, **Kobi**, **Amma** *and* **Belle** *hang back outside the window.*

Zafer   Told you. It's all a lie.

An air of deflation.

Tom Joy   *(with more force)* **HELLO?!**

Kobi   Ssssh!

Zafer   He's not even real.

Amma   Still spooky though.

Tom Joy   We should make him real. Make a film. About the mad tramp who lives in the basement. Bring him to life.

Scene Seven: A Plan

PRESENT DAY – Emre's Kitchen. A growing tension. **Vee** *peering out of a window to the street beyond. It's still lashing down.* **Amma** *continues to neck the vodka.*

Vee   Maybe we need to speak to the police, say we're concerned.

Belle   With evidence of what exactly? Look, he's probably tagged. Probably got a curfew. The chances of him turning up here are so slim.

Stefi   They get those tags off all the time.

Belle   No they don't.

Stefi   They can just slip them off. Bit of Vaseline.

Belle   Always the drama, Stefi.

Stefi   I know people who've done it!

Ray   Why did you bring us here? You trying to scare us?

Stefi   Course not.

Ray   You could've just sent us a message.

Stefi   'Oh hey, long time no see, by the way Tom Joy is out, watch your back . . .?' I'm looking out for you, obvs.

Ray   You suddenly feel a moral duty to us after years of no contact?

Stefi   Why the attitude?

Ray   Dragging all this up again! I can't.

Stefi   You don't think I'd rather be at home now, looking after my brother? Like I don't have enough going on?!

Beat.

I brought you here because we need to come up with a plan. I don't trust Tom Joy for a second and nor should you. But together we can protect each other, protect Zafer, okay? Because this is literally the last thing he needs right now, he has to focus on getting well, and the stress of this is going to make everything impossible. More impossible.

Belle   What sort of plan?

Stefi   There's a lot of interest in Tom because it was a big thing here, everyone remembers it. I think there's a way we can stay one step ahead; tell our story. Our side of the story.

FLASHBACK – suddenly young **Ray** *is in the space, lit as if in a cold, clinical police interview room. Older* **Ray** *is in the role of* **Officer***, questioning him. Like a warped memory has punctured the reflection.*

Officer   Ray, remember what we said. This is a very serious incident. You need to tell us everything that happened. You need to tell us the truth. You won't get anyone in trouble.

Ray   I don't know anything.

Officer   I think you do.

Ray   Dad, can you tell them?

Officer   Ray, look at me.

Ray   Stop hassling me!

Officer   Where were you on 24 October between the hours of 4.30 and 6 p.m.?

PRESENT DAY –

Amma   We did that already.

Stefi   Yeah but I mean, publicly. There's a podcast, a true crime podcast, and I spoke to the producer, and they're interested.

Belle   What?

Stefi   They want to talk to us, they want to do an episode. On us. And that time. In the town. And what happened.

Beat

Amma   Oh my God. We are gonna be famous.

Kobi (*taking the vodka from* **Amma**)   Let's slow down.

Stefi   Just think about it. All we need to do is stick to what we said, the truth, and we put a message out there – to Tom – and we say, we've still got each other's backs, and we won't be messed with.

Belle   There's already been so much in the press, Stef, I mean, it's not really in the public interest is it?

Stefi   No it's in *our* interest. And the way they pitched it / is that –

Ray   Wow.

Stefi   We were a group of friends, young, innocent, and something tragic happened, and it splintered our friendships – and you moved away, Ray, you were taken out of school, Vee, and everything . . . *changed.* And we, we were so *young*, and it's about us and how we've *survived.* And you, Kobes, with the religious thing, y'know – that is a really powerful story, that is really inspiring, how you've made the best out of an awful situation. And Belle being a child genius, and training to be a lawyer . . . How we are all doing really well now in spite of everything.

Ray   Doing so well. Having nightmares, flashbacks. Moving to a town where everyone knew who I was. Never settling in. Never making friends.

Vee   What else do you suggest, Ray? That we just wait to see what he's got in store for us?

Kobi   What if it just antagonises him? He'll know it's us.

Vee   Good, he should know.

Kobi   Don't you think we've done enough to him?

Vee   We didn't *do* anything to him, Kobi.

FLASHBACK –

Stefi, **Kobi**, **Zafer**, *hanging out after school.* **Tom Joy** *bouncing a ball too hard.*

Tom Joy   Are you going?

Kobi   Course. Aren't you?

Tom Joy *shakes his head.* **Kobi** *delights in this.*

Kobi   Oohhhhh burn!

Tom Joy   Fuck off.

Zafer   Dad says I can only invite five.

Tom Joy   Why not me?

Zafer   No, just because, because of five, and because I've . . . already been invited to their parties, so I have to invite them to mine. So it's just five people.

Tom Joy   But the café's massive.

Zafer   Yeah but it's a rule. Sorry.

Tom Joy   Maybe one of the others won't come.

Pause.

If one of them can't come, can I come?

Zafer *shakes his head. Awkward silence.*

Tom Joy   It is 'cause I've never had a party?

PRESENT DAY – Emre's Kitchen.

Belle   I don't think it's wise, bringing attention to it.

Vee   Fine, then don't *you* do it.

Stefi   They want all of us. For the content. Multi-voiced narratives, or something.

Belle   Even Zafer?

Stefi   No, obviously, but. I'll speak for him.

Belle   I don't think my mum would even let me.

Vee   You're eighteen, Belle, she can't stop you.

Belle   Our parents have already been through so much with us.

Kobi   She's right.

Belle   It's not fair on them.

Amma   Screw our parents.

Belle   Can't we just let it lie?

Stefi   You're not the one getting threatening phone calls.

Amma   I'm in.

Stefi   Thanks, Amma.

Vee   Personally, I don't think they should have *ever* let him out. So maybe it's our duty, our responsibility to remind people about what he was like, about the kind of kid he was.

FLASHBACK – Outside the Ansten House, way before the incident. A wild energy being plumbed into a game: British Bulldog.

Stefi   **You're never gonna get past me.**

Amma   **Watch me.**

She gets tagged.

Stefi   **Got you, got you!**

Ray *makes a run for it, gets to the other side.*

Ray   **Yaaaaaaaas.**

Zafer *uses the diversion to race past.*

Stefi   **Amma – concentrate!**

Amma   **That wasn't me!**

Tom Joy *begins his race: instead of trying to avoid them, he simply runs straight at* **Amma**, *roaring as he does – sheer intimidation tactics, so that in the end it is* **Amma** *who is screaming and running away from him.*

Stefi   Oh no you don't!

She tags **Tom**. *Now it's the three of them against* **Belle**, **Kobi** *and* **Vee**.

Vee   Go on, Belle!

Belle *takes a run; as she does* **Vee** *is chased by* **Amma**. **Tom** *and* **Stefi** *create a pincer-like movement to cut* **Belle**'s *run off.*

Stefi   Get her, get her, get her!

They clumsily crash into her.

Belle   Owwwwwww!

Stefi   Tom! What you doing?

Tom Joy *clumsily trying to get her up to her feet, but she's crying.*

Stefi (*to* **Tom Joy**)   Apologise then.

Tom Joy   Sorry, but –

Vee   You okay, Belle?

Belle *cradling her hand, whimpering.*

Stefi   Why you gotta be so rough?

Tom Joy   I didn't do nothin'.

Kobi   Is it broken?

Amma   Let's call an ambulance.

Stefi   No.

Amma   I want to call an ambulance.

Tom Joy *reaching out to* **Belle**.

Stefi   Just leave her alone.

Vee   You're such a crank, Tom.

Tom Joy   You are.

Zafer   It was an accident.

Kobi   If it is broke you'll have a wicked cast.

Tom Joy   Want me to carry you?

Stefi   Just give her some space.

Tom Joy   You give her space!

He pushes **Stefi** *in frustration.* **Stefi** *reacts with theatrics.*

Stefi (*under her breath*)   Little shit.

LEAP TO –

Older **Belle** *in the role of her* **Mum***; she questions her younger self.*

Mum   How did this happen, Belle?

Belle   It was a game.

Mum   Was someone playing dangerously?

Belle *shrugs.*

Mum   Look, you're not being disloyal or grassing or anything like that. Was it Tom?

Silence.

Mum   Tom Joy? I knew it. I'm going to have to have a word with his mum. Not that that will make an ounce of difference, but. You need to pick your friends more wisely, Belle. I see a lot of young boys like Tom in my job and he's got to learn he's responsible for his actions. And if he hurts you, even if it's an accident, then you shouldn't protect him, okay?

Beat.

Tom Joy   Just playing.

FLASHBACK – Older **Vee** *in role as* **Officer***.*

Vee   He's crazy, and he's always doing crazy things.

Officer   What sort of things?

Vee   He breaks things, he breaks people, he's always going mad. He broke someone's hand.

Officer   Whose hand?

Vee   Ages ago. Ask him.

Officer   I'm asking you.

JUMP TO – Older **Ray** *in role as* **Officer***.*

Ray   I can't remember.

Officer   How did he break someone's hand?

Ray   It was a game. I don't know. Ask him!

Officer   Ray, calm down.

Ray   He's always fighting everyone!

Officer   Okay, take a breath.

Ray   He'll kill me if I tell you.

Officer   He can't hurt you now.

FLASHBACK – School. **Belle**, *with her left hand in a cast.*

Tom *with his left hand in a homemade bandage – cobbled together from whatever he could find – his sports kits, some foil, some bubble wrap. It is almost comedic.*

Tom Joy   So you don't feel left out.

Pause.

I made it.

Belle   I can see that.

Tom Joy   I'm going to keep it on. 'Til yours comes off.

Belle   That's weeks away.

Tom Joy   Doesn't matter. Does it still hurt?

Belle   Only when I bang it.

Tom Joy   Hard to get dressed innit?

Belle   You don't have to do that, Tom. Your skin will go all pale and manky and it won't be nice.

Tom Joy   Mine gets hot, does yours get hot?

She nods.

Tom Joy   Just didn't want you to feel alone.

Belle   I don't feel alone.

Tom Joy   Don't you?

Pause.

Also good for punching things with *(he demonstrates by punching the wall).* **And I can give someone the finger without them knowing.**

Belle   Are you giving me the finger right now?

Tom Joy   Yep.

Pause.

Are we friends, Belle? Again?

She shrugs.

Tom Joy   Why don't people like me?

PRESENT DAY – Emre's Kitchen.

Stefi   If we are gonna do this we need to make sure we're on the same page. It was a long time ago and it's easy to get muddled.

Amma   Trauma affects your memory doesn't it.

Stefi   And Tom did a lot of stuff that they'll want to know about; he was violent, he was always stealing stuff.

Amma   He stole cigarettes for me.

Belle   His mum sent him out to steal though, she taught him, but obviously no one ever mentioned that.

Vee   It's not really the point.

Belle   Isn't it?

Vee   It's not like him stealing was an isolated incident.

Stefi   Everyone steals stuff. You can't blame his mum.

Belle   She sent him out to steal because she relied on it.

Stefi   Well, I was never 'taught' to steal, and I did it.

Belle   Well if everyone steals stuff, even 'good' kids like you, Stef, then how is that relevant?

Stefi   Can you stop being a lawyer for one minute please.

Kobi   Hang on, hang on. Maybe Tom is trying to reach out to us, and we should be open to that, and extend the hand of friendship instead of . . . *this*.

Amma   That is very Jesus of you.

Kobi   Has anyone ever been in touch with him?

Amma   As if.

Kobi   I have. I wrote to him.

Amma   When?

Kobi   A couple of years ago. It felt like the right thing to do. I wanted him to know that I'd forgiven him.

Ray   That you forgave *him*?

Kobi   'Do not judge, and you will not be judged. Do not condemn and you will not be condemned. Forgive, and you will be forgiven.'

Vee   Some things are unforgivable, Kobi.

Kobi   Look, there's every chance my life could've turned out differently, I'm not saying I was a bad kid, but yeah, I stole things. I could have got myself into trouble. We don't know what path has been laid out for us, do we? But I feel like I was saved because of the lessons I was able to learn. It was horrible but . . . It changed my life. And maybe Tom is the same, maybe he is on a different path now. Maybe he's *new*.

Belle   Of course he will have changed, he'll have been given a new identity for starters. But he hasn't been going to Sunday School these last five years, Kobes, he's been in *prison*.

Amma   Is it fair that he's got a new identity and we haven't? He can find us, and we can't find him.

Kobi   You're asking me to condemn him again, and I don't think I can do that.

Beat.

Stefi   I respect that, Kobi. I must say, I thought your loyalty to us would win out over Tom. And I thought the money would have come in handy but . . .

Kobi   What money?

Stefi   Oh the producer said they'll pay. We'll each get a fee. For contributing.

Amma   So you're saying . . .

Kobi   We profit from this?

Stefi   I'm saying we look after ourselves, Kobi. A bit of extra cash to help your nan. Take some pressure off. Vee, you could afford to move out, make the 'flatshare' a reality. God knows my family need the money. We'll never be able to undo what happened five years ago. But that's no reason to suffer more than we already have.

Scene Eight: You Need to See This

FLASHBACK – everyone bar **Tom Joy** *and* **Kobi** *inside the Ansten House. A shadowy den. A perfect set for a horror movie.*

Amma *carrying a jar of homemade slime.* **Belle** *with a notebook.* **Stefi** *carrying a rucksack.* **Vee** *holding her mobile in her hand.*

Zafer   I think we should go. What if someone saw us come in?

Ray   We barricaded the door.

Stefi   No one is gonna find us here.

Amma   Apart from the mad tramp.

Ray   Look, it's just one scene and then we'll go.

Stefi *grabbing torches out of her rucksack. They hear a noise coming from outside. They freeze. She shines a torch into the far corner – nothing there. Palpable relief.*

Belle   Who's gonna shoot it?

Ray *and* **Vee** *in unison.*

Ray & Vee   I am.

Vee   My phone is better.

Ray   Really? You've never mentioned that.

Vee   Is.

Ray   But it's my idea.

Vee   No it's not.

Ray   It's my words.

Vee   Only the first bit.

Belle (*holding up the notebook*)   'Scene one' – you wrote that bit.

Zafer   Stop arguing and just do it.

Belle *has picked up* **Amma**'*s jar of slime; when she tilts it, it stays put.*

Belle   Amma – it's solid. Did you put enough glue in it? Looks nothing like brains.

Amma   Just shake it.

Belle   You can't even get it out the jar.

Kobi   Just smash the jar.

Vee   Gonna have to re-write the whole scene now, Amma!

Zafer   Let's leave it.

Ray   We're not leaving it!

Stefi   She's right, we need to get this scene done and get out.

Kobi   Okay, okay, okay, listen up, right. Scene one – take one. We see the mad tramp is in his basement, hunched over a table.

Vee   Who said 'he'?

Kobi   Oh come on. He's a he.

Ray   I told Tom he could do it.

Kobi   Why?

Ray   He'll make it real.

Vee   I could be a mad tramp.

Kobi   You're directing.

Ray   No, I'm directing.

Vee   IT'S MY PHONE.

Ray   I don't care it's my idea!

Kobi   And he, she, whatever, is sharpening up his knife.

Vee   Do a nice close-up of the knife glinting.

Amma   We don't even have a knife.

A door slams.

Belle   Thought you said it was barricaded?

Ray   It was.

Tom Joy *enters carrying a plastic bag.*

Tom Joy   Wait 'til you see this, this is next level!

He opens up the plastic bag. Everyone bar **Zafer** *gathers around to peer in. Everyone recoils/explodes. Delight versus disgust. Responses tumble on top of each other.*

Ray   Oh my God!

Amma   What is it?

Tom Joy   It's intestines.

Ray   WHAT.

Kobi   That is sick!

Tom Joy   For the scene.

Belle   Where did you get it?!

Tom Joy   From the butcher's.

Vee   This is insane. You are insane!

Belle   Where on earth do you come up with these ideas?!

Tom Joy   And a heart.

Another explosion of awe and disgust. Their faces a series of mini-bombs going off: is this the best thing to ever happen or the worst thing?! Freaking out. **Zafer** *frozen.*

Tom Joy   I'm gonna make it so good!

Stefi   Zafer! You need to come and see this.

Zafer   I don't want to.

Scene Nine: Stick Together

PRESENT DAY – Emre's Kitchen.

Stefi   The podcast producer seemed like really, like, they're not going to do a sensationalised version, they're going to be sensitive. And if it's too traumatic to talk about certain parts, then you can just say that – that's why we all need to do it together, to help each other out, to share the responsibility.

Ray   It'll make everything worse.

Stefi   How could it be worse?

Ray   Because one day – maybe – we'll have kids of our own. We'll have to teach them about right and wrong. And somewhere online there'll be a podcast *episode* about the worst thing that ever . . . It'll exist forever. A document of it. . .? I don't want any kid of mine to ever know.

Vee   If I have children, I'm gonna use it as an e*xample* to them. I'm going to teach my kids resilience, Ray.

Ray   Do you remember the police interviews, Vee?

She shrugs.

Because I do. I can remember the room and the tape recorder, and the way they looked at us. And the feeling it was never going to end. So don't talk to me about resilience.

Kobi   Can't remember any of their faces, but I do remember his voice. The main guy.

Amma   My dad having a go at him. So embarrassed that he was standing up and shouting at them. I just wanted to die.

Ray   I don't remember being scared of much at that age. But when we were hauled in for questioning, they didn't know a thing, everyone looked at us like we were the experts. And we were *thirteen*. For the first time in my life, I was meant to know more than the adults. And that was terrifying.

Vee*'s phone rings*.

Vee (*answering*)   Hi, Dad . . . Whoa. Calm down. What are you on about? I can't 'bring the car back' because I don't have the car. Yeah, I know you need it, that's why I didn't take it?! Have you had a stroke or something, it's in the driveway . . . What? Are you for real? (*Speaking to everyone*.) My car's gone!

Kobi   What?

Vee (*to phone*)   It was there when I left. Yes! Dad! (*To everyone*.) It's gone. It's been – (*to phone*) – no. (*To everyone*.) It's been stolen!

Beat.

Kobi   Call the police.

Vee (*to phone*)   No, I'm with friends. Have you called the police?

Stefi   No don't.

Vee (*to phone*)   No, don't call the police. (*To* **Stefi**.) Why? (*To phone*.) What?

Amma   Do you think he's taken it?

Vee   Shit. (*To phone*.) Sorry, yeah. No. Erm. LR08 OZP. Yeah, Dad. I'm positive!

Kobi   Definitely call the police.

Vee (*to phone*)   Definitely call the police though. I don't know?! Half six. . .? It was definitely there!

Ray   How would he know her address?

Belle   She never moved.

Amma   He's got the car, he's got her car! Tom Joy is joy-riding!

Vee (*to phone*)   Dad! I don't need a bloody lecture right now. Just call the police! Or I'll do it! I'll call the police.

Stefi   No, let him do it.

Vee (*to phone*)   No, you do it. Call me when you . . . Yes!

Belle   That car cost her eight grand.

Kobi   How can she afford an eight grand car?

Belle   Well, when your mum runs the council . . .

Vee (*to phone, exasperated*)   Dad . . . Yeah I'm leaving soon . . . Okay! (*She hangs up.*)

Silence.

Vee   He's targeting me! Right?

Belle   He'd break his parole.

Vee   Well, you explain why my car is no longer in the sodding drive then, days after he's released?!

Kobi   Anyone could've taken it.

Vee   Oh really?! He knows where I live, he knows where we all live!

Stefi   Seeking retribution. This is exactly what I'm talking about. Y'see?

Amma   What if this is just the start?

Vee   My car is literally my only source of freedom!

Amma   He's probably on his way here right now.

Stefi   This is why we need to stick together.

Ray   No.

Vee   I need to leave.

Stefi   I wouldn't.

Vee   What, are we gonna just stay here forever?

A loud bang at the door.

FLASHBACK – **Tom Joy***, in the dark, holding a torch. Wildness creeping in.*

Tom Joy   **It's a place where only bad things happen. And he lives there. And he's weird and evil and he stinks like death and he's sets traps for you. And if he catches you he cuts you up. He'll tear up your skin. He'll pull out your organs, all of your insides. And he'll eat you. Every bit of you that ever lived.**

Beat.

Zafer   Why you always got to take it so far, Tom?

Tom Joy   Because I want to make it good.

Scene Ten: What We Did

PRESENT DAY – Emre's Kitchen. Another loud bang on the door that makes the space vibrate. All eyes on the entrance.

Vee   Does anyone else know we're here?

Stefi *shakes her head. Bang again.* **Stefi** *moves toward the door tentatively.*

Ray   Leave it.

Vee   Turn the lights off.

Bang.

Stefi (*calling*)   Hello . . .?

Bang.

Stefi *reaches out to open the door.*

Amma   Don't.

Grips the handle, opens a crack. **Zafer** *pushes the door open further, thrusts himself through the doorway, soaking wet, agitated. A palpable sigh of relief.*

Zafer   What you playing at?!

Stefi   What are you playing at? You terrified us!

Zafer   You wouldn't answer your phone!

Stefi   Okay, chill.

Zafer   You leave me standing out there like a –

Stefi   How'd you even know we were here?

Zafer   Dad knows the keys have gone!

Stefi   Shit.

Zafer   He's livid. I was trying to call you!

Kobi   Sorry, Zafer. We thought . . . You okay?

Belle   You're soaked. Do you want my coat?

Zafer   I'm fine.

Beat.

They look at **Zafer** *with something like concern, pity, fear.*

Belle   It's been a while.

Zafer   Yep.

Ray   You want to sit down?

Zafer   No.

Kobi   You look well.

Zafer   I don't. But thanks . . .

Amma   Can I give you a hug?

She is maudlin drunk. She clings on to **Zafer**.

Ray   I'm really sorry about your –

Zafer   Yeah I know you're sorry, and everyone is sorry, but there is no reason to be sorry so you don't need to apologise. You don't need to do that face.

Belle   How is it all . . . going?

Zafer *shrugs.*

Kobi   Your sis said about your treatment – going to America or something? That'd be cool. If it wasn't so. Bad.

Zafer   That's nothing to do with me.

Amma   What d'you mean?

Zafer   My parents make all the decisions.

Kobi   Why?

Zafer   Because I'm still a child.

Kobi   So . . .

Zafer   I'm not. It's not. My dad has, like, this has taken over his life. All this random treatment stuff. Making a huge public thing about it. And that is so not me.

Amma   You wanna get better though.

Zafer   I just want to be able to make my own decisions. About *my* treatment. But when it comes to my own body, and *my* health and *my* blood, I'm not in charge. So I'm just waiting. Until I'm old enough.

Ray   And then what will you do?

Beat.

Amma   But at least your dad is . . . looking after you. Mine. He just lies. Has affairs. Gets me to lie for him. Buys me vodka. I just hold it all in. Hold it hold it hold it. God it's so good to see you guys. I've missed you guys! This is like old times isn't it? I mean. It's not, but. It was easier then wasn't it. It was easier and then it was awful.

She touches **Zafer**'s *face tenderly.*

Amma   I've never been so glad to see someone in my life. We thought you were Tom.

Zafer   What?

Amma   He knows we're here. He's coming.

FLASHBACK – **Amma** *instantly in role as her* **Mum**, *grilling her younger self.*

Mum   How on earth did he get her phone?

Amma   He stole it!

Mum   When?

Amma   When we were playing. He took it, ask anyone, ask Vee.

Mum   Amma, you know this is incredibly serious, don't you?

Amma   Don't shout at me!

Mum   I'm not shouting!

JUMP TO – Older **Vee** *in the role as her* **Mum**.

Vee   He was pissed off about not / being in the film –

Mum   Watch your language.

Vee   And then he started kicking off and everything so I left –

Mum   You left.

Vee   To go and tell an adult.

Mum   Okay.

Vee   Or, like, get someone. So I came home. And that was the last I saw of him.

Mum   Were you on your own?

Vee   No, I was with Amma the whole time, she never left my side. Ask her.

Mum   Victoria, you know that Tom is in a lot of trouble don't you? And because he is an acquaintance of yours, and because of the law, if you had any involvement, or you could've stopped it , well – you could be in just as much trouble as Tom. It's very serious.

Vee   Honestly.

Mum   Okay. You just have to tell the truth to the police, just tell them what you told me, okay? And I'll make sure you don't get into trouble.

Vee   Okay.

FLASHBACK –

Amma   Yes, I was with her the whole time!

Mum   At Victoria's.

Amma   Yes!

Mum   So you left the Ansten House together.

Amma   Yes! I just said that!

Mum   Look – this is nothing compared to what the police are going to ask.

PRESENT DAY – Emre's Kitchen.

Amma   He's following me.

Vee   He's stolen my car. Seriously.

Belle   Speculation.

Vee (*mocking her*)   Speculation, your honour!

Zafer   But he's –

Amma   He wants revenge. But we've got a plan.

Zafer   You're paranoid.

Amma   We are deadly serious.

It feels like there's not enough air in the room for **Zafer**.

Vee   Maybe we should get out of here. Go to mine. My mum. She can help.

Stefi   No, we're not getting our parents / involved.

Amma   Like, go to a safe house.

Kobi   Y'okay Zafer?

Zafer *shakes his head.*

Vee   Look, my mum is going to know because of the car –

Stefi   No! I'm across this, alright? (*To* **Kobi**.) Just give him some space.

Zafer   Can't.

Kobi   What?

Zafer   Can't breathe.

Kobi   Okay, okay. Take a deep breath in.

Ray   You should phone your dad.

Stefi   Stay out of it, Ray.

Ray   He's not well!

Kobi   Anyone got any water?

Amma *passes him the vodka.*

Stefi   Don't crowd him!

Zafer   Can't do it.

Kobi   Slow breaths, mate.

Amma   We'll protect you, Zafer.

Stefi   You all panicking is making it worse. Leave him alone.

Ray   Look at me, Zafer. Look at me.

He breathes with **Zafer***, slowly in and out.*

Ray   That's it. It's okay.

Stefi   I told you, I'm going to sort it. But you shouldn't be here. You should be at home.

Kobi   That's it. Nice and calm.

Zafer   I can't do this.

Kobi   What do you mean?

Zafer   All of this. I have treatment. And I feel rotten inside. Don't even know if it's the drugs anymore. Nights I can't sleep. Thinking about everything. Maybe I deserve to be sick. Or maybe it made me ill. Maybe this is punishment.

Belle   You can't think like that.

Zafer   I said he was a monster.

Belle   No you didn't. They did.

Ray   We all did.

Belle   We were kids.

FLASHBACK – **Zafer** *being interviewed by an unseen Police Officer, with his* **Dad** *in attendance – embodied by older* **Zafer***.*

Officer   Go on, Zafer.

Dad   Tell them what you told me.

Officer   Tom is a good friend of yours, isn't he?

Dad   He's never been to our house or anything. He isn't a close friend is he, Zafer?

Officer   Let Zafer answer the question please.

Dad   Sorry.

Zafer   Not a good friend. But I know him from school.

Officer   But you were with him at the Ansten House that day.

Zafer   He just turned up. We were making a film.

Officer   Did he know you were making a film?

Zafer   Yeah. We were trying to do it. And he was getting angry. Because he wanted to do it.

Dad   Tell her what you told me. Go on.

PRESENT DAY – Emre's Kitchen.

Belle   Look, I'm really sorry that you are ill, it must be really scary, and I'm sorry we've not been here for you properly, and maybe you have a right to be angry with us. (*Looking to the group.*) But we are going to help aren't we? With your treatment or whatever you decide to do. (*To the others.*) This is the best thing we can do with the fee isn't it? We donate it to Zaf, for his medical bills or . . . (*To* **Zafer**.) I don't know – maybe you want to go on a blow-out holiday?! But we use the money to do some good.

Zafer   What money?

Stefi   I think we should stop talking about his treatment, it's private.

Vee   We could all do with that money, Belle.

Belle   Yeah we can all spend it on something totally self-serving, or we can do *this*.

Zafer   What money?!

Belle   From the podcast.

Stefi   I told you – I am managing this / so he doesn't need to worry.

Amma   We are going to go on the record, Zafer.

Stefi   Can't you see he's already in a state?

Ray   We are going to re-live the whole thing on a true crime podcast for the sheer entertainment of it all.

Amma   We do the podcast, and we leave it there forever.

Belle   And we give you the fee.

Zafer   What podcast? Why would / we do that? That's insane.

Ray   You didn't know?

Stefi (*to* **Zafer**)   You don't need to be involved in this, you need to go home. I'll talk to you later.

Zafer   When did you come up with this? / Why didn't you –

Stefi   Do as you're told, Zafer. Listen to me / you will thank me for this. Okay?

Zafer   Were you going to tell me? No, I'm not going home. You're – what has gotten into you?

Stefi   I will explain everything, but now / I need you to just

Zafer   No. No.

Stefi   Back off!

Zafer   Stop telling me what to do!

Stefi (*snaps*)   Well, stop behaving like a child!

Zafer   I'm going to the police.

Beat

That's what I came here to say. It ends here. Right now. I'm going to tell them what we did.

Scene Eleven: Too Late

FLASHBACK – their younger selves flood the space; we are back to that day at the Ansten House, they are shooting their horror scene with a clumsy urgency. A camera phone propped up somewhere, a bunch of torches suspended from points, a makeshift 'set', but despite their efforts there is zero order to proceedings. No one is focused and tempers are beginning to fray.

Ray (*looking through the camera*)   Hold, hold, hold! No, I can't see you there.

Kobi   Someone saw us come in y'know.

Amma   We need to hurry up.

Kobi   From over the road.

Stefi   Well, it's not illegal to be here is it?

Kobi   Isn't it?

Stefi   I dunno.

Ray   She probably thinks you're the mad tramp.

Tom Joy   But I'm the mad tramp!

Ray   Yeah you are in the film but – forget it.

Vee   We need to start now.

*She is going through a bag of costumes that **Zafer** has brought with him.*

Vee   Okay, this will do.

Zafer   Tom, keep a look-out.

Tom Joy   You do it.

Stefi *is frustrated about the positioning of the torches.*

Stefi   They are totally going to be in shot there, we need to move them.

Tom Joy   Leave them, leave them.

Vee   Tom, you need to get into this costume.

Kobi   Where's the script?

Tom Joy   We're not using a script are we? We are gonna act it! You're not going to say anything, you're not even going to be in it! (*To* Stefi.) DON'T MOVE THE LIGHTS.

He grabs a torch out of **Stefi**'s *hand.*

Ray   Belle, can you get the heart out the bag?

Tom Joy   No! I'm doing it, it's mine!

Ray   Okay, get on with it!

He wrestles the bag from the butcher's out of **Belle**'s *hand.*

Belle   Oi!

Tom Joy   I own it.

Ray   Whatever.

Amma   Just hurry up!

Vee   Okay, let's start.

Kobi   Am I in this scene or what?

Amma   No! You're in the background.

Tom Joy   I'm the boss, I'm the guy, I'm the mad tramp.

Vee (*still trying to get* **Tom Joy**'s *costume on him*)   Put this on now. Or we'll recast you.

Tom Joy   I'm not wearing that. Stinks.

Throws it on the floor.

Ray   Okay, Kobi – you do it, you be the mad tramp.

Kobi   Okay.

Tom Joy   No way.

Vee   I'm directing this first bit, Ray. Let's do a practice shot – RECORDING.

Amma (*to* **Kobi**)   Get in position.

PRESENT DAY – Emre's Kitchen.

Zafer   We should go together, all of us.

Vee   No way.

Stefi   We're not going to the police.

Zafer   We have to.

Stefi   Look, I have got a plan!

Zafer   Some plan?! You just want to control everyone, everything, you're worse than Dad.

Stefi   What?

Ray   He's right, you manipulated us to get us here / lied to us.

Stefi   For your own safety!

Zafer   You go behind my back, you come up / with some outrageous plan –

Stefi   I'm doing it for you! Dad has never forgiven me for not 'protecting you'. Barely minutes older, but I'm meant to look after *you*. And now . . . you might not have noticed this, Zafer, but if you don't have cancer in our family you're kind of irrelevant. So this is what I'm doing. To sort it. Fuck off and let me do it.

FLASHBACK – Ansten House. **Vee** *looking through camera lens.*

Vee   Okay, action!

Kobi *steps forward, but* **Tom Joy** *runs in front of the camera holding a knife.*

Amma   Hey!

Vee   Get out of the shot!

Tom Joy   It's my film! I'm doing it.

Zafer   Tom, cut it out!

Amma   Where'd you get that knife?

Tom Joy   Found it.

Stefi   Zafer brought it. He stole it from home economics.

Zafer   I borrowed it.

Tom   I'm doing it.

Vee   This is ridiculous.

Kobi   Are we ready or not?

Ray   Clearly not!

Tom Joy   This is my scene, I'm the mad tramp!

He grabs the camera phone from **Vee.**

Tom Joy   You said I could do it!

Ray   We changed our minds!

Tom Joy   But it's my turn!

He throws it on the floor.

Vee   You idiot!

Tom Joy *starts kicking down the 'set' they have erected. Like a toddler having a tantrum.* **Belle** *has picked up the thrown mobile.*

Belle   Got it! It's still recording.

PRESENT DAY – Emre's Kitchen.

Ray   I'll come with you, Zafer.

Belle   Wait, wait, wait – if you go –

Amma   You can't.

Stefi   We have to stick together!

Zafer   We did that already remember!

Ray   Come on, Zaf.

Stefi *gets to the door first and locks it.*

Stefi   Tom was not some innocent kid who got done!

FLASHBACK – Ansten House. **Tom Joy** *is wilfully dismantling everything he can. He's lost it.*

Tom Joy   I'm the mad tramp!

Stefi *gestures to* **Belle** *holding the phone.*

Stefi   You need to get this! This is mental.

Belle *recording* **Tom Joy***, who is immersed in his 'tramp' character.*

Tom Joy   Anyone dares to trespass here!

He rips open the butcher's bag and pulls out the prized heart – he stabs it with the knife.

You will never leave!

He advances on them, they squeal – scatter, duck, try and hide. Kind of hysterical. **Belle** *is still filming.*

Tom Joy   I will tear you into shreds!

Suddenly a bang from outside. Everyone freaks.

Zafer   What's that?

Creaks and footsteps.

Ray   It's the tramp, it's the real mad tramp?!

Terror. They move like bullets. Torches knocked over. Near darkness now.

Kobi   He's coming for us!

Vee   Help!

Belle   Tom!

Amma   Quick!

Stefi   Get him!

Tom Joy, *hyped-up, no longer sure what's the 'film' and what's reality.*

A door creaks open.

PRESENT DAY – Emre's Kitchen.

Ray   Open the door, Stefi.

Stefi   No.

Ray   Open the door!

FLASHBACK – Ansten House – their younger selves attempt to exit through a door.

Kobi   It's locked!

They find a place to hide – crouching, scrambling, breathless and petrified.

Tom Joy, *backed in a corner, holding the knife.*

PRESENT DAY – Emre's Kitchen.

Ray *tries to grab the keys off* **Stefi**, *they tussle.* **Kobi** *tries to break them up.*

Kobi   Stop it!

FLASHBACK – Ansten House.

Tom Joy *screams at an unseen figure.*

SFX clinical voices of new **Reporters** *start to filter in. Alternate moments crashing into one another.*

Reporter One   A policeman has been stabbed to death in a derelict housing estate on the edge of the town.

Tom Joy *scrambles away, holding a knife. He leaps, he ducks, he needs to escape.*

Reporter Two   The Ansten House remains cordoned off as forensic officers continue their investigation.

Everyone bar **Tom Joy** *gathers in the dark, out of breath; they talk at pace over each other.*

Amma   Oh my God, oh my God, / oh my God.

Kobi   Where is he? Where has he gone?

Ray   We just said the skip, the big skip behind the house / is it still there?

Belle   But you said meet here – did you say meet here?

Stefi   No because what if he doesn't / what if he . . .

Vee   He was – oh my God.

Kobi   You can't trust him!

Ray   He lost it, we tell the police.

Amma   I thought we were waiting for him?

Ray   No we need to get home, but run yeah, because it has to look like we've run from him.

Amma   Do we say anything / do we tell anyone?

Ray   Don't text each other. Just meet up here, tomorrow.

Amma   But what do we say?

Ray   Just say what happened, he went mad and we ran away.

SFX.

Reporter Three   Known locally as a site where young gangs congregate, local police are appealing for witnesses to come forward urgently.

FLASHBACK – The voice of their parents echo around the space:

Mum   Victoria, can you come downstairs for a moment?

Nan   Kobi, what have you been playing at now?

Mum   Amma the police are here.

Dad   Stefi! Zafer! Get down here now!

Nan   Of course, officer.

Mum   Belle, this woman wants to ask you some questions, okay?

PRESENT DAY – Emre's Kitchen. It's heated, everyone trying to separate **Stefi** *and* **Ray***.*

Amma   We can't go back there.

Zafer   Maybe they'll understand!

Stefi   I've got this under control, okay?

Zafer   We were just kids.

Belle   It didn't help Tom did it?

Vee   We were terrified and we didn't know what was happening – we did our best, and y'know what – I'd do it again.

Amma   We did the right thing.

Kobi   Did we?

FLASHBACK – **Kobi** *in role as his stern* **Nan**, *questioning his younger, panicked self.*

Kobi   I didn't do anything!

Nan   You could go to prison! Do you want to go to prison?

Kobi   But you said –

Nan   The law is the law. I can't protect you!

PRESENT DAY – Emre's Kitchen.

Vee   Think about it, Zafer. For Tom. I mean statistically, he's not going to have a good life now, a normal life – is he, Belle? Back me up here. You know about child offenders, right?

Belle   Yeah yeah.

FLASHBACK – **Vee** *in role as* **Officer**, *grilling her younger self.*

Officer   You had no idea he had a knife with him?

Belle   No.

Officer   He didn't mention it or talk about it, or say anything at all?

Belle   No. But he was always stealing things. So we come to expect it.

PRESENT DAY – Emre's Kitchen.

Vee   They don't get rehabilitated. It's a cycle. They get stuck. So even if we did go to the police, we won't be able to change that. That's happened. To him. The damage has been done. Right? Coming clean . . . doesn't save him. And I know you're struggling. I know you're sick. But maybe you would have a better chance of fighting . . . recovering . . . if you stopped torturing yourself.

FLASHBACK –

Stefi   If we both say we saw him with it.

Zafer   Yeah.

Stefi   Before.

Zafer   Okay.

Stefi   That he had it in his bag.

Zafer   In his bag.

Stefi   That he stole it. Because then.

Zafer   Because –

Stefi   Yeah.

Zafer   We didn't do anything wrong.

PRESENT DAY – Emre's Kitchen.

Vee   He was off his head. He'd always been off his head.

Zafer   But we lied.

Amma   No we didn't.

Belle   We did, Amma.

Amma   Did we?

FLASHBACK – Police interrogation.

Belle   We've told him so many times to leave us alone, but he follows us everywhere, so when he arrived, we were just, we just said, y'know, leave us alone, and he wouldn't listen. He was just off on one and saying he was going to kill someone.

SFX of news report.

Reporter One   News today that a thirteen-year-old boy has been arrested in connection with the violent murder of PC Trent Powell, with local residents here expressing their disgust at the crime by attacking his family home.

PRESENT DAY – Emre's Kitchen.

Vee   Now he's out, you think it'll matter to him? Five years too late? He won't care. Ray's still traumatised by it, we all are, and we didn't even do time, you think Tom is going to bounce out of prison and be okay?

*FLASHBACK – **Tom Joy**, in a police interview room, distressed and pleading with his unseen mother.*

Tom Joy   Mum! I don't wanna answer no questions no more! Please! Tell them to stop! Please, Mum! I didn't do it! I didn't! Please.

PRESENT DAY – Emre's Kitchen.

Zafer   You've got to let us go, Stef.

Stefi   Not unless we all agree we do the story. We do the story.

Vee   We do it because it's the only thing we can control.

Ray   Another nail in the coffin for him.

Vee   Oh put your bleeding heart away, Ray! I'm over it.

Zafer   I had to look at his face on the front of the newspaper every day, and every time his name is mentioned in the news I feel like I'm going to throw up. It's the end, okay?

Stefi   You can't make this decision because it affects all of us!

Belle   Look. The law is messed up, Zafer. I know that. If this had happened somewhere else, maybe Tom might have had a chance. There was a case in Sweden, okay? Some kids – five years old – they kicked a girl to death. She was a friend. It was a game, and it got out of hand. And those kids were *protected*, the community looked after them. Because it was tragic, and they were too young to know the consequences. But that's not . . . *Here*. It's bad luck for Tom, because he was accountable because that's the law. We can't take responsibility for *that*, Zafer. I mean, Jesus, you can't even *vote* yet. You can't even elect the people who make the laws. It's not your fault. It's not our fault.

FLASHBACK – **Tom Joy** *visibly distressed.*

Tom Joy   Why can't I talk to them?

Officer   You're not allowed to communicate whilst we're questioning.

Tom Joy   Can I just speak to Ray or Kobi or Belle, or anyone?

Officer   No.

Tom Joy   They'll tell you.

Officer   Oh yes, they've told us. How you stalk them. Harass them. How you attacked Belle last year.

Tom Joy   But I didn't.

Officer   We've taken statements, Tom.

Tom Joy   Ask Zafer. He knows me. Properly. He'll tell you.

SFX headlines.

Headline One   Devil Child Kills Local Bobby in Cold Blood!

Headline Two   Real Life Horror Movie as Killer Child Goes on Rampage!

Headline Three   Born Bad: Teenage Tearaway Turns to Murder

PRESENT DAY – *Emre's Kitchen.*

Belle   What would've been worse? One life – his life – ruined, or all of ours? All of us in the dock.

FLASHBACK – **Tom Joy**, *jarringly formal in a suit that is slightly too big for him, like a shrunken version of himself.*

Prosecutor   Members of the jury, you may think you see a naïve young boy in the dock before you, but let me assure you that Tom Joy is a devious and violent criminal.

Reporter Two   It took the jury less than three hours of deliberation to return a unanimous verdict of guilty.

Reporter Three   Tom Joy sat motionless in the dock as he was sentenced.

Judge   The severity of the crime you have committed belies your age; it was a heinous and hateful act of violence against an innocent man, for which you will pay dearly.

PRESENT DAY – Emre's Kitchen.

Ray   I don't wanna be scared anymore.

Stefi   Suck it up and stick together, and after that, we'll never have to see each other again. But if you go to the police now . . .?! He probably would've ended up in jail anyway! (*To* **Zafer**.) And you. I'm asking you. To look after *me*. For once in your life!

The jangling of **Vee***'s phone disrupts. She answers.*

Vee   Yeah I'm coming . . . What? Are you . . .? Okay . . . okay. I will.

She ends the call.

The police have found the car.

Pause.

It was my brother, he took it.

Belle   Can he even drive?

Vee   Not legally.

Belle   Is he okay?

Vee   He's fine, he's probably going to get grounded for the rest of his life but – yeah. The car is fine. And. He is. So.

Kobi   No sign of Tom?

Amma   You gonna press charges?

Vee   Against my brother?!

Beat.

Ray   That's that mystery solved then isn't it?

Amma   It doesn't mean he's not out.

Zafer   Maybe he's outside the door right now. (*Taunting* **Stefi**.) Go on, open it. Open it.

Stefi *unlocks it. No one there.*

Zafer   Tom?

Amma   Ssssh!

Zafer   Tom, you there?!

Vee   Cut it out!

Zafer   Tom, it's us!

Beat.

Tom, I'm sorry!

Silence but for the rain. They wait.

Ray (*to* **Zafer**)   Let's go.

Ray *and* **Zafer** *look at them, one by one, expectant. The weight of a decision.*

Ray   Kobi?

Kobi   Yeah, yeah, can you just give me a second.

Pause.

I know what I should do. But. It's my nan. I'm all she's got. This would kill her. Please. I know I don't have the right, but. I've tried so hard to do everything right since then.

Zafer   I don't want to hurt you.

Kobi   I know.

Belle   This is my whole career. I cannot be involved in this, I don't see how you don't get that?! I can't throw it away, for him. But I can make up for it. When I'm older, when I'm qualified, when I can change things from the inside, I'll make it up to Tom, to other kids like him. But I want that chance. I don't see why we should all have to pay. Why?!

Stefi   She's right.

Amma   What's the point? We won't become good off the back of it.

Ray   But maybe it will get rid of . . . this feeling. Of pain. Or something.

Stefi   But it's not fair, Zafer, to any of us. Especially you. Because he's out now, he gets his life back, his whole life back, and you go from test, to test, to hospital, to treatment, from bad news to worse – and you think that's justice? That he can start again and you don't get to?

Zafer   I don't wanna live with this anymore, Stef.

Stefi   Do it for me.

Zafer   And I don't want to die with it either.

Stefi (*quietly*)   You're not gonna die.

Zafer   I don't know what the police will do. I just need to tell them. That we were there. That we lied. We wiped the blood off his hands and wiped the knife, and forced him to take it, and hide it because we already knew. He was just a scared, sad kid. And we treated him like every shit adult had ever treated him. It was so easy.

Vee   He did it! He was guilty.

Zafer   Yeah. We made sure of that.

He walks towards the door. **Ray** *follows him.*

Stefi   Don't leave me.

Zafer   I'm sorry.

Ray   Maybe we should be sorry.

Stefi   Please.

They walk out. A moment where no one can bear to breathe.

Vee   My parents find out I've been lying about this, and lying about everything, I am so screwed.

Belle   We should never have come here.

Stefi   I was trying to make it better.

Vee *heads to the door.*

Vee (*to* **Belle**)   Come on, Belle.

(*calling out towards* **Zafer** *and* **Ray**)   Zafer! Wait!

Belle *runs after them.*

Vee   Jesus.

Kobi   I thought I was lucky. To get them years. As a kid. Total freedom. Tom never had that. But we were lucky weren't we?

He goes to leave.

Amma   Where you going?

Kobi   Home. Where else?

Amma   Can I come with you?

Kobi   If you like.

Amma   If I'm alone, I'll just . . .

Kobi   Sure.

Amma   Maybe I can help? With your nan or something. Do something.

Kobi   Siphon off her vodka, you mean?

Amma   Everyone just betrays everyone in the end, don't they?

Kobi   Not always, no.

Amma   What if we're never normal again?

Kobi   Then we have to bear it.

He holds out his hand to **Amma***; she grips on to it. They leave.*

Vee   Stef. I'm panicking here. You just gonna sit there?! Stef!

She waits, gives up, storms out.

Stefi, *entirely alone. Afraid to move. As if her whole body is a bruise.*

A creepy ringtone on her phone. It's an unknown number. She lets it ring.

From the open doorway, the shadow of a figure cast. It stretches across the floor, as big as a ghost, as big as a giant.

Stef *looks into her future.*

Blackout

End.

Old Times

BY MOLLY TAYLOR

Notes on rehearsal and staging, drawn from a workshop with the writer,
held at the National Theatre facilitated by director Jade Lewis, October 2022

How the writer came to write the play

> I wrote the play because I am really interested in the state and the relationship
> between state and individuals . . . And also because I'm fascinated by how
> we develop.
>
> Molly Taylor, October 2022

In a conversation with lead director Jade Lewis, Molly talked about how she was researching for another project about looked after children and ended up looking into children in the criminal justice system in the UK.

Children in the UK have criminal responsibility at a younger age that other European countries and it brought her to question why this is, what is justice and what is fair? How does society treat young people and 'are we as a nation particularly rubbish to our young people'?

Young people's brains are still developing at thirteen and are actually drawn to risk taking. What is maturity and when can people be deemed responsible?

When Molly was starting to write the play, it was during lockdown in response to Covid-19 and on a walk she saw a local park with police tape around it. The image gave her the idea of something awful happening to a group of young people and the impact that has on their lives.

Why this play?

Everyone in the room discussed why they decided to work on this play with their groups and the responses fell into similar categories:

Characters:
> The characters were considered to be relatable for the young people in the groups.
>
> Tom Joy in particular stood out as a child that the participants recognised in young people they had worked with.
>
> The relationships and power dynamics between the characters and between teenagers.
>
> The young performers also playing adults.
>
> The language of the dialogue felt authentic.

Form of the piece:
> The challenge of the memories/flashbacks appealed to lots of groups.
>
> Parallel timelines.
>
> Fast pace of the play.

Performance opportunities:

    To develop detailed characters.

    Challenge of switching from eighteen-year-olds to adults.

    To work out how to create the different worlds and times.

    Fun of the cast sharing the same character at two different points in their lives – working together to make decisions.

    Opportunities to skill share across age ranges – with older members of the group mentoring the younger members.

Themes:

    Exploring why young people get into trouble when they don't mean to.

    Implications of choices.

    Lies and truth.

    Responsibility and the systems we live under as young people and adults.

    No nice and easy resolution but a complex subject to explore.

The world of the play

In small groups everyone discussed what they knew about the world of the play and what questions they had.

Depending on your rehearsal time this could be something you do as a director and make decisions before starting rehearsals, or you could do this as a company at the start of your process.

Here are some of the things we know from the text

Two worlds/time periods – friends (aged seventeen/eighteen or thirteen/fourteen)
Past and present
Locations – that we see and don't see:

- Emre's Kitchen – kebab shop – somewhere this group knows and has a sense of ownership over.
- Ansten House – a derelict house that kids hang out in
- court house
- prison
- church
- hospital
- school

Things that exist in this world:

- social media
- mobile phones

- computer games
- religion
- police
- morality
- children (Tom Joy is thirteen) can be criminally responsible.

It is raining.

The characters have different cultures and context. They are brought up in different ways by different types of families.

There is experience of trauma.

Education as a route of progression.

There is a monster – whether it is the tramp or illness or Tom Joy – they are all scared of something.

What don't we know – or questions we might want to consider?

It talks about raining – is it ever sunny?

How does this group fit into the world of the town/school?

How affluent is the area they live in?

Is it rural or urban?

Has this group lived through Covid-19?

Where in the UK is it set?

What have they all done in the last five years?

What is prison like in this society?

Exercise: Solidifying the world

Jade suggested an activity where you solidify what the world is by completing the sentence 'This is a world where . . .'

For example, this is a world where there is social media.

This is a world where there is a hospital.

Exercise: Getting into the world of the play

Choose eight participants for this activity – one for each of the children – but you could have everyone take part or do it in two groups and use it as an opportunity for those playing the same character to observe their counterpart.

Eight people in the space walk around to music. Once they have explored each direction, move them on to the next stage.

- Walk in straight lines – sharp turns – where is your eye line?
- Walk in curves – circles – move eye line in circles as well.
- Play with dynamics, levels, pace and begin to fuse lines with curves.
- Begin to be more aware of the others in the space – make eye contact with them.
- Return to a more naturalistic walk but retaining an awareness of these elements.

- Add in some given circumstances – it is freezing cold, for example.
- Count down from ten to zero and on zero come to a stop.
- Start walking again but now it is getting hot. Start to add in location information – walking down the street, walking past the derelict house, see the church – visualise the kebab shop. See everyone – you haven't seen them in years.
- Still considering all these elements, go back to your seat and when you arrive, you are sitting in the kebab shop.

This exercise is a direct way into the world of the text – the company can start to picture it and feel it.

You can start to find a geography.

It is a way to start to develop the characters in the space. Each character may have a very different response to the same thing.

It allows the actors to question their character's response to the locations.

Extension – you can control the levels of reaction to something by giving them a number on the scale (1–10).

Characters

In groups (one group per character), participants discussed what they knew about them. With the passage of time they noted what they knew of them in the present and in the past and things that might have changed.

Note – you could get the actors who play two different ages of the same character to do this together to see what they share and how they change. By starting to build those characters together they can discover how that character progresses and how they could show that through their performances.

Amma
At thirteen:
Makes slime
Steals glue from art
Smokes – Tom Joy stole cigarettes for her
Had a sleepover for her thirteenth birthday
Is frightened when they go to Ansten House
Is a fast runner
Won't share her nuggets
Amma's dad shouts at the police – she has someone who will stand up for her

At eighteen:
Smokes and drinks – refers to herself as an addict. 'Addiction is an illness'
Has had a few drinks before she arrives to the reunion
Posts on socials
Wants to be famous
Image concerned
Seeks validation
Doesn't want to be alone
Writes poetry

Disregards Kobi's faith
Scared of Tom Joy coming back
Rebellious – 'screw our parents'
Justifies her behaviour
Gets annoyed that Tom Joy gets a new identity – perception of fairness
Awareness that theirs is only a version of the truth – 'trauma effects your memory'
Her dad is having an affair
Her dad buys her alcohol

Kobi
At thirteen:
Lives with his nan
He is all his nan has
Says things to get a reaction
Is impulsive
Doesn't trust Tom Joy
Questions – What happened to his parents? Why is he in the care of his nan?

At eighteen:
Religious – was taken to the church by his nan after everything happened
His nan has dementia – she is doing things that are causing money problems for
    them
He is sensible/pragmatic
Has a moral responsibility
He is more sympathetic towards Tom Joy
He wrote to Tom Joy in prison
'Do not judge, and you will not be judged. Do not condemn and you will not be
    condemned. Forgive, and you will be forgiven'
Question: Is he totally against the idea of making money from their story or is he
    interested due to money issues?

Belle
At fourteen:
Obedient
Trusting
Quite mature compared to the others
Not a rule breaker
She lives with her mum who has a job working with young people
Her hand was broken during a game of British Bulldog
Belle told the police that Tom Joy was always stealing things
She tells the police that Tom Joy said he was going to kill someone – which he
    doesn't say
Question: Does she deliberately lie about Tom Joy or is this how she views their
    relationship?

At eighteen:
Did her A Levels early
Fast-tracked to university
Training to be a lawyer – the application of the law can make her slightly clinical.

She embodies the law to protect herself from her feelings of personal responsibility towards the crime. She can think dispassionately about the situation

Talks about changing the system from the inside

Big picture thinker – morality and justice

Doesn't want to take personal responsibility

Best friends with Vee. There is some tension between them as their paths have moved further apart

Judgement on others' life choices

Lives with her mum

Question: Does Belle choose to be a lawyer because of her experiences and guilt?

Ray
At fourteen:

Confident

Encourages the others to do risky things

His dad is with him when he speaks to the police

Suggests to the police that Tom Joy will kill him if he tells on him

Wants to shoot the film and convinces everyone to use Ansten House as a location

Gives Tom Joy a role because, 'He'll make it real'

He is the one that tells everyone else the story they should tell when the incident happens

He knows that this story isn't true – 'it has to look like we have run from him'

After the incident his family moved him away

He was lonely when he moved

Was it only his dad or is his mum around?

Close with Zafer

At eighteen:

Anxious

Kind

Has a moral voice in the room

Could be seen to have changed the most in the five years

Struggles to get involved

He doesn't want to be filmed for social media

Doesn't want to be there but keen to see Zafer

Still has nightmares and flashbacks – trauma

Vee
At thirteen:

High status and interested in status and being grown up

Best friends with Belle

Has a younger brother

Had braces – she tells Amma that she had them taken off

Following the incident her parents send her to a fee-paying school

Mum and dad both around

Has sleepovers all the time – suggests she has a stable home life that can cater for
    other children being around
Gluten free

At seventeen:
Concerned with her looks – plans to get a nose job
Older boyfriend – perhaps she looks a bit older than the others
Lies to her family about having an older boyfriend
Independent
She appears to have completely distanced herself from the incident. She
    strongly stands on the side of he was wrong and it shouldn't be discussed or
    ambiguous
Close to Belle but can feel judged by her
Wealthy
Spoilt?
Has a car

Stefi
At thirteen:
A natural ringleader
Her birthday is coming up
Non-identical twin – older by just over two and a half minutes
Her family run/own a kebab shop
In control

At seventeen:
Brings everyone together
Wants to raise money to help Zafer get the treatment he needs
Feels invisible and useless due to Zafer's illness
Wants to solve the problem
Abrasive
Question – is the podcast and producer a real thing?
What has Stefi said to make this group come together? Or is it just her as a person?

Zafer
At thirteen:
Thoughtful
Diligent
Non-identical twin to Stefi – younger by 2 minutes and 38 seconds
His birthday is coming up – he doesn't want to have to share a party
Close friends with Ray
Is initially concerned about Tom Joy feeling left out by not being invited to the
    party
Stole the knife which killed the policeman

At seventeen:
Has cancer which needs extremely specialist treatment
Spends a lot of time in hospital

Wants to be able to make his own medical decisions – which he can't do until he is eighteen

Hasn't been in touch with the others since being ill

Does not want to do the podcast

Tom Joy

At thirteen:

Lives with his mum – who isn't spoken very well of by others

Dad is absent

He steals for his mum

Seeks validation and belonging

Has no filter

He is vulnerable – neglected

Has never had a birthday party

Caring

Energetic and creative

Is written off by adults as a bad kid to hang around with

We don't meet Tom Joy at eighteen but we know he has spent nearly five years in prison and we believe he has now been released under a new name.

Once you have found all the information from the script you could start to ask some questions of your characters; for example:

What is your nickname?

How does your character display affection? (Older and younger might be different)

Is your character competitive?

What is your character's biggest fear?

What haunts them?

What would your character stand up for?

Does your character keep promises?

What advice would your older character self give to your younger self?

Molly spoke about the difference between the younger and older versions of the characters. The younger group is really activated – they are creative and busy making a film. They are the freest they will ever be – 'they are having a boss time'.

The older group are all imprisoned in some way – already dealing with very grown-up things. Zafer isn't allowed to make his own medical decisions due to his age. Stefi feels the responsibility of being the older sibling but has no power to help. Vee is lying about her age. Amma is holding on to family secrets and struggling with addiction. Kobi is looking after his nan. Ray is stuck in the past. Belle is fast-tracking her life and escaping her youth.

Jade spoke about how you should think about each character's 'wants' and 'objectives' in each scene as well as their overall 'super-objective'.

There is a lot to explore in the subtext of the dialogue – what tactics are people using to get what they want?

Exercises to explore character

Exercise 1: Run the dialogue of a scene. At any point the director can CLAP and you switch to saying what is actually in your character's head at that moment. CLAP again and you go back into the scene.

Exercise 2: Set up some improvisations around the 'missing years' – what has happened to these characters since they were last all together?

Exercise 3: Look at the play chronologically so each actor knows what information their character has at each point.

Exercise 4: Make a list of everything that is said about your character and who by? What does your character say about others?

Exercise 5: Make a play list for your character – how does their taste change over the years?

Exercise 6:

- Those playing the younger version of each character move around the space playing with moving in curves (as per the earlier exercise on exploring the world of the play).

- Add in a ball. Throw the ball to someone and say your character name – while continuing to walk around the space.

- Older version of the character observe from the outside. See how the character already begins to develop just with the power of a name.

- The group who are playing progress to explore how you receive and pass the ball. Stop when you receive it and add in a gestural movement.

- Older group can now join in. If you get passed the ball, you must remain still. You can only pass to a younger version of any character who will gesture that they want the ball. Older selves can explore how much they want to interact with their younger selves or if they want to observe from afar.

This exercise allows the pairings to start to explore the similarities and differences between the two ages and the journey they have been on. How does their experiences impact the quality of movement/their awareness of space or their responsibility for the space and others in it?

Exercise 7: Zombie
Walking around the space – one person is a zombie – They walk like a zombie to your victim. To be safe the victim has to shout out a character name before the zombie gets them. The character that you have shouted then becomes the zombie. But if you don't do it in time, you sit down.

This game has a great element of danger but also the sense of dropping someone else in it to save yourself . . . no one wants to be the zombie.

Exploring transitions

Transitions are really important in this play and happen in a number of different ways – the group looked at three different types:

1   Through time – for example from Scene Two into Scene Three where they remain in the same location but go back in time.

2   When an actor transitions from one character to another – for example where Stefi takes on the role of Dad.

3   When lots of actors are becoming different characters – for example, when reporters and police and parents start getting involved.

Jade and the group tried some ideas out in the room.

For each scene they read the section they were looking at, including the stage directions and mined it for the information available.

They then set up the location and did a first draft of the staging.

Everyone talked about what they felt or observed and what they might want to change.

They then did a second draft with these alterations.

Each version opened up more questions.

Transition 1 (page 265)

Where do people enter from? Are they here all along? When they aren't speaking in the space are they still activated? Can you use movement as a transition between characters? If you are transitioning between characters, who are you walking as?

As you try different versions continue to explore that 'What ifs'.

What if the younger characters did some sort of physical handover with the older characters?

What if the younger characters can't see the older characters but the older ones can see them?

Once you have tried some versions you can select what worked best – the pace of version 1 but with the physical handover of version 4 for example. How does each version support the story you are telling?

The play explores form and is asking for something to break – you don't have to come through established naturalistic doorways, etc.

Decide the rules that you want to give your company but then you can also decide to break them.

You could create a fixed language for your transitions, but it doesn't have to be the same each time.

Transition 2 (page 267)

Is it a physicality or a prop that creates the adult character?

How grotesque and huge can you take it?

How do the others respond to that person?

Could it be delivered out front to audience rather than to the character? This is a form that can then be used for the interrogation/police, etc.

Exercise: Storytelling

Ask your company to tell a story about an adult in their lives and then part-way through become that adult telling the story. This will allow them to try this technique with someone they are familiar with before creating the adult their character is representing.

Transition 3 (page 272)

Which character are you travelling as? Be clear when the change is being made.

How do different characters in the different time zones engage with the set? Where are the memories created? Where are they physically located? Do all the adults appear in a certain location?

Do you step forward if you are in a memory? What is the physical space between the two worlds?

Do the others turn away or stop watching them? Can it be achieved by a shift in eyeline?

Consider who the lines are for and in which world. Make sure you are clear on that.

Jade suggested that rather than freezing when a character isn't 'activated' they exist in a living stillness – still part of the story even if not part of that bit of action.

Casting

The group discussed the challenges and opportunities in casting this play.

Age

We meet these characters at two points in their life, thirteen/fourteen and seventeen/eighteen, intended to be played by two different sets of actors. The seventeen/eighteen-year-olds also play the adults in their life.

Taylor is interested in adult legacy and how at this stage in the characters' lives they are drawing on what they have learnt from the adults in their lives as they embark on adulthood. Taylor would invite you to explore the form of that in relation to the subject of the story and keep the adults played by the same actors playing the seventeen/eighteen-year-olds.

It is a fun challenge for those actors to show the characters in flux and parroting the adults in their lives – this is a young persons' interpretation of an adult rather than playing that person. However, if your company size means that you want different actors to play the adults then there will be a version of this that works – just keep in mind the idea of adult legacy and the impact it has on the younger characters.

You may be working with a youth group that spans these two age groups or school year group that is a smaller age bracket. If you are casting actors playing older or younger than themselves it is good to approach this physically. Observe the movement of people the age they are playing – find a physical way into the character. The earlier exercise of movement dynamics whilst exploring the space could be used for this.

Gender and ethnicity in the same character at different ages

In this play there will be two actors playing the same character at different points in their life. You may want these pairings to be the same ethnicity and gender but that might not always be possible in your company. Cast the people that are best for the role in your company and when building the character find the links in how the character is played. They are both the same character – how do they express that?

Potential cultural issues

Some of the characters may be partaking in activities that are of cultural sensitivity. Molly discussed how it is important that the characters are going through those journeys – Amma is partaking in adult vices because she is dealing with adult problems and it would be great to retain that. However, if something specific – for example, alcohol – causes problems for your company then consider how you retain this element of the story without that specific element.

Production, staging and design

There are several elements that you can consider when thinking about how you tell this story through your production. Jade reminded everyone that making a production provides great opportunities to expose your young companies to other roles in theatre making.

The groups split and focused on four elements – set, costume, light and sound – and discussed how they could tell the story with that design element.

What does the script suggest – does a light flash, phone ring or someone come through a door? When you know what is in the text you can chose how to interpret that.

Set

The play moves rapidly between time periods and locations so discussions centred around an awareness of the pace of the play and not wanting to slow it down with scene changes.

- Is there one naturalistic space (the kebab shop) that every flashback/memory happens within?
- Is it a more abstract space that can be turned into lots of locations?
- Do you divide up the space it to the different locations?

- Do you keep it minimal, representing locations with props?
- Can you explore the functionality of the set – if you have a counter for the kebab shop does it rotate to be something else?

Enjoy the theatricality in the form of the piece and how that can be reflected in the set. Other things to consider:

Where are the adult characters located and is there a physical space for the older versions of the characters to watch their younger selves – are these separate or do they happen in the same space?

Who moves and creates the space? Is this stage management or the characters? What is the story if the present-day older versions create all the spaces? What if it is the past younger selves?

Costume

Costume could be a way of bringing together both versions of the same character – do both Vees wear the same colour or is there an item that they still have a more worn version of?

Colour could be used to show the passage of time – bright colours of youth dulled down. Vividness of the memories.

'Same but different' – enough similarities to make the connections but not exact replicas as a lot of time has passed.

How have their changes in circumstances impacted their style? Have they consciously or subconsciously made a big shift from who they were before?

Do you have costume items for the adult characters? If so, how do you facilitate this as it is very quick? Could you have small items – glasses, a hat, a prop – that is easily stowed in a pocket or bag?

Is this a world of school uniform for the younger group?

Again, due to the pace of the piece, costume changes are probably best kept quite simple, and Jade suggested that you should try costume ideas early on so you can build them into the piece and make sure that they work with the language of the piece you are creating.

Light

As with all the elements of production, the resources available for each company could be different. Develop your ideas with the resources you have.

Characters can have light within the story – phone screens, torches, etc.

There is filming in the piece – do we see this? Do we see the red 'recording' light? Are the characters setting up light for their own filming?

Light could be a great medium to aid transitions between time and location and can create atmosphere.

- Is there a different quality of light in the past and present?
- Could you light from different angles or in different colours for when the eighteen-year-old group play their parents/reporters/police, etc.?

Use of light to support the story – for example, if they don't want people to know that they are in the kebab shop are the full shop lights on or not?

Lighting could also be a good way of building the panic of the stabbing moment; for example, a strobe could add to the confusion of the movement or is it totally black?

Shadow could be used to great effect in this piece. At the end the text talks about the shadow of a figure in the doorway. Shadow could also be used to make the adult characters look like they are looming over the children.

Sound

The group discussed the sounds that are in the script – phone ringing or vibrating, sirens, knock at the door, doorbell, recorded lines of characters, etc.

There are also potential environmental sounds – rain, for example: does this stay the same or does the rain build?

Is there a radio on or music playing in the kebab shop?

There is reference to a specific phone ringtone – how is this obviously different to the others?

Once you know the sounds that are needed how could you interpret them to support your story:

- Is the sound literal or abstract? Is the sound quality different in the past and present?
- You can use sound to support the tension building – do noises get louder, higher, more distorted?
- Where does the sound come from (directional) and is that literal or abstact?
- You could use a noise to support the changes in time – a buzz or whoosh?
- You could use songs to locate your audience in the different time periods.

For each element the important thing is what story you are wanting to tell with it and how does the use of it or not using it support the story. Which element is most prominent in each moment – is there sound coming through a blackout?

Important things when approaching the play

Molly spoke about the things she thinks are the most important to retain in your versions of the play.

The stakes: Shared enterprise laws could have an impact on all of them and so the stakes are really high – there is a lot to potentially lose, and the group know this as they come back together.

Joy and energy of the past scenes: In contrast to the present, the characters in their younger past state are full of youth, freedom and vitality. They are playful and creative – they are choosing to make a film together for fun. This is the opportunity to see them before they are tarnished.

Tom Joy's humanity: It is important that Tom Joy is a fully realised character. It isn't about over-sentimentalising him, but he is not a villain. He does lovely things for his friends and others in the group make questionable decisions in hindsight, but it is a combination of factors that leads to Tom Joy ending up in prison.

Form: The theatrical language of memory is totally up for grabs. Enjoy playing with that.

Final questions

Q: How do we show the heart and blood on stage?
A: This could be stylised rather than realistic. If you want something realistic, workshop this early on – the group offered suggestions of playdough, a sponge with fake blood and having fake blood and objects in a carrier bag so you never see it directly. You could also consider whether the audience ever have to see it, but it is all in how the actors react to it.

Q: Does the game have to be British Bulldog?
A: It doesn't have to be British Bulldog specifically, but it needs to be a game that goes wrong in a way that can cause a physical injury.

Q: How do we pronounce Zafer?
A: Whatever works for you as a company – each region will have different 'a' sounds so go with that.

From a workshop led by Jade Lewis
With notes by Leigh Toney

Samphire

by Shamser Sinha

Shamser Sinha writes about people at the wrong end of money, fortune and the wars we fight. Outside of theatre, he works as a sociologist and child/youth worker with young asylum seekers and refugees, those living in children's homes and those with additional needs. His plays include *Our White Skoda Octavia* for Eastern Angles/Derby Theatre and national tour, *Three Sat Under the Banyan Tree* for 7+ for Polka Theatre/ Tara Arts and national tour, nominated for Best Production at the Asian Arts, Culture and Theatre Awards 2019, *The Dissidents* for Tricycle [now Kiln] Young Company and *Khadija is 18* (Finborough – Pearson Playwright Award). Sinha recently won a Writers Guild of Great Britain award and as a consequence is now under commission to the egg, Theatre Royal Bath for *Marjana*, *Sinbad* and *The Jewel of the Lost Lagoon*.

When reading this play for the first time you are advised to read it very slowly and carefully. Keep the glossary provided by your side and refer back to it regularly. Unless you are familiar with the rural Suffolk vernacular, you will have to.

A message from the dramaturg:

Dear director

If I may, a brief word on Samphire *before you begin.*

I think it is worth you knowing that this is a double espresso of a play – in as much as it is dark, strong, and stimulating – and if you're not used to it, it pays to start slowly, by sipping it.

Like Shakespeare, (a lot of) the text in this play is unique and not instantly recognisable to the unfamiliar eye and ear. Like Shakespeare the key is to relax, trust the author and the words and find the rhythm – or rather, allow the rhythm of the words and the world to find you and then go with the flow.

Read it phonetically – i.e. if you encounter the word 'yew' (like the tree) then say and hear the word 'yew' in your mind, whilst simultaneously knowing that what the character and author mean is the word 'you'.

Once the character intentions in this play are understood by director and performer alike, in performance I believe this play will reveal a world that is complex, harsh and authentic, covering themes of immense importance whilst revealing a perceptive understanding of the lived experience of a distinct group of young people growing up in a rural as opposed to an urban context.

So, pick it up, put it to your lips and savour it, and discover the richness and deep resonance of the characters, actions and themes of this play.

Ola Animashawun
July 2022

2023. A Suffolk story. A rural story. Alicia lives in a children's home, with her best friend Sofia, while her boyfriend Jake lives in a shed. Alicia and Jake rob local farms for animals to eat. But when they steal a piglet from the wrong farmer their dreams of a houseshare in Leiston are put in jeopardy. A story with dogs, demons and the rural Suffolk vernacular. Take your time. Use the glossary as much as you need to.

Characters

There are twenty-one roles comprising humans and animals. Those playing Alicia, Jake, Sofia, Chelle and Rob can't double. The rest can. That choice is up to you. The German Shepherd and the Demon Dog are played by the same person. So, that person must double. You can make a choice concerning if you want Sam to also play the German Shepherd and the Demon Dog – so this would be a triple. The adult roles do not have to be played by bigger people, and you can cast ethnicity and gender freely. Shaq is Muslim but there is absolutely no imperative for the person playing this role to share the same faith as the character.

Alica, Jake, Beth, Chelle, Rob, Mel and **Bus Driver** speak in a rural Suffolk vernacular.

Alicia (*sixteen*) – *Alicia doesn't lie. And she doesn't keep secrets. But now, she's made a promise to keep a secret. Alicia happens to be a person who is neurodiverse.*

Jake (*fifteen*) – *Jake needs secrets keeping. He doesn't talk much. Good with butcher's knives. Loves a dog called Luna.*

Luna the Lurcher – *Jake's dog. Great sense of smell. Partially sighted, clumsy, affectionate, gentle, likes eating pheasant. Foolish.*

Sofia (*sixteen*) – *Protective of the only person she loves – Alicia. Wary, sharp, and fears being abandoned.*

German Shepherd – *Vicious. The alpha dog. One of Chelle's dogs. The actor playing the German shepherd should also play Demon Dog.*

Demon Dog – *A demon dog. German shepherd. According to Suffolk myth, Leiston has a demon dog.*

Four Rottweilers – *Chelle's dogs. Vicious.*

Alsatian – *Chelle's dog. Vicious.*

Beth (*eighteen*) – *Finds dogs, for bad, bad works.*

Chelle (*sixteen*) – *Chelle wants to do bad, bad works. Clever, influential, fierce.*

Rob (*sixteen*) – *Enjoys a privilege accruing to him as Chelle's cousin. Does what Chelle says.*

Mary – *Alicia's birth mother. A reformed character? Wants Alicia to come and live with her. Why does she wear that necklace?*

Sam – *Schoolteacher. Has difficulty understanding and appreciating some of her more educationally lower-achieving pupils. Or might not want to.*

Parminder (*sixteen*) – *Studious, eco conscious, wealthy. Fancies Sofia. Looks after her gran.*

Mel (*sixteen*) – *Studious, eco conscious, wealthy. Animal rights activist.*

Ed – *Jerk. He would love to be a member of Ipswich's J block gang, but is probably actually scared of catching a bus to Ipswich.*

Shaq – *Shares Ed's illusions of being 'urban'. A stereotypical illusion at that. Not conscious of his own privilege.*

Bus Driver – *Believes everything he's told in the* East Anglian Daily Times. *Wary of those short of money, different and young.*

Language

Some of the characters speak in a rural Suffolk vernacular. To understand the character is to understand the language ... whether the young people perform them in this vernacular or not is entirely up to you. I certainly wouldn't want some of the protagonists talking in a rural Suffolk accent putting you off.

Glossary in alphabetical order

Here is a phonetic glossary to help you understand the language of those speaking in a rural Suffolk vernacular. Having it helps you understand the characters even if you decide to play them in accents you are more accustomed to.

Abandun – abandon
Bin – been
Boi – boy
Dawdlin' – dawdling
doinut – doing it
Dussen't – doesn't
Foind – find
Gab – gob
Git gorn – get going
Gorn – going to, gone
Huld on a minut, howd yew hard – hold on a minute, let's think about it
Innut – innit
Int – isn't or ain't
Int ser loikely – not so likely
Loik – like
Marn't – must not
Minut – minute

Moind – mind
Nuffun – nothing
Oi – I
Oi'd – I'd
Oi'm – I'm
Oo – who
Probly – probably
Puttun – putting
Rekun – reckon
Sharn't – should not/ought not
Speakun – speaking
Suffun – something
Tha' – that
Togither – together
Wroight – write
Yew – you
Yew rum are ya'? – reckon you're bad do you?

A / indicates overlapping dialogue. This means the character whose line is beneath the one above speaks at the same time from the point at which the slash occurs.

[words enclosed in square brackets] are silent and are not to be spoken, but are there simply to assist in understanding and clarifying the intention behind the line.

Movement

You will have to think about how the dogs move and their mannerisms. Much fun could be had.

Some terms you may not know

Farrowing crates – Farrowing crates are small cages where sow are kept to give birth to their piglets. They are sometimes used to keep the sow caged to separate them from their piglets, while allowing the piglets to suckle when they want to.

Sow – There is one reference to 'sow' in the play. This is an adult female pig

Scene One: Children's Home, Evening

Alicia *is doing her homework and eating a flapjack.*

Offstage **Sofia** *screams.*

Alicia *continues working and does not react.*

Sofia *emerges panicked, breathing deeply, with soaked Pikachu pyjamas and carrying some wet bedsheets.*

Pause.

Alicia   Pikachu? They're / Pikachu!

Sofia   Are there any bedsheets downstairs?

Pause.

Alicia   *Oi* can't help you.

Sofia   They're wet-through.

Alicia   Pikachu pyjamas int age appropriate! Give me your earbuds.

Sofia   No.

She walks away.

Alicia   Was it . . . the one where yew was drowning. The one where yew open your mouth, no words come out. The one where –

Sofia   Alicia ! I've got sheets with wee on them. Got it? I need / new ones.

Alicia   *Oi* can't / help.

Sofia   I'll have to drag / these downstairs.

Alicia   *Oi* int allow!

Sofia   And all the way up, if basket ain't there.

Alicia   Care worker say, 'Yew do your own, okay?' And *Oi* say 'yes'.

Sofia   She never meant you / can't tell me!

Alicia   We're responsible [for] our own bedsheets. We do it our [on our] own!

Sofia   She meant you make / your own bed!

Alicia   Responsible our own sheets! Is yew gorn borrow me your earbuds or / int yew?

Sofia   No!

Alicia   *Oi'm* doing maths! *Oi* need toons.

Sofia *walks away.*

Sofia   Bedsheets!

Alicia   You were in water.

Sofia *turns.*

Alicia   Nut deep water. Shallow. Yew can see your mum and dad speak [to] each other, but they *dussen't* hear yew, they nut speakun yew, they abandun yew.

Silence.

Oi int abandun yew.

Sofia *refers to the bedsheets.*

Sofia   That's not helpin' with these. How d'you know?

Alicia   Cos *Oi* int.

Sofia   No! Which nightmare it was! how d'you – how d'you know?

Alicia   *Oi* know yew.

Sofia *is sceptical. She's sizing* **Alicia** *up.*

Sofia   Where you been going after school?

Pause.

Alicia   *Oi* go in the mud.

Sofia   Don't come home till late.

Silence.

Say

Alicia   Say waa?

Sofia   Say.

Alicia   Say / waa?

Sofia   Answer innit.

Alicia   Yew dussen't ask nuffun. *Oi* told yew where *Oi* go. The mud. Yew int ask a / question.

Sofia   Where you been?

Alicia   'Don't come home till late' is a statement –

Sofia   O my –

Alicia   – int a question. 'Where yew bin?' Tha's question.

Beat.

River, *Oi* bin.

Sofia   Where? What part?

Alicia   Near Sizewell.

Pause.

Sofia   Saltmarsh.

Alicia *is bursting with the truth.*

Sofia   You smell of saltmarsh.

She realises it needs to be a question.

Okay. Have you been hanging out at the saltmarsh?

Alicia   Yes. Can *Oi* have / your earbuds?

Sofia   No.

Alicia *is bursting even more.*

Sofia   And there's something else.

She realises.

Jake. Have you been meeting Jake on the saltmarsh? I know you have.

Alicia   If yew know, why yew askun?

Sofia   Why didn't / you say?

Alicia   Promised Jake *Oi dussen't* say *Oi* been meeting him. And *Oi* int no liar girl.

Sofia   You just did.

Alicia   No. Yew guessed! Still hasn't said.

Sofia   Idiot. They're trying to put you in special needs school. Get excluded, they ain't bothered, fine, that's good enough for them.

Alicia   So. Probably *Oi* int roight for normal school.

Pause.

Oi still love yew. Big. Even though *Oi* see him. When Jake say he do suffun, he do.

Sofia   Me too.

Alicia   And *Oi* can do things with him waa *Oi* dussen't do with yew.

Sofia*'s unimpressed.*

Sofia   Good for / you.

Alicia   *Oi* show Jake. Yew and Parminder can do tha'. She's hot / on yew.

Sofia   I've weed the sheets. Where are the clean ones?

Alicia   *Oi* said [to] care worker *Oi* dussen't help!

Beat.

She passes a tampon to **Sofia**.

Sofia   Tampon?! What / you doin?!

Alicia   *Oi* know it's piss! But *Oi* know yew spent all your money again. And *Oi* know waa's coming up for yew.

Pause.

Sofia   Earbuds on my table, yeah.

Pause.

That means you can borrow them.

She turns and goes.

Here yeah, so you know, my clean PJs / are Sonic the Hedgehog.

Alicia   Int appropriate, Sofia! Int appropriate [for] / your age.

Sofia *laughs and walks off.*

Sofia   Here I go! Down the stairs what I probably don't need to go, yeah.

Alicia   Do yew –

Sofia   Yes! I love you. Big.

Scene Two: Classroom

Parminder, **Jake** *and* **Mel**. **Sofia** *and* **Ed** *are on different sides of the classroom, with* **Alicia** *between them.* **Sam** *is looking at some of* **Mel**'s *animal liberation leaflets.*

Ed *is eating crisps.* **Jake** *can't help but stare at the crisps.* **Ed** *offers some to* **Shaq**.

Shaq   Why's he staring? (*Referring to* **Jake**.)

Ed (*to* **Jake**)   Reach out.

Ed *offers,* **Jake** *doesn't take any.*

Ed   Reach out innit.

Shaq (*to* **Jake**)   What you waiting for?

Mel (*to* **Shaq** *and* **Ed**)   Leave him alone.

Sam   No eating in class. And if you were going to, why would you eat crisps?

She extends her hands and **Ed** *gives her the packet.*

Sam *refers to the leaflets.*

Sam   Nobody wants to see the state of these lambs.

Mel   / Free speech.

Sam   I'm taking these off you, Mel.

Parminder   It's the truth / Miss.

Sam (*to* **Parminder**)   It's triggering.

Beat.

Sam (*to* **Mel**)   You think it's a good idea giving these out. D'you want to be called in by the police?

Mel   Free speech.

Shaq *puts his hand up.*

Ed (*to* **Sam**)   My dad's was one of the farms robbed! How Mel know we was lambing this early?

Parminder   Shutup.

Shaq   Mel's Insta says milking cows is torture.

Mel   Shut yer gab!

Sam (*to* **Shaq**)   Leave it to the police. How'd you know it's animal liberation who've been robbing the animals? Radio said they found dead chicken parts on one farm.

Parminder (*to* **Ed** *and* **Shaq**)   / See.

Mel   Int me then, is it idiot? Int killin' / animals!

Ed   Don't mean nothing. Could've been foxes.

Parminder   Yeah, yeah. Could've been Demon Dog of Leiston. Fool.

Ed (*to* **Mel**)   If pulling cows' tits is torture yeah, how comes your mum's got that girlfriend?

Ed *and* **Shaq** *laugh.*

Mel   Whatever / Ed.

Parminder (*to* **Ed** *and* **Shaq**)   Shutup.

Sofia *whispers.*

Sofia (*to* **Alicia**)   That's what – Have you – you ain't been eating at home. You and Jake been robbin' farms ain't you?

Alicia   Yes.

Sofia (*to* **Alicia**)   You're getting catch. And expelled.

Alicia   Everything's Armageddon with yew. Well.

Beat.

Arma-gedding on with it.

She chuckles.

Sofia   Not even funny. Not even funny, yeah.

Shaq (*to* **Mel**)   You don't get gay sheep or chickens or nothing do you?

Mel   Fool.

Ed   Ain't / natural.

Shaq   Sex and gender are the same.

Parminder   Better tell your mum then.

Shaq   Why?

Parminder   Cos I had gender with her last night.

Parminder *and* **Mel** *laugh it up.*

Sam (*to class*)   Work!

Alicia *tries to show* **Sofia** *the maths booklet but* **Sofia** *ignores her.*

Alicia   Sofia, Sofia. What's the answer to this?

Ed (*to* **Alicia**)   Two.

Sam *turns round and* **Sofia** *stops talking.*

Sofia (*to* **Alicia**)   No –

Alicia (*to* **Ed**)   Is it?

Sam *puts her head down and continues looking at an exercise book.*

Sofia (*to* **Alicia**)   Heh, no.

Sam   Do your / work Sofia.

Ed (*to* **Alicia**)   Put what you want, it's your problem innit?

Sofia (*to* **Alicia**)   No! That's not –

Sam   Sofia!

Sam (*to class*)   Get your homework out. For those going to the library after school. I want no noise. I'm coming in to check.

She is looking at **Alicia**'s *work.*

Sam (*to* **Alicia**)   So, one third of the animals are goats in June's flock. The rest are sheep. There's twelve more sheep than goats. How many animals are there in June's flock?

Alicia *takes a moment to search her mind.*

Alicia   Two.

Ed *and* **Shaq** *laughing.*

Sam   Two. How is it two?

Pause.

Alicia   Sheep and goats.

Shaq   O / my gosh.

Ed   Dumb as a sheep.

He makes a sheep's baa sound.

Ed   Jake, Jake are you the robber?

Silence. **Jake** *looks up.*

Ed   Which farm you steal her off?

Shaq *and* **Ed** *laugh it up.*

Sam (*to* **Ed** *and* **Shaq**)   Enough! Okay! Both of you. See me at morning break tomorrow.

Sam (*to* **Alicia**)   You shouldn't be doing these. I didn't set these for you.

Sam *continues to collect the homework from the class. She stops at* **Jake**.

Sam (*to* **Jake**)   Jake. Where is it?

Jake *looks down and is silent.*

Sam *then continues to go round the class collecting the homework from the rest.*

Sam (*to everyone*)   Alright, get out you lot.

Class exits and goes to the library. **Sam** *stands over* **Jake**. **Alicia** *hangs back.*

Sam (*to* **Alicia**)   Can you leave please?

Alicia *goes and* **Sam** *turns to* **Jake**.

Silence.

Sam   Show me your work.

Silence.

Show me your work.

Silence.

Where is it?

Silence.

Jake. Answer.

Silence.

Sam (*to* **Jake**)   I give up! Detention! Walk out that door and I'll be straight on to your grandad.

Sam *exits the classroom.*

Scene Three: School Library

Sofia *is on one side of* **Alicia**. *Near* **Alicia** *on the other side are* **Mel** *and* **Parminder**. **Shaq** *and* **Ed** *are further away from* **Sofia**, **Alicia**, **Mel** *and* **Parminder**. **Alicia** *is intently reading. All the rest are studying with their textbooks and exercise books out.*

Parminder *puts her pen down, and sniffs her hands. She reaches into her bag.*

Mel   No. Your hands dussen't smell. Stop it.

Parminder's *brings out some perfume. She ignores* **Mel** *and sprays her hands.*

Mel   Stop it!

Parminder   Shhussh.

Mel   Yew up then last noight?

Parminder *returns the perfume to her bag.*

Parminder   Five times.

Mel   Can't go on loike tha'.

Sam *enters and starts walking over to* **Mel** *and* **Parminder**. **Sam** *hands some work back to* **Parminder**.

Sam (*to* **Parminder**)   Wrong work.

Parminder   Oh. Sorry.

She retrieves the correct work and gives it to **Sam**.

Alicia   Int no need for shame, Parminder.

Parminder   What?

Alicia   With your hands, red raw they are. With your gran being how she is.

Parminder   Keep out of it.

Sam *passes by* **Alicia** *and notices the book she's reading.*

Sam (*to* **Alicia**)   You reading that book?

Alicia   Yeah.

She carries on reading while **Sam** *watches.*

Sam   Give it 'ere. Give.

She looks inside and flicks through.

You can read this?

Alicia *doesn't respond.* **Sam** *sighs.*

Sam   Alicia. Even if you can, it's not appropriate for you.

Pause.

Somethings are safe for you to know and somethings are not. It's okay to learn about sex but it's got be in an appropriate context.

Pause.

Alicia   She's masturbating, tha' waa / she describing 'ere.

Ed   Oh shit!

Alicia   Tha' sex? [It's] Only her doinut.

Shaq   O my gosh.

Parminder (*to* **Ed** *and* **Shaq**)   Grow up.

Ed   You're nasty Alicia, yeah. Don't you know what's normal?

Shaq (*to* **Ed**)   Serious / man.

Parminder   Leave her alone.

Sam   Shutup all of you.

Sam (*kindly to* **Alicia**)   Anne Frank is for the A Level students. I'll get the PSHE lead to speak with you, okay?

Alicia   Girl in this book's thirteen. *Oi'm* older / than her.

Sam   There's things you can't understand like others. People'll take advantage of you. Shaq and Ed did it in class today.

Alicia   Masturbating. Dussen't need other people.

Sam   Heh. It's not your fault. Not at all. Okay?

Beat.

You should rethink. Take that place in the special needs school.

Alicia   No. It's my decision.

Sam   I'm trying to protect you, Alicia!

Beat.

Fine! Can you put this back on the shelf?

Pause. **Alicia** *does not move.*

Sam   Go on.

Reluctantly **Alicia** *gets up and shelves the book.*

Mel   Is yew gorn take my books off me? She can read tha'. Why yew giving her primary school books?

Sam   Melanie Thorpe. You're mum's a teacher. You're not. You don't get to decide who reads what.

She goes back to the classroom. **Alicia** *sits down, pauses and suddenly collects her books.*

Sofia   What you doing?

Alicia   Time she let Jake go.

She goes.

Sofia   You ain't gonna help Jake by kicking off at teacher.

Scene Four: Classroom

Sam *stands over* Jake.

Sam   What do you want me to do?

Silence.

You know, I'm gonna have to contact your grandad again.

Jake *stares at* **Sam**.

Silence.

Jake *bends down to open his school bag.*

Sam   Put your pen back. Put the exercise book back. You're not allowed to do your homework in detention. Not homework club, is it?

Jake *knocks everything off the table.*

Sam   Pick all that up.

Jake *clasps his hands round his ears.*

Sam   Pick it up.

Silence.

Jake!

Pause.

You've knocked those on the floor, so pick 'em up!

Jake *complies. But one pencil remains on the floor.*

Sam   Pick that pencil up!

She barks like a dog.

Pick it up!

She barks viciously. **Jake** *clasps his hands round his head tighter.*

Get your hands off your ears and pick it up.

She barks more viciously.

You listening to me? Am I gonna have to call your grandad?

She barks and snarls like a dog about to attack.

Alicia *arrives.*

Sam (*to* **Alicia**)   Get out.

Alicia   No.

She walks towards **Sam**. **Alicia** *and* **Sam** *confront each other.*

Silence.

Alicia   Detention finish five minut ago, Miss.

Sam *looks at her watch. And decides not to confront* **Alicia**.

Sam (*to both*)   Fine. I've got better things to do.

She leaves.

Jake   Look see, is yew hearing tha?

Alicia   Waa?

Jake   Sounds teacher making.

Alicia   Shouting.

Pause.

Jake   That all yew hear?

Alicia   Yeah.

Jake   Nuffen else.

Alicia   No. Waa she saying?

Silence.

Don't *moind* her. Let's have us some fun, *Oi'm* propa hungry.

Jake   We int done Shadwell farm yet.

Scene Five: The Farm

Alicia *and* **Jake** *enter the farm. It's raining heavily and windy as. They are hiding in the field with* **Luna**. **Luna** *is excited and* **Jake** *is trying to calm her.*

Two **Rottweilers** *circle in front of the piglet pen.*

Piglets snorting and squealing in alarm.

Jake *holds* **Luna**'s *collar.* **Luna**'s *ears prick up.* **Luna** *barks.*

Jake (*to* **Luna**)   Huld on, Luna girl! There. Pheasant.

Jake (*to* **Alicia**)   After Luna bolts, git piglet and git gorn! Luna's *moind* on tha' pheasant. All them guard dogs see a' Luna is enuff to bark and give chase.

Alicia   Give her the spell.

Jake *whispers the spell lovingly in* **Luna**'s *ears.*

Jake (*to* **Luna**)   An egret at dawn, a robin's songs worn all around me.

Luna *bolts.*

The **Rottweilers** *who were in front of the piglet pen gnash, bark and chase* **Luna**.

A kind of dance occurs where **Luna** *sniffs the dogs, evades them, gets spotted by them and evades them again. Whenever the* **Rottweilers** *near* **Luna** *they gnash and bark.*

They're communicating. When they get really near they go quiet. **Luna** *sniffs and evades but two further* **Rottweilers** *appear in front of her. They form a square around* **Luna**. **Luna**'*s blocked. She whimpers as the dogs close in.*

Jake   Go in shed / and git a' piglet.

Alicia   No!

Jake   Who see [to] these dogs?

He goes towards the dogs surrounding **Luna**. *They start barking at him.*

Alicia   Yew can't do nuffun with 'em. Luna'll / foind a way [out]

Jake   Git in shed!

The sound of piglet squeal comes from the shed. **Alicia** *goes towards the shed.*

Alicia   *Oi* hear suffun. *Oi* git veg 'stead

Jake   No.

Alicia   Spinach. Git yew some iron.

Jake   Waa?

Alicia *doesn't go into the shed but goes off into the spinach field.*

A **German Shepherd** *suddenly emerges where* **Jake** *and the other dogs are. This dog is particularly aggressive.*

Jake *stamps his foot at the dogs closing in on* **Luna**. *The dogs flinch before quickly re-grouping to bark and gnash again. The only farm dog that doesn't flinch is the* **German Shepherd**. *It's baring its teeth and ready to attack. The other dogs take their cue and gnash harder.*

Jake (*to* **German Shepherd**)   Okay, boi, yew rum are ya'? Yeah? Looking at me? Looking at me are yew, boi?

Jake *extends his arm making a fist. He walks towards the* **German Shepherd**.

Jake Tha' roight, boi!

He puts his arm and fist into the **German Shepherd**'*s mouth.*

Jake   There yew go, *boi*. Take a bite. Take a bite. C'mon take a bite.

The **German Shepherd** *withdraws and whimpers.*

Jake *turns to eyeball all the dogs who back down. The piglets are still making 'oink' sounds offstage.* **Jake** *walks towards the shed, where the sound of the piglets is. He draws out a butcher's knife and a hammer but stops as* **Luna** *has not run off.*

Jake   Git yew gorn Luna

Luna *barks.*

Jake   Go!

Luna *stays.*

Jake   Go!

Luna *bolts.*

Off stage an **Alsatian** *starts barking.*

Jake *walks off stage, i.e. to where the piglets are oinking.*

Scene Six: Tractor Shed

Chelle *and* **Rob** *are in the tractor shed with* **Beth**. **Chelle** *is looking over dog collars, while* **Rob** *is sharpening butcher knives.* **Chelle** *has an* **Alsatian** *at her side. The* **Alsatian** *is barking.*

Rob   Waa is it, boi?

Beth   Clever dogs, *Oi* got. Three a' them. Unchipped.

Chelle   Unchipped?

Beth   Feral. Vicious. Do waa you wan with them.

Rob   Waa is it with this dog?

Chelle   Bark over anything that one.

Chelle (*to* **Alsatian**)   Heh!

Alsatian *stops barking.*

Beth   Yew wan my dogs or nut? [I can] Git 'em 'morrow.

Silence.

Norfolk lads reckun they're whitest county in England. Yew got work [to] do catching up.

Pause.

Chelle's **Alsatian** *starts barking again.*

Chelle (*to* **Rob**)   Yew hear noise?

Chelle (*to* **Alsatian**)   Waa is it, boi? Eh?

Rob's *looking out from the tractor shed.*

Rob   Suffun' there, Can't see nuffun.

He jokes.

Maybe it's the Demon Dog!

Chelle (*to* **Alsatian**)   Waa is it now?

Rob   Kestrel?

Chelle   No kestrel staying tha' low for tha' long. Fox or suffun. Int a kestrel.

Chelle, Rob *and her* **Alsatian** *emerge from tractor shed.*

The **Alsatian** *becomes even more agitated.* **Rob** *puts on his binoculars.*

Rob   A lurcher over there. Ragged lurcher.

Chelle   Be chasing foxes then.

Rob   Suffun chasing it . . . our dogs.

When **Chelle** *says 'this ere dog's seen', this refers to her* **Alsatian** *by her side.*

Chelle (*to* **Rob**)   Huld on a minut.

Pause.

We bin robbed. Jake own a lurcher. [A] ragged lurcher. Int many own lurcher. Lurcher's distracting [the] dogs by the piglets, Jake can git in there, rob piglets an' git gorn. Clever Jake!

Beat.

[He's] bin watching. He know we took the sow out to boar. He know piglets alone. [He] Int stealing piglets with their bone-munching mums nearby, is he? Go and count [the] piglets.

Rob *departs.*

Beth *laughs.*

Beth   Looks loik yew [could] do with some propa dogs, [to] do a propa job.

Scene Seven: The Saltmarsh

Sizewell Nuclear Reactor is opposite. **Jake**'s *got a fire going. He is emotionally cold and still. He is looking out across the saltmarsh.*

Alicia *enters and sets the successfully snaffled vegetables down on the bank and laughs.*

Alicia   Why yew lookun' in river loik tha'?

Jake   Like waa.

Alicia   Way yew stand, yer bones are rememberin' suffun. Sofia's [the] same [as you].

She starts to jump between the solid bits of the saltmarsh.

Jake   Yew see Luna? Think they moight a' spot her.

Alicia   No. She's quick.

Jake *whistles.*

Jake   Luna-girl see nuffun [in] those woods. Half bloind she is.

Alicia   She int bloind.

Jake   Roight eye glaze grey.

Alicia   She see other universes, spirits all sorts outta tha' eye.

Jake *fries samphire.* **Alicia** *looks over to the forest.*

Alicia (*to* **Jake**)   Luna's sniffing her arse by beech tree.

Jake   Yeah?!

After his excited moment he quickly goes back to being cold and still.

Jake   Saw two farrowing crates on tha' farm. Call theirselves free range, they do, tha' farm. [And yet they're] Keeping sow in a cage.

Barking noise. **Jake**'s *dog* **Luna** *comes barking and leaping.* **Jake** *was cold, stiff and apparently unemotional before. He is effusive now and laughing.* **Luna** *shakes herself off and* **Jake** *gets wet.* **Alicia** *laughs.*

Jake   Luna!

He stands over **Luna**.

Jake (*to* **Luna**)   How many toimes *Oi* tell yew nut [to] soak me!

Alicia *laughs and starts jumping again between the multiple, different banks of the saltmarsh.*

Jake   They see Luna. They know it's me thieving.

Alicia   They int see Luna. Even [if] they see a lurcher, Luna int only lurcher in Suffolk.

She is still jumping. **Jake** *is butchering the piglet and frying it up.* **Alicia** *yelps as she misses her footing and gets wet and muddy.*

Jake *and* **Alicia** *laugh it up.*

Jake   Yew ever have trotter's ears?

Alicia   No.

Jake   Do it roight, they crispy [and] tasty. *Oi* want trotter's ears tonoight. Crispy tasty. Kill it, should eat every gland n' toe.

Luna *rolls over on her back, paws in the air and does the 'submit' pose.* **Jake** *scratches* **Luna**'s *tummy.*

Jake *strokes* **Luna**.

Luna *licks him.*

Jake *laughs.*

Jake (*to* **Luna**)   There yew go, girl, there yew go.

Alicia   Yew do your homework at moin tonight.

Jake *passes* **Alicia** *the food.*

Jake   No!

Alicia   How long we git away [with] this? Yew says [if] they see Luna, they know its yew, tha' waa yew say.

Jake   Yew say they *dussen't* see her!

Alicia *knows the answer to her next question.*

Alicia   Yew going back [to] your grandad?

Jake   No!

Alicia   Well then. A shed int no home.

Beat.

Only way out is yew do your homework, don't git excluded, and come into care home with me.

Jake   No.

Alicia   When you're sixteen, we can move out.

Beat.

Every day yew be gittin' detention cos yew int do [your] homework. Toime yew git 'ere it's too dark [to] do homework! So next day yew gittin' detention again! Either yew gittin' excluded from school, caught by police or both.

Beat.

No GCSE, no job, no room in Leiston togither. Dussen't yew wan [to] be with me?

Silence.

Oi need words, Jake. Need tellin'. Words connect up my brain. Make it work propa.

Jake *summons his best attempt.*

Jake   *Oi* think a lot [of] people be worse than yew.

Silence.

Oi duessen't *moind* being with yew. Cook samphire with animal for yew, dussen't *Oi*?

More **Jake** *and* **Luna** *cuddling.*

Jake   Why yew going on loik tha?

Alicia   You love Luna, cos yew dussen't have [to] tell her yew love her. She just go woof, you chuck her chicken, or suffun. Words, Jake!

Pause.

Oi wan tell social worker.

Jake   Yew dussen't say nuffun! They int' [gonna] catch me. Yew say Chelle dussen't know its Luna. No problem!

Alicia   Keeping secrets is a shed a shame!

Jake   You promise / nut tell no one!

Alicia   A shed a shame.

Jake   Yew promise [to] keep [it] secret. Yew says to me, '*Oi* int no little liar girl'!

Alicia   You int got /choice.

Jake   Yew says! *Oi* int go care home. Why you come here!

Silence.

Alicia   *Oi* know yew love me.

Jake   Yew git samphire cook, cos *Oi* think yew okay.

Alicia   More then tha'. Cos when yew say yew do suffun see, yew do it. If yew say yew gonna be somewhere, yew are. Yew loike a dog. Faithful.

She laughs.

Jake   *Oi* int no dog me! *Oi'm* a person. Nut no scrappin' bone-eating dog!

Alicia   Curl up loik a dog's / been beaten.

Jake   Int no dog.

Alicia   Loik! *Oi* never say yew was. Loik!

Pause.

Jake   Jus' for doing homework *Oi* go care home. Then *Oi* come back 'ere.

Alicia   You *dussen't* look in to tha' river you. Loik tha. Look loik yew seeing demons.

Jake   How yew know waa *Oi* see? See in my brain, can yew?

Pause.

Alicia   Everything you're lookin' for is lookin' at yew.

They're looking romantic.

Spud

They spud.

C'mon. Best git gorn.

Jake *gets ready to go.*

Pause.

Alicia   Jake. Me an' Sofia, waa's in her head, *Oi* know, [and] she know waa's in moin.

Jake   Waa yew on about? Who'se dawdlin' / now.

Alicia   She know yew live by saltmarsh.

Jake   No!

Alicia   Secret is for / shame, Jake.

Jake   Yew tell her.

Alicia   No. She guess.

Jake   Little liar girl is for lying.

Alicia   No. *Oi, Oi* – secrets / is for shame!

Jake   Little liar girl!

Luna *is whimpering.*

Alicia   *Oi* int lying.

Jake   Git gorn yew.

Alicia   She guessed!

Jake   Liar girl!

Alicia   No. / Yew don't get it.

Jake   Git gorn! Go! Go!

Alicia   Screw yew then.

She goes.

Yew int understand nuffun.

Luna *comes over to lick* **Jake**.

Scene Eight: Bus

The next morning. The bus stop and the bus. **Bus Driver** *is in the driver's seat.* **Alicia** *is sitting with* **Sofia** *on the bus.* **Sofia** *has a painting in a transparent folder.* **Rob** *is on the bus.* **Jake** *is at the bus stop. He is not on the bus yet. Gradually, when indicated below,* **Parminder**, **Mel**, **Ed**, **Shaq** *and* **Chelle** *get to the bus stop and on the bus. They will sit with people as the script indicates.*

Alicia *opens up the bag and gets a flapjack for* **Sofia**.

Alicia   Eat a propa breakfast next time. And don't let driver see.

Sofia   Why you still got condoms in your bag? Jake ain't even speaking to you.

Alicia   Just left 'em in there. He was practising. Without putting it in. Puttin' it on an' masturbating.

Sofia   It's called a posh wank, if you wanna know.

Alicia   A posh wank? Why they call it posh wank?

Sofia   Boys at posh schools do it.

Alicia   Yeah?

Sofia   Yeah. All the boys at Woodbridge.

Beat.

Alicia   Okay.

Pause.

Oi think *Oi* see my mum tonight. Yew *dussen't* start.

Sofia   You don't / need her.

Alicia   Everyone *Oi* wan [to] see, yew say *Oi* sharn't. Anyway, *Oi* int decided.

Ed *and* **Shaq** *get on.* **Chelle** *gets on. She will sit next to* **Rob**. **Parminder** *and* **Mel** *turn up.*

Parminder (*to* **Mel**)   Stand in front of me.

Parminder *gets on hiding her burger. They will sit next to each other.*

Mel (*to* **Sofia**)   How ya gittin on? Alroight?

Jake *gets on.*

Bus Driver (*to* **Jake**)   Take your hood off.

Pause.

Take it off.

Jake *puts hood down.* **Jake** *shows his bus pass and moves on.*

Bus Driver   Heh. Stop, give it 'ere.

He examines it.

Oi thank yew show me tha' propa. Thirwhistle? Tha' your name?

He returns pass.

Tell me the name, *Oi'll* tell yew the sort.

Ed (*to* **Jake**)   Bruv, / whatsup, bruv.

Jake *puts his earphones on and sits down.*

Shaq (*to* **Jake**)   What you listening to?

Mel (*to* **Parminder**)   Speak to her. She loike[s] yew. Just shy, she is.

Parminder (*to* **Mel**)   Do I look good?

Mel (*to* **Parminder**)   No. But yew int gorn look no better.

Parminder   Idiot.

Beat.

Parminder (*to* **Sofia**)   Sofia, let's see. Show us.

Sofia *shows her painting to* **Parminder**.

Parminder   Let me take it out.

Parminder *offers her burger to* **Sofia**.

Sofia *gawps.*

Parminder You need to hold the burger.

Eventually **Sofia** *does.*

Parminder Try it

Parminder *takes the folder.* **Sofia** *takes a bite.*

Parminder   Mel changed the soy mix.

She looks at the painting.

Wow.

Sofia   Just a painting.

Parminder *refers to the burger.*

Parminder   What d'you think?

Sofia   You're hot. It's hot, it's hot.

Parminder   Banged the chilli sauce on.

Alicia   *Oi'll* open the window.

Mel   It's freezing!

Alicia   Oh, yeah, no, *Oi* won't, *Oi* won't.

Mel *prods* **Parminder**.

Parminder (*to* **Mel**)   Okay!

Parminder *tries to act casual.*

Parminder (*to* **Sofia**)   D'you want to come to the vegan caff? If you want. Saturday. It's just a – thing, hang out . . .

Sofia   No.

Shaq *makes the sound of a plane crashing and burning.*

Parminder   . . . thing. Eat some lentils.

Mel (*to* **Parminder**)   Style / it, style it out girl.

Parminder (*to* **Sofia**)   Cool, cool, cool.

Ed (*to* **Jake**)   'A', 'A', 'A', what you listening to? Heh!

Shaq *knocks* **Jake**'s *cap off his head and picks it up before* **Jake** *can get it.*

Jake   Give it 'ere.

He keeps going for the cap, but **Shaq** *keeps evading him.*

Shaq   Is it? Is it? Take it, innit.

Shaq *baits him again but evades* **Jake**'s *lunges.* **Jake**'s *headphones and mobile drop.* **Ed** *picks them up and listens.*

Ed (*to* **Shaq**)   Not even on.

Shaq (*to* **Ed**)   No tunes.

Ed (*to* **Shaq**)   Nothing.

Shaq   Why you got headphones / on with no tune!

Alicia (*to* **Sofia**)   *Oi* int havin' tha.

Alicia *gets up.*

Jakes *grabs his phone and headphones back.*

Sofia *pulls her back.*

Sofia   / Stay out of it.

Alicia   / Bullying.

Shaq (*to* **Jake**)   Take your / headphones off.

Ed (*to* **Jake**)   Heh, heh.

Jake (*to* **Shaq** *and* **Ed**)   Piss off!

Ed   Found some bollocks.

Shaq   Cut 'em off that lurcher.

Jake   Luna's / a girl.

Ed (*to* **Shaq**)   He told you [to] piss off, bro.

Shaq (*to* **Jake**)   How about yeah, I put the dog down.

Jake (*to* **Shaq**)   No. Dussen't touch her, yew.

Shaq (*to* **Jake**)   Scrawny anyway, can't even keep him proper.

Ed (*to* **Shaq**)   Dog or his grandad.

Shaq *and* **Ed** *laugh.*

Shaq   Rude, nah man, rude.

Alicia *gets up.*

Ed   He's gonna cry, innit.

Sofia (*to* **Alicia**)   What are you doing?

Sofia *pulls* **Alicia** *down.*

Chelle (*to* **Ed**)   Yew lot, think you live Ipswich. Puttun on how you speak loik tha'.

Silence.

Speak loik tha' t' me now.

Silence.

Keep your gab shut, Shaq. Else, *Oi* put a dog prong round your neck. Electrocute ya, for fun. Maybe *Oi* do yew too, Ed.

Silence.

Chelle *moves nearer to* **Shaq**.

Chelle (*to* **Shaq**)   Bark.

Silence.

Chelle   Bark

Shaq *barks.*

Chelle   Now pant.

Shaq *pants.*

Chelle   With yer tongue out.

Shaq *pants with his tongue out.*

Chelle   Give me paw. Give me paw. Give!

Chelle'*s hand is open and relaxed when she extends her hand for* **Shaq** *to 'give paw'.* **Shaq** *gives* **Chelle** *his 'paw'. This is like a dog 'giving paw' to show its submitting to a human. This means* **Shaq** *puts his fingers on* **Chelle**'*s fingers.* **Shaq**'*s fingers go no further on to* **Chelle**'*s hand than that.* **Chelle**'*s hand remains relaxed.*

Chelle   Dussen't touch his lurcher, yew.

Chelle *returns to her seat next to* **Rob** *and beckons* **Jake** *over.*

Rob (*to* **Jake**)   Come 'ere, *boi.*

Pause.

Jake *goes to sit with* **Chelle** *and* **Rob**.

Chelle   Tell us about this lurcher. Only one person got a scruffy lurcher loik one *Oi* see on my farm yesterday, *Oi* think.

(*Whispers.*) Thief.

Silence.

She smiles.

Oi said tell us about this lurcher then.

Jake   She's mine / alroight.

Rob (*to* **Jake**)   Ah yew / alroight, *boi.*

Chelle   Who say *Oi* after your dog? If *Oi* wan, [to] *Oi* take her. Where yew git tha' lurcher? Cuppla grand them.

Jake   Why?

Beat.

Owner was beating her. *Oi* beat him. Then *Oi* took dog.

Chelle   Took his dog?

Jake   And Alsatian and Staffy.

Chelle   Yew have got some bollocks.

Jake   Give other two rescue home.

Chelle   Waa yew go school for? Why *dussen't* yew jus' bunk off?

Pause.

Least yew can do is have a conversation with me after raiding my dad's farm.

Pause.

Jake   Been boning cows heads since *Oi* was ten. Need GCSE[s].

Chelle   Yew?

Jake   Work EDF, Sizewell.

Chelle   [Yew] can't hardly wroight.

Beat.

My dad says yours and 'im were on tour togither.

Chelle *asks* **Jake** *whether he's got a tattoo.*

Chelle   Bin inked?

Jake   No.

Chelle   Forces let your family down. 'Britain First' they said, nut yew or me though. Born poor in Suffolk loik us, how much chance yew got? Nut loike Shaq. Them Muslims. Take your job. Now they wanna kill your dog, take your house.

Rob   Jake int living there tho'.

Chelle   No. We bin askun around, boi. We know.

Beat.

Waa yew see in tha' girl yours?

Jake   Not my girl.

Beat.

Chelle *sniffs* **Jake**.

Chelle   Smell a' saltmarsh. You bin living feral? Have ya, *boi*?

Beat.

Git yourself round my farm tonoight.

Pause – **Jake** *isn't sure.*

Oi int tell police nuffun.

Beat.

Oi'd a tell 'em already if *Oi* waa going 'oo.

Beat.

Oi got plan for yew. Won't be living [on the] saltmarsh, or having put up with this school no longer.

Alicia *sits behind* **Parminder** *and* **Mel***. She stares at them and they at her.*

Parminder   What?

Alicia   Yew dussen't need to be ashame. Everyone deserve [to] have fun. Sofia loike yew.

Parminder   What you on about?

Alicia   *Oi* heard yew in library. *Oi* know waa its loike t' care for people.

Parminder   Nothing to / do with you.

Alicia   Spraying perfume on your hands [to] git rid a' smell urine / and faeces.

Parminder   / Shutup.

Mel (*to* **Alicia**)   What yew doin?

Ed (*to* **Shaq**)   What they on about?

Parminder   / Can you shut up?

Alicia   Nuffun wrong with waa / yew do!

Parminder   Shut / up!

Alicia   *Oi* help Sofia when she do it –

Sofia   No!

Alicia (*to* **Sofia**)   Yew say show empathy.

Ed (*to* **Shaq**)   Sofia craps herself?

Shaq (*to* **Ed**)   / Gross.

Parminder (*to* **Alicia**)   / Go! Just go.

Mel   Piss off, Alicia.

Ed   Sofia, yew crap / yourself?

Sofia (*to* **Ed**)   / No.

Shaq   Errrrr. She does.

Alicia (*to* **Shaq**)   No, / no, it's wee!

Shaq (*to* **Sofia**)   You crap / the bed.

Alicia (*to* **Shaq**)   / It's wee!

Ed (*to* **Sofia**)   Tha' waa you do [in] your country?

Sofia (*to* **Alicia**)   I can't believe you / said that.

Mel (*to* **Parminder**)   Can't believe she said that.

Alicia (*to* **Sofia**)   We gotta talk about / our problems!

Parminder   I'm gonna / deck her.

Mel (*to* **Parminder**)   No.

Alicia (*to* **Parminder**)   Nut keeping secrets!

Parminder *tries to deck* **Alicia**. **Mel** *grabs her back.*

Bus Driver (*to* **Alicia**)   / *Oi* stop this bus, *Oi* will.

Parminder (*to* **Mel**)   / Get off.

Bus Driver   Shutup, the lot of yer.

Alicia *puts her hands over her ears.* **Bus Driver** *stops the bus and walks over.*

Sofia (*to* **Alicia**)   What's / wrong with you?

Bus Driver (*to* **Alicia**)   Bother yew cause, yew do.

Sofia (*to* **Alicia**)   Your mum's not coming. She don't care / about you.

Bus Driver (*to* **Alicia**)   Troublemaker!

Sofia (*to* **Alicia**)   No one does. I don't.

Bus Driver *stands over* **Alicia** *shouting.* **Jake** *gets up and walks towards* **Alicia**.

Bus Driver (*to* **Alicia**)   Hands off your ears. *Oi* should put you off here – get your hands off those ears! – get your – you listening? Get your hands off them ears.

Bus Driver (*to* **Jake**)   Waa yew want?

Jake *sits next to her.*

Jake (*to* **Alicia**)   Everything yew looking for is looking at yew.

Bus Driver   Get off bus, both of ya.

Jake *repeats.*

Jake (*to* **Alicia**)   Everything yew looking for is looking at yew.

Bus Driver *pulls* **Alicia** *and* **Jake** *off the bus, and they walk on.*

Bus Driver (*to* **Sofia**)   *Yew* can git off in all. *Oi* int jokun'. Move.

Bus Driver (*to rest*)   Rest a' *yew* lot, keep *gab* shut.

Sofia *gets off too and lags behind.*

Pause.

Alicia   Waa tha' Chelle wan?

Jake   *Oi* still want to git tha' houseshare. *Oi* thought *Oi* best say. After last noight. One tha' take Luna and us. *Oi* dussen't loike her living feral.

Alicia   Your dog hate tha'.

Jake   She knows how to foind dry place. Foind tha' shed for me, she do.

Alicia   So. Waa tha' Chelle wan' then?

Jake   Jus' talkun 'bout dogs cos Shaq threaten [to] put Luna down.

Alicia   How come tho?

Jake   She's got dogs. She loikes dogs, *Oi* reckun.

Alicia   Waa she want?

Jake   Nuffun.

Alicia   Dussen't know we rob her farm then?

Pause.

Jake   No.

Pause.

Alicia   My mum ask to see me tonoight.

Pause.

Oi think *Oi* say 'yes'.

Jake   If yew wan'.

Alicia   After samphire.

Alicia *turns round to look at* **Sofia** *lagging behind.*

Sofia   What you looking at?

Alicia   Yew!

Alicia (*to* **Jake**)   Box her head in, *Oi* oughtta. Sofia say 'show empathy'. So *oi* do. And she goes off all bazonkers on me!

Scene Nine: Saltmarsh, Sunset

Mary   Could've met in a cosy coffee shop.

Alicia   Why yew wearing tha' necklace?

Mary   Just wear it. Freezing.

Alicia   Don't drink coffee me. Over there is Sizewell, where *Oi* gorn work. *Oi* weren't gorn see yew today, *Oi'm* busy, *Oi* got lots [to] do these days.

Mary   Glad you did. Heh. Come here. Got some pics.

Alicia   What of?

Mary   I'll show you!

Alicia   D'yew loike it, 'ere?

Mary   Yeah, yeah, just a bit cold! But yeah, it's / beautiful.

Alicia   Take tha' necklace off.

Mary   No.

Alicia *bends down to the samphire.*

Alicia   Yew can eat samphire.

Pause.

You had a few wrong uns int yer, Mum.

Mary   Men?

Alicia   *Oi* int goin' on at yew.

Pause.

Oi met someone.

Mary   Oh yeah.

Beat.

Boy, girl, they, I don't mind.

Alicia   Not your place to *moind*! Take tha' off.

Mary   You just tell me when you wanna say whatever.

Pause.

Alicia   His name's Jake.

Mary   Sloppy teenage snogs is it?

Alicia   Yew having a go. Yew / making fun a me?

Mary   No / love.

Alicia   If *Oi* wan' boyfriend *Oi* have one.

Mary   Just / trying –

Alicia   Yew dussen't stop me.

Mary   Okay, jus' trying to enjoy the time we got. Have a little fun before I die kind of thing.

Alicia   We don't kiss – with tongues anyway. *Oi* dussen't loike tha'.

Mary   That's okay, you're growing.

Alicia   Int asking yew. They say *Oi* sharn't, cos how Oi am. But tha' int my fault. *Oi* reckun, *oi* remember yew drinkin' from womb.

Mary   Nowadays, ginger n' lemon tea is all.

Alicia   Jake loike samphire too.

Pause.

Mary   I tried protecting you, when you were in the womb. And after. I was in too much pain to handle, Alicia. So I drunk.

Beat.

I can see your raptor senses lighting up. You can trust me.

Pause.

Alicia   *Oi'm* in trouble.

Pause.

Oi gotta keep a secret *Oi* dussen't wan 'oo.

Mary   It's not good to have secrets.

Alicia   But *Oi* sharn't break a promise. Sharn't lie. It's Jake.

Beat.

He was living his grandad, see. But his grandad say things too him waa split his head, call him 'little shit'. And worse. Mum left his dad, then his dad left.

Pause.

Mary   What's the secret?

Alicia *looks at* **Mary** *accusingly.*

Alicia   No. Yew let me down. How many toime? Breakun promises.

Mary   I was crap.

Pause.

You share in your own time.

Pause.

C'mon, c'mon. Look at these. Brought 'em for you to see. This lot are lifesavers! The commune women I live with.

Alicia *looks at the photos.* **Mary** *shows her another.*

Mary   And this one . . . .

Alicia   A deer!

Mary   Yeah, loads up in Holkham. Big herds.

Alicia   Tha' how close yew git!

Mary   / Yeah.

Alicia   No way!

Mary   I've been talking to your social worker.

Alicia   No. Int ser loikley. You an' a / social worker.

Mary   And the school. I'm ready to take you back.

Beat.

It's true.

Pause.

Alicia   *Oi'm* sixteen. *Oi* decide now. Nut social worker.

Mary *shows her more photos.*

Mary   That's the spare room.

She offers **Alicia** *the photo to hold in her hands. She doesn't take it.*

Mary Those deer are from the window. I printed the photos. So you can feel them in your hands. Let's you know they're real. I know you like that. I won't let you down again.

Alicia *takes the photo.*

Alicia You talk Suffolk, 'Int ser loikely'. Talk like that, people think you're stupid enough anyway. You wanna watch that.

Mary *laughs.*

Mary After I had you, social worker said – thought I couldn't hear – 'loves her drugs more than her daughter'.

Beat.

I've always loved you.

Alicia *gives the photo back to* **Mary**.

Alicia *Oi* probly done some things *Oi* sharn't do, yew know with Jake. If *Oi* say waa secret is, tha' make me a little liar girl, cos *Oi* promise Jake.

Mary Go on.

Alicia If *Oi* dussen't, [tell, I'll] git in worse bother with school or police probly.

Mary / Oh, love.

Alicia Now *Oi* think he was doin' lyin', cos, cos he was talkin' to this girl, Chelle. And she's bad news her. And her cousin. If he's talkin' [to] them too, he be gittin' in worse bother.

Pause.

Mary I know what I done wasn't good. But there's a difference between a decision and a choice, know what I mean? I don't think you can choose to do something you know is bad for you. You can decide to do it. But that's a lack of options. Not a choice. Don't think those daughter-grabbing social workers get that. You ain't got proper choices. Come and live with me, eh?

Pause.

Alicia Take tha' necklace off.

Mary Why? You speak how you want. I didn't mean that earlier.

Alicia Shame. You trying to shame me for my words, how *Oi* speak. Yew say 'people think you're stupid enough anyway'. Shaming tha' is!

Mary Sorry, okay, sorry.

Pause.

You're fine as you are. Great, I mean.

Alicia Take off tha' necklace.

Mary No.

Silence.

Alicia   Say suffun good about me.

Pause.

Mary   I love you.

Alicia   No! Say suffun good about me.

Pause.

Take off your necklace.

Mary   No. Why am I gonna do that? That's Declan.

Beat.

I always keep my necklace / on.

Alicia   No. No you don't. Tha' /a lie.

Mary   Don't worry / about that.

Alicia   Roight 'ere you be lying. And yew call me a 'a little liar girl'. Yew a little liar!

Mary   / No.

Alicia   *Oi* see them photos. *Oi* int see no necklace.

Mary   He was my son.

Alicia   *Oi* know why you wear it. *Oi* love Declan. Not my fault. Yew blaming a four-year-old, *Oi* was then. Yew was out on drink an' drugs.

Mary   I'm not letting go / of him.

Alicia   Every time yew see me, yew be wearing tha'. Yew know that necklace trigger me.

Mary   It's past / now.

Alicia   Take it off then.

Mary   / I can't.

Alicia   *Oi* gave Declan headache pills cos *Oi* seen yew takin'em! After your brandy! All the toime!

Mary   You lied –

Alicia   Yew / weren't waking up.

Mary   You shoulda shook me. Used to bang the pot n' pans / all times a day.

Alicia   *Oi* was scared.

Mary   And when you did wake me, you lied about what happened.

Alicia   Don't say tha'. Don't / say tha', Mum.

Mary   You said you never give him pills. Hid in that shed.

Alicia   *Oi* was four!

Mary You lied.

Alicia Yew int got tha' necklace in none of them photos.

Mary So.

Alicia But everytoime you seen me last eight years yew wear it. Go!

Mary No, I – I – wear it so I can have all my family together.

Alicia Go! *Oi'm* saying yew to go. *Oi* know waa *Oi* feel. And *Oi* wan' yew to go.

Mary Alicia, you're not –

Alicia Don't contact me.

Mary Don't be / like that.

Alicia *Oi'm* stopping contact. You're dead!

Mary / No.

Alicia Dead!

Scene Ten: Forest

Jake *is by an oak tree. Twilight. A dog barks from the forest and* **Jake** *is nervous, frenetic even.*

Luna *is looking at* **Jake** *as the dog continues.*

Jake Waa?

Luna *whines.*

Jake It's okay, Luna-girl.

Jake *sees red eyes amidst the branches in the dark. He blanches.*

Luna *gripes.*

Jake Tha' alroight girl.

A menacing growl emerges from where the red eyes are.

Jake *grabs his butcher's knife.*

Luna *jumps at* **Jake** *and starts pawing and licking him.*

The eyes disappear, barking stops, and they pensively wait, until the red eyes appear elsewhere.

Jake *turns frantically to try and see where the barking is.*

Gnashing sounds and red, demon eyes.

A **German Shepherd** *appears. It's the same* **German Shepherd Jake** *faced off with on the farm. But this time it's got* demon *eyes and ears pricking preternaturally up. Think the demon dog in Spike Lee's* Summer of Sam.

Demon Dog *gnashes, growls and barks throughout this segment. How and when are worked out in rehearsal.*

Demon Dog   Yew little shit.

Jake   No. / Noooo.

Demon Dog   Is yew a little shit?

Jake   No.

Demon Dog *approaches.*

Jake   *Oi* int! *Oi* int!

Demon Dog   Is yew a little shit?

Luna *whines.*

Demon Dog *gnashes – this gnash has to be here because it precedes* **Jake** *submitting – what the submission 'pose' is is worked out in rehearsal.*

Jake *submits.*

Jake   *Oi'm* a little shit. *Oi'm* a little shit.

Demon Dog *gnashes.* **Luna** *whines.*

The sound of other barking dogs. **Demon Dog** *goes silent.*

Chelle *emerges with two of her* **Rottweilers***, and the* **Demon Dog** *morphs back into the* **German Shepherd***.*

Chelle   *Oi* says yew come farmhouse! If *Oi* can foind yew, how easy's tha? Even my daft dogs [can] smell your stink.

Jake*'s looking at the* **German Shepherd***, as it plays with the rottweilers.*

Chelle   Heh. Heh. Waa yew lookun at?

Beat.

Waa? this one?

She pats the dog.

Boo Boo. Expect yew met him anyhow, when yew robbed me piglet! Why int yew come?

She bends down to stroke the **German Shepherd***.*

Chelle (*to* **German Shepherd**)   C'ome 'ere, Boo Boo.

The dog starts nuzzling into **Chelle** *playfully.*

Chelle   Lookun scared, boi. No wonder. Hanging round [this] forest [at] twilight. [Yew] got demons in your head, boi. Scared a' everything.

Pause.

Oi ['d] be scared [if], *Oi* was yew. Police know it's yew, my dad [told me] say. [If you] come see me, yew int gorn be bothered by no police, no more. Else yew be in a jail cell [with] your demons.

Jake   O'll think 'bout it.

Chelle   Think? Yew know, *your* girl gorn see her mum, int she? *Oi* see her. On way 'ere.

Beat.

Yew think she gorn hang round yew? She know she git in bother [with] yew.

German Shepherd *jumps up for a cuddle n' nuzzle and* **Chelle** *responds affectionately.*

Chelle (*to* **German Shepherd**)   Heh! Alroight, boi.

Chelle (*to* **Jake**)   This one's a roight devil.

Chelle (*to* **German Shepherd**)   Int yew.

Jake *withdraws sharply, but recovers his poise.*

Chelle *advances to* **Jake**. **German Shepherd** *does not.*

Chelle   When *Oi* say, yew come see me, tha' how yew do. *Oi'll* expect yew 'morrow.

She walks away but turns.

O! Stay off school. Otherwise *Oi* think yew be in cop shop fore 'morrow evening. [You'd] be no use [to] me then, boi.

She walks away and makes a phone call.

Chelle (*to* **Rob**)   Rob. *Oi* found 'im. *Oi* got a job for yew.

Luna *jumps up on* **Jake** *to lick him, and* **Jake** *holds her close.*

Jake   It's alroight, it's alroight, Luna-girl.

He laughs because **Luna***'s still licking him.*

It's okay, Luna.

Beat.

Oi'm hungry, girl. Yew gorn have [to] foind me a pheasant.

Jake *whispers the spell lovingly in* **Luna***'s ears.*

Jake   An egret at dawn, a robin's songs worn all around me.

Luna *bolts off.*

Scene Eleven: Forest

Luna*'s sniffing around. Night-time.*

Rottweiler One *is circling.*

Luna *hears a noise. She stands up and her ears prick up.*

Luna*'s more wary now.*

Rottweiler One *closes in on* **Luna**.

A kind of dance occurs where **Luna** *sniffs* **Rottweiler One**, *evades it, then gets spotted by it, and evades it again. Whenever* **Rottweiler One** *nears* **Luna**, **Rottweiler One** *gnashes and barks. When* **Rottweiler One** *is really near* **Luna**, *it goes quiet.*

Rottweiler Two *emerges and starts barking.*

Rottweiler One *starts barking too, as though they're communicating with each other.*

Both close in on **Luna**.

Luna *moves towards* **Rottweiler Two**, *because* **Rottweiler One** *closes in on her.*

Luna's *looking right at* **Rottweiler Two** *closing in on her but can't see her.* **Rottweiler Two** *can see her though.*

At the last **Luna** *evades* **Rottweiler Two**, *and* **Rottweiler One** *but unwittingly runs near to the* **German Shepherd** *that emerges into the audience's sight, and out of the shadows.*

Rottweiler Two *closes in on* **Luna** *from one side. The* **German Shepherd** *is on the other.*

Luna *can't see the* **German Shepherd**, *and walks right into his sight. Now* **Luna** *can.* **Luna** *whines. The* **German Shepherd** *is gnashing and barking with ferocity.*

Rottweiler Two *and* **One** *surround her barking and* **Luna** *whines more.*

The **German Shepherd** *closes in.* **Luna** *faces her and rolls over on her back in the 'submission' pose she's done before with* **Jake**.

Pause.

The **German Shepherd** *does not attack* **Luna**. *The* **German Shepherd** *eats her. Tummy first.*

After the **German Shepherd** *has eaten for a while* **Rob** *enters.*

Rob   Tha's enough, Boo Boo, leave suffun for Jake to foind.

The **German Shepherd** *doesn't desist.*

Rob   Heh!

He drops a dog-toy in front of the **German Shepherd** *which the dog playfully takes in its mouth, while the* **Rottweilers** *bark for attention.*

Scene Twelve: Forest, Before Dawn

Jake *is walking in the forest trying to find* **Luna**. *It's night-time. And raining.*

Jake *whistles.*

Jake   Where are ya? Luna! Luna-girl!

Beat.

Luna!

He sees **Luna***'s head. He collapses to his knees. He puts his hands on his ears like he did when* **Sam** *had him in detention. He crosses his legs and rocks back and forth. He lets out a low, quiet, squeal.*

Jake *starts hitting his head with his hand, as he rocks back and forth.*

Scene Thirteen: Outside the Classroom

Alicia *is sitting down alone.* **Mel** *enters.*

Mel   Why [did] Jake do tha' damage [on] Shaq's house?

Alicia   He think Shaq's killed his dog.

Mel   [That] about as loikley as the demon dog of Leiston.

Alicia   Why yew talkin' [to] me?

Mel   Cos *Oi* know [about] police. Takin' my leaflets off me, an' all sorts.

Beat.

Teacher gonna call yew in. If she say yew gotta go police station, they int got roight t'question yew without [an] appropriate adult. Okay. Remember that. Cos a' your special needs.

She leaves.

Sofia *exits the classroom and stands in front of* **Alicia***. They look at each other in silence.*

Sofia   Just so you know, you're still a dickhead.

She sighs and goes to sit with **Alicia***.*

Sofia   I never tell teacher nothing, yeah. Don't react when you go in.

Alicia   *Oi* saw the therapist Friday. She say *Oi'm* impulsive. *Oi* never punch her.

Sofia   You're not impulsive. Don't take that!

Beat.

Alicia   So *Oi* should punch her?

Sofia   No!

Beat.

And you don't have rejection sensitivity disorder either.

Alicia   *Oi* do. *Oi am* sensitive. She say *Oi'm* developmentally delayed. This time she held my hand when she say it. *Oi* git even more angry. But *Oi* never hit her

Sofia   Good.

Alicia   Chucked my Diet Coke on her, see.

Sofia   / Alicia!

Alicia   So obvious, *Oi* got tha' rejection disorder.

Sofia   Knowing when someone's not on your side's a skill. It's your raptor brain. Just gotta learn what to do with it.

Alicia   Sometoime my senses work' propa, innut. When *Oi* been gittin' love, [I] feel safe.

Pause.

D'yew love me?

Sofia   Yes. Big.

Alicia   How big?

Sofia   This big.

Sofia *moves to hug* **Alicia**. **Alicia** *rejects the hug in a perfunctory fashion.*

Alicia   No hugging!

Sofia   Okay.

Scene Fourteen: Tractor Shed

Chelle *is inking* **Rob** (*i.e. giving him a tattoo*).

Rob   *Oi* had [to] spend propa hours cleaning blood off tha' German Shepherd.

Beat.

After he's seen tha' dog dead. Almost dislocated his shoulder, tryin' [to] batter Shaq's door down.

Chelle *laughs.*

Chelle   He'll come. Where else he go?

School

Inside the classroom. There is a can of Diet Coke on the table.

Sam   Police'll have Jake soon enough. You say where he is, what you done with him, I think I can get you out of bother.

Silence.

He's going youth offenders' institute.

Pause.

How do you think this is gonna end for you? I saw the condoms in your bag. He's using you. None of this is your fault. Police won't see it like that though.

Silence.

Alicia   *Oi* need to study, miss. / Can I go?

Sam   Where is he? And don't lie to me.

Alicia   *Oi* int no little liar girl!

Sam   Tell me / then.

Alicia   You hear!

She picks up the can.

Sam   Okay!

Pause.

Breathwork. Put it down.

Pause.

Alicia *does her breathwork.*

She puts the can down.

Sam   Good.

Tractor Shed

There's four empty beer bottles. **Jake**'s *got his baseball cap on.*

Jake *enters.*

Chelle   Sit.

She offers **Jake** *a chair near some beer bottles.*

Chelle   Sit.

Jake *sits. He's nervous and hyper-alert.*

Chelle   Best hope Ipswich Youth Court. Worst Crown Court. *Oi'll* tell you suffun, Chelle boi – wear tha' cap in court, you're guilty.

Chelle (*to* **Rob**)   Rob. Take them bottles. Put 'em in cellar.

Rob   Waa? Muslim, is he?

Chelle *laughs.*

Chelle (*to* **Rob**)   [I'll] Electrocute *yew* with tha' dog prong. Cheeky.

Rob *takes the beer bottles away.*

Chelle (*to* **Jake**)   They call it alerting behaviour. Too many sounds make you hyper, so yew wear earbuds, block it out. Jus' loik sight of alcohol. Git yew nervous. *Oi* used [to] be [the] same. My dad dussen't drink now.

Beat.

Tha' girl a' yours, be shopping yew [to] police now. *Oi* guarantee it. My dad [will] call' em off if yew wan'. Listen [to] my dad, coppers do.

Beat.

They int bother yew, if yew with us.

School

Alicia   *Oi* wan [to] go.

Sam   You can't.

Beat.

I told the police you're special needs.

Beat.

Well, you are. Police'll go easy if we say he's manipulating you. But you've gotta tell 'em it was him, how you robbed the farms, and where he is.

Silence.

Alicia, are you listening? You don't want this trouble.

Alicia   *Oi* say where he stay, and waa happen, then *Oi* int git arrested?

Sam   Yeah but –

Alicia   *Oi* wan normal loife, like others. Job at Sizewell / *Oi* want.

Sam   Love, you're not getting a job there. There's places – Sainsbury's got a scheme – for those with disabilities.

Alicia   Yew sayin' *Oi'm* / disabled.

Sam   Difficulties, learning, processing.

Alicia   *Oi* got – *Oi* – *Oi* got different way yew know, a' thinkin'.

Sam   You agree to go to the special needs school in Ipswich, say it was Jake's fault. Everything'll be okay.

Pause.

Alicia   Yew always sayin' suffun wrong me, if yew on my soide see, yew int do tha'.

Sam   I am!

Alicia   Yew int. *Oi* gotta raptor brain. If police [could] prove anythink *Oi* be in cop shop.

Sam   They're gonna find out whether you / say or not.

Alicia   Yew *dussen't* loike me, yew wanting me outta this school.

Sam   I do like you. Else, I'd have let you go off with that Coke can just now. Itching you were.

Tractor Shed

Jake   *Oi* says, *Oi* says *Oi* move in with her.

Chelle   Got money, have ya?

Jake   Gonna work at Sizewell.

Chelle *and* **Rob** *laugh.*

Rob   Sizewell, he say. EDF energy. Them jobs go the Asians with the tech skill, live in Martlesham *innut*.

Beat.

Chelle   *Oi* need yew train some dogs for me. Feral. Unchipped.

Jake   Tha' it.

Chelle   No.

Beat.

See this. Waas it say?

Chelle *rolls up her sleeve.*

Jake   EDF.

Chelle   Int Sizewell, *boi*. Not that EDF. This is English Defence Force. Join us.

Jake   Waa you need unchipped dogs for?

Chelle   People we need to set 'em on. People be turning Suffolk Muslim. Start with Shaq and his dad [if] yew wan. Up to yew. Was sayin' he'd put your lurcher down.

School

Sam (*Kindly*)   Tell me where he is.

Pause.

It's not your fault, you can't get on in this school, or that Jake gets away with what he wants with you. Don't feel guilty about it.

Alicia   Waa?

Beat.

Say again.

Sam   Don't feel guilty.

Beat.

Police'll take you in, Alicia! They'll manhandle you, claim you're resisting arrest, speak to you without a social worker, cos they get away with it.

Beat.

Your brain didn't grow properly in the womb, cos of the alcohol.

Beat.

It's a reality.

Beat.

You're vulnerable. You've been manipulated.

Pause.

You like this Jake? Was he aggressive? Did he promise you things? We've talked /
about this, haven't we?

Alicia   Can *Oi* go?

Sam   Are you sexually active? You got seen in your school uniform few days back
being physical with him by Loompit Lake.

Alicia   Physical?

Sam   Not appropriate.

Pause.

Alicia   *Oi* do my homework first. Int yew allow to have sex in school uniform?

Sam   You're sexually active aren't you?

Alicia   Not very active at all. Mostly, *Oi* loik chilling when *Oi* do it. *Oi'm* on me
back, or there's / other things we do you know.

Sam   Okay, okay. Alicia –

Alicia   Or me front.

Sam   Is that appropriate? There were condoms in your bag. Did you have sex with
him? Are you sexually active?

Pause.

Alicia   *Oi* don't know.

Sam   Consent! what I say about you? Consent! How can you actually consent to sex
if you don't know if you've had it?!

Alicia   Yew confusing me.

Sam   If I am, what about Jake?

Alicia   We used a condom.

Sam   He put you under pressure? Did he wear one before you had intercourse? Did
you think that meant he loves you? Cos he used a condom?

Alicia   No. *Oi* just wondered why.

Sam   Why?! You wondered why he used a condom?!

Alicia   Yeah.

Pause.

Sofia said it's called a posh wank.

Beat.

Boys at private school do it. They got loads of weird traditions at Woodbridge, don't they?

Beat.

Think he was practising how to put it on.

Tractor Shed

Chelle (*to* **Rob**)   Rob. Warm tha' stew up.

Chelle (*to* **Jake**)   She be making plans to leave you jus' loik your mum, and your dad. Where you be then, *boi*?

Beat.

Yew never choose live feral, steal animals. Yew call making a choice yew know is gonna do you harm a choice? Self-harm, *innut*.

Beat.

Yew int had [a] choice. Yew had to rob this 'ere farm, didn't yew? Shaq's dad's got shop, cash n' carry. Own tha' cab firm in Ipswich too. That Shaq's family got lot 'oo answer for. Waa they done [to] your dad.

Beat.

Your dad treat you bad. That's all he could do. Went off to war to foight the Muslims. Then a Muslim screws him over here too. Takes away his job. How many Mussers work in tha' cab firm?

Pause.

Jake   *Oi* look in river, sometoime. And see a dog. Red eyes barking. Dad used to chain me up with angry dogs when he go drinkin'. *Oi* try an' block 'em out.

Chelle   Set them dogs on Shaq an' his dad. Tha' pain yew got make yew angry. Use it on Shaq. *Oi* can keep yew. When you're with us, this Alicia girl, she duessen't, she marn't know. Not kind of work we do. You marn't see her anymore. No way.

Beat.

Waa yew say?

Pause.

If *Oi* wan' *Oi* could say, yew join us or we shop yew 'oo police. But *Oi* int do tha'. Kind of work we got, need commitment, int do it 'cos *Oi'm* blackmailing yew. Join us, not out of fear. Cos yew believe. Cos you're with us.

Pause.

Jake   No. No.

Beat.

Alicia's my girl, see. No.

School

Sam   You're not capable of making these decisions

Alicia   *Oi dussen't* know waa *Oi* feel?

Sam   You think you do.

Alicia   Tha' waa yew say?

Sam   He's taking advantage.

Alicia   Tha' be abuse! Only abuser say your feelings and words int roight [to] git waa they wan'. Tha' waa yew doin' now. Abuse! Abuse!

Beat.

Yew take my words off me in library too! Took my Anne Frank book!

Sam   Alicia –

Alicia   Just cos it got masturbation in it. Natural tha' be. Why / can't *Oi* do waa natural.

Sam   Alicia –

Alicia   You git spotted in Southwold drunk with your tongue in some / woman's mouth. Not your wife.

Sam   Not appropriate, Alicia.

Alicia   And your hands were –

Sam   Alicia!

Alicia   Yew even split / up [with] your wife?

Sam   Boundaries!

Alicia   Yew tell her truth? Int jus' me keepin' secret.

Beat.

Just because you're a lesbian, doesn't mean you're less of a being.

She laughs.

Sam   It's not funny, Alicia.

Alicia   Everyone know everyone business in Southwold. It's loik a panopticon. Yew know waa a panopticon is?

Sam   We're not here to discuss me.

Alicia   Wass a panopticon?

Sam   You need to be / in special needs school.

Alicia   Wass a panopticon?

Sam   Never mind that. There you'll get –

Alicia   Dussen't know, yew.

Sam   Your phonics'll get better. Listen to me! It's better if you decide to go.

Alicia (*to* **Sam**)   Fuck phonics.

Alicia *laughs.*

Alicia   Get it. Fuck phonics. *Oi* int say nuffun to yew.

She gets up.

Sam   Sit down.

Alicia *leaves.*

Scene Fifteen: Saltmarsh, Twilight

Alicia*'s cooking the samphire.*

Jake *enters.*

Jake   Did the police come?

Alicia   No.

Jake   Yew tell teacher?

Alicia   No. She say they gorn foind yew anyway.

Jake   'Ow they know it's us?

Alicia   Never say.

Beat.

Jake   Why yew cookun' samphire? Tha' how *Oi* do.

Alicia   Cos *Oi* don't wan yew [to] be my boyfriend no more.

Silence.

Routine int enough. Int enough Jake. Without out words.

Pause.

Jake   Yew int a dog –

Alicia   Waa? *Oi* / know tha'.

Jake   But now my dog dead, *Oi* know waa.

Pause.

Yew int Luna –

Pause.

But *Oi* think.

He tries to summon the words.

Yew alroight anyway.

Alicia   *Oi'm* sorry about Luna-girl. *Oi* know yew love her.

Pause.

Yew look loik yew got suffun to say.

Silence.

Oi cook this 'ere Samphire, not loike a spell, make yew say precious words. Nut words yew can't say. Sofia say '*Oi* love yew big'. Every day. Too many toime.

Pause.

Oi keep my mouth shut at school. But *Oi dussen't* do tha' no more. *Oi* have to be me with my boyfriend, see.

Pause.

Jake   *Oi'm* here. *Oi'm* here now. Look.

Alicia   Waa tha mean?!

Jake   It means *Oi* taking risk being here. Police, or Chelle an' her dogs, who knows moight come and grab me. See

Alicia   Waa, yew wan [to] do now you're here?

Pause.

Suffun to say?

Pause.

Int nowhere we can go anyway.

Pause.

Jake   Care home. *Oi* go back in care. *Oi* still be able to see yew.

Alicia   Yer bones are rememberin' demons, way yew move. *Oi* seen your demons, an' *Oi* seen Sofia's. *Oi* can handle hers. Cos of words. Truth and love. *Oi* needs words Jake.

Silence.

Jake *conjures something up.*

Jake   Everything yew looking for, looking at yew.

Alicia   It int.

Jake   If yew – yew know – love someone, they go. Loik Luna.

Alicia   Yew made out yew weren't seeing Chelle but yew was. Yew was fearing *Oi* leave yew, if yew git involve with her.

Jake   Yew doin it, yew are leavin'!

Alicia   Cos yew done lying, cos a' your demons, cos *Oi dussen't* wanna live in a lying way. *Oi* wanna live in a '*Oi* love yew way'. See.

Beat.

When people say '*Oi* love yew' make my brain grow. Neural pathways loight up. Nerves jangle. Different nerves than waa on my clitoris. Tho' *Oi dussen't* need yew for them. No Jake. Eat up. And *Oi* go my own way. And *Oi* thank yew, watch where you're standing, *Oi* jus' pick them samphire.

They eat. **Alicia** *gets up and goes.*

Jake
    Noight draws
    Lolike a bull through my skull
    My head's in my hands and Oi'm lonely
    Samphire. An' a curse for this life
    A bark in my breath cold and boney
    But if yew took
    To me
    Loike
    A heron take to the wind
    Oi'd have swung
    Loike
    The breeze
    And
    Danced loike
    An egret at dawn. A robin's song worn
    All around me

Gnashing, grunting, barking. **Demon Dog** *enters and walks towards* **Jake**.

Jake *pulls up his sleeve, stretches out his arm and fist and walks towards* **Demon Dog**.

End.

Samphire

BY SHAMSER SINHA

Notes on rehearsal and staging, drawn from a workshop with the writer,
held at the National Theatre facilitated by director Katherine Nesbitt, October 2022

How the writer came to write the play

'Where are the stories about experiences of those without a lot of money in rural areas?'

When Shamser Sinha was approached to write for Connections, he wanted to write about this subject. There were a few articles/stories which inspired him.

The first was a word-of-mouth story about the cycle that some rural young people found themselves in where they received a detention for not doing homework. The detention meant they then missed their bus home, and because of the irregularity of buses in rural areas, this meant they got home late. They then had to do chores, have dinner and help their family, which meant it was late when they came to do their homework. So, they either didn't do it and got detention again, or got tired and struggled in school, sometimes getting more detentions. Sinha started thinking about where punishment is more a show of power than about supporting young people.

The second was a story in the news about the treatment of young people in special educational needs departments in Suffolk. It was about the mistreatment of young people in those departments, and whether it was right for young people with these needs to be separated from their peers, to be written out of institutions.

With the character of Alicia, Sinha wanted to consider how neurodiverse people are treated. To start conversations about their right to relationships and to sexual relationships, and how this might mean that (especially in institutions) there may need to be check-ins around whether they fully understand choices they are making. In this play Alicia is very capable, a good reader and knows her own mind, yet because of how people perceive her, she is constantly told who she is and treated in certain ways. Sinha talked about the term 'vulnerable adults', and how we now shift towards talking about people who are 'at-risk'. This doesn't mean someone like Alicia is *always* at risk, but might be in certain situations.

He also talked about how he wanted to explore how chaos in family life can be cyclical, and when writing about Alicia and her mother's substance abuse and her brother's death, he wanted to look at the complexities of that. And to look at how the care system doesn't always end these cycles, but can perpetuate them.

As a playwright, Shamser Sinha is always interested in how individual characters are, and having an audience consider where they might share things with these characters and where they don't. For him, the paradoxical reason a character is so resonant is them being vivid and particular. He didn't want a series of talking heads on the subject, but a rich story, one which could provide young people doing the play with a rich subject and rich characters for them to go on a journey with.

Approaching the play

Lead director Katherine Nesbitt recommended gathering your initial response to the script by finishing the following sentences:

- This is a play about . . .
- This is a play that asks me to . . . (i.e. as a director, practically and formally what do you need to check off your list)
- The themes of the play are . . .

Here is what the group in the room came up with:

This is a play about . . .
finding home
overcoming trauma, and bettering yourself
vulnerability
growing up without guidance
lack of care (informal and formal)
choice and who gets to have choices and options?

This is a play that asks me to . . .
consider the relationship between the real and the abstract
consider how to direct the dogs and their physicality
consider how to manage a speaking and non-speaking cast
work within a dialogue
manage multi-roling
holding space for themes and questions about consent and sexual experiences of characters
dive deep into the text and invite young people to understand it.
be true to Alicia and cast who may have neurodiversity.
be true to students with difficult backgrounds and hold their vulnerability safely and responsibly in the room.

The themes of the play are . . .

- Hierarchies and power
- Education
- Neurodiversity
- Guilt and lies
- Consent
- Care system
- Love and friendship
- Line between people and animals
- Power
- Freedom

Nesbitt invited the group to talk about what their first thoughts and reactions to the play were.

Participants said they were drawn to the real world and the real characters, and were struck by the challenge of the dogs and how they might be achieved. Are they dogs with human characteristics? Are they humans with animalistic aspects? How realistic are they? They also noted that, since Covid took hold, many students are facing the challenges around money that these characters are.

Nesbitt talked about other ways to read through the play or understand the play as a cast when beginning rehearsals. She recommended two or three read-throughs, and many of the participants noted that the script felt much clearer on a second read, mostly due to understanding the particular dialect of the characters.

Here are some approaches to help your cast approach the script, to learn the logic and the narrative of it:

- Tell the cast the story as a fairy tale to help find a way in.
- Share the dialogue round the room so people don't read their own character at first; this can take the pressure off getting things 'right' and allow for creativity.
- Put chairs in the middle of the circle and people enter when they are part of the scene being read and leave when their character leaves the scene.
- On a second or third read-through, why not put signs with the locations in the play around the room and invite the characters to go and wait in their next location. This helps them consider their journey through the play and to start to think about where they are when they are not in the current scene.
- Another option is that you divide your cast into groups. Each group reads a scene together, then each reports back to the whole cast.
- Draw a map of the town.
- For non-speaking roles like the dogs, Katherine recommended challenging the dogs to write an internal monologue in the Suffolk accent.

Once you've done a read-through or two, read the entire play again and stop every time you find a fact or had a question. This will help you identify the things you definitely know about them, and what you need to know. This might be something you do by yourself as a director, or something you do with your cast as a whole or in groups.

The group read through Scene One, and anyone could shout 'fact' to stop and mark it in the script. It's important to note that everything in the stage directions is a fact, and the opening stage directions are all facts. You can also stop to write down questions. You may find some of these get answered later, or they may be something you have to decide on with your cast.

Here are some of the facts and questions the group discovered about Scene One:

Facts

- Sophia is wearing Pikachu pyjamas.
- Alicia isn't allowed to go downstairs.
- Alicia knows the nightmares Sophia has.
- Alicia has been doing something out of routine. Sophia has noticed this.

- Sophia knows she must ask the right question to get an answer.
- Alicia made a promise to keep the secret.
- Sophia has Sonic the Hedgehog pyjamas.
- Alicia lived at home until she was four.
- Alicia has been talked to about going into a special educational needs department.

Questions

- Why doesn't Alicia react to Sophia's scream?
- Why has Alicia been told explicitly to do her own? What previous conversation happened? How was it said and how Alicia has taken that?
- How recurring are those nightmares? How much is Alicia and Sophia's intense understanding of each other intuitive? How much is it interpretive? How long have they known each other? How long have they lived in the same place?
- Why is Alicia so obsessed with rules about what is age appropriate with Sophia? But against Sam?
- Why does Sophia have comic pyjamas?
- How long has Alicia been in the children's home?
- Has she only been in this one? Has it been since she was four? Has she been in and out?
- Is Sophia jealous of Jake? Or does Alicia just think she is? Because of Alicia's reassurances.
- What energy do Sophie and Alicia have? The audience won't know their age at this point. Are they younger mentally than their age? Or older?

Shamser talked about how important it is to research and understand the saltmarshes, samphire and the Demon Dog (sometimes known as the Black Shuck) which has supposedly haunted East Anglia. This might be a task you set for your students.

Language

Shamser Sinha talked about how integral the way the characters speak is to them and how they think, and their location is a key part of the script. This means you cannot change the words in the script to suit your cast's accent. Instead, Shamser has provided links to resources to help with learning the Suffolk accent, which are at the end of these notes.

Sinha added how the characters speak is part of who they are, so understanding them in their accent helps you bring them to life – this is regardless of whether you choose to perform them subsequently in standard English or not. It is important to consider the characters with their accents and look at how they speak and their thought processes.

Sinha wanted to clarify that Alicia always says I as '*Oi*' and italicisations in his script are not stressed. They are just highlighting the accent, not a stress on the meaning she intends.

Characters and characterisation

The group read Scene Two, dividing up characters between them. They then came up with three statements that began 'I am . . .', and then 'he is . . .' or 'she is . . .' or 'they are . . .' to show how they feel about other characters in the scene. Katherine noted that this was a task she'd often set overnight for the cast to do for their characters. Ask them to also write down why they came to these conclusions.

Here are some examples of what the group wrote:

Mel:
I am caring
I am reassuring
I am the daughter of the teacher
I am righteous (because she speaks up for animal rights)

Parminder:
I am self-conscious
I am responsible (because she is the first one to tell Ed)
I am strong

Parminder on Ed and Shaq: They are childish
Parminder on Sam: She is unfair
Parminder on Alice: She is in need of help

Sam:
I am impatient
I am uncomfortable
I am condescending

Sam on Shaq, Parminder and Ed: They are immature
Sam on Alice: She is not very clever and stubborn
Sam on Mel: She is self-righteous

This exercise is useful because it asks questions about when you are aware of what other people think of you and when you are less aware. Who does each character have an opinion on? They may have a small opinion about some people, and a bigger one about others. Relationships are weighted differently. This task flushes out their assumptions.

It also pushes less experienced people to understand their character's relationships at different times. Then when they are in a scene, they can use these choices to help them think about when they are reacting, and how would they react.

Further character work suggestions

Image research – ask them to bring in images of any place their character mentions in the play, such as a childhood bedroom or the house they live in. Ask them to share these in rehearsals so you can see similarities and differences between different characters, and how each feels about those places.

Song – bring in a song they associate with their character.

Think of texture – choose a material or substance they associate with a character.

If they were a colour what would their character be?

What smell would they associate with their character?

What sounds might they associate with their character?

If they were any animal, what animal would their character be?

What's their character's star sign?

What's their character's favourite food? And if they were a food what food would their character be?

What are their character's hobbies?

What is their character's goal?

What makes their character happy?

What makes their character sad?

If their character could change one thing about themselves, what would it be?

If their character could change one thing about someone else in the play, what would it be?

You might not want to share all of these with the whole cast but get them to pick three of these that feel really important and share them.

You could improvise scenes around the text to understand how relationships came to be a certain way, think about what events from before the play get mentioned, or what happens offstage. Can you ask your cast members to improvise around what they know about these scenes and their character? Don't be afraid to invite them to try it more than once if it doesn't quite work the first time.

In the workshop, Alicia was particularly discussed, and her relationship with her mother, Sophia, and Jake. The group talked about how when Alicia meets her mother, she is very aware of the games her mother is playing, or the fact that her mother doesn't seem to want to make Alicia happy, rather just to get her home and prove that she (the mother) has recovered. They talked about how Alicia spots the shaming in her mother's words.

The group discovered questions like:

Is her mother trying to annoy Alicia with the necklace? Or is she not doing it on purpose?

Does she want her to move in?

Has she forgiven Alicia?

Does she want Alicia to come live with her for selfish or unselfish reasons?

They talked about how Alicia clearly had a chaotic family life where older siblings looked after younger siblings.

The group also talked about Alicia's relationship to Sophia, where they seem to know each other so well that it's almost magic, or intuition. Alicia knows what dream Sophia's been having. They talked about how this might be played. Is Sophia surprised or does it seem totally normal? Is Alicia reading tiny things in Sophia's face and body language? How long have they lived together in this care home? What do they mean to each other?

When considering how the dogs might be achieved, the group talked about other dogs and animal performances they'd seen. Examples included the National Theatre's

Jane Eyre and *Peter Pan* (both available online), *Animal Farm*, *Equus* with English Touring Theatre, directed by Ned Bennett, *War Horse*.

Katherine Nesbitt answered a question about helping the cast achieve the dog sounds without straining their voices. She suggested:

- Use the voice work sparingly.
- Think about breath, and panting, though she noted it was important to be careful with panting as some people could faint. She recommended making noise on the out breath.
- Use the resonators in the body – placing the dog noises in different places from mouth, throat, chest and in the nose. Switch between them to save voices.
- Explore the different noises dogs make, not just barking or growling. For example, whining is very nasal, but barking or growling can be in the throat or chest.

Another thing that was raised was playing the adults, and how different they should feel. Sinha said simply to approach it truthfully for your production.

You could also ask actors to use animal work to help them find characters. This is something which can be used for dog characters and human characters, the difference is how strong the animal influence is. Ask the company to write a list of adjectives about their character, sitting with that list and thinking about what animal suits that list. Then invite them to watch YouTube videos about that animal. Some will already have animals, and for the dog actors there are differences between breeds. This might be a task you want to set overnight or between rehearsals and ask them to come in prepared.

Set up thirty minutes of them moving round the room as if they are their chosen animal. As they move, provoke with these questions and statements:

Where does the animal carry its weight or heaviness?
Remind them they don't have to go on all fours to create that heaviness or weight.
Think about the feet they have; how do they find balance in their bodies?
Think about the tempo of their movement?
What's their hide like? Do they have fur or feathers, so how do they experience temperature?
How do they experience the world? Is it through sight, hearing or smell? Which of these senses are less strong? How does that lead them through space?
How do they greet other animals?
What is it like for them to relax and let go?
What happens when they are tense?
Do they hunt?
Do they play?
If they are a pet, how differently do they behave with their human? Do they always behave? Or do they act out?

For those playing humans, ask them if there are things they could use from this animal exploration that can inform the way their character moves, or the speed they move at? What can they tone down to be slightly more pedestrian?

This task can be useful for the cast to understand their character and make choices. Katherine pointed out that different people access characters in different ways: some are more into conversation and some want to discover it physically.

Casting

Some of the participants raised questions about neurodiversity and casting the character of Alicia. The playwright shared that for him, her neurodiversity comes from in utero exposure to alcohol which can affect how the brain develops. The group talked about honouring her intelligence and understanding of the world, while also seeing how she misunderstands things. Capturing her nuance is integral to helping you understand her and her complexities.

If you needed to, you could double cast the roles of the Demon Dog and the German Shepherd, and potentially triple cast Sam with them too, depending on your cast size.

Here were some of the questions raised by this:

Whose eyes do we see the links between Sam and the Demon Dog from?
Will the doubling moment with the Demon Dog feel like a literal moment or a magical/metaphorical moment?
Where is the line of demonising Sam too much?
Does she deserve demonising?
How much does Sam mean to exert power?
How much is she just following orders?

The group talked about how she struck them as a relatively young teacher (perhaps thirty) who is overwhelmed and inexperienced, and perhaps not thinking fully about her actions. How could you explore this in the production? Does this matter?

For Shamser, the link between Sam and the Demon Dog is to show how threatening adults can feel to Jake and other young people. The participants talked about finding other ways to link Sam to the Demon Dog, and red-framed glasses to give a glimpse of red around her eyes was suggested as an example.

If you have a smaller cast than the number of characters and need to do other doubling, then Sinha noted that these doublings should not feel meaningful to each other. Rather they should be clearly differentiated.

Production, staging and design

Katherine Nesbitt talked about how to approach complicated sequences, and drawing each stage of non-verbal movement for yourself and/or with the company members involved.

They looked at Scene Eleven to explore this idea. In the scene is Rottweiler One (R1), Rottweiler Two (R2), Luna, German Shepherd (GS) and Rob. Below are the beats of the sequence that were drawn:

1   R1 is circling Luna.
2   R1 and Luna back and forth at each other.

3 R2 enters.

4 R1 and Luna still back and forth, R1 and R2 barking at each other.

5 Luna is pushed back towards R2 and can't see them.

6 Luna sees R2 and evades R2 and runs into GS who has just emerged. Luna does not see GS.

7 R2 follows Luna towards GS. Luna sees GS and begins whining.

8 R1 and R2 circle, and them and GS surround Luna.

9 GS closes in.

10 Luna faces her, and does a submission pose to GS (the one she has done to Jake).

11 GS eats Luna's stomach. R1 and R2 are keeping guard.

As you begin to stage it, think about the possibilities of the stage directions. Shamser said there should be moments where we think she might escape, but they are lost. Hit those moments of danger, and the dramatic irony of us seeing the other dogs while Luna doesn't. What do we know about what is about to happen, which Luna doesn't know?

The group talked about how the design could communicate that Luna can't see them – Nesbitt suggested one option might be creating shadows in the lighting state for this scene.

One particular element of the production which drew discussion was how the participants wanted to approach the dogs, and whether Shamser had a specific vision. Sinha said that with any costume choices you make and don't make, always: Do they help you feel anything about the story? Or is it distracting from the story? For your performers, what will help them get into the role?

Here are some suggestions which came up in the room:

No dog-like costumes, maybe they dress like humans but have matching plain T-shirts to look like a uniform. And the dog-like nature is brought through movement. For the Demon Dog red eyes – you could use handheld lights.

You might use big dog head shapes and human clothes.

You could use studded collars.

One participant asked about puppetry. Sinha said that for him, when writing the play, there was something that felt more of the body than puppetry. However, he said if you feel like you can best tell the story with puppets, then go for it.

Another moment which came up was how to stage the killing of Luna, and Sinha answered the question of why Luna is eaten and not killed. He talked about how eating is a function of life and animal instinct, it's not cruel, just functional. It is an invitation to consider these things against each other. What is cruel? Is it cruelty that is part of life or unnecessary? Where is it both? For this reason, he suggested that this moment not be gratuitously horrifying, particularly as we are not seeing it through Jake's eyes, just Luna's. So, you might stage this moment with the other dogs hiding the action of Luna's death and do it through sound. Or you might find another way.

Exercises for use in rehearsals

Two truths and a lie

Lead Director Katherine Nesbitt asked each person to tell two truths and one lie about themselves, and the rest of the group had to try and work out which was the lie.

This is a good game to play after reading the play at least once. It's interesting because Alicia won't tell a lie, as well as being an ice breaker for your company.

Afterwards you might consider discussing:

How do you feel about lying?
Are you good at lying? How does it feel to admit that?
Why might someone refuse to lie?
Why has Alicia decided not to lie?

Hunting games

The group thought about games which might be good for getting the groups into a stalking or hunting mindset.

Grandmother's footsteps

A game where the group sneaks up on one member of the group. They start at one end of a space, and they have to stop and freeze every time the person turns round. If they are seen moving, they have to move back to the beginning and start again.

Bomb and shield

Ask the group to walk around the room, silently picking one person in the room to be their bomb. Keep walking around the room but ask them to always be aware of where this person is. Encourage them to use their peripheral vision. Then get them to pick another person as their shield. Encourage them to walk around being aware of both these people. When you clap, they have thirty seconds to get their shield between them and their bomb. Once the time runs out the bomb explodes. Get them playing that with different paces, and how soon the bomb is going to go off. How does this change the danger?

Pass the click

Get in a circle. One person flicks their hand and clicks, as if throwing it to someone across the circle. The person receives the click with a click and then will click to send it on. Get each person to catch it with the energy it was sent with and then send it with a different energy.

Eye-contact listening game

Make eye contact and switch places with the person you make eye contact with, hold the eye contact until you are fully in their spot, so you circle each other and walk backwards towards your new spot. The person who was invited to switch picks a new person to switch with.

Acting exercises

Seven levels of tension

This is a Lecoq exercise which could be useful as a warm-up for scenes like Scene Eleven for example. Get people to walk around your rehearsal room and explore the seven levels of tension in their body, 1 being no tension and 7 being complete tension. A link to more detailed instructions can be found at the end of these notes.

Eye-contact chase

Get in pairs. A can look at B and wants them to look at them, B can't look at A. Both can move. A must try and get B to look at them. Switch over halfway through. No shutting your eyes or facing a wall.

Play again but this time A has to stay in one spot.
Play again but this time a group of people are trying to get A's eye contact.
What happens if one person tries to get three different people to look at them?

This game can be useful when applied to scenes where a character might be avoiding or trying to get eye contact. It is best played once your actors are off script, or are being fed lines by people on the side. What happens if you flip it? What if you do it and they hold eye contact the whole time? What feels right or wrong? What might you use from these exercises and when? Explore the physical rules and try them out, then see where they might change. Who's allowed to move? Who has to ask for permission?

The group looked at Scene One. First, they tried where Alicia can't make eye contact, and Sophia wants her to. It was noted that this game made Sophia more energised, while Alicia was in her own little world. It brought out the awkwardness, and for Sophia brought out her urgency for connection: 'I need you to pay attention to me so we can solve this.' What happens if you change it over and Alicia is trying to get Sophia's attention? The group found this made Sophia more avoidant and Alicia more direct. There might be different moments in your final staging of the scene where they use elements of eye contact discovered through this exercise.

This game might also be good to explore with Sam and Jake in Scene Four.

Acting questions

Here are some questions to use when your actors are off script and you might find them not listening to each other and getting into predictable loops.

Practise setting up these questions with them so you can use them in a scene. And when you feel like they aren't in the moment or listening, use them to provoke them into redelivering the line they just said. They can then carry on the scene.

Questions to ask

If they say something and it doesn't feel like they are having the thought in the moment, the question is 'When did you think of that?' Their response is always 'Just now'. Then they should say the line they last said again. And this time try to deliver it like they had that thought in the moment.

When the actor uses a name or description, but it feels like it doesn't mean anything or feels non-specific, ask them, 'Is there something else you could call them/it?' The answer is always 'yes' because they could call it something else but they chose this, so they should make it meaningful. They should then deliver the line with more intention.

If the actor has a line which lists a few things, but they all sound the same in their delivery, ask them, 'On a list or comparison, are those the same thing?' The answer is always 'no' from the actor and then they must deliver that line with the list or comparison, so they sound like specifically different things.

If they state a fact but it doesn't feel true, the question is, 'Is that true?' The answer is always 'Yes', even if it isn't. Then they must repeat the line they just said and say it as if it is true or not true to their character, and think about how much their character wants to be believed.

If they state an opinion but it doesn't feel meaningful, ask, 'Do you really believe that?' and the answer is always 'Yes'. Even if they don't! They should then repeat the line with the appropriate level of belief.

If they say something in the script about what they want, but you are unconvinced, ask them, 'Is that what you really want?' They should always say 'Yes' even if it isn't true, then repeat the line with the appropriate level of want or need.

If you can't tell if something they say is a good or bad thing, ask them, 'Is that a good thing?' The answer is always 'Yes'. But then they should repeat the question with the appropriate level of good vibe or bad vibe.

Here are some examples of how that might work in this script:

A   Did the police come?

B   No.

Director   Is that true?

B (*to* **Director**)   Yes. (*Returning to script.*) No.

The answers should be directed at the director. This exercise can be done slowly or more quickly. The actors can have a little time to ruminate before they repeat the line, if needed.

Whatever/I don't care/Not that it matters

Add 'whatever' or 'I don't care' or 'not that it matters' after every line when they speak the script. Do it once for practice. Do it a second time, but this time really say the script as if you don't mean it. Then a third time where it really matters but you still say that it doesn't at the end of every line.

You can also explore where one actor means what they say, and the other doesn't. And one where they are saying it and they mean it, but don't want the other person to know they mean it.

This exercise can help an actor to explore about what a character is saying and what they mean, and how they feel about what they are saying. You may make unexpected discoveries in these exercises.

Question and answer with Shamser Sinha

Q: What do you think about music or underscoring with this play?
A: Is it supporting the storytelling? Would it be made by other company members? Shamser said he could definitely see how rhythm can work, and suggested that it could come from the rest of the cast or from recorded music. If you are introducing musicians, you might need to consider whether you are confusing the storyline.

Q: Why dogs?
A: Shamser told the group how his son had recently gotten into dogs, and when Shamser had gone to a rescue centre, he had seen there were these clear hierarchies within the dogs' relationships. He wanted to explore these hierarchies in people and the dogs in the play allow for them to be highlighted. He had written the play without them, but he said it suddenly occurred to him that they could help Jake as he's struggling to express himself. He also knew that in the area he had set the play there were lots of people who felt similarly about their dogs. There is also lots of dog kidnapping and reselling of dogs without chips in rural areas.

Q: What is the difference between beat, pause and silence?
A: A beat is the shortest, then a pause, and then a silence. A beat is little thought or a little shift, a pause is a bigger thought and it's more active. Silence is an absence of knowing what is next or a bigger intention in that silence. A pause is suspended, a silence is sometimes a removal of potential.

Q: How do we best approach the overlapping text?
A: Shamser asked them to consider why it overlaps. It's natural to overlap, but why does the thought rush in or why do they speak over someone else? It can bring a sense of argument, but it might be a normal part of how two characters talk. How does the person respond to someone who has interrupted the other? And for the actors, the challenge is to keep listening while continuing to talk over the top of someone.

Safeguarding

The group was joined by a member of the National Theatre's safeguarding team. Here were some of the things that were discussed.

The participants acknowledged that it was important to set up a relationship with the safeguarding leads in your teams, and noted that large organisations could be more difficult. They may have teams who don't have enough time to look at the play fully and understand the nuance. This could leave to rehearsals being postponed when safeguarding teams caught up, or threatening the performance completely. Most participants found that with good communication problems were quickly resolved in previous productions, and that the safeguarding teams often applauded the work which was going on.

How do you hold the varying backgrounds and lived experiences of a group?

How do you lead discussions where you might talk about intimate subjects, and how do you create a space where difficult subjects can be talked about?

There are particular conversations to have around consent and capacity, and in this script it raises issues around neurodivergency and consent, a subject which is complex and developing in our current society.

Alicia is clearly cleverer than Sam gives her credit for, but at the same time there are some elements where she misunderstands things in the play because of her neurodivergency.

There are also lots of moments in the play where things happen with consent or without consent, for example when Alicia talks about how she was left as a child to care for her four-year-old brother (something she was too young to give consent for), and the play leaves space to have a conversation with young people about what consent is and how different people approach it. What is an informed and fair approach, and what is more problematic? Also, when might consent still not be enough, or when might consent be withdrawn? Who can give consent? And who can't? An interesting resource for talking about consent is the consent and tea video in the references below.

There was a discussion about radicalisation with regards to some of the characters, and some resources about this issue have been provided below. Be aware of the community you're talking with, and whether anyone in the group might be vulnerable to this.

Be aware that some of what happens to Alicia might trigger young people. Make sure you have space to check in with students and not rush through these discussions. Feel empowered to call a break at any time in these heavier moments.

The group discussed how some young people in the room might have experience of the care system and how they might bring those experiences into the room safely. It's always about making sure they know that it's not a requirement for them to bring that into the room, just as every actor should know that they don't have to bring their traumatic experiences and they don't have to share anything they aren't comfortable with.

It's important to remind them that once it's out there, you can't take it back, because lots of people tend to be really open, but sometimes people can be surprised by how it feels after that moment of sharing. Nesbitt suggested keeping the focus of the discussion on the play, rather than sharing personal stories. Remind them they are playing these characters, and it's not them saying or doing these things if they feel uncomfortable.

Lead director Katherine Nesbitt recommended using tapping in and out for emotional scenes, even if it's not something from personal experience. This might be double high fiving before and after as a physical marker of entering and exiting this emotional space. This means you can really signpost when you are entering emotional territory, so people aren't blindsided by big things. You want the young people to feel ready to face the world again after finishing rehearsals.

Nesbitt also mentioned focusing on the funny and lovely bits of the scene, not just the sad bits. This is a funny, beautiful and moving play too.

The aim is to give young people permission and freedom to explore in rehearsals, and they should be encouraged to ask any questions that feel appropriate to the process.

The group talked about 'calling in' and 'calling out', and how as a company it's important to call each other 'in' to work as a company and resolve issues that arise. Ned Glasier, Artistic Director of Company Three, talks very well about this. Calling out feels much more like an act of announcing publicly a mistake that isn't being fixed within a group of people, while 'calling in' is the action within the group of someone raising an issue to be dealt with and responded to. If someone does or says something you are unhappy with, you call them in. Company Three also frame the act of calling in as one of generosity, an act which is welcomed within the group and by anyone who receives a call in. It is an invitation to see things differently.

Suggested references

Guardian article: https://www.theguardian.com/education/2022/sep/26/ofsted-concerns-physical-restraints-on-pupils-in-special-needs-school-warren-school-lowestoft-suffolk

Documentary: *Boy in the Woods* on BBC iPlayer, an example of a chaotic family life and the effects on children.

Tea and Consent video: https://www.youtube.com/watch?v=pZwvrxVavnQ

Seven levels of tension exercise: https://dramaresource.com/seven-levels-of-tension/

Company Three, young people's theatre company: https://www.companythree.co.uk/

For Suffolk accent references:

BBC Voices Archive: https://sounds.bl.uk/Accents-and-dialects/BBC-Voices

British Library Sounds Archive: https://sounds.bl.uk/

From a workshop led by Katherine Nesbitt
With notes by Stephanie Kempson

Strangers Like Me

by Ed Harris

Ed Harris is an award-winning, dyslexic playwright, poet and comedy writer based in Brighton. Before finding his feet as a writer, Harris was a binman, care worker, and even once spent a winter as a husky trainer in Lapland! His first major play *Mongrel Island* opened at Soho Theatre in 2011 to great critical acclaim, and was later produced in Mexico as *Perro Sin Raza*, where it ran for six months. His other plays include *The Cow Play*, *What the Thunder Said* (which won the Writers' Guild Award for Best Play for Younger Audiences) and *Never Ever After* (shortlisted for the Meyer-Whitworth award). He wrote his first opera, *A Shoe Full of Stars*, with composer Omar Shahryar. It was described as a 'comic opera for children ... about terrorism!' and won the international YAM Award in 2018 for Best Opera.

Harris has also become one of BBC Radio Drama's most regularly commissioned and highly acclaimed dramatists since his first radio play, *Porshia*, was produced in 2007. His first sitcom, *Dot*, a popular wartime spoof about the misadventures of some of the female staff of Churchill's War Rooms, has run since 2015. Between 2011 and 2015 he won a Sony Gold/Radio Academy Award for *The Resistance of Mrs Brown*, a Writers' Guild Award for *Troll* and a BBC Audio Drama Award for *Billions*.

He is a Royal Literary Fellow and has recently been awarded an Arts Council Grant to write his first children's novel, *The Night Is Large*. Harris will also be adapting a season of Kafka's novels for radio and stage for both BBC Radio 4 and Oxford University's *Global Kafka Festival*, commemorating the centenary of Franz Kafka's death in 2024.

For all of us who were there, and everyone who wasn't

Characters

Narrators
N1
N2

People
Elbow
Amira
Rupert
Mum
Dad
Donut
Teacher
Shona
Held Girl
Various pupils

Voxes[1]
Skrik
Crumb
Calico
Pug
Character descriptions overleaf

Trigger Warnings
Strong language
Death (unwitnessed, offstage)
An act of (non-naturalistic) violence

---

1 *'Voxes' comes from Latin and is the plural of Vox: Voice.*

A few things before we begin . . .

A note on text: Although some of the characters are presented here as identifiably female or male, this is only – roughly speaking – how they presented themselves to me while I wrote it. Your Elbow, your Skrik, Crumb, Calico, Pug, Rupert or Amira might not look the same as the ones who I've had knocking around inside me these past few months. Feel free to change pronouns or gendered names and titles. Similarly, I've referenced a towpath on a canal-side here, but feel free to change that to a riverside, lakeside, beach or whatever is most geographically relevant to the area of the production.

A note on performance: The serious subject matter of this play might give a company the impression that they should lean towards sentimentality in their performance and production. But while light, shade and especially emotional truth are vital, I would suggest resisting this urge, as it can lead to creating the kind of 'earnest, schmaltzy' drama Elbow takes the piss out of in Scene Nine ('I just, y'know, really feel . . . Things?'). A lot of the emotional impact of this play will come from its playfulness, mischief and everydayness.

A note on characters: The Voxes are a community of personified personality traits that together make up Elbow's mind. It's a bit like in Pixar's *Inside Out*, except that these aren't personifications of emotions, but more like personifications of ways of being and/or seeing. For that reason, I don't want to assign the Voxes overly specific character traits – but, if you're interested, I would invite you to consider the following artworks as inspiration-points in relation to understanding each Vox. Skrik: Munch's *The Scream* (1893), Pug: Miró's *The Sun* (1949), Calico: Rockwell's *Girl at Mirror* (1954) and Crumb: Bacon's *Man with Dog* (1953).

A note on staging: Personally, I picture the play taking place in a white box space, with the whole cast onstage throughout, sat around the edge of the playing space when not performing. All props look like line-drawings, so a real three-dimensional birdhouse would be painted white with simplistic details and 'outlines' painted on in black to give it the impression of being two-dimensional, from any angle. Same goes for chairs, benches, games consoles and books, etc. You may have a better idea.

A note on notes: Take what works, leave the rest.

Enjoy!
Ed

Scene One

Darkness.

The pre-show music (suggestion: 'One is The Loneliest Number' by Three Dog Night) is interrupted by the sound of a mirror smashing. Lights up.

There are big crack lines across the stage (floor and walls), like a mirror has been smashed – into five distinct parts. Throughout the play, the cracks in the stage are never openly acknowledged, but all characters are always forced to step over them as if they are real cracks in the earth. Same goes for any cast or crew helping scene changes.

The **Narrators**, **N1** *and* **N2**, *are clowns (but not the red-nose and silly wig type). They bicker like siblings, and are only rudimentarily prepared for their jobs as narrators. However, now and then, they can manage a little gravitas:*

N1   When the news hit,

N2   it was like a meteor.

N1   Like something shattered:

N2   Something as tiny as a single hair left on a pillow

N1   Or as big as the Big Bang, broke the world open

N2   . . . like an egg.

Beat.

N1 (*to* **N2**, *mouthed*)   'Like an egg'?

N2 (*mouthed*)   'Like an egg.' What?

N1 (*rolls eyes/tuts/similar*)   Broke open – like *an egg* – never to fit back the way it had been.

Scene Two

Changing rooms. Through the wall, sound of sports, plimsols squeaking on school hall, or shouting on a muddy field.

Elbow *talks to us. Standing in each of the 'shards' created by the cracks on the stage are* **Calico**, **Pug**, **Skrik** *and* **Crumb**. *They are collectively known as the* **Voxes**. *They are all, in some way, identifiably similar to* **Elbow** *(same cap or coat, same school tie, etc.) – in this section, they mirror his movements exactly.*

Elbow   That day at school, I smashed a mirror. It was only a school mirror, so I didn't get the bad luck. Not myself. I guess everyone did, everyone in the school; like when everyone has to stay behind in PE because one kid's naughty.

The pieces of the mirror lay there on the scuffed tiles of the changing-room floor. I had on my plimsoles and red and green socks like watermelons. Five mirror pieces, staring back at me.

And then the PE teacher came in and found what I'd done and everyone had to stay behind after PE while I cleaned up; even though my mate had just died, and no-one else's had; even though only me had smashed the mirror and no one else had; even though he should have been in PE with me except he died. Even though I'd only found out he'd died cos of a hashtag.

N1   There was a Big Empty Superunknown . . . space.

N2   Like an abyss.

N1   Like his internal . . .

N2   'ness'?

N1   Like his internal-ness was an expansive, echoless abyss.

Elbow *is revealed as a doll/puppet astronaut and animated by the* **Narrators/Voxes**.

N1   In which he hung, like an astronaut.

N2   Or a deep-sea diver.

N1 (*firmly, through a smile*)   Or an astronaut; one will do.

N2   Just a boy named Elbow.

N1   In the Deep Nothing.

Elbow *looks into the smashed mirror on the fourth wall or floor; the various hims move at the same time.* **Pug** *is the first to break from the union-in-unison.*

Pug   Most of all though, I like the smell of the soil when the rain hits it. It's like warm dust in an airing closet.

Calico   Shh.

Pug   Like when we were little and we used to hide at Nana's? Do you remember hiding in her airing closet?

Calico   *Shh.*

Pug   Her towels were scrapey. Standing on the cold bathroom floor and her, like, really roughly sort of shaking you dry? Do you remember that scrape-iness on your goosebumps? Do you?

Crumb   It was nice and not-nice at the same time. Like extreme close-up loud feelings – like she'd rawed you.

Pug   Yeah, and –

Calico   We Are Grieving!

Pug   Oh. (*Tries to be quiet. Beat.*) I think I'm horny.

Calico   Oh, please!

Pug   I'm not saying I'm going to do anything about it, I'm just saying a feeling that I'm feeling, that is felt.

Calico   This really isn't the time to be talking about towels or airing closets where we'd hide or – 'anything else'. Especially anything else. Is that really the person you want us to be, the one who finds out their Best Friend dies and –

Crumb   Best Friend?

Calico   One of our best friends.

Pug (*still on same subject*)   I wasn't going to do anything about it!

Calico   I should hope not. We are to remain here solemnly and think respectful thoughts about one of our best friends – and, at a sensitive, possibly moonlit moment, cry. While looking at a framed photo . . .

Crumb   How do you know?

Calico (*beat*)   They do it in films.

Pug   Just so we all know: I wasn't proposing a wank.

Calico   *Please*!

Skrik   We don't have a framed photo of him.

Calico   I just mean . . . whatever we do will be What People Do. It will be like a film.

Skrik   I miss Nana. I prefer cremations to hole-in-the-ground ones. The ground ones make you feel how heavy the earth is.

We haven't cried yet. Is that weird? Don't people find out and cry, instead of –

They watch the astronaut/diver **Elbow** *floating around in The Nothing.*

Calico   I shall have a look in my Book! Everything's in here. Now . . . (*Flicking through.*) 'How Long After the Death of a Best Friend – '

Crumb   Best Friend?

Pug   Best In-School friend.

Skrik   At Primary. I mean.

Crumb   Not recently.

Skrik   Not since –

Calico   'of a Long-Serving Friend – how soon until one should cry?'

Skrik   Why aren't we feeling anything?

Crumb   Because everyone's yammering on!

Skrik   Only two people don't feel anything: Psychopaths and Robots.

Pug   If we don't feel anything –

Skrik   – if we Never Feel Anything –

Pug   – does that. . . do we. . . are we a Psychopath?

Calico   We Are Not a Psychopath. Wait, it'll be in The Book somewhere.

Crumb   Have you seen *American Psycho*?

Calico   Can you just shut up and bloody well grieve, please? I'm trying to find the right page.

Crumb   Or Hannibal Lecter. Or The Dude from *Clockwork Orange*. Sometimes psychos are just cool. James Bond's a psycho.

Calico   James Bond is *not* a psycho – (*Beat.*) Okay, he is a bit, but we're not here to discuss James Bond! Can we please all stop our mind wandering? Just sit patiently and we shall grieve. This is a Defining Moment, perhaps the Most Defining Moment. Of our Lives. (*To* **Pug**.) And don't pick your nose!

N1   Elbow had never thought before about how he thought, but the further he thought into the Great Deep Nothing, the more clearly he heard them:

N2   as if they'd just arrived,

N1   like the Universe and the Big Bang and stuff just all arrived one day, out of nowhere;

N2   like a smash in a mirror just appeared one day; and made five pieces out of one . . .

Scene Three

School.

A kaleidoscope of uniformity circling **Elbow**. *Pupils, school uniforms, corridors, doorways, etc.*

N1   School is a strange thing when your friend's just died.

N2   There's something about the uniformed lines of uniformed kids . . .

N1   All moving together when the bell sounds, the colossal all-at-once scraping of chairs;

N2   like a dawn chorus of grunting, squeaking furniture across the whole school . . .

N1   like a hive of trolls creaking out from under their bridges.

N2   Like a whole morgue farting, all at once.

N1   Or like a hive – like we'd agreed.

N2   Or like a whole morgue, because I didn't agree, only you did.

A school bell.

Teacher (*over the noise*)   ERM – THANK YOU! That was the First Bell –

A classroom forms.

Teacher   I *didn't* say go. SHONA, DANIEL? Books remain open, please. Thank you, isn't that nice? In summary, people used to believe that the smallest thing in the universe is the atom; that an atom is One Thing, that cannot be divided up into any smaller parts. But now we know it's actually quite a busy bunch of separate things, all hanging out together and making up One Individual Thing.

Second bell. Class file out.

Teacher   Books away! Thank you everyone! (*To* **Elbow**.) Actually, I wanted a word, Elbow? Before you go. It's nothing bad. (*Beat.*) I know you and Hamster were Best Friends. Death is . . . Well, you're probably feeling So Much Right Now . . .?

Elbow *shrinks into himself.*

Teacher   I just think . . . if it were me, at your age? I would have just shattered into a million pieces. I think it shows real strength that you're able to stay in one piece during this.

Elbow   Thanks, Miss/Sir.

Teacher   Before you go. We're holding a short afterschool service on Friday. Just for students and staff who want to. But so people can come and pay their respects. Hamster's mum specifically asked if you'd speak. As Hamster's best friend.

Scene Four

Elbow   He'd never said I was his best friend. We were close-ish, but I thought we'd both just . . .

Calico   Drifted.

Pug   Peeled away.

Skrik (*bluntly*)   We thought we were better than him.

Calico   Balderdash!

Skrik   That's what we said. We said we'd outgrown him. That's essentially –

Pug   It was a dumb argument!

Skrik   It was the last thing we said.

Crumb   If we were his best mate, we'd know. Right?

Calico   If we were, there should have been some sort of ceremony.

Skrik   Maybe he kept it secret from us.

Calico   With witnesses and signatories. (*To* **Skrik**.) How preposterous – a secret! – why?

Skrik   Because he didn't trust us.

Calico   Why wouldn't he trust us?

Skrik (*nothing*)

Pug   C'mon! We're awesome! People can tell us anything! We're not like Shona and those fakers –

Skrik   Then, why don't we feel anything?

Pause.

Calico   Hamster's mum's simply confused. We *were* best friends, at primary, but – and it's not her fault – things simply change at high school. It's a far more sophisticated eco-system of relationships and –

Skrik   He was our Best Friend, till Amira.

Scene Five

Elbow *is on the side of the road. Sound of traffic, etc.*

N1   You can see them a mile off, all lit up like Christmas shopfronts:

N2   The buses float through the dark towards you, like something glowing underwater;

N1   these strange sad whale pods, red mouths open; scooping up kids and uniform and muddy shoes and damp.

N2   And sicking them up, up the road.

On bus. Sounds of: kids, phones, games, clashing music from phones. **Elbow** *is pinned between various conversations. It is a hive of action around him; they talk over him, lean over him, hustle and bustle him, while he sits in the middle, knocked and rocked about.*

1   *Oh my God*, give that back!

Shona   *Oh my God*, get off!

2   Ah! That's Daniel's house!

3   What Daniel?

1   I'm serious, Shon-a!

2   I swear I told you about Daniel like yesterday.

Shona   Get off!

1   It's *mine!*

3   Oh, *that* Daniel. 'Daniel'-Daniel.

2   Amira.

Amira   Yup?

2   You and Elbow fancy coming?

Amira   When, what?

2   Friday. After the school have done their thing, we're doing something for Hamster.

3   She just wants everyone to meet 'Daniel'!

2   Piss off! He won't be there. No. It's like, Purely a Hamster Thing. I thought we could –

3   *We* thought we could . . .

2   Like, do a Thing. I dunno. Like a thing with candles. Like, I dunno.

3   I dunno, like – cos the school are like 'naming a tree after him' or some crap . . . why can't we do a thing, like Our Own Thing?

Shona   What's this?

3   We had an idea?

1   Give me. I'm serious, Shona!

Amira   Like a sort of remembrance thing? (*To* **Elbow**.) What d'you reckon?

2 & 3   Yeah! Like, share memories and do songs and like –

Shona   Whatever happens this weekend, I'mma gonna get wrecked.

3   Who put a pound in you?

Shona   I sold all my sister's Barbie Extra on eBay. I'm basically loaded.

Amira   What's Extra?

Shona   Pink braids.

2   You sold her crap?!

Shona   She's eight: She should learn to lock up what she loves.

1   Shona.

3   We can do it at mine? My folks are away.

1   Sho-w-n-*Ahh!*

Shona   Oh my days, can we?

Amira   I mean, it'd be great. What d'you reckon, Elbow?

4   It'd be sick. Hamster and me used to go to primary together, so y'know . . . we're pretty old school. Friends. Old school friends. (*Laughs.*)

Amira *laughs.*

Shona   I haven't finished with it!

1   Shona, I swear I'm gonna fucking *drown* you! (*Gasps. To everyone.*) Oh my God, I'm sorry. It's not me it's my brain. I keep saying really inappropriate – (*To* **5***, with a smile.*) Don't laugh-uh, I'm serious!

The crowd around him become slow-motion, and **Elbow** *is pushed about more slowly. From somewhere (under his seat?) the* **Voxes** *emerge with the astronaut version of him. He soars slowly away from the crowd.*

He swims for the exit. As he does so he passes two or more other pupils. One of them, **Held Girl***, is crying and the others are simply holding him/her. They barely move; we see them breathe as one.* **Elbow** *and the* **Voxes** *all notice them as they pass; slightly spellbound. They all move on except* **Pug***, who lingers longest.*

Pug   Held.

Calico   What?

Pug *interacts with* **Held Girl** *and his/her friend/s. She moves a hand or an arm so that the cuddle is slightly more 'holding'.*

Pug   Held.

Crumb *drags her away. The sounds of the bus fade; we are underwater. The sky above the water shines brightly.*

Crumb   Remember what Hamster said.

Calico   If you're ever on holiday,

Pug   In the Arctic.

Calico   And you fall through the ice,

Pug   Don't just head for the light.

Calico   It's a sheet of ice.

Crumb   Find the dark spot.

Skrik   Head for the hole.

From a watery distance:

Amira   What do you reckon, Elbow? Some people round to Sean's on Friday? For Hamster? Don't go, Elbow!

Scene Six

The **Narrators**.

Elbow *sits on 'Hamster's bench' by a canal towpath. People walk past, not looking at him.*

N1   And people were around.

N2   People were around.

N1   Physically.

N2   But you kind of go: 'who am I gonna talk to?'

N1   'All my mates are my age. So they're like me, except either they haven't been through the thing I'm going through.'

N2   'Or they're going through the same thing. But probably how you're supposed to, like in a film. With less of this . . .'

N1   'Nothing.'

N2   'And the grown-ups. We don't . . .'

N1   'I don't . . .'

N2   'Like, we haven't . . . 'done'. . . that kind of talking before.'

N1   And sometimes if you do try, when you do try talking to someone –

N2   And they look at you, and this Fear in their eyes,

N1   It's like they're watching a crack appear in the fabric of the universe behind you . . . and all this empty rubbish Nothingness pouring out – pouring *in* . . .

N2   Like you're on the *Titanic* and it's the Arctic Sea flooding into the room . . .

N1   And they're there, nodding with their Listening Face on . . .

N2 (*does impression*)   Blink, blink, blink.

N1   While kinda actually working out the best escape route.

N2   Nothing scares people like Nothingness does.

N1   Nothing.

N2   So it gets like violence. Speaking. It shatters them.

Scene Seven

Home. Probably the kitchen.

The doll/astronaut leads us here through the sound of lapping water; ascends.

Mum *and* **Dad** *spend all their time on their phones (or staring into other shining rectangles; iPads, laptops, televisions, refrigerators).* **Elbow** *comes home, he is struggling to find the confidence to talk to them.*

Elbow   Mum. Dad.

Mum   Did you see Rupert Next Door?

Elbow   What?

Mum   Did you drop round his stuff? You saw the Family WhatsApp?

Elbow   Yeah.

Dad *chuckles at something on his phone.*

Mum   Hm? Did you?

Elbow   Yeah, I said yeah.

Dad (*chuckles at something on his phone*)   Did you see that?

Mum   What? From Baz?

Dad   His video he sent. Of his cat falling over.

Still without eye contact, they each do an impression, to themselves.

Elbow   Erm, Mum – ?

Mum   How was he?

Elbow *doesn't know if she's talking to him or Dad.*

Elbow   Me?

Dad   Elbow. C'mon.

Mum   How was Rupert Next Door? You *did* see him, didn't you?

Elbow   Yeah. He's yeah.

Mum   Good. Agoraphobia.

Dad (*chuckles at something on his phone*)   What's agoraphobia?

Mum   Rupert Next Door.

Dad   I know.

Mum   I know you know. But it's official now. There was a woman – well, girl – with a clipboard. She had a pixie cut with a bit of a mulletty fluff at the back. I thought: you don't imagine that of a doctor. But, course, these days, you get anyone being anything.

Dad   Maybe Rupert Next Door will weave his magic on her.

Mum   Rupert Next Door's got Mental Health, he's not a Lothario.

Dad   'A man in his lifetime plays many parts.'

Mum   Must get lonely. Rattling around like a bean in a can. Agoraphobia or not, it's just Care isn't it? People just need Care, don't they?

Elbow   Mum?

Mum   Love?

Elbow   At school today – (*Rumbling sound. Everyone's aware.*) Mum, you know Hamster who I used to hang out with – (*Rumbling intensifies.*)

Mum   I thought you still did –

Elbow   No, we (*Rumbling intensifies.*)

Dad   Can anyone else hear that?

Elbow (*pitching over the rumbling sound*)   How do you cope, Mum, when someone's died?

A crack appears and Nothingness comes flooding in like water into the Titanic. *Screaming, panic, everything destroyed.*

Elbow   Okay!

Everything goes back the way it was. We rewind to:

Elbow   Mum?

Mum   Love?

Dad   Is sixteen-ninety-five too much for a sprinkler?

Mum   Hm?

Dad   eBay. Sprinkler. Sixteen-ninety-five.

Elbow *leaves around this point.*

Mum   When do you ever step foot in the garden?

(*To* **Elbow**, *who she doesn't realise has left the room.*) Well, I'm glad you popped by on Rupert. His mum was So Decent to me when my back went. And everyone needs company, don't they? Trendy little doctors or no trendy little doctors. Elbow?

Dad   Elbow, your mother's talking to you!

Scene Eight

His bedroom.

Elbow *is playing PlayStation/Xbox/whatever. It's a very violent, shooty-shooty game.*

Pug *is playing with something she can practise 'holding' with – even if it's only a controller for the PlayStation, she's trying to cuddle it and give it sympathy.* **Skrik** *is reading a book called 'How to Spot a Psychopathic Killer'.* **Crumb** *watches the computer game over* **Elbow**'s *shoulder, miming shotguns, body wounds, blood spurting out, etc.*

Pug   Do you remember the time we played hide and seek and hid in Nana's wardrobe for, like, *ever* before she found us?

Calico   Wrapped in Towels. She always knew where we were.

Pug   We only ever hid in one place.

Crumb   Why do you two keep going on about Nana?

Pug   I don't know how memories work.

Skrik   Maybe . . . (*Pause. They all look at him.*) we can't talk to anyone, because we're scared they'll understand.

Pug   Understand what?

Skrik   Understand us. Better than we do. Understand maybe we made this happen, by arguing at him, because we weren't with him when it happened . . . and weren't with him because we wanted him to suffer –

Calico   Oh for God's sake, please!

Pug   We didn't want him to suffer –

Skrik   Then why did we say we hated him? Why did we say –

Pug   Please don't go through what we said again.

Skrik   Because it hurts?

Calico   Listen. I'm the Keeper of the Book of Shoulds, and there's nothing here about beating ourselves up over a silly misunderstanding.

Skrik   'A silly misunderstanding.'

Calico   What?

Skrik   We told him we don't want to see him again, and now we won't. That's not a grey area, is it?

Pug   Will someone please stop him.

Skrik   They're only thoughts.

Calico   Ignore. Ignore, ignore, ignore – it's what I do. We didn't mean to say anything so final.

Skrik   Don't they say 'there are no accidents'?

Pug   No one says that – who said that?

Calico   It was Sigmund Freud in *Persistence of Identity.*

Crumb   It was Master Oogway in *Kung-Fu Panda.*

They all get on with what they're doing, knowing **Skrik** *will start up again. Eventually:*

Skrik   I just think maybe we don't feel anything because, y'know, on some level, we don't care. Earlier, one of us mentioned psychopaths – ?

Crumb   Yeah, *you.*

Skrik   It got me thinking, maybe this is the first sign. Cos it's at this age kids start to show . . . *tendencies*, isn't it? Like of us becoming a serial killer. We'll end up being some dead-eyed hitchhiker on a motorway, or something creepy like the CEO of, like, Facebook or something.

Pug   How dare you?

Calico   Can everyone *please* ignore him?

Skrik   You're right. We should go into Denial. Cos, if anything; it's probably thoughts like this that trigger the urge.

Calico (*to* **Pug**)   Don't.

Pug   What urge?

Calico   Don't. Ask.

Skrik   The spree.

Calico   *Please!*

Pug   I can't handle this! Is this going to be forever now, him just banging *on* and *on* and –

Calico   Okay – I'm putting a new Should in the book! 'We shouldn't spread paranoid thoughts.'

Skrik (*helping*)   'They only make things worse.'

Calico (*writing it down*)   Precisely.

Skrik   'Some urges are better kept un-looked-at.'

Calico   Quite. No! We're supposed to be As One. Not falling apart. Not shattering. Remember what Miss said. Look, there must be something in here. (*She opens 'The Book of Shoulds'.*) I am The Keeper of the Book of Shoulds, Oughts, and Rightful Behaviour. Everything we've ever needed to know is in here. I've been compiling it ever since Elbow was a baby. (*Opens book.*) Page One, Should Number One – 'We should cry if we want milk. (*Turns page.*) We shouldn't poo ourselves Too Much: It

Gets Itchy. (*Turns page.*) We should cry if we get itchy.' Oh, they were simpler times . . . Right to . . . (*Skims forward.*) Ah. Yes. Just a couple of weeks ago. Learned the hard way: Shouldn't Number Fourteen Thousand Eight Hundred and Sixteen: 'We shouldn't look Alice Bowman in Year 13 in the eye, Just in Case.'

Voxes *nod/mumble, remembering.*

Pug   She was really mean.

Crumb   I'm running out of patience with your book. All we've got are a million Shoulds, like a million little policemen going 'ello ello ello' whenever I scratch my arse or don't put paper in the bloody paper recycling thing. Half the crap in there contradicts the other half of the crap in there!

Calico   Hey! Shouldn't Number Fourteen Thousand Eight Hundred and Seventeen: 'We shouldn't spread negative thoughts.'

Skrik   Oh! I've just realised!

Pug   What?

Skrik   This is great!

Crumb & Calico   What?

Skrik   We've gone into Denial. Look at us. We're hardly thinking about being a psychopath at all!

Calico   Oh my good Lord, just a moment of silence – *please!*

Pug   But what can we do? We're stuck with him.

Sudden door open/slam offstage.

Pug (*sniffs*)   Wait. Wait! It smells like . . . Africa. (*Pause.*) Lynx Africa.

Calico   It's Him.

Skrik   Is He – ?

*They listen/***Pug** *sniffs.*

Pug   He's coming.

Small ripple of fear/dread, especially between **Pug** *and* **Calico.** **Donut** *enters and picks up the second games controller and automatically joins the game. Both he and* **Elbow** *stare at the screen.* **Crumb** *increasingly hangs off* **Donut**'s *words.*

Donut (*of the game, routinely*)   You watch the windows, I'll stay on stairs.

Elbow   Shoot the barrels.

Donut   Er. No shit, Sherlock. (*Beat.*) Cake.

Elbow   What?

Donut   That's what you've got. A great, big old, oozing, squelchy, fat-arse Death Cake, with cherries and icing and jelly babies drowning it in. That's what you've got. (*Beat.*) Amira mentioned. Hello? Your Girlfriend? Told me about whatsit. Hamster.

Elbow   Oh. (*Feigning disinterest.*) What's Death Cake?

Donut   Ha. Wait and see. All the cool kids know. Cos you've got the Golden Ticket, baby.

Elbow   What you talking about?

Donut   You don't have to be interesting to be interesting anymore. You're Authentic. You're cool by association, and they're gonna want a slice. Parties, drinking, maybe even get yourself a little (*Mimes something sexual. Beat.*) I mean, I know you and Amira are A Thing, but. (*Beat.*) Your mate? The one with the shit hair. No? Someone said he died.

Elbow   Oh. I guess.

Donut   No one wants the whole Death Cake, you have to carry that on your own – but everyone wants to look at it. Lick it.

Elbow *gives him a 'you're weird' look. There is then some action onscreen and they react quickly and violently.*

Donut   Top Left!

Elbow   I am, you twonk.

Donut *punches* **Elbow** *on arm.*

Elbow   Ow.

Donut   This is the trick, yeah. Do Not let it undo you, yeah. Thing is, all your emotions right now – they're like junk yard dogs. They'll pull you apart.

So you don't go about being all mimpsey-pimpsey with like bows and ribbons for them to play with – they'll eat you alive. You gotta go in like Head Pooch, man; Billy Big Bollocks. You gotta be able to hold down their stare and if they're getting any clever ideas – thwack – back in their place. It's training, mate. *Top Left! Are you even playing?* Respect. Keep off the furniture. Obey.

Elbow   And you're the oracle are you? Who do you know who's ever died?

Donut   Y'know Craig with the Gi-norm-ous Head? Yeah, well. His mate. Phil. Or Pete. Or something. Craig blubbed for like, weeks about it. I told him to pull himself together. Man up. Best advice he ever got. His words, not mine.

More violence. **Donut** *tosses the controller away in disgust.*

Donut   You can't even watch the windows.

Donut *shoves* **Elbow** *and walks away. By now,* **Crumb** *is practically in love. He's found his role model.*

Crumb   'Junkyard Dogs'.

Calico   Oh good grief, don't listen to him. Elbow's big brother is an absolute . . . donut. There's even a Should in here about ignoring him. Remember when he said his friend had a real gun and he'd touched it?

Pug   Plus, we're not taking advice from someone who smells of Lynx Africa.

Calico   Not in the book, though, and that's the important bit.

Pug   It's in . . . the Bible!

Calico   Is not!

Pug   'And lol! Noah cameth down from the hill and proclaimed; alleth thee who smelleth of Lynx Africa shalt not have thy opinion pinioned lest thy opinion doth be prickish –'

Crumb   Yeah, but shut up. The Donut's right though, isn't he? It's like Miss/Sir said – we've got to stay together. One Thing. Independent. I mean, look at Donut! He doesn't need anyone! And he's, like, the strongest guy we know.

Pug   Let's not be like Donut.

Crumb   He's not the one fighting amongst himself, is he? He's got No Bullshit, Zero-Tolerance Authority.

Skrik   Agreed – plus which, it's exactly those authoritarian and sadistic tendencies in us that make me think we're onto a winner with the whole 'We're a Psychopath' idea.

Beat.

Crumb   I've warned you, haven't I?

Skrik   You have. More than once. In fact, you –

In a horrific moment, **Crumb** *attacks* **Skrik** *and pulls his tongue out.* **Calico** *and* **Pug** *stare in shock.*

Crumb (*looks at tongue*)   Head Pooch.

From this point, whenever we see **Crumb**, *he has adopted mannerisms from* **Donut**, *as well as one clearly identifiable item of clothing – a brightly coloured cap or beanie, for example.*

We don't see **Skrik** *again until Scene Eighteen.*

Scene Nine

Rupert's *room in his house. Pot plants, trailing plants, etc.* **Elbow** *comes in with a bag of stuff.*

Rupert   Wasn't sure if I'd see you again.

Elbow (*dumps bag*)   They didn't have Baby Bio, but I got the rest of the stuff off the list.

Rupert   I like you coming round to play carer, Elbow, / but

Elbow   S'okay.

Rupert   . . . because I know your mum offered on your behalf, so –

Elbow   S'alright.

Rupert   It's just . . . Because you're inconsistent, which is okay – you've got your own life –

Elbow   What?

Rupert   Well. The Baby Bio. It was three weeks ago I asked for it. Don't worry, I always tell your mum you dropped by. Even when you don't.

Elbow   Okay.

Rupert   It's kinda the contact more than anything. You can get companies to drop anything to your door these days. Except company. But you're not meant to be cooped up being someone's 'carer'. Right?

Elbow   I said okay.

Uncomfortable silence.

Rupert (*looking out window*)   Do you know what that lot are doing down by the canal?

Elbow   It's some sort of candle-lit 'sharing' for a kid at school who snuffed it.

Rupert   You not going?

Elbow *shrugs.*

Rupert   Didn't know 'em?

Elbow   They're not really my friends, so.

Rupert   What about the one who died? I was gonna shout over the fence that I've got brownies or hot-water bottles or something. Just to . . . (*Trails off.*)

Elbow   But?

Rupert   I don't know any of them. Or the lad who died.

Elbow   You'll get on great then.

Rupert   Hmm?

Elbow   All that crying – those girls didn't even know him, and they're like some wailing, blubbering funeral procession. See her? By the tree, with the weird bunches and the guitar? Shona. She sat behind him in French and for the whole of Year 7 she'd gob-up little bits of paper and try and flick 'em into mine and his collars. Now look at her. She's 'written a song about him'. And you see those two soapy, squeaky-clean 'popular girls' who're sharing the same scarf – they Missed School cos of it. They used to barge him in the corridor. But they missed school, so they could stay in and put their crying faces on Instagram! They made him into a hashtag. That's how I heard about it. As an algorithm. It's –

Elbow *feels he's gone too far. Clams up. Perhaps* **Crumb** *has appeared/made himself known, or given him a signal . . .*

Rupert   What was his name?

Elbow   Whose?

Rupert   Your mate. You sat next to him in French – the spit-balls in your collars? (*Beat.*) You were close?

Elbow   No! What's 'close'? We never had Deep & Meaningfuls – like, skimming stones at sunset, and being all (*overly earnest*) 'I just, y'know, really feel . . . Things?' He lived round the corner, so we . . . hung out. We just did, because we did. And then we didn't.

Rupert   Why did you stop? (*No response.*) Was it recent? (*Beat.*) I reckon feelings can get like headphones. Sometimes too loud, too quiet – but if you don't look after them properly, you have to spend for-bloody-ever untangling them, and –

Elbow   I just use earbuds.

He heads for the door.

Rupert   Oh come on, I thought that was quite good! It was on-the-spot. (*Beat.*) Well. Nearly. I have A Lot of time to myself. But it was menna sound on-the-spot!

Elbow (*deadpan*)   Sorry about the Baby Bio.

Rupert   Well. Don't be. I've run out. (*Shakes bottle.*) Near enough. So if you ever see some . . .

I'd appreciate it.

Scene Ten

Elbow (*to us*)   One day, the mirror I'd smashed in PE was whole again. It wasn't the same mirror. I'd swept up the broken bits and let them smash into the bin – it sounded like a round of applause. The caretaker or someone must have replaced it overnight. But it didn't look new. It looked just like the old one. I'd wondered if they'd taken it from the girls' changing rooms. Like for like. Everything gets replaced and no one notices the difference. It's like people can't just let things be broken. Or missing. They can't let there be an absence, like it scares them. When Miss calls the register, they just skip Hamster's name now. And I know, like *obviously*, they have to, but. All absences get sealed over. And I have to pretend I'm sealed over too, or they'll be scared of me. My Nothingness.

Movement piece representing everything getting sealed over and moving on. The empty chair next to **Elbow** *is removed, or there's someone new sitting in it. Lessons go on, lunchbreaks happen, people play and laugh again.*

As a final image, in antithesis to this, **Elbow** *sees the two or three students from the bus again, the one or two holding* **Held Girl**. *We can hear them talking very intimately; but it's too quiet to be audible except as a soft murmur or whisper.* **Pug** *gets closer to them, and their conversation becomes slightly audible. We hear repeated words and phrases like 'Hamster', 'How does that feel?' 'I just feel . . .', 'How do you feel?', 'That must feel horrid', 'It's no one's fault', etc.* **Crumb** *signals for* **Pug** *to return, which, reluctantly, she does.* **Held Girl** *is left alone by the others.* **Elbow** *looks at her. She is aware she's being stared at and meets his eye.*

Elbow   Faker.

Scene Eleven

Hamster's bench, on a canal towpath.

There are a couple of trees and somewhere to sit. People have put flowers, cards, notes and trinkets round the bottom of the tree. **Elbow** *and the* **Voxes** *enter, minus* **Skrik**. **Pug** *enters as a plane, dog-fights, etc. . . .*

Pug   Do you remember when we were kids and did planes here? Hamster did sick loop-de-loops. I can still smell the jet-fuel.

She stops when she sees the cards around Hamster's bench. **Elbow** *picks one up. The other* **Voxes** *look at cards.*

Crumb   Tourists.

Amira *enters unseen.*

Amira   So you don't answer your phone anymore? That's alright, I'm the same sometimes. But if you ever spot my little name coming up when it rings, that's just a little clue that it's me. Everyone asks after you. (*Beat.*) Seen the cards?

Elbow   Yeah.

Amira   We didn't know where to put them and I was like here – I mean, it's his bench, isn't it?

Elbow   Is it?

Amira   He carved his name in it. Actually, Shona and me made something. You're not allowed to take the piss . . . (*She opens her bag, reveals a birdhouse.*) What do you think?

Pause.

Elbow   Is it your first birdhouse?

Amira (*laughs*)   We thought we'd put it in the tree. Y'know. Birds. Song. Life.

Pug (*to* **Elbow**)   Tell her. Tell her: It's just hard – the emptiness and the Nothingness and the gnashing, mashed-up inside-iness. . . (*To* **Amira**.) You know we haven't even cried yet? Like, nothing. Not even selfishly –

Crumb   Do I need to have a word?

Pug   But she's just here! We love her!

Crumb   You really think she wants some little dribble of a child, who leaves a watery trail behind him wherever he goes? She wants someone more like . . . Donut.

Pug   No one. Ever. Has ever. Wanted –

Calico *puts her hand over* **Pug**'s *mouth.*

Calico   Shh.

Crumb   Tell her you feel Nothing and she'll Know You're a Monster.

Amira *looks at* **Elbow** *a moment. He is staring at the water, or the birdhouse. She takes his hand.*

Beat.

Amira   Sorry. Clammy.

She wipes her hand and re-takes his. Smiles.

Amira   You didn't come to the school thing. Or the candle-lit thing we did here. If it's, I dunno, maybe you think it all sucks, but not everyone could make it, so we're going to have another? This Friday. We're going to take turns sharing some stories about Hamster. Maybe you might find it useful.

Elbow   Stories?

Crumb   What 'stories'! We literally hung out in his room and played Xbox the whole of last summer.

Calico   And the three summers before that. Not a thought to fresh air.

Crumb   We shot Nazi Zombies eight hours a day.

Pug   And then we stopped hanging out with him.

Calico   We didn't 'stop'.

Pug   We did when we started hanging out with Amira.

Crumb   He stopped hanging out with us too.

Calico   Quite. We could have hung out . . . as a three.

Pug   So why didn't we invite him?

Calico   Oh come on, you're turning into . . . you-know-who, with all this misery-talk! (*To* **Crumb**.) She doesn't mean it.

Amira   Just dumb stories. Like . . . Savannah was saying about the time him and her tried to shoplift from Smiths and the guard chased them and they even got out the door but then they tripped over a cockapoo. Y'know, stories. (*Beat.*) It helps. Sometimes seeing other people feel things helps me feel things? I dunno, it's dumb. We're gonna dress the bench. With things we remember –

Elbow   Nah.

Amira   – you can get bunting that has, like, your photos printed on them? So we're going to make Hamster Bunting™, and poems and stuff to stick up and –

Elbow   Why? (*Beat.*) That's not what he was like.

Amira   I think that's what he was like.

Elbow   How would you know?

Amira (*she takes her hand back*)   Okay.

Elbow   Did you ever even hang out outside of school?

Amira   Okay. Erm.

Elbow   But you didn't, cos you didn't get on, cos you weren't actually friends – just like him and Savannah weren't Actually Friends – cos he didn't even like her, just like he didn't even like – (*He stops himself.*)

Amira   Go on. Finish what you were gonna say.

Elbow   He. He didn't even like you. He said you were soapy. Like, some earnest little squeaky-clean *Blue Peter* girl, who –

Amira *gets out a cigarette.*

Elbow   He said smoking made you a Try-Hard/Pick-Me.

Amira   Wow.

Elbow   I'm not having a go at *you*, I'm –

Amira   Really? Cos it sounds like you kinda Are.

Elbow   I'm trying to explain he, *he* was –

Amira   What? (**Elbow** *goes quiet.*) Eventually, y'know, people will stop asking you if you're okay.

She begins to head.

Pug   HELP! AMIRA!

Amira *stops at the sound of* **Pug**'s *voice. Everyone's surprised/shocked.* **Calico** *and* **Crumb** *restrain* **Pug** *again.*

Pug   Please! AMIRA!

Amira *looks back a moment.*

Amira (*to* **Elbow**)   Sorry? Did you say something? (*Beat.*) Elbow?

Amira *and* **Elbow** *look at each other.* **Calico** *restrains* **Pug** – **Pug** *writhes.*

Amira   Okay. (*She scrunches up the fag box and chucks it.*)

She turns and exits. **Elbow** *watches. He realises she left the birdhouse. Beat. He kicks it – damages it, but doesn't destroy it. Then he picks it up, and holds it to him.*

Scene Twelve

Suddenly, the world ends.

Oxygen and gravity are destroyed and, in slow motion, the characters grab hold of the bench or tree, etc. so they don't float away as the world is pulled apart around them.

The **Narrators**. *The astronaut doll.*

N1   In Space, no one can hear you scream . . .

N2   But in the emptiness, Elbow could hide anywhere. Because everywhere he looked –

N1   No one was looking.

N2   And whatever he said –

N1   there was no one to contradict him. You can feel as safe as you would in a fortress –

N2   sitting in a pile of your own shit.

N1   We never agreed to That Word.

N2   *You* never agreed to That Word.

The characters spot **Elbow**'s *bed or bedroom or X-box, and 'swim' for it. Once they land and have a firm grip of it (bed/X-box, etc.), they are back in the real world. Such as it is.*

Scene Thirteen

Elbow *is asleep. The remaining* **Voxes** *are asleep too.* **Pug** *wakes up.* **Pug** *climbs over to where* **Elbow** *is sleeping; she starts invoking a dream:*

Pug   Lovely blue skies and white clouds and everything's fresh and bright, and the colours of a toothpaste advert. (*Makes the sound of water, or simply says 'splash,*

splash, splash'.) You can hear the water lapping. And . . . (*Makes noise.*) a log fire, like the one Hamster showed us how to make when we went camping . . .

When **Pug** *has made her amateurish sound effects, they magically appear around her as pre-records.* **Elbow** *responds, asleep. He finds it unsettling.* **Pug** *stays close, trying to reassure him.*

Pug   Oh, but the lake's lovely, splash splash, and the fire's lovely, crackle crackle, and the air's nice . . . (*Tries blowing on him – raspberries.*) And it's the loveliest dream in the whole wide **Amira** begins to head off. And you can smell popcorn . . .

Elbow *reacts.*

Pug   And it's like popcorn but it's not quite because it's

Elbow (*still asleep*)   Amira's hair.

Pug   And she smells like popcorn and Benson & Hedges that she stole from her dad's big North Face jacket with the hole in, in the hallway where you first kissed.

Elbow *goes in for a kiss. Maybe* **Pug** *avoids it, maybe* **Pug** *holds out her hand and he kisses that, while she stands around, awkward/embarrassed.*

Pug (*reassuring him*)   And you know it's okay and it's okay to say . . . whatever to her. About the angriness. And the emptiness.

Elbow *shakes his head – is sad, broken.*

Elbow   Too much.

Pug   Too much for her or too much for you?

Elbow   Too much.

Pug   No, no, cos it'll be okay, cos nothing's so bad you can't tell her, and maybe that's why you're angry, at her; she might make it okay. Remember the niceness of –

Elbow   It's Too Much.

Sound of storm-clouds, etc.

Calico *wakes up, sees* **Pug** *and desperately tries to stop her. They fight as silently as they can manage, so as to not wake* **Crumb.**

Pug (*hushed*)   Tell her everything, tell her, tell her, tell her – mind control! subliminal messages! – tell her, tell her, tell *someone* –

Calico *pulls* **Pug** *away from* **Elbow**.

Calico   Don't. Play. Games. This is absolutely not in the Book of Shoulds.

Pug   There are no Shoulds anymore, except whatever He says –

Calico   Do you want me to tell him you said that? You know what'll happen.

Crumb   Tell me what?

Scene Fourteen

Elbow *and* **Crumb**. **Crumb** *is playing on the console.* **Elbow** *start toying with the birdhouse he broke.*

N1   The other thing you notice is, even the weather doesn't notice you.

N2   Which obviously you kinda knew, if you'd ever thought about it. But on TV or whatever, it's always rainy when the main character is sad.

N1   'Prophetic fallacy' – (*flexing*) GCSE Drama.

N2   So, because it's sunny, you start to think, logically, maybe you're not the main character after all. And the real main character must be off being happy in like lovely sunshine somewhere, slaying dragons or snogging royalty or, like, getting a record deal, cos . . . sun.

N1   And there are good bits and hard bits about thinking like that.

N2   On the plus side. Life is going on. And on the other,

N1   it goes on, and on, and on.

N2   With or without your participation.

N1   Until –

Beat.

Elbow (*to* **Crumb**)   Where are the others?

Either **Crumb** *keeps playing on the games console, too absorbed to acknowledge him, or:*

Crumb (*still playing*)   Who? We don't need anyone.

Scene Fifteen

Mum *and* **Dad** *on their phones.* **Elbow** *enters with* **Crumb**.

Crumb (*waves hand in front of a parent's eyes – no reaction*)   Pathetic.

Elbow   I feel like a ghost.

Crumb   Welcome to my life.

Elbow *and* **Crumb** *chortle.*

Mum   Your dinner's in the thing.

Elbow *and* **Crumb** *look at each other with disdain: 'What's that supposed to mean?'*

Mum (*correcting herself*)   On the thing.

Dad (*chuckles*) 'Thing'.

Mum (*chuckles. To* **Dad**)   What? (*To* **Elbow**.) Microwave.

Elbow   K.

Dad   Two and a half minutes, then take it out, peel back the umm . . .

He is distracted. Pause.

Crumb   Lid.

Dad   Lid, and give it a stir with a . . .

Again.

Crumb   Fork.

Dad   Fork. Then pop it back in for a . . .

Crumb   Eternity? Until the Sun detonates and sucks the whole solar system into a Black Hole? Until Christ rises again, to win *Dancing on Ice* by beating Kim Jong-un and 'That Presenter off of *Springwatch*'?

Elbow   It's alright, Dad.

Dad (*suddenly remembering: to* **Mum**)   Did you see – ?

Mum (*to* **Dad**, *with eye contact.*)   The erm – ?

Both   That video!

The both do the same impression of a video they saw. For example, they both mime a person climbing to the top of a ladder, looking around like they're a bit stupid, and then the whole ladder leaning over in one direction, and the person realising they're falling/about to fall. Both parents laugh, with a brief moment of eye contact, then hold hands, then return to their phones – hands still held.

Crumb (*under his breath*)   Miserable.

But maybe **Elbow** *isn't so sure.* **Donut** *enters.* **Crumb** *perks up. He points him out to* **Elbow**, *as if he's a celebrity.* **Elbow** *doesn't care.*

Donut   Alwight.

Mum   Squidge! You're back! How long for? (*Sees bag. Tries to sound upbeat.*) Oh, laundry!

Dad   Did you get caught in the rain?

Donut (*to* **Elbow**)   Alwight, dickhead. (*He ruffles his hair/thumps him.*)

Elbow   Piss off.

Donut   'Piss off.'

Mum (*not looking*)   Hey! *Elbow.*

Donut *gives* **Elbow** *the typical sibling face meaning: 'Ha ha ha, you got caught and I didn't.'* **Crumb** *sniggers, clearly taking* **Donut***'s side.* **Elbow** *thumps* **Crumb**.

Mum   Oh. Did you pick up the Baby Bio?

Elbow   Erm, yeah. That was ages ago, Mum.

Mum (*not registering him*)   Hm? Donut, I asked if you got the plant food for Rupert Next Door?

Donut   I'll take it round later.

Elbow *is offended.*

Elbow   You what?

Donut   What?

Elbow   I do that, Rupert asks me to do that; Mum – that's what I do.

Mum   Yeah, but you stopped bothering. And that's okay. But it's good someone cares now, isn't it?

Elbow   I care.

Donut   Awwww, baby.

Crumb (*joining in with* **Donut**)   Awwww, baby 'cares'.

Elbow   You wouldn't know. Rupert's alright.

Dad   Kids.

Donut   Yeah, I know Rupert's alright, Twonkmeister. Bangs on about his rhododendrons a bit, but he's a laugh.

Elbow   Mum! Rupert was my thing.

Mum   It's not your thing if you don't care.

Elbow   I do care.

Mum   You don't! Caring's doing, it's not just sitting there thinking about it.

Donut   He doesn't even do that. (*Another annoying thump/mime/hair ruffle, etc.*) He just sits at home seeing how many farts he can squeeze into his bedroom.

Crumb *sniggers again.*

Crumb   Come on, that was good. You couldn't've thought of that.

Elbow   You *are* me!

Crumb   You're on your own here, mate.

Elbow (*to* **Mum/Dad**)   Well, I wanna start again.

Dad   'Stop, start; stop, start . . .'

Mum   It's Friday night, Elbow. You must have better things to do than care-work for your next door neighbour. Enjoy yourself. Donut doesn't mind, do you, Squidge?

Donut   After Rupert's I'm headed round Christine's.

Mum   Aww. Send love. And tell her mum we'll see her for the shindig on Sunday! Glad-rags: on. Hair: done. Face: less said, the better! Can't wait.

Dad   I ruddy *love* Karaoke Sundays with the gang.

Donut   Oh oh oh – did you see?

All   The video!

All three do the same mime from earlier (ladder, climbing, looking round, falling) – all laugh. **Crumb** *watches it all, eyes twinkling as if it's magic.*

Crumb (*Laughs. To* **Donut***, unheard*)   Do it again.

Donut   Did you see that? Hilarious!

Dad   His expression!

Mum   Maddy took that. You can come if you like, Elbow? One thing about Christine's dad is he can laugh at himself. Broken arm or no broken arm.

Dad & Donut   He can't climb a ladder though!

Mum, **Dad**, **Donut** *and* **Crumb** *laugh.*

Mum   When you can't even laugh at yourself, I mean you're a lost cause.

Elbow *grabs the Baby Bio from* **Donut** *and marches out.*

Donut   Oi! You little plum!

Scene Sixteen

Rupert *'s flat.*

Elbow *arrives, alone, dejected.* **Rupert** *is preparing a table for a nice dinner – laying out plates and wine glasses (x2), flowers or candle, that kinda thing.*

Rupert   I thought you'd be your brother.

Elbow   Sorry. (*He hands him the Baby Bio.*) It wasn't me who found it.

Elbow *sits on a chair – he is obviously sitting at the 'romantic dinner table', oblivious.* **Rupert** *observes. He tries to make it obvious he's setting up for something important – loud clattering of cutlery, lighting the candle right in front of* **Elbow** *'s face, etc.*

Rupert   I'd offer you a drink but I'm –

Elbow   S'alright. I should get going. (*He goes nowhere.*) You and the plants probably have big plans to watch *Strictly*.

Rupert   Not quite. I'm –

Elbow   No?

Rupert (*pause*)   No.

Rupert *checks the time. Beat. He sits down.*

Rupert   What's up?

Elbow   I've realised something, finally. I hate him.

Rupert   Your brother?

Elbow   Hamster.

Rupert   Ahhh-kay.

Elbow   Yeah, I fucking hate him. He told his mum we were best friends. He never told *me*. Why'd he never tell *me*? We weren't best friends.

Rupert   Okay.

Elbow   I just thought his actual best friend was someone, I dunno, someone better. Isn't your best friend meant to be someone you share crap with? Y'know? Inner-stuff.

Rupert   I don't know. Guess, best friends can / come in all –

Elbow   And I hate how everyone's talking about him. Like there's this whole 'community' now of these kids, and all they ever do is talk about him and pretend they knew him.

Rupert   Why's that a problem?

Elbow   The problem is Hamster wasn't this skippy, kitteny, rainbow-boy they're making out. He was a wind-up merchant, he was snarky . . . he was a shit about Amira when he found out I liked her –

Rupert   Your girlfriend?

Elbow   Kinda. Was. He just made all these bitchy comments about the fact she had green hair – *once* – or her feet.

Rupert   Well –

Around this point, **Elbow** *potentially pours himself a glass of wine.*

Elbow (*ignoring*)   How can you have a problem with someone's feet? They're feet. And he says all this trash while we're playing Cuphead – which is crap anyway – and I just chucked my controller and was like: 'Mate: game over.' Which I know is a dick thing to say. And I went. And that was the *Last Thing* I said to him . . .

Rupert   But you didn't mean it.

Elbow   No. No: I did. I felt it, like I was on fire with it. So, No. I can't be this perfect fucking saint his disciples want me to be and tell them he was a saint too; he was a prick. And dying was a prick-ish thing to do too. And me being his best friend? Is that it? Am I all he got? Someone who . . . actually hated him.

Rupert   Did you?

Elbow   Yes, cos when I told him it was over . . . he was meant to argue. Like he did about everything – everything! Hair! Feet! Cuphead! He wasn't meant to . . . it wasn't meant to be over. I wasn't meant to Win. But you play stupid games, you win stupid prizes, right?

Beat. **Rupert** *glances out the window.*

Rupert   The girl you pointed out? Last time you were here, with the guitar? If all the strings were the same – no, hear me out – if all the strings were the same, you couldn't make a chord. You couldn't make a song. Even when we really love someone, there are other feelings there too. Everything is a mix. And the fact you're trying to block out what your friends are saying . . . makes me think there might be other voices you're blocking out too. Feelings. That maybe don't hate him. Or maybe love him. Listen to them, talk to them. Everything's a two-way process.

Elbow   So you're saying I've got to let in this shit-arse bunch of soppy idiots, just so I can be happy?

Rupert   I'm saying wholeness requires others. We are each a mix of us, and the people we do us with. And the more kinds of people you let in, the more kinds of you you discover. Strangers lighting up strangers.

At this point, **Rupert** *makes another effort towards getting ready for his romantic evening.* **Elbow** *notices the table. The wine glass in his hand.*

Elbow   Did you know I was coming?

Rupert   I have a date.

Elbow *vacates the chair quickly.*

Elbow   But – you've got agoraphobia.

Rupert   I know, aren't I greedy?

Elbow   Is it the doctor? With the clipboard and the hair? My mum said about her.

Rupert (*amused*)   She's not a doctor, she's an admin assistant from a care agency. They organise home visits and stuff. She's my age. We clicked. And she might leave the clipboard at home.

Elbow   I'm such a dick.

Rupert   Elbow. Everyone. The World Over. Is a dick. And we can still love them. (*Smiles warmly. Beat.*) Now. Be a mate, and fuck off.

Elbow   Right!

Rupert (*looks out window*)   The candle-lit hordes are back. By the canal. Maybe you could go and hear what they have to say. On the off-chance it lights up any new voices in you.

Scene Seventeen

Elbow *is alone. He wraps himself in his duvet, or a big coat; he looks small. Perhaps* **Crumb** *is playing PlayStation throughout, back to* **Elbow**. *There is a representation of the candle-lit horde onstage – perhaps walking past/circling them in procession.* **Elbow** *is trying not to cry:*

Crumb   Don't.

Elbow   What?

Crumb   You know what.

Elbow *tries to stifle himself crying.*

Crumb   Do that and we're done. You'll be a faker like them.

Elbow   So?

Crumb   This isn't about Hamster, it's about you – it's about you being all 'victim', when you're not. You can't cry. You ended it. You did / not want him.

Elbow   He was meant to fight back.

Crumb   Why?

Elbow   Because –

Elbow *fights the tears.*

Crumb   Don't.

Elbow   I wasn't! Because, I don't know why! Because! I wasn't thinking! Because I'm allowed not to think, and be wrong, and say dumb-ass crap I don't mean, and then break down about it like a . . . (*He cries.*)

Crumb   Like a hypocrite!

Elbow (*with conviction*)   Like a hypocrite! I can be both things, I can disagree with myself!

Crumb   Don't you — don't you dare – what would Donut do? You wouldn't see Donut being all . . . – you're a faker!

Elbow   Donut's the faker, pretending to be Just One Thing – like this stone god who just floats about, being all untouchable and / invincible!

Crumb   You cry and I'm off. You cry and I'm walking, I swear. Do that and . . . Mate: Game over.

Silence: **Crumb** *and* **Elbow** *realise what he's said. They stare at each other.* **Elbow** *stands, not aggressively. Immediately,* **Crumb** *sits – scared.*

Beat.

Crumb   Sorry.

Elbow   What have you done with the others?

Crumb   Cross my heart, I don't have that power. They just escaped one night.

Elbow   Where?

Crumb (*points*)   The cracks. But that's The Nothingness! You'll never make it back! They could be anywhere.

Elbow   There's only one place they'll hide. And I'll get back. Cos you're gonna help. Unless you wanna walk? (*He gestures to the door.*)

Crumb   I've stood by you through everything! No one protects you like me!

Elbow   Then we should be on the same side. Right? (*No response.*) Right, soldier?

Beat.

Crumb (*removes the* **Donut** *cap/hat*)   Dib dib dib.

Elbow *leads the way.*

Scene Eighteen

Elbow *follows* **Crumb** *through one of the cracks in the stage (it might be, conveniently, a crack that runs through a wall and down a cupboard, for example). The following movement sequence is performed using* **Elbow** *and the astronaut/diver doll interchangeably and/or simultaneously.* **N1** *and* **N2** *animate the doll as* **Elbow** *enters the abyss.*

N2   In your life,

N1   every new loss contains, inside it,

N2   your dumb, white-knuckled grip on all the other crap you've ever had to lose;

N1   or had stolen; or that's died.

N2   Dead gerbils found all stiff and doorstoppy in their nest one morning.

N1   People you found kissing someone else.

N2   *Prick.*

N1   That Actually Really Good stripy jumper you packed before you moved house, but that wasn't there when you unpacked.

N2   Whole oceans of loss, crashing into ponds and smashing through rivers.

N1   Swallowing swimming pools and spitting out waterfalls.

N2   Every time you grieve, you go back. Not to the last time you grieved. Right back to the first time,

N1   The first time you ever got lost there,

N2 (*dramatically*)   In the Lost Sea . . . of Loss.

N1   This is the Important Bit. You're ruining it.

N2   Am not!

N1   Bloody are.

N2   Bloody ain't.

N1   I'm not arguing about this.

N2   Good, then I win.

N1 *isn't sure how/if to proceed.*

N2   So as Elbow swam through the abyss,

N1   he had to be very quiet . . . and listen . . .

N2   He had to be as quiet as the whole Antarctic,

N2   quiet as a paperclip in a drawer . . .

N2   I like that one.

N1   Thanks. Just thought of it. (*Beat.*) So very quiet . . .

N2   he could hear where the voices were hiding.

N1   Like they say, if you're going through hell,

N2   keep going.

*On **Elbow**'s journey through the abyss (during the above dialogue), there is a bus like a whale that gloops through the darkness; **Elbow** hides and, as it passes, we can hear the commotion of kids onboard, coming home from school.*

*There are strange dark figures representing **Mum** and **Dad**; they hold hands and, as if the connection is electric current, they are both up lit by their phones.*

Elbow *passes the group from the bus,* **Held Girl** *and her friends. He watches them, mesmerised – possibly touches them, as he passes.*

Eventually, **Elbow** *finds a door, and opens it. It's Nana's linen closet, where all the* **Voxes** *are hiding.* **Skrik** *is clutching a jar that contains his tongue.*

Calico   He found us!

Pug   I knew he would!

Skrik (*tongueless and inaudible: 'Yay, he's back!'*)

Elbow   Oh guys. All this, all this mess – none of it is your fault. (*To* **Skrik**.) I'm so sorry. I should have talked to you. I don't know how it all works, and when you came in with all your . . . really downbeat . . .

Calico   *Really* downbeat . . .

Pug   Oh my days, so downbeat.

Crumb   I literally wanted to shoot myself . . .

Elbow   *Alright* . . . I just wanted to block it out. I just wanted you silent. But I needed to talk with you, back and forth; all of you, and I acted like you were something to be stamped out, and that just . . . I'm sorry. If any of us are missing, there's no balance.

Skrik (*talks in a sensible way, but we can't make anything out*)

Elbow (*to* **Calico**)   Do you know how to, um . . . do . . . the tongue? . . . back in?

Calico   We know how.

Pug   We've always known how.

Calico   We just . . .

Pug   Well, we can't, can we?

Calico   Not without making a horrible mess.

Elbow   Well, what do we do?

Calico   We can't do anything.

Pug   Only you can.

Elbow   Me?

Calico   It's all you. The cupboard, the jar, the Nothingness, everything.

Skrik *is hesitant, but* **Elbow** *takes the jar from him and puts his hand in. He takes the tongue and puts it back into* **Skrik**'*s mouth.*

Skrik (*miserably*)   I just think it's all my fault we're here; I should stay here, forever, and let the Nothingness swallow me up like I deserve.

Pug   He's back!

She squeezes him.

Elbow   We have somewhere to be.

Scene Nineteen

*Students and others are gathered around 'Hamster's bench', holding candles, etc.
When* **Elbow** *and the* **Voxes** *arrive,* **Shona** *is talking.*

Shona   Hamster probably only knew me as that little brat who'd gob up bits of Rizla
and try and get them down his collar in French. Till one day he turned round and it
looked like his eyes were gonna pop and he just went *'va te faire foutre!'*. Which, if
you don't know, is rude in French. But even though all that, he still walked me home
sometimes, when it was dark. So. To me. He was The Best.

Various echoes of 'The Best' from the crowd. **Amira** *gets up, less sure, encouraged by*
Shona *(and others).*

Amira   I don't know. He never walked me home, or anything, so. . . (*Chuckle.*) I
thought we got on, but I heard now maybe we didn't. I always liked him though.
(*Shrugs.*)

Amira *sits – other people encourage her to keep going, but she stays put.* **Elbow** *gets
through the people to the standing spot.*

Elbow   I need to speak to you.

A kind of hush. The students have all formed opinions of him during his absence.
Amira *indicates the group.*

Amira   Mate. We're in the middle of something. If you want to say something
– (*Indicates group.*)

He looks at **Shona** *and she encourages him to speak. He opens his mouth:*

Crumb, **Calico**, **Pug** *and* **Skrik** *speak through/for* **Elbow***:*

Elbow   Sometimes, I hated Hamster. That was the feeling.

Crumb   Cos he could be a right dick.

Pug   Like all of us –

Calico   – he was a mix.

Crumb   And some of those bits I hated, sometimes.

Skrik   Maybe that's a limitation of mine, I don't know.

Pug   But I can't boil him down into one singular thing.

Crumb   Not yet.

Calico   But you're right about one thing.

Elbow   This was his bench, and he did carve his name into it –

Crumb   but only after he'd tried to burn it down about eight times with his mum's
lighter and some Glade air freshener.

Some unexpected chuckles from crowd.

Skrik   I feel ashamed of myself if that ruins anything for you, when everyone else can just talk about him as if he was just . . . The Best; I love that he's like that for you. For me it's messier.

Elbow   But I know I feel like I've lost something that should be Right Here, next to me.

Calico (*looking at* **Pug**)   Like a really annoying shadow. Usually smiling, cos he had something smartarse to say.

More small chuckles of recognition.

Crumb   He wasn't just One Thing.

Pug   I just don't want him to go anywhere with us forgetting that. It doesn't feel fair somehow,

Calico   on him. Or any of us left behind either.

Skrik   He was a rattle-bag of contradictions and snarky comments and . . .

Calico   bossiness and worry,

Pug   silliness, sensation

Crumb   loyalty, anger

Skrik   and four-in-the-morning, frosty-morning, honesty

Elbow   the stuff I didn't always wanna look at. (*To* **Amira**.) Of course he liked you. He just didn't always like how much I liked you. So he said some dumb things. And if you can forgive him, maybe you can forgive me for being . . . literally, a shit.

Amira (*smile*)   You are a shit.

Crumb   I just wanted things outside to hurt like all the things hurt inside.

Pug   I think I wanted to see someone shatter like me.

Skrik   Sorry I pushed you away.

Calico   I shouldn't have.

Elbow   The way we treat Them Outside ends up being how we treat Us Inside. And vice versa.

Pug   And that's it.

Skrik   I don't know what else I'm feeling.

Calico   Yet.

Pug   Definitely love too, but.

Elbow   I'm just starting.

He cries. **Amira** *holds out her hand.* **Elbow** *takes it. Beat.*

Elbow   Sorry. Clammy.

Wipes hand, takes it again. **Amira** *and* **Shona** *come to him, and he is held. Everyone joins the hug. They all form a big hug around* **Elbow**. *The* **Voxes** *join.*

Amira   About what you said –

Elbow   Amira, he was angry at me, not you and –

Amira (*genuinely, mischievously*)   No, I mean – and thanks and everything, I believe you, but – I'm serious . . . if that's what he wanted: Shall we burn the bench down?

The crowd laugh/cheer/respond variously – but with positivity.

N1   And so, as the sun set, over the canal; [however many] students and friends, gathered, held one another and

N2   lovingly set fire to Hamster's bench.

N2   Or didn't, you decide.

Again, probably 'One is the Loneliest Number' by Three Dog Night. Or not. You decide.

End of play.

Strangers Like Me

BY ED HARRIS

Notes on rehearsal and staging, drawn from a workshop with the writer,
held at the National Theatre facilitated by director Andrea Brooks, October 2022

Icebreaker

The group went round and said words that felt resonant for them with regards to *Strangers Like Me*:

deeply felt · recovery · sincerity · heard · balance · relatable · affinity · lost · expansive · technical · silence · comedy · shattered · humour · void · absence · heart · many voices · mischief · mess · conflict · reflection · heart · raw · fish tank · nuance · unheard · hopeful · inclusive · human · universal

Puppetry workshop

Andrea Brooks introduced that this workshop sprung out of her experience of training in the Republic of Georgia, and explained how her passion and speciality in puppetry was able to develop and expand working with a group of artists at Battersea Arts Centre, under the artistic leadership of Tom Morris.

Andrea Brooks invited the group to use the terminology of *animation* rather than puppetry: the etymology comes from 'moving' and 'spirit'. She explains that puppetry is doing just that.

There are three fundamentals of animation:

1 Breath

2 Focus

3 Gravity

And the fourth floating idea is moving the soul.

Exercise: Little creatures

Everyone was invited to walk around the room and find a space to sit down, placing their writing hand on the floor, preferably taking jewellery off. Brooks then led some orchestrated breathing as a group. Breath in for four, hold for four, out for six. This regulates breathing.

The group were invited to see what sounds they could identify – both inside and outside the building. Brooks guided the attention into the room in terms of sounds and invited the group to start taking deep belly breaths. The group were invited to notice that as they breathe deeply, the heel of the hand wants to lift off the floor, and their descending breath wants to let it move back towards the floor. Then let this happen in their hand as well.

When Andrea Brooks clapped and the group opened their eyes to become aware that what they are looking at was not their hand, but a little hand creature.

The group were invited to go forward with curiosity rather than ambition as they manipulated their little creatures: if these little creatures want to move around, they have to do that with the gift of weight through the wrist.

Each hand creature was given a small ball to move with. The participants were encouraged to follow the creature, ensuring its means of locomotion are absolutely justified by the ground. These creatures can't do anything that a real creature couldn't do.

Andrea Brooks counted down from sixty. During the counting, the hand creatures retreated to where they were born and the puppeteers let them go. The hand creatures are then pushed back into the ground and thanked for coming.

The group were asked to get up and shake it off.

Reflections from little creatures exercise

Responses from the group included:

- Once you start to make a connection with the creature you have created, you start to anthropomorphise their existence. It starts to yearn for a connection with our reality.
- We often think about animation as interacting separately to the 'real' world, but actually the arc narrative of learning to walk and going off into the world, and dealing with the commotion of the world, gave it reality.
- The struggle of gravity gave it sense.

Andrea concluded that these exercises were passed on by a Georgian puppet mistress and she urged that if you are to pass it on you should always underline the foundational preciousness of the work.

Exercise: Summoning the soul into an object

This exercise requires careful regulation and, just as above, there should be a sustained sense of its preciousness.

The group were instructed to each take a scarf and lay it out on the ground. The group then folded their scarf four times, one hand doing the job of manipulating the life of the scarf, the other assisting. On the count of three, two, one on a quick in-breath by participants, the creature comes up and to life, but always keeping contact with the ground.

Andrea instructed the group to keep focus, keep contact with the world, and keep using breath to let the creature find its own way.

The descent back to where the creature came from happened over the count of thirty. The group were instructed to allow the scarf to fall as a pile, not to spread it out. They pushed with both hands the creature back into the ground and shook the scarf out and the spirit away.

Reflections after summoning the soul exercise

The focus was on curiosity not ambition, making the creatures real and alive. Get that right and you can use anything – even a lollipop stick, successfully. But if the foundations aren't there, it doesn't matter how impressive or elaborate the material puppet might be, it will not have the same animating effect and feel alive.

Brooks suggested that puppeteers would ideally have thirty seconds to a minute to prepare, to avoid rushing around on stage moving from character to puppeteer too quickly.

The text

Andrea Brooks and Ed Harris lead a close-reading text workshop with free-flow questions afterwards.

Brooks introduced the exercise as not only an important way to appreciate the text but also for the young people to become familiar with the lines and the script as a whole. A 'close reading' of the text is a reading that takes a similar level of care and attention as the work being done with the creatures and puppets.

The same principles of being led by curiosity rather than ambition applied and Andrea Brooks explained that in her experience, a close reading of the text will yield lots of questions.

The exercise began with Scene Ten: Elbow's Speech.

Brooks asked what participants noticed about it, and what their interpretation of this section of the text might be. Some thoughts were:

- Through the speech a new mirror might be being put in place: a sealing over, becoming not quite as it was.
- That there is a habit and culture of going on, despite events, and the emotional impact of this on Elbow.
- There is a real sadness to the line and Elbow is expressing how no one cares – it is just another mundane day.
- Elbow might speak with disconnect and distance.

The group were invited to look at one specific line within the speech:

I'd swept up the broken bits and let them smash into the bin – it sounded like a round of applause. The caretaker or someone must have replaced it overnight.

Some thoughts were:

- Elbow needs professional help but the caretaker offers care to a material inanimate object, rather than to Elbow. It isn't the care Elbow so desperately needs.
- The very name caretaker is interesting: within it is this concept of care and yet the profession is not directed towards caring for bereavement.
- There are feelings of jealousy from Elbow.

Close-read exercise in groups

The group split into smaller groups of five to each do a close reading of a chosen scene, annotating the script and finding three key questions they don't have the answer to but feel important to ask.

Scene Four close reading

The conversation around Scene Four looked at how the Voxes are all the same person and that it is useful to keep in mind during directing the play: they are having the same thought process and emotional journey throughout. Groups discussed that it is truly an internal monologue and the language of the scene is organic. It contains lots of textures and objects concerning the natural world.

Different language is used from 'best friend', which might feel rigid and hierarchical, and there are themes of expression and who is allowed to express themselves within the scene.

Questions included:

- What is the interpretation of Crumb, how do we understand them?
- 'We said we'd outgrown him . . .' – what are his intentions with this question?
- How did Hamster die? And therefore with this answer, is the guilt being carried sensical or misplaced?
- Why is the word 'Balderdash' used?
- Is the character Pug a representation of feelings towards girls in their own class?
- What feelings would Elbow accept as authentic?

Scene Seven close reading

The conversation around Scene Seven was to do with the appreciation of the complex depiction of Elbow's family dynamic: the parents aren't horrible or intentionally neglectful but are rather people with busy day-to-day lives and distractions. There is comedy as well as a seriousness to this scene where you gain a deeper understanding of the loneliness and isolation that grief and bereavement have brought to Elbow.

The use of irony is very present here: Mum speaks about everyone 'needing care don't they' and yet Elbow doesn't receive any at this moment. It seems that Rupert having 'mental health' gives him the right to have feelings that Elbow does not have the space to have.

Questions included:

- How do we do the moment of the rumbling and breaking through of the water?
- How might we do the rewind?
- What is the viscosity of nothingness? Is it thick and rushing like water?

- Are the Voxes always present?
- Dad mentions that he can hear something – does he know something is there? Can he sense it?
- Does the image speak to the fact that death is universal and involves all?
- Rupert has 'mental health' – gives him the right to have feelings, but because Elbow is 'normal' he doesn't get the same space to have those feelings.
- Why does this *Titanic* moment happen? Perhaps it shows that rather than it being a momentary expression – 'my parents don't care about me' – it is more about the fact that a moment is missed.
- How might you stage the idea of something being missed?
- What are the cracks? Are they physical or use portrayed by sound, light or another element?
- What is Dad's tone and intention? Is he an absent father in an accidental way or in a more active toxic-masculinity way? Or is he recognising discomfort and shying away into his phone?
- Dad says 'a man in his lifetime plays many parts' which feels tonally different here to some of the other parts of this scene – is this significant?
- What might the 'okay' mean? Who is it addressed to? What tone is it?
- Why did the school not ring ahead to let them know?
- Is the logic of the story world that everyone except Elbow just carries on with the day to day?
- If Elbow was not a he/him – would that affect the scene or the play?
- Capitalisation of the text concerning 'Rupert Next Door' – how might this literary decision inform the way we interpret the text and direct it?

Scene Nine close reading

Conversation on Scene Nine focused on the relationship and significance of the audience seeing Rupert and Elbow interact for the first time. Rupert is the first naturalistic name that comes up, and the groups discussed the potential significance of this. The scene also describes the plants inside the house bring the outside back in – a significant image for a boy who stays indoors. It was observed also that Rupert has a lot more time for Elbow than any other character in the play, despite the fact they are forced together by Elbow's parents rather than choosing it by their own volition.

Questions included:

- Who is that uncomfortable silence for?
- How old is Rupert? The same age as Elbow (fourteen/fifteen?) or younger/ older?
- Does Rupert know about the death?
- Is there a passive aggressive quality to Rupert?

- What room are we in in Rupert's house?
- Is Rupert intentionally provocative?
- How conscious was the Baby Bio?

Visual prompts for characters

A short discussion took place around the prompts in the script for character – on p. 392 of the script it reads:

> I would invite you to consider the following artworks as inspiration-points in relation to understanding each Vox. Skrik: Munch's *The Scream* (1893), Pug: Miró's *The Sun* (1949), Calico: Rockwell's *Girl at Mirror* (1954) and Crumb: Bacon's *Man with Dog* (1944)

Each of these images were on the wall of the room during the day and the participants were invited to look at them and consider how they informed the room's understanding of the identity of each of the characters.

Andrea Brooks asked everyone to form a shape to the sound of the names of some of the characters as a visual and visceral aid to interpreting their function. For Pug there were a lot of closed-off shapes. For Skrik it was more exposed and pointed. For Calico it was curvy, and for Crumb there were a lot of heads and bodies turning away.

Question and answer with Ed Harris

Q: When was the play written?
A: It was written from October 2021 to October 2022. It has in it a hangover from the goodwill that we decided to have as a nation during Covid just briefly. And now it has become a tick-boxing duty for neighbours.

Q: What is Rupert's personality like and how old is he?
A: I imagine he spends a lot of time alone, and listens to a lot of Radio 4, but he is written to be in the age range of about twenty. It is deliberately kept vague so you can make that decision. He is very intelligent, and although he might not be a natural empath, humans have become a fascination for him and he wants to get how people work.

Q: Could Rupert be understood as trans?
A: Absolutely.

Q: How are you imagining the socio-economic status of Rupert? Is this a factor in Rupert and Elbow's dynamic?
A: It is not prescriptive – it is left to what feels true to you in the area you are and what makes most sense for your company.

Q: What was lost/changed/adapted during the process of writing the play?
A: So much! The play didn't write itself in any chronological order.

Q: How did you come up with names of characters? Particularly Hamster?

A: Hamsters as a family pet are often kept in the corner or in the bedroom away from the centre of things. They almost become part of the furniture.

Andrea invited the participants to interpret the name too. Some responses including the image of a hamster being small, generic, and an animal that kids take home from school to look after but also have short lifetimes.

Q: Could Amira and Elbow be a same-sex couple?
A: Absolutely.

Q: Why does Amira have a name so unlike the other characters in Elbow's group at school?
A: I had a strong sense that that was her name: she felt so clearly not quite from the same world as groups of friends with nicknames that Elbow's gang has. The naturalism of her name sets her apart.

Q: Do you have experience of the sort of internal dialogue you write for Elbow? As a younger person? And did you research it?
A: Yes, yes and yes! As a person, whether we take it as a metaphor or being able to audibly hear the internal monologue – the inner community, the village of voices that is internal to us and the community external to us are so central and important in this play.

Q: On the role of narrators: very early on the word 'clown' is used to describe them. Where is the link between clowns and narrators as you imagine it?
A: Laurel and Hardy, Morecambe and Wise. There is a humanity and insistence to them: they are trying things over and over again. They don't take a direct route, but they are earnest and not duplicitous.

Q: Do you see the narrators as always the same two narrators or could they be different pairs?
A: I do see them as the same two. It is useful that they are set characters because if the voices got spread around it might not do the same job.

Q: How would you feel if Elbow was played by different actors?
A: I wouldn't mind that as much!

Q: And if they are the same characters, but different actors portraying them?
A: I wanted to create something a bit like a fanzine, almost like a collage. Moving to different moments and times without having to explain oneself. I like that we are moving through different styles, like a torn-together collage.

The important thing is having them very clearly delineated. So when they change, we wouldn't have to be in any doubt that it is the same character.

Q: Are the cracks on the stage essential?
A: Yes!

Q: Does the box have to be white?
A: No! It doesn't have to be!

Q: How do you imagine the astronaut puppet?
A: It is Elbow – an astronaut or deep sea diver.

Q: How identifiable do the puppets have to be as astronauts?
A: The headgear aspect feels very useful to me.

Q: How do you envisage the 'sealed over' movement piece?
A: I invite you to work that out!

A word on scene changes: the fanzine element of it is a youthful, disruptive and slightly disorganised energy. You can embrace that as much as you like in terms of the scene changes being chaotic, so long as the cracks are stepped over and have consequences and so long as it is not actual chaos!

It might be useful here to refer to Pina Bausch and Complicité's work – they are great examples of how you can incorporate the ensemble in movement and play.

Q: Do you imagine the play as end-on, thrust, traverse or in the round?
A: All options are possible!

Q: Could the puppet movement be indicated by ensemble rather than physical single puppet?
A: Absolutely. You can move a single puppet with an ensemble group.

At this point Andrea Brooks demonstrated this with shoes, a coat and multiple participants. Each manoeuvring one item of clothing of the full 'person' demonstrated how multiple people could operate a single puppet.

Q: How long does the story happen over and when in time is it set?
A: It is set now and in terms of timescale I have been deliberately loopy about it. Literal/naturalistic time is not important.

Q: Could Hamster be present on stage?
A: I think not!

Q: Could the topics of grief and death be potentially triggering for young people?
A: This isn't about trying to shock anyone; it is more about the mind and how the mind works. We don't talk about the death itself; we talk about the fallout which feels so important to be talking about.

Whilst this content is serious and emotional, try to move away from the idea of it being 'triggering', rather being aware of its content and sensitive to what this might bring up.

Suggested references from Andrea Brooks

Book: *The Wild Edge of Sorrow* (2015), Francis Weller
The work of Pina Bausch and Complicité

From a workshop led by Andrea Brooks
With notes by Sammy Glover

The Heights

by Lisa McGee

Lisa McGee, an award-winning screenwriter and playwright from Derry, is the creator, writer and executive producer of the acclaimed *Derry Girls*. She co-created, co-wrote and was executive producer on *The Deceived* with her husband Tobias Beer and was creative director, executive producer and wrote an episode of the BBC monologues on poverty *Skint*. Her other TV credits include *London Irish*, *Raw*, *Being Human*, *The White Queen* and *Indian Summers*.

Characters

Lillie
Dara
Jacob
Boyle
Webb
Jimmy
Bizzy
Pat
Matt
Mother
Sampson

Scene One: Darkness. A Shadow Appears

Lillie   I make up stories. That's what I do. Sometimes they're funny. Sometimes they're sad. Sometimes they're wonderful. Sometimes they're terrible. But they're always just stories.

Scene Two: Night. Lillie's Bedroom

Lillie *lies in bed.* **Dara** *stands at the foot of the bed aiming a gun at her.* **Jacob** *appears. He looks at the* **Lillie**'s *bedroom before continuing downstage. He speaks directly to the audience.*

Jacob   Most people, if they woke up in the middle of the night to find a stranger standing at the foot their bed, aiming a gun between their eyes . . . well, most people would do one of three things I think. They would either scream, faint or try to escape somehow. Not Lillie . . . Lillie sat bolt upright, smiled at her intruder and simply said.

Lillie   Hello. Can I help you?

Jacob   Lillie wasn't like most people.

Lillie lived here. Here on The Heights estate.

Lights come up revealing a street and a large run-down tower block building.

There's never anything to do up here. There's nothing to do and nowhere to go. We all just sit around waiting for something, for anything to happen. It never does. Nothing ever happens on The Heights.

Scene Three: The Street

A group of boys and **Dara** *race onto the street.* **Dara** *is holding an old gun.*

Boyle   Give it back, Dara!

Dara   In a minute I said. Fucking relax.

Webb   Where'd you find it?

Boyle   Moses gave me it.

Dara   Where'd he get it?

Boyle   I dunno. He found it. I think. Give us it, Dara.

Webb   Moses just gave it to you?

Boyle   I bought it off him.

Dara   You paid money for this piece of shit, Boyle?

Boyle   It's not a piece of shit.

Dara   The thing must be a hundred years old.

Webb   How much did you pay for it?

Boyle   Twenty.

Dara   Pence I hope.

Boyle   Piss off. Quid.

Dara   He robbed you, Boyle.

Boyle   You know fuck-all about guns.

Dara   I know enough about Moses.

Webb   What do you need a gun for, Boyle?

Boyle   I just liked the look of it.

Dara   You liked the look of this rusty piece of shit?

Boyle   Give me it back now, Dara, I'm serious.

Dara   Oh he's serious now!

Boyle   I'm not gonna ask again.

Dara   What are you gonna do then?

Boyle   I swear to God, Dara, if you were a fella . . .

Dara   You'd fuck me. I know.

Boyle *lunges at her.* **Webb** *steps in between them.* **Dara** *backs away laughing.*

Boyle   Tell her to give it to me.

Dara   I'm not gonna break it.

Jimmy *enters.*

Dara   Jim Bob!

Jimmy (*to* **Dara**)   Ma's looking for you.

Dara   Let her look.

Jimmy   What's going on?

Webb   Boyle bought a gun.

Jimmy   Fuck me – I'm impressed.

Boyle   I'm glad someone is.

Jimmy   I told Mosses he would never get rid of that thing – bastard proved me wrong.

Boyle   Piss off.

Jimmy   Give us a look at it then.

Webb   Dara! Throw!

Boyle   Dara, do not throw.

She throws the gun to **Jimmy**. *He catches it.*

Jimmy   Jesus . . . It's not light is it? That's a beauty, Boyle – they don't make them like they used to do they?

Boyle   Ha ha!

Jimmy *throws it to* **Webb**. **Webb** *catches it.*

Boyle   Stop it.

Webb   Though, Jimmy. I'd say this thing could still do a lot of damage.

Webb *throws it to* **Dara** *– she catches it.*

Dara   Yeah if you threw it at someone . . .

Jimmy   Or force fed it to some poor bastard.

Dara *throws it to* **Jimmy**.

Boyle   Dickheads.

Jimmy *throws it to* **Webb** *again.*

Jimmy   We're dickheads are we?

Webb *pulls* **Boyle** *towards him. He gets him into a headlock and points the gun at his head.*

Webb   Say that again, fuckwit. Let me hear you say it again.

Dara *laughs.*

Jimmy   Come on, Webb

Boyle *pushes* **Webb** *off.*

Boyle   Hilarious. As much as I'm enjoying the gun-related humour – it's mine and I want it back now please.

Webb   Yeah you're right. Sorry.

He approaches **Boyle** *to give him the gun. At the last moment he snatches it away and throws it to* **Dara**.

Dara   Sucked in!

Boyle   Wankers. You're all wankers. A collection of wankers that's what I'm looking at. That's what I have before me. You are the elite of the wanker world.

Bizzy *walks onto the street reading a book.* **Dara** *doesn't see her and walks backwards with the gun.*

Dara   Aw you want it back? You want it back, Boyle? Here.

*She throws the gun to **Jimmy**. As she does so she walks backwards into **Bizzy** causing her to drop her book.*

Dara   Fuck, sorry.

Bizzy   You're alright.

Dara *picks up her book and hands it back to her. The boys continue to argue amongst themselves.*

Dara   Reading again, Biz?

Bizzy   There's no law against it.

Dara   It's dangerous though – I mean look what just happened – lucky one of us wasn't injured.

Webb   Dara!

*He hurls the gun at **Dara** – she catches it.*

Bizzy   Reading's dangerous but playing catch with a loaded weapon, that's perfectly safe is it?

Dara   This? This isn't a weapon – this is a historical artefact. It doesn't even work –

She raises the gun in the air.

Boyle   Don't, Dara . . .

Dara   And it's not loaded.

She fires the gun. A loud bang.

Dara (*laughing*)   Shit!

Boyle   What did I say?

He runs towards her and takes the gun from her hands.

Boyle   What did I tell you?

Jimmy   Relax, Boyle – nobody died.

Dara   Holy shit. (*To **Bizzy**.*) You alright?

Bizzy   Yeah. Fine. I'm fine.

Jimmy *hits **Boyle** across the head.*

Jimmy   What are you doing walking about with a loaded gun? Prick.

Bizzy *looks to a flat in the tower block behind them.*

Bizzy   Look. The Countess is at her window; you got her attention anyway, Dara.

Dara   What?

Jimmy *realises what* **Bizzy** *is referring to. They all look up at one of the windows in the tower block behind them.*

Jimmy   So she is.

Webb   She creeps the fuck outta me.

Jimmy *gives the flat the finger.* **Boyle** *points his gun towards it.*

Boyle   You're next Show White!

The boys and **Dara** *all run off laughing.* **Bizzy** *sits down on the pavement and continues to read her book.*

Jacob   Lillie lived on the sixth floor. She never left that flat. Never really left her room. She was so sick you see. Allergic to the sun, at least that's what everyone said. Apparently if her skin saw daylight she would swell until she was three times her original size – then she would just drop dead. So Lillie never came outside. She just sat at her window all wrapped up looking down on the street. Occasionally people down here would shout things up at her. They'd shout 'Dracula' or make the sign of the cross with their fingers, original stuff – groundbreaking material. Most of the time though she just got ignored . . . but that all changed because . . . well . . . Dara had an idea.

Dara *and the boys are gathered on the street again.* **Boyle** *is playing with his gun, the others are messing around with a ball.* **Bizzy** *sits with her book as before.*

Jimmy   It's a stupid idea.

Dara   Says who?

Jimmy   Me. Just then. Did you not hear me?

Webb   She'd fucking freak out though, Jim.

Jimmy   Nah, you're better keeping away.

Boyle   It would be funny, Jimmy.

Dara (*to* **Jimmy**)   They think I should.

Jimmy   Oh, well, if the intellectual heavyweights think you should . . . go ahead . . . don't listen to your brother.

Boyle (*re gun*)   I want this back though, Dara.

Jimmy   She won't need it . . . she's not doing it . . .

Dara   Don't tell me what I can and can't fucking do, Jimmy.

Bizzy (*quietly*)   I think you should listen to him.

Dara   What? Who asked you?

Bizzy   I don't think you should do it, that's all.

Webb (*to* **Bizzy**)   Just you read another chapter, Limpet. (*Beat.*) It'll be a laugh, Dara.

Bizzy It won't though – not for her. It'll be frightening.

Webb That's the point, fuck features.

Dara It's just a joke, Bizzy.

Jimmy (*to* **Webb**) If you're so keen why don't you get up there and do it yourself, big man?

Dara Are you not listening to me, Jimmy? I said I'm doing it.

Boyle You tell him.

Webb Good woman, Dara!

Dara I just need to wait until it gets dark first.

Scene Four: Lillie's Bedroom

Lillie *lies in bed.* **Dara** *stands at the foot of the bed staring at her. She has the gun in her hand. She points it at her.* **Lillie** *stirs in her bed. She opens her eyes. She sits up. She stares at* **Dara**. *Silence.*

Lillie Hello. Can I help you?

Dara *doesn't respond. She simply stares back at her.*

Lillie Can I help you?

Dara I don't know.

Lillie Are you planning to kill me?

Dara No. No of course not.

Lillie I only make the assumption because . . . well, you're pointing a gun at my head.

Dara *looks at the gun. She lowers it.*

Dara I'm sorry.

Lillie It's okay.

Dara I'm so sorry.

Lillie The thing is . . . if you were . . . planning to kill me I mean, well, I wouldn't mind. Honestly I wouldn't.

Dara Are you mental?

Lillie You broke into my room in the middle of the night and pointed a firearm at me while I slept. Yeah, I'm the mental one.

Dara It was . . . it was supposed to be a joke.

Lillie I don't get it.

Dara   Yeah neither do I, not really. Not anymore.

Lillie   It wasn't a joke, Dara.

Dara   How do you know my name?

Lillie *shrugs.*

Dara   We wanted to scare you. It was a joke.

Lillie   I don't think it was. I think it was an excuse. You didn't want to scare me – all you really wanted was to see me, to look at me – to observe the freak in her natural environment – that's the truth of the matter isn't it?

Dara   No.

Lillie   You don't need to lie. It's fine.

Dara   If I had wanted to scare you I wouldn't have managed it.

Lillie   I don't scare easily.

Dara   You knew I was coming.

Lillie   How could I possibly have known that?.

Dara   You knew. You knew I would come sooner or later. I see you. Every day I see you sitting in here staring out at me.

Lillie   And every day I see you. I see you standing *out* there staring *in* at me.

Dara   This was stupid. I'm sorry. I really am.

Lillie   Don't be.

Dara   What's you're name?

Lillie   You don't know my name?

Dara   I've never heard anyone use it. Out there . . . well, they call you the Countess, you know like . . .

Lillie   Dracula, yeah I get it. (*Beat.*) My name's Lillie. Lillie Lee.

Dara   Well, I think I should go now. (*Beat.*) It was nice to meet you, Lillie Lee.

She walks towards the window.

Lillie   Don't go, Dara. Stay.

Dara   Why?

Lillie   Stay and talk to me. Stay and tell me everything . . . tell me anything.

Dara   I can't. Nothing ever happens. Not really. There's nothing out there. I don't have anything to tell you, Lillie.

Lillie   That's okay. Just make it up.

Dara *sits on the end of* **Lillie***'s bed.*

Scene Five: The Street

Jacob   I knew Lillie. Not many people can say that. Before Dara there was me. Though it was all over before it even really started. (*Beat*.) One day last summer I was just hanging around the street as usual, hoping for something to break the boredom, hoping for a miracle, and I got one. It was just a little thing but it was miraculous all the same. A piece of pink note paper floated past my shoulder and landed on the pavement. I picked it up and read what it said.

Lillie   Once there was a nice woman.

Jacob   Once there was a nice woman.

Lillie   The nice woman had lots of nice things but she wasn't happy.

Jacob   It was the first line of a story.

Lillie   Because it didn't matter how many nice things she had. She was still all alone.

Jacob   So I went back there every day.

Lillie   What she really wanted was a baby.

Jacob   I went back to that exact same spot every day and every day the next line of the story would float down from her window.

Lillie   So the nice woman, hoped and wished and prayed.

The **Nice Woman** *appears.*

Nice Woman   Please God. Please give me a baby. I'll love it, I'll look after it. I promise. Please God, please.

Lillie   One day there was a knock at her door. She opened it and screamed with delight – a cradle sat on her step. She looked inside and there she was – her very own beautiful baby girl.

The little girl appears and goes to the **Nice Woman**.

Lillie   However, she wasn't like other babies, this little girl was different, she was special. This little girl was made entirely from glass. She had little glass hands and little glass fingers, little glass feet and little glass toes, a little glass mouth and two little glass eyes . . . even the hair on her head was glass. The nice woman didn't mind at all – she looked at her and said . . .

Nice Woman   You're the most beautiful thing I've ever seen. You're perfect.

Lillie   But she knew she had to be careful. She was so frightened her little glass girl might break that she made her lie still in a room full of feathers –

Nice Woman   It's safe in here. Nothing can hurt you in here.

Lillie   The nice woman sat beside her and read her stories but she never touched her.

Nice Woman   I might damage you, without meaning to, I never want to damage you.

Lillie   One night the little glass girl had a terrible dream –

The glass girl screams in horror.

Lillie   It was a strange dream too, for although she'd never seen the ocean she dreamt she was drowning in it. She screamed and cried – she was so scared that the nice woman put her arms around her without thinking –

Nice Woman   There, there, ssh now, ssh.

Lillie   She comforted her until the little glass girl wasn't frightened anymore. They lay back together on the fluffy white feathers.

A while later sunlight poured into the room. The nice woman opens her eyes. She must have fallen asleep. She's warm and wet. She looks down at her body – and for a moment she's confused. The fluffy white feathers have all turned red. They stick to her skin. Horrified she realises they're soaked in blood – her own blood – her arms and legs are decorated with hundreds of tiny cuts, her body is covered in the smallest shreds of glass. The little glass girl is gone. The nice woman starts to cry . . .

Nice Woman   All I did was fall asleep.

Lillie   . . . She whispers. Poor, poor nice woman – she held her little glass girl too tightly –

Nice Woman   Now I'm all alone again.

Jacob   When I'd collected all the lines – when I'd pieced the entire story together – she invited me to visit. So I did.

Scene Six: Lillie's Bedroom

Lillie *and* **Jacob** *sit at the window staring down onto the street.*

Lillie   I know everybody wonders what I do up here all day. How I keep myself occupied. How I stop myself from going mad. The truth is I make up stories. That's what I do. Sometimes they're funny. Sometimes they're sad. Sometimes they're wonderful. Sometimes they're terrible but they're always just stories.

Jacob   You're good at it – you're really good.

Lillie   You've only read one.

Jacob   I liked it though.

Lillie   I have hundreds, thousands, hundreds of thousands.

Jacob   Hundreds of thousands?

Lillie   You don't believe me?

Jacob   No I believe you. It's just . . . well that's a lot of stories.

Lillie   I have a lot of time on my hands.

Jacob I suppose.

Lillie It's like a prison . . . this room.

Jacob It's not much better out there you know, Lillie. I mean there's a pub that we're too young for, a club that we're too old for – sitting on the street drinking cider is as exciting as it gets.

Lillie At least there's people out there.

Jacob They're not very interesting, Lillie.

Lillie At least you have people you can talk to, Jacob.

Jacob Doesn't your ma talk to you?

Lillie Yeah of course. There's never anything new though. I think we might have used up all our conversation – now we're just repeating ourselves. (*Beat.*) She'd go mad if she knew I had you up here.

Jacob Why doesn't she let you have friends, Lillie? Why doesn't she let people visit?

Lillie She's afraid I'll catch something.

Jacob *laughs.*

Jacob I should be offended but I've a feeling she's right. (*Points down at the street below.*) You could probably catch something from Boyle just by looking at him.

Lillie No she's okay . . . she means well . . . she thinks she's looking after me . . . I mean she is looking after me . . . I just wish . . .

Jacob What?

Lillie Nothing.

A silence.

Jacob So how do you get your ideas then . . . for the stories.

Lillie From this window. I sit at this window and I look out at people – I imagine things about them – about their lives . . .

Jacob Like what?

Lillie Like secrets they might be hiding, that type of thing.

Jacob I see. So which of them have you written a story about?

Lillie A few of them. But mainly that one.

She points down to the street.

Mainly that girl who's always with the boys.

Jacob Dara.

Lillie Dara? Is that her name?

Jacob   Yeah, Dara lives two doors down from me – I know her brother Jimmy. He's in my class. He's in my class when he bothers to turn up. He's okay but Dara . . . I don't know, I never really . . . –

Lillie *covers his mouth with her hand.*

Lillie   Don't. Don't tell me anything. I don't want to know.

Jacob *removes her hand and holds it for a second. She pulls it away and goes back to looking out the window.*

Jacob   Have you ever written about me?

Lillie   Not yet. I probably will . . . although . . .

Jacob   Although what?

Lillie   I think you'd make a better narrator, Jacob.

Jacob   How do you mean?

Lillie *doesn't answer – she returns to her window.*

Lillie   Do you notice how Dara's always running about. She's always moving. Always needs to be doing something, to be going somewhere and she's always talking. I think she's afraid to be still. Because stillness means silence. People like Dara hate silence – they always want to fill it – silence scares them.

She turns to **Jacob**. *He stares out the window. He hasn't really been listening to what she's said. A long silence follows.*

Lillie   You're not afraid of it though are you, Jacob?

Jacob   Sorry?

Lillie   Silence. (*Beat.*) What's wrong?

Jacob   What? (*Beat.*) Sorry I was just thinking . . .

Lillie   Right.

Jacob   Don't you want to know what I'm thinking about?

Lillie   I already do.

Jacob   Really?

Lillie   You're thinking this is boring now. For a while it was fine but the novelty has worn off. You're thinking you'd rather be out there with the others.

Jacob   No!

Lillie   It's okay.

Jacob   I love coming here, Lillie.

Lillie   You don't have to.

Jacob   I want to.

Lillie   Promise?

Jacob   I promise. (*Beat.*) I love coming here . . . being with you.

Jacob *looks at* **Lillie***.* **Lillie** *smiles at him then quickly decides to change the subject.*

Lillie   If you could have a superpower what would it be?

Jacob   What?

Lillie   Any superpower.

Jacob   I . . . don't . . . I'm not sure.

Lillie   Just pick one.

Jacob   What's the point?

Lillie   It's a game.

Jacob   I don't want to play.

Lillie   Pick one, Jacob!

Jacob   Flying.

Lillie   Flying?

Jacob   The ability to fly – that would be my superpower.

Lillie   That's a terrible choice – the ability to fly – why would you choose that?

Jacob   I . . . I don't know. I . . .

Lillie   That's an awful choice, Jacob. (*Beat.*) Do you know what mine would be?

Jacob   No.

Lillie   Time control. The ability to rewind, fast forward or freeze time. That's a good one isn't it? That's better than flying. Admit it, Jacob.

Jacob   I suppose.

Lillie   I mean you could travel to the past, visit the future and pause the present. Imagine all the things you could see . . .

Jacob   Lillie . . .

Lillie   Just imagine . . .

Jacob   Lillie, I don't want to imagine anymore.

Lillie   What?

Jacob   I don't want to imagine, I don't want to pretend, I don't want to play games.

Lillie   What do you want?

Jacob   I want you to tell me something real.

Lillie *stares at him for a moment.*

Jacob   Something true – a memory – something that actually happened to you – something real.

Lillie   I . . . I can't think of anything.

Jacob   Try.

Lillie   I don't want to.

Jacob   Please Lillie . . .

Lillie   Why?

Jacob   I need you to.

Lillie   Why do you need me to?

Jacob   You talk all the time without really saying anything. Every night I leave this room feeling I know less than I did the night before . . . and I hate that.

Jacob *cups* **Lillie**'*s face with his hand.*

Lillie   Jacob . . .

Jacob   Tell me something real.

Lillie   I can't.

Jacob *kisses* **Lillie** – *she kisses him back for a moment, then pushes him away.*

Jacob   What's wrong?

Lillie   You shouldn't have done that. (*Beat.*) I think you should leave now.

Jacob   And I did. I left. I hoped that she would ask me to come back. She never did. Anyway soon her new playmate would arrive.

Scene Eight: Lillie's Bedroom

Lillie *in her bed* – **Dara** *looking out the window.*

Lillie   What else?

Dara   Nothing else.

Lillie   That couldn't be it.

Dara   I'm telling you it is.

Lillie   If I came over there I bet I'd find something else.

Dara   Webb and Boyle are playing football. Jimmy is hitting Dave the debt . . .

Lillie   You said he was shouting at him . . .

Dara   He was the first time you asked, now he's hitting him.

Lillie   What else?

Dara   Mags is drying out mats on her balcony.

Lillie   Still – she was doing that yesterday.

Dara   These are different ones . . .

Lillie   How many mats does she have?

Dara   Fucking shit loads by the looks of it.

Lillie   Where does she put them all?

Dara   Oh . . .

Lillie   What? (*Beat.*) What is it, Dara?

Dara   One of the fat twins has just got up.

Lillie   Which one?

Dara   Pat.

Lillie   Is he the one with the glasses or without the glasses?

Dara   With.

Lillie   Lazy bastard.

Dara   Lazy fat fucker.

Lillie   Lazy fat dirty brute. (*Beat.*) What's he doing?

Dara   Pulling his curtains – Jesus . . .

Lillie   What?

Dara (*disgusted*)   He's standing at his window with no fucking shirt on.

Lillie   He's disgusting.

Dara   Yeah . . .

Lillie   He makes me sick.

Dara   I can't see the other one. I can't see Matt.

Lillie   Oh, he'll be there somewhere – he'll make an appearance – you don't see one without the other – they might as well be Siamese. You'd think they'd get sick of each other . . .

Dara   No . . . not fat Matt and fat Pat.

Lillie   They both turn my stomach.

Dara   I don't know them. Bizzy does . . . she says they're alright.

Lillie   Bizzy?

Dara   She's my friend.

Lillie   The one that's always reading.

Dara   Yeah that's her. Yeah Bizzy says they're okay – that they're harmless.

Lillie   I don't care what Bizzy says.

Dara   I'm sorry. I thought . . . I just thought you might be interested.

Lillie   I'm not.

Dara   Okay.

An awkward silence for a moment. **Lillie** *goes and joins* **Dara** *at the window.*

Lillie   You know Dara . . . sometimes I think that I'm the only real person. Sometimes I think that I've made everyone else up – all those people down there – I imagine that they're only in my head – that when I stop thinking about them they stop existing. (*Beat.*) Do you think I'm mad?

Dara   No . . . of course not. (*Beat.*) Do you ever think that about me? Do you ever think I'm not real.

Lillie   I have done. There are times when I know what you're gonna say before you even say it. It's like I know what you're thinking – it's like I see it coming.

Dara *places her hands gently around* **Lillie**'s *throat and then suddenly begins to choke her.*

Dara   Did you see that coming, Lillie?

Lillie *struggles and falls to her knees.* **Dara** *continues to choke her.*

Dara   Did you fucking see that coming?

She releases her grip, laughing. **Lillie** *catches her breath.*

Lillie   Bitch. (*Beat.*) Fucking bitch.

She starts to laugh. She turns her neck towards **Dara**.

Lillie   Did you mark me?

Dara   No. Did you want me to?

Lillie *nods her head.*

Dara   We're not like the rest of them are we, Lillie?

Lillie   No. It would probably be easier if we were.

Scene Nine: The Street

Bizzy *sits on a wall reading.* **Jimmy**, **Boyle**, **Jacob** *and* **Webb** *sit on the pavement having a drink and playing a game of cards.* **Dara** *walks past them.*

Dara   Alright.

Jimmy   Ma's looking for you.

Dara   Let her look.

Jimmy   She's going mental. I can't listen to her – you get yourself home – you hear me?

Dara   I will . . . not just now though. Okay.

Jimmy *shakes his head.* **Dara** *goes to walk on.*

Boyle   Why don't you have a game, Dara?

Dara   Na . . . I'm alright

Webb   Come on, Dara. We haven't seen you in ages. You hiding on us?

Dara   No. Course not. I've stuff to do that's all . . .

Boyle   It can wait can't it?

Webb   Sit down. Have a drink.

Dara   Later maybe.

She goes to walk on. **Webb** *smirks.*

Webb   Later maybe . . . she can't tear herself away.

Jimmy   Fuck up.

Dara   What did you say, Webb?

Webb   I just . . .

Jimmy   Go say it. Go on say it and it'll be the last thing you fucking say.

Webb   Nothing.

Dara   What's going on, Jimmy?

Jimmy *stands up and walks towards her.*

Jimmy   We know where you've been going, Dara, who you've been with. Everybody knows.

Dara   And what of it?

Silence.

Dara   And what of it?

Webb   You're spending a lot of time up in that thing's bedroom . . . that's all I saying.

Dara   When really I should be down here drinking lager and playing switch . . .

Boyle   Poker.

Dara   Shut up, Boyle.

Jimmy   Shut the fuck up, Boyle.

He looks at **Dara**.

Jimmy   I want you to stop going up there.

Dara   You're serious?

Jimmy   I'm serious.

Dara   Why?

Jimmy   People are talking about you. People are saying shit about you and about her . . . about you both.

Dara *laughs.*

Dara   Jesus . . . well, at least we've given them something to talk about. There's not exactly a lot else going on is there.

Jimmy   It's not funny, Dara.

Dara   It is. It's a bit funny,. (*Beat.*) What's the big deal – I go up there and I talk to her . . .

Jimmy   That's not what people are saying.

Dara   I don't care.

Jimmy   Well, I do. It's embarrassing. You're shaming me. Is that want you want?

Dara   Of course not.

Jimmy   Promise me you won't go up there again.

Dara   I can't.

Jimmy *turns away from her. He addresses the boys.*

Jimmy   Come on. We're going.

He starts to walk away. The boys begin to gather their things and follow him.

Boyle   Why?

Jimmy   Because I said so, prick. Come on!

Boyle *starts to gather up the cards.*

Jimmy   Leave them . . .

He kicks the cards – they scatter over the pavement.

Leave them and come on.

He walks off. The boys follow. **Dara** *watches. When they've gone she sees* **Bizzy** *sitting on the wall reading.*

Dara   How's it going, Bizzy?

Bizzy   Oh you do remember my name do you? I was starting to think you'd forgotten all about me.

Dara   Not you too.

Bizzy   Not me what?

Dara   Everybody's talking about me apparently.

Bizzy   I've got more interesting things to talk about than you, Dara.

Dara *smiles.*

Dara   I'm glad to hear it. (*Beat.*) New book?

Bizzy *nods.*

Dara   Any good?

Bizzy   Haven't made up my mind yet.

Dara *snaps the book out of* **Bizzy**'*s hand.*

Bizzy   Hey!

Dara   Maybe I'll read it.

Bizzy   I don't think you'd like it.

Dara   You don't think I'd understand it you mean.

She looks at the book.

Bizzy   Dara . . .

Dara   Hmmm?

Bizzy   What's she like? The Countess?

Dara   Her name's Lillie.

Bizzy   What's she like?

Dara   She's nice –

Bizzy   Really.

Dara   She's, you know, funny . . . she's different but contrary to popular belief she doesn't have two fucking heads and a tail.

Bizzy   Take me to see her.

Dara   No.

Bizzy   Please. Take me. Take me to see her.

Dara   She's not a painting in a museum, Bizzy.

Bizzy   Just once.

Dara   Not happening.

Bizzy   Why not?

Dara   She hasn't invited you.

Bizzy   You could invite me though.

Dara   No.

Bizzy   You said she was nice . . . if she's nice she won't mind.

Dara *gives* **Bizzy** *back her book.*

Dara   Let it die, Bizzy.

Bizzy   Fine.

Dara   Look, I'll see you about. I have to go.

She leaves.

Bizzy (*under her breath*)   Yeah . . . Of course you do.

Scene Ten: Lillie's Bedroom

Dara *stands at the window staring out –* **Lillie** *lies on her bed.*

Dara   Seriously, Lillie, this is strange. This is very strange. It's been two days now and still no sign of fat Matt. They've never been apart for this long. Fat Pat's in there all alone. What the fuck is going on?

Lillie   What were you talking to her about?

Dara   What?

Lillie   The girl on the street. What were you talking to her about?

Dara   The girl on the street?

Lillie   The book girl. The girl who's always reading. I saw you talking to her earlier.

Dara   Oh Bizzy.

Lillie   Yeah.

Dara   Maybe he's gone to visit someone – but if he did surely Pat would have gone too. I mean surely they know all the same people.

Lillie   What were you talking about?

Dara   I dunno. I can't remember.

Lillie   You were talking about me . . . weren't you?

Dara   No . . .

Lillie   You were . . . I saw her look up here. And you were laughing . . .

Dara   No . . .

Lillie   Were you laughing at me, Dara?

Dara   Don't be paranoid.

Lillie   Were you laughing at me with her?

Dara   Lillie, don't be ridiculous.

Lillie   You come up here – you listen to my stories – you pretend to be my friend and all the time you're going down there and you're laughing at me.

Dara   That's not true. I would never laugh at you

Lillie   I saw you.

Dara   You saw me talking to her.

Lillie   Talking about me.

Dara   Not the way you think, Lillie. I swear. But if you don't believe me . . . If you want me to go . . .

Lillie   No. No, I'm sorry.

Dara   It's fine. Let's just forget about it okay. Let's forget about it and get back to the matter at hand.

Lillie   The matter at hand?

Dara   Fat Matt. The mystery of the missing twin. Any theories?

Lillie   Maybe Pat killed him.

Dara   Why?

Lillie   Maybe they had a fight about something.

Scene Eleven: Fat Pat and Fat Matt's Place

Fat **Pat** *and fat* **Matt** *sit beside their* **Mother** *who lies in her bed. She is very ill.*

Jacob   Mathew and Patrick were always fighting. For forty years they did little else. They lived on the first floor of block three with their mother and they tortured her with their constant arguing and bickering. When the poor woman's time came she lay quietly on her death bed and asked just one thing of them before she passed away . . . . .

Mother   Boys . . . Promise me you'll stop fighting. Promise me you'll look after each other and love each other.

Pat/Matt   We promise, Mammy.

Jacob   And they meant to keep their promise. Three years passed without so much as an angry word – they were perfect gentlemen. Then one day they went into Sampson's shop to buy the newspaper.

Scene Twelve: Sampson's Shop

Sampson   Hiya, Matt – Hiya, Pat – How are you?

Matt   Not bad, Sampson, not bad.

Jacob   Normally they bought the same thing on every visit.

Pat   We'll have the *Daily Mirror* – two cans of Fanta – two packs of Maltesers, a Lion bar and a Twix please, Sampson.

Jacob   But today Matthew's feeling adventurous.

Matt   Will we buy a Lotto ticket, Pat?

Pat   But we never buy a Lotto ticket, Matt.

Sampson   You never know your luck, lads. What is it they say . . .

Jacob   If you're not in you can't win.

Sampson   If you're not in you can't win.

Pat   You have a point there, Sampson.

Matt   Will we get one, Pat?

Pat   Do you think we should, Matt?

Matt   I think we should, Pat, yeah.

Jacob   Eventually . . . after hours of deliberation over numbers, the twins left the shop – lottery ticket in hand.

Scene Thirteen: Pat and Matt's Living Room

Jacob   And later that evening tension and excitement filled the air as they settled down to watch the results.

Pat *passes a plate of chocolate biscuits to* **Matt**.

Pat   Hobnob?

Matt   Cheers.

They watch the TV.

Voice of Presenter   Which brings tonight's lottery jackpot rollover to a grand total of . . . wait for it . . . ten million pounds, ladies and gentlemen. . . .What do we think about that?

Matt   Jesus but I hate that bastard.

Pat   Me too, Matt.

Matt   If there's one bastard I hate it's that bastard, Pat.

Pat   Fruity orange fucker. (*Beat.*) More tea?

Matt   That would be lovely.

Pat   Still though . . . if he was handing you a cheque for ten million . . .

Matt   If he handed me a cheque for ten million I'd marry the bastard . . .

Pat *passes* **Matt** *a cigarette. He then takes out a lighter.*

Pat   Light, Pat?

Matt   Cheers, Matt.

Pat   Imagine what you could do with that money.

Matt   I'd buy a boat.

Pat   A boat?

Matt   Like a big yacht thing.

Pat   What the fuck would you do with a yacht?

Matt   I'd sail it.

Pat   You don't know how.

Matt   I'd learn.

Pat   They cost a fortune them things.

Matt   We've ten million, Pat.

Pat   I know. But still . . . think about it first that's all I'm saying.

Matt   I have thought about it.

Pat   You have not – you're buying this yacht on impulse that's what you're doing.

Matt   I am not.

Pat   You're out there throwing our money about like it grows on trees.

Matt   No I'm fucking not!

Pat   Don't raise your voice to me. Remember what Mammy said.

Matt   Sorry, Pat.

Pat   You're okay, Matt.

Matt   A yacht's a good investment though.

Pat   How?

Matt   Cos you can live on it as well.

Pat   I'm not living on a boat.

Matt   Why not?

Pat   I get sea sick, Matt.

Matt   Once you got sea sick, Pat.

Pat   Once was enough.

Matt   You'd get used to it after a couple of weeks.

Pat   Why should I have to? I'm not living on a boat and that's the end of it.

Matt   Fine. Don't.

Pat   I won't.

Matt   Won't stop me.

Pat   What?

Matt   I'll take my five million buy a yacht and live on it myself.

Pat   Oh will you now?

Matt   I will.

Pat   Is that how it is?

Matt   It is.

Pat   Well, I'll take my five million and buy a big fucking mansion.

Matt   Good for you.

Pat   And I'll put a big electric fence around it so you can't get in.

Matt   I won't want in.

Pat   Oh you will. You'll want in when your big stupid boat sinks.

Matt   Yacht!

Pat   You'll come crying to me then. 'Let me in, Pat . . . please, Pat . . . I'm sorry.' And I'll say, 'Fuck away off – I told you not to buy that boat' . . .

Matt   Yacht . . . it's a fucking yacht and I won't need to come crawling to you. It'll be the other way round. You'll beg me to let you stay . . .

Pat   Never.

Matt   You will, you'll have to when your mansion burns down.

Pat   My mansion won't burn down.

Matt   It will. Your faulty electric fence will blow up and your house will burn down.

Pat   There's nothing wrong with my electric fence.

Matt   It's faulty!

Pat   Shut your mouth.

Matt   Everything will go up in flames.

Pat   Shut – up.

Matt   You'll have nothing again.

Pat   Stop it.

Matt   Nothing, nothing, nothing.

Pat *throws a punch, knocking* **Matt** *to the floor. Silence.*

Jacob   Patrick only hit Matthew the once. That was all it took. He banged his head on the corner of the coffee table as he fell to the ground.

Scene Fourteen: Lillie's Bedroom

Lillie *lies on the bed,* **Dara** *sits at the window as before.*

Dara   I don't know.

Lillie   I'm only telling you what I think . . .

Dara   I don't think Pat's the killing type.

Lillie   Why not?

Dara   I don't think he'd have the energy.

Lillie   So what? – Matt just disappeared did he? Forty-odd years living in the same place, unemployed and overweight, and suddenly he decides to take himself travelling – suddenly he decides to get up and do something.

Dara   If Pat did kill him what did he do with the body? We've been watching his flat for days now – we'd have noticed him try to dispose of his clinically obese twin.

Lillie   He must . . . he must still be in the flat somewhere.

Dara   Bullshit.

Lillie   I'd put money on it, Dara.

Dara   You're not even joking are you?

Lillie   He's in there. I know it.

Dara   You might know it but you can't prove it.

Lillie   I can if you help me.

Jacob   Getting yourself into an unbelievably horrifying and slightly surreal situation is much simpler than you might expect.

Scene Fifteen: Night. Pat and Matt's Place

Jacob   You begin by taking a really stupid idea – like . . . I don't know, breaking into your neighbour's home while he's at bingo to look for the body of his murdered twin. Then you put that stupid idea into action.

Dara *walks in. She begins to poke about.*

Jacob   And after thirty minutes of searching, when all you've managed to find is a bulk supply of Cadbury's Dairy Milk and a box of 'specialist' porn . . .

Dara *looks in a box.*

Dara   Urgh! Dirty bastard.

Jacob   You're suddenly startled when you hear a key turn in the lock and realise your neighbour has come home early.

Pat *enters singing to himself.*

Dara (*whispers*)   Shit, fuck, balls, fuck, shit, shit, bollocks.

Jacob   You run upstairs and hide in his bedroom – you plan to escape when the coast is clear.

Pat *looks around his living room.*

Pat   What the fuck is going on in here?

Jacob   Unfortunately for you, your neighbour isn't blind . . .

Pat *looks around the ransacked living room.*

Pat (*shouting*)   I know you're in here. I know your still in here, you fucker. Come out, you slimy bastard – come out here and face me like a man!

Jacob   Panic sets in. All you want to do is get out of there. You rush out of the bedroom only to be met by your now understandably angry neighbour at the top of the stairs.

Pat *and* **Dara** *come face to face.*

Pat   And just what the hell do you think you're playing at?

Jacob   You didn't mean it – you were just trying to push past him that's all. You didn't mean for him to lose his balance, you didn't mean for him to fall backwards, thumping his big, fat, heavy head on every stair as he went. And you stand there just looking at him, he's not breathing, he's not moving, you stand there and you think to yourself . . .

Dara   Holy fuck!

Scene Sixteen: Lillie's Bedroom

Dara *and* **Lillie** *sit looking out the window.*

Lillie   I can't believe you killed fat Pat.

Dara   Will you stop saying that please?

Lillie   Sorry.

Dara   It was your fault anyway. 'I know there's a body over there, Dara.' (*Beat.*) Body my hole.

Lillie   You're the one that threw him down the stairs.

Dara   I did not throw him down the stairs – it was an accident. Anyway how could I have thrown him down the stairs . . . I mean look . . .

She points out at the street.

Dara   Look at the size of that coffin. What am I the bionic fucking woman?

Lillie   There's a big turn-out isn't there?

Dara   Yeah, well, people round here love nothing better than a funeral. Sad bastards.

Lillie   Who found him?

Dara   Sampson the shopkeeper – he hadn't gone to pick up his newspaper. Pat always collected his newspaper.

A pause.

At least it's the funeral. At least it's over today. Once he's in the ground that's it. There's nothing they can do . . .

Lillie   Unless they dig him up again.

Dara   Why would they dig him up again?

Lillie   I dunno.

Dara   Why would you say that?

Lillie   No you're right. Why would they dig him up? I mean everybody thinks it was an accident.

Dara   It was an accident!

Lillie   Yeah. I know.

Dara   Don't say things like that, Lillie – I am of a very fucking nervous disposition at present.

They watch the funeral procession for a few more moments.

Lillie   What did it feel like?

Dara   What do you mean?

Lillie   When you watched him lying there. When you saw him dying. What did it feel like?

Dara   It was all so quick, Lillie. Though . . .

Lillie   Though what?

Dara   I'm sure I saw a little smile on his face – just before he went – it was as though he was thinking, 'This is it, I'm out of here, I'm finally leaving this shit-hole behind.'

They return to watching the procession.

Lillie   Isn't that your brother?

Dara   Yeah that's my brother and all his little bitches.

Lillie   Is he still not talking to you?

Dara   No.

Lillie   All because of me.

Dara   All because he's a prick, Lillie.

She notices something.

Sweet Jesus!

Lillie   What?

Dara   Look who's showed up!

Lillie   Who?

Dara   Standing behind my brother. Big guy. Big fat fella – looks a lot like the guy who's now lying in that coffin – only without the glasses.

Lillie *realises.*

Lillie   Oh. I suppose I was wrong.

Dara   You think?

Jacob   I never did finish that story.

Scene Seventeen: Pat and Matt's Living Room

The two brothers sit in front of the television watching the lottery results. They are in the middle of a heated argument.

Pat   You'll come crying to me then, 'Let me in, Pat . . . please, Pat . . . I'm sorry.' And I'll say, 'Fuck away off – I told you not to buy that boat' . . .

Matt   Yacht . . . it's a fucking yacht and I won't need to come crawling to you. It'll be the other way round. You'll beg me to let me stay . . .

Pat   Never.

Matt   You will, you'll have to when your mansion burns down.

Pat   My mansion won't burn down.

Matt   It will. Your faulty electric fence will blow up and your house will burn down.

Pat   There's nothing wrong with my electric fence.

Matt   It's faulty!

Pat   Shut your mouth.

Matt   Everything will go up in flames.

Pat   Shut – up.

Matt   You'll have nothing again.

Pat   Stop it.

Matt   Nothing, nothing, nothing.

Pat *throws a punch, knocking* **Matt** *to the floor. Silence.*

Matt *lies on the floor for a second before sitting up and clutching his head in agony.*

Pat   I'm . . . Jesus, Matt, I didn't mean . . .

Matt   What did Mammy say?

Pat   I know . . .

Matt   The one thing Mammy asked us to do, Pat.

Pat   I'm sorry.

Matt   What good is sorry? What good is sorry now? It's ruined, Pat. We've broken our promise. Our poor Mammy's dying wish.

Pat   I shouldn't have lashed out. I shouldn't have lost my temper.

Matt   No you shouldn't have.

He gets up and starts to walk out of the living room.

Pat   Where are you going, Matt?

Matt   I'm leaving, Pat. I can't even look at you. I can't bear to be around you. I never want to see you again.

Jacob   And he didn't – If Matt had known those would have been the last words he would ever get to say to his brother – he probably would have chosen different ones.

Scene Eighteen: The Street

Jimmy, **Jacob**, **Webb** *and* **Boyle** *are playing football.* **Dara** *walks past.*

Jimmy   She finally blew you out then, Dara?

Dara   Fuck! Breaking your vow of silence are you, Jimmy?

Jimmy   You're taking it well.

Dara   What are you talking about?

Jimmy   You don't know.

Dara   Clearly I don't have a clue what you're slabbering on about. So are you gonna continue to sprout shit at me or actually fucking tell me.

Jimmy   Your friend the Countess . . .

Dara   Her name's Lillie.

Jimmy   She's got herself a new best friend. She's dropped you like you were on fire.

Dara   What?

Jimmy   She's been waving Bizzy over all morning. She's in there with her now.

Dara   Bizzy's in Lillie's room. What? Now?

Jimmy   Jesus it's bad if someone with no other human contact gets bored listening to you, Dara.

He laughs. **Dara** *rushes off.*

Jimmy   Dara . . . Dara . . . get back here . . .

Dara   Fuck off and die, Jimmy.

Scene Nineteen: Bizzy's Flat

Jacob   The night that poor fat Pat met his untimely death, Lillie noticed something which worried her ever since. From her window she watched Dara make her speedy exit out Pat's front door and down the steps of the tower block but she soon realised she wasn't the only one watching.

Bizzy *walks out of her bedroom with a torch and a book.*

Jacob   Bizzy who shared her bedroom with her three sisters had come out on to her balcony to read by torchlight in peace and quiet.

Bizzy *sits on the balcony and starts to read – something at the other side of the tower block catches her attention. She watches.*

Jacob   At the time it was both intriguing and confusing . . . at the time it didn't make sense . . . it wasn't till a few days later that Bizzy understood, that she knew what happened that night . . . that she knew what Dara did. The thing is, Bizzy isn't sure if it horrified or excited her.

Scene Twenty: Lillie's Bedroom

Bizzy *is tied to a chair in the middle of the room. She's bound and gagged.* **Lillie** *points the gun at her.* **Dara** *enters.*

Dara   Lillie . . .

Lillie   She knows. She saw you. She saw you run away. She knows what you did.

Dara   You can't do this, Lillie . . .

Lillie   I have to. She'll tell someone.

Dara   She won't. You won't will you, Bizzy?

A terrified **Bizzy** *shakes her head.*

Lillie   Yeah . . . like she'd say anything else.

Dara   I trust her.

Lillie   You shouldn't.

Dara   Put it down Lillie.

Lillie   I'm trying to protect you, Dara.

Dara   I don't need you to protect me. Lillie, look at me . . .

Lillie *looks at her.*

Dara   Listen to me. This is mad. You're not gonna actually do it. I know that and you know that. Put it down.

Lillie *lowers the gun.*

Dara   Because they all know she's up here, Lillie. They all saw her up here. So if anything happens her they'll know you did it, Lillie. They'll put you in prison . . .

Lillie   I already am in prison.

Dara   This isn't a game.

Lillie   I know.

Dara   Let's just put a stop to it.

Lillie   Yeah it's time to put a stop to it. I'm tired now. It's time for the ending I think.

She quickly aims the gun at **Dara***'s head.*

Lillie   Bizzy, apparently before Pat died he smiled. He smiled because he was leaving all this behind. He smiled because he was escaping, escaping all the boredom, all the monotony, all the shit – he was moving on.

She fires the gun, shooting **Dara** *in the head.* **Dara** *falls to the floor. She then turns the gun on herself.*

Lillie   Watch me, Bizzy. Watch me smile.

Blackout. A second gunshot sounds. In darkness **Jacob** *and* **Lillie** *speak.*

Jacob   There's never anything to do up here. There's nothing to do and nowhere to go. We all just sit around waiting for something, for anything to happen. It never does. Nothing ever happens on The Heights

Lillie   I make up stories that's what I do.

Scene Twenty-One: The Street

Dara, **Jimmy**, **Boyle** and **Webb** scuffle over the gun – exactly as they did in their first scene.

Jimmy   Give us a look at it then.

Webb   Dara! Throw!

Boyle   Dara do not throw.

She throws the gun to **Jimmy**. He catches it.

Jimmy   Jesus . . . It's not light is it? That's a beauty, Boyle – they don't make them like they used to do they?

Boyle   Ha ha!

Jimmy throws it to **Webb**. **Webb** catches it.

Boyle   Stop it.

Webb   Though Jimmy. I'd say this thing could still do a lot of damage.

He throws it to **Dara** – she catches it.

Dara   Yeah if you threw it at someone . . .

Jimmy   Or force fed it to some poor bastard.

Dara throws it to **Jimmy**.

Boyle   Dickheads.

Jimmy throws it to **Webb** again.

Jimmy   We're dickheads are we?

Webb pulls **Boyle** towards him. He gets him into a headlock and points the gun at his head.

Webb   Say that again, fuckwit. Let me hear you say it again.

Dara laughs.

Jimmy   Come on, Webb.

Boyle pushes **Webb** off.

Boyle   Hilarious. As much as I'm enjoying the gun-related humour – it's mine and I want it back now please.

Webb   Yeah you're right. Sorry.

He approaches **Boyle** to give him the gun. At the last moment he snatches it away and throws it to **Dara**.

Dara   Sucked in!

Boyle   Wankers. You're all wankers. A collection of wankers that's what I'm looking at. That's what I have before me. You are the elite of the wanker world.

Bizzy *walks onto the street reading a book.* **Dara** *doesn't see her and walks backwards with the gun.*

Dara   Aw, you want it back? You want it back, Boyle? Here.

She throws the gun to **Jimmy**. *As she does so she walks backwards into* **Bizzy** *causing her to drop her book.*

Dara   Fuck, sorry.

Bizzy   You're alright.

Dara *picks up her book and hands it back to her. The boys continue to argue amongst themselves.*

Dara   Reading again, Biz?

Bizzy   There's no law against it.

Dara   It's dangerous though – I mean look what just happened – lucky one of us wasn't injured.

Webb   Dara!

He hurls the gun at **Dara** *– she catches it.*

Bizzy   Reading's dangerous but playing catch with a loaded weapon, that's perfectly safe is it?

Dara   This? This isn't a weapon – this is a historical artefact. It doesn't even work –

She raises the gun in the air.

Boyle   Don't, Dara . . .

Dara   And it's not loaded.

She fires the gun. Nothing happens.

Dara (*laughing*)   See!

Jimmy   I think Boyle actually just shat himself.

Boyle   I did not.

He runs towards her and takes the gun from her hands.

Webb   Give me twenty quid I'll give you my belt, Boyle – it would do more damage than that thing.

Jimmy   My sock would do more damage than that thing.

They all laugh except **Boyle**.

Boyle   You're all such funny bastards aren't you?

Bizzy *looks to a flat in one of the tower blocks behind them.*

Bizzy   Look. The Countess is at her window again

Dara   What?

Jimmy *realises what* **Bizzy** *is referring to.*

Jimmy   So she is. Not that she needs an excuse to look at us. Creepy bitch.

He gives the flat the finger. **Boyle** *points his gun towards it.*

Boyle   You're next Show White!

Webb   What the fuck do you think you're looking at!

Dara   Give it a rest.

Jimmy   What?

Dara   She's not doing any harm is she?

The boys and **Bizzy** *start to walk away –* **Dara** *remains staring intently up at* **Lillie***'s window.*

Jimmy   You coming, Dara?

Dara   Yeah . . . I'm coming.

She follows them.

Scene Twenty-Two: Lillie's Bedroom

Lillie *stands at her window looking out at the street.*

Lillie   Sometimes they're funny. Sometimes they're sad. Sometimes they're wonderful. Sometimes they're terrible. But they're always just stories.

The End.

The Heights

BY LISA MCGEE

Notes on rehearsal and staging, drawn from a workshop with the writer,
held at the National Theatre facilitated by director Des Kennedy, October 2022

How the writer came to write the play

Lisa McGee wanted to create something fast-paced with swearing and interesting female characters. McGee is interested in storytelling and why we need to tell stories; she wanted to write about a writer, a narrator and a reader.

She talked about her love of thrillers; you get a lot of them in TV and movies but less so in theatre. She is interested in how those who perform this play will put together the puzzle of the story for the audience. She hopes the mixture of mystery and comedy will challenge the young performers' storytelling skills. She also talked about how growing up in a conflict zone affects your 'DNA' as a writer; there is a thread of violence in the work, but groups of all backgrounds can find their own slant on it.

Lisa McGee wants *The Heights* to be a creative experience for young people; she hopes that companies will be able to put their own spin on the play. There's a lot of opportunity to tell the story your way. It's almost a modern myth, and those can happen anywhere.

Approaching the play

Read-through with the actors

Lead director Des Kennedy said: 'First read-throughs are a funny thing. Sometimes people are really nervous or disappear into the script and mumble their way through. Try and go for it, be strong and wrong.'

To read through the play, you could read around the circle, so the first person reads the first character, the second person the second character, etc. Each person who is reading keeps the character for the length of the scene. Every time there's a new scene, shift around the circle and reallocate characters so that everyone gets a chance to read.

Read the stage directions as well.

Lisa McGee originally imagined *The Heights* as being in Northern Ireland, but it could be set anywhere. You'll need to find a way to make it work for the accents of your young people that is funny, has its own rhythms and is comfortable to perform.

She talked about how rhythm is central to comedy, it's like a piece of music, there's a lot of repetition and build (like in the Matt and Pat scenes). The accent it's performed in is not as important as finding a rhythm that works.

Lisa McGee also talked about how the timeline of the play is not necessarily the timeline of the story. A great rehearsal activity could be to decide as a whole company what you think the timeline is.

Themes

Lisa McGee summed up the play in three words: imagination, storytelling, escape.
Other themes identified by the group:

- Loneliness
- Control
- Freedom
- Violence
- Comedy
- Appearances

Structure, style and transitions

Des Kennedy talked about how the play shifts genre from thriller to farce to comedy.
He suggested that directors of this play celebrate the way it plays with genre.

> Don't be afraid of genre and playing into the genre. Familiarise yourself with
> the different genres in the play. There's no shame in saying – this bit is going to
> be a bit like that reference or this film.

Lisa McGee talked about the need to balance the loneliness with the comedy.

> You have to make the comedy work really hard so that the emotional punch
> lands; we want to feel like the build is natural and not a cheat.

The group talked about the challenge of young performers understanding the comedy
and working out how to perform it. To find your way in for your young people, you
could use existing references to help them. Once they get going, and it's fun and
energetic they will get it. Find what 'reads' and is clear by getting some of the cast to
sit out and watch each other.

Language

Lisa McGee spoke about the fact that the play is not set in Northern Ireland, although
it uses those expressions. You should be able to lift it and adapt it to suit your group.

Characters and characterisation

Character questions exercise

You can do this exercise for any character in the play, even the small characters like the
shopkeeper and the mother. Everyone can work on their own character, or you could
have people work in a small group on a particular character.

1 Something your character would want other people to think or know about them

2 Something your character wouldn't mind people thinking or knowing about them

3 Something your character wouldn't want people to know or think about them

The exercise explores the idea that there are three versions of everyone: the person we want people to think we are; the person we think we are; and the person we actually are. It helps actors discover the inner life of their character.

Reflections from the group about some of the characters

The only characters who are 'real' in the play are Lillie and Jacob. The rest are from Lillie's stories. Lisa McGee spoke about how Jacob almost became 'too real' for Lillie and so she banished him. Not much is revealed about him. He is the only real person Lillie interacts with; everyone else she is writing or creating in her head.

McGee says: 'Jacob keeps a bit of distance from the rest of the young people on The Heights. That's why he's drawn to Lillie; he's her narrator'. For the person playing Jacob it could be hard to be present and open and to have a connection with the audience. She talked about how narration can be very playful and mischievous, Jacob can have fun as well.

It is important for the actors to find the reality within their characters. Even though the stories are imagined, for the actor they need to be a real person. Des Kennedy says the best way for an actor to play any character is to find their inner life. Although the characters are in Lillie's head, their wants, needs and desires are absolutely real to them.

Lillie is the writer, Jacob the narrator and Bizzy is the reader. All the characters are trying to escape in some way. Kennedy talked about how all locations in plays are metaphors. The group talked about The Heights being an inner-city street, an estate, a rural village or a caravan park.

Casting

Before casting, Kennedy suggested that you could get the company together and everyone reads the play; they don't necessarily read a specific character, they go through it for the 'sense' of it. It might be useful for your group to read it through a few times before casting, have everyone read a few different parts to give the group a sense of the play and the characters.

Ways of approaching *The Heights* with a large cast:

- You could split the gang up, make them into more characters.
- Be careful about having more than one actor playing Lillie; it could be confusing as we don't know what's true and what's not.
- You could have two different gangs, one for the scene at the beginning and one at the end, and have a real and imaginary gang. If you're going to do this Kennedy and McGee suggested that you make the staging of both scenes exactly the same

- You could double the cast (have two people assigned to each part) and then the actors could do one performance each.

Lisa McGee said: 'Remember that the piece has to move as one thing, and gather pace, ensemble is so important, much more than who has the biggest part.'

Des Kennedy talked about the importance of group dynamics, especially getting the gang to gel. You can use the icebreakers below to help your actors work well as an ensemble.

McGee talked about how important the energy of the gang is: 'the gang is hard, it's physical, if the energy stops you go back to zero again. You need to be shocked by the energy of it. The ensemble needs to be together. It's about the physical performance and the rhythm of the text. It's almost like a dance, once they know it they'll know it.'

With all your casting choices, they stressed that clarity is the most important thing. The storytelling needs to be clear or it won't work. The audience needs to understand it. That being said, if you need to shift characters' ages, pronouns or gender, do what you need to do for your cast.

Production, staging and design

The stories that Lillie tells are great opportunities for interesting design choices. Lisa McGee talked about how exciting it is for young people to experience other roles in theatre such as design, choreography or stage management.

Possible ways to stage the glass baby story include various types of puppetry, a white cloth which turns red, an actor in a blanket, lighting. Consider that the version of the story where you have a realistic glass baby prop is arguably the least interesting one.

Exercises for use in rehearsals

Des Kennedy offered that making theatre is not about following a recipe. The most important thing is the creativity of the director and the creativity of the young people.

Exercises to build the ensemble and prepare your actors

Exercise One: Remote control

Walking around the space, constantly changing direction; as a group make sure you're filling the entire space. The leader has an imaginary remote control where 1 is the slowest and 10 is the fastest that the group should move. The leader calls out various numbers to get the group moving together.

Exercise Two: Buzzy bees

Building on Exercise One, imagine the remote control breaks and it goes up to 11. This makes the group move so quickly they start to buzz and grow wings like a bumblebee. When the leader shouts freeze, they choose a letter of the alphabet. The bumblebees have to create a statue with their bodies of something beginning with that letter. So if the letter is D there might be dogs, dinosaurs, daffodils, etc. If more than one bumblebee picks the same word (e.g. dog), they are out.

Exercise Three: A to Z

Everyone stands in a circle. The leader says, 'to the left of me is A, to the right of me is Z'. The group have to order themselves around the circle in alphabetical order of first names. Then go around the circle and hear back everyone's names. Do it again with clear voices and a beat in between everyone's names so it's clear; go Z–A, keep it slow and clear. After a few rounds everyone try and say each name all together – go A–Z and Z–A.

Exercise Four: Names in a circle

Leader (person A) walks towards someone (person B) in the circle, making clear eye contact. Before they reach that person, B says A's name really loud and clear. Then person B walks towards someone else (person C) who has to say person B's name before they reach them and so on. This can happen in any order. If you don't know the name, you can ask! Try and do it before they reach you.

Return to the A–Z game after you've played this and see if the group has improved.

Exercise Five: 1,2,3 and giving gifts

Working with a partner the group are going to count to three taking it in turns as in the script below:

A: 1

B: 2

A: 3

B: 1

A: 2

B: 3 and so on

Hear a few groups have a go and reflect on what it's like to do the exercise. Change the partners each time you shift to the following. Every time you do another version go around and watch a few pairs doing the exercise.

This time instead of saying the number 2 you clap

Instead of 2 you clap and now instead of 3 you stamp your foot

Same as above but add: instead of 1 you nod your head

Des Kennedy talked about how actors can struggle with the fact that you can't control your co-performers. A key challenge as a director is how to get actors acting *with* each other without feeling like someone has to lead.

Kennedy said: 'Openness should be what we strive for in theatre, not concentrating. We want living, breathing people who are responding to each other.'

Ask your actors to do the same exercise (1,2,3 but replaced with nod, clap, stamp) but thinking of it as if you're giving it to your partner as a gift.

The group in the workshop found it a lot easier, Des talked about the fact that when you're stressed it's much harder to get it right. If something goes wrong, so what? It has to be alive. So in scenes, ask your actors to think about gift giving.

Exercises to analyse the script and understand the play

Exercise One: Units and objectives

Directors often break the play into more manageable chunks called units.Some directors have a new unit every time someone enters or exits, others have a new unit every time an event happens. You might label your units or make a list of them so you remember where they are and what happens in each unit.

When you have broken the play and scenes down into units, you could use the objectives exercise to understand what the character wants in each moment of the play. Break it up into smaller portions. What do they want in every small moment?

An objective is what the character wants. You can start working the objectives out by using these questions:

- What does the character want in their life?
- What does the character want in the story of the play?
- What does the character want in the scene?
- What does the character want in this unit?

Each character will have different objectives throughout the play and in each scene. This makes everything really active because the characters want different things; this is how you start taking the drama from the page to the stage. The different wants or objectives help you to make the performances active.

Exercise Two: Tactics improvisation

One of the ways that actors can play their character's objective is by using different tactics. This improvisation can assist a cast in exploring different tactics.

Scenario
A is on a chair, their objective is to stay on their chair.
B doesn't have a chair, they want the chair.
Rules: you can say whatever you like to try and achieve your objective, but there is to be no physical contact in the scene.

Reflect on the improvisation with the whole group.
Possible questions to ask:

- What did you notice about the interaction?
- What different responses did you see?
- What different tactics were used by the actors?
- Who has the power in the scene?
- Did the status of the characters shift in the scene?

Tactics used by B in the workshop included: my grandma wants the seat, I've broken my leg, someone's calling your name . . .

It's interesting when characters don't get what they want, or they only get it at the end. How many different endings can your group of actors come up with for this one scene?

Exercise Three: Actioning

Working through the scene, decide on transitive verbs for every line in the scene. You should end up with a sentence in this structure for each line: I _____ you.

Examples could be: I charm you, I flatter you, I threaten you, I control you, etc.

When you read the scene, actors say the line and then add their action at the end of the line; e.g. 'I've hundreds, thousands, hundreds of thousands. *I charm you*' and work through the scene affixing the actioning statement at the end of each line.

Actioning can be a great rehearsal tool, especially if a section isn't specific enough or when actors are getting lost.

Sometimes young people find it easier to externalise their performance when they are clear about the internal world of their character.

Exercises to build the world of the play, create scenes and devise transitions

Exercise One: Stage pictures with chairs

This exercise can be a way to start creating stage pictures. As a director, stage pictures can help you be consistent, cohesive and thorough with your storytelling.

Create a stage and audience area. Everyone closes their eyes and the leader arranges four chairs on stage in a line. Ask the audience to open their eyes and reflect on the following questions:

- What do you see?
- Is there a story?
- Which is the most powerful chair? Why?

Develop the exercise by asking a few volunteers to rearrange the chairs to make one chair the most powerful. How many different stage pictures can the group create with just four chairs? What stories do you see with the rearranged chairs?

Even though you're just looking at four identical chairs, depending on the positioning, you can tell massively different stories. Positioning on stage is a very powerful thing. If you're upstage or centre you can pull focus. The fact that we read left to right is a very powerful thing; the difference between a character speaking whilst walking left to right as opposed to the other way will affect how the audience experiences it. We are narrative creatures and we read stories into everything we see.

To develop the exercise further:

- Imagine a chair is a scorpion or a bus driver or something else – how does that change your original take on the scene?

- Add people one by one into the chair scene – each actor's job is to make themselves the most powerful; each person needs to try out/do the previous one.

Exercise Two: Running into shapes

A group of about seven actors stand at the back of the stage. The audience close their eyes and the actors move forward and create a stage picture in which everyone is touching one other person. The audience open their eyes and discuss what they see, and what stories they read into it.

To develop the image further:

- Keep the image the same but all actors hide their faces from the audience.
- One person looks directly at the audience but everyone else keeps their face hidden.
- Everyone looks at one specific person (A), A hides their face.
- Everyone looks at each other except person A.

Now go back to the start of the exercise with seven actors running from the back but this time there is a stimulus word, such as 'escape'. As you build these images you can also add other instructions around where the actors are looking. In the workshop Des used floor, sky and a specific point on the ceiling.

In staging *The Heights,* there might be specific moments where all the characters are looking up at the Countess (Lillie), or at the funeral; this exercise could help you shape these moments or other transitions.

Exercise Three: Building stories out of sculptures

There are several stories in *The Heights:*

The story of the glass girl
The story of Matt and Pat
The murder
The true story of Matt and Pat
The girl in tower and the pink notes

In groups of five or six make the story out of stage pictures. Think of them as sculptures. There will be the same number of moments as group members – so that there is one sculpture for each moment and one created by each different group member. Each person in the group should direct their shape/sculpture and then step into that. Everyone in the group should be in the picture. Don't worry about where the audience is, just focus on the picture.

Make sure the group carry through the work from the making stage pictures exercise; be detailed, think about shape and composition – what stories are you telling?

Getting ready for performance
Between each sculpture moment will be a transition; everyone in the group is responsible for one transition each. The structure of the piece is made up of a series of eight beats. So you hold an image for eight, transition for eight and repeat until the group has shared the whole story.

Sharing back the stories as an ensemble performance

Everyone walks around the room with the commands stop and go. Each group has a name (fish, chips, onions, gravy, peas). When a group is called they go to the middle and perform their sequence; everyone else is still and watches from the outside. Then the walking resumes.

The sculptures don't need to be exact, the counts of eight don't need to be exact. The purpose of this is performance that is outside-in. So when performing, Des wanted the group to emotionally feel what they're doing. He asked the group not to worry if it's wrong, and to try not to concentrate too much. Openness is the thing to strive for.

Developing the exercise

- The group decides when to stop and when to go again; there should be no leaders or followers.
- When the leader says 'Countess', look up a pre-agreed point in the room as if looking at Lillie's flat.
- When the leader says 'audience', make a big clump and eyeball the audience.
- As the group walk around the room they should make eye contact and then turn away with everyone that they pass.
- When the leader says 'Glass', you have had something precious made of glass in your hands and it has just broken.
- Everyone with blue eyes is actively seeking eye contact; any other eye colour is avoiding eye contact.
- Everyone is seeking eye contact with one specific person; they try to avoid everyone else.
- Everyone is avoiding eye contact except one person who seeks it.
- Once everyone has performed their sequence once, start asking groups to reverse them, to layer up multiple groups at a time.

Question and answer with Lisa McGee

Q: Can we edit out the swearing?

A: You can edit the swearing – do what you need to do with strong language. The most important thing is that the actors are comfortable. Have a look at the rhythm to try and make it still work. McGee would rather young people do the play than not.

Q: How can we bring The Heights *to life for students who can't imagine the city setting?*

A: If you want to keep the city location then references might be really helpful for your students. Rural places can be terrifying in different ways – could you lean into the horror/ thriller genre in a more rural setting to bring it to life for the students? The Heights is Lillie's imagination so it could be anything, a fairy-tale world, or anything at all. Isolation can exist in rural settings too – caravan sites, the middle of nowhere, places with no transport.

Q: How can we safely stage the kiss?

A: The most important thing is that no one should do anything they're not comfortable with. You can signpost the story beat in another way. Des Kennedy talked about how intimacy directors are now the industry standard and so in a school or youth organisation it would be important to bring the safeguarding team into this conversation. Everything should be discussed in advance, with the young people taking the lead about what they feel comfortable with. Directors should make sure there is always another adult in the room when rehearsing any moments of intimacy and the kiss should only be properly rehearsed two or three times before the show. Lisa McGee pointed out that in TV, a moment of intimacy will be treated as a stunt or a piece of choreography. Actors should also check in with each other at every rehearsal so it's very clear how they are feeling and whether they are happy to rehearse that section.

Q: What do you think the most special moments of the play are?

A: Lisa McGee said that for her, the opening section is probably hardest; the tight comedic work which establishes the world of the play is harder than the story of the glass baby because it relies on everyone's timing being so good. For her, the most beautiful moment is probably the glass baby section.

Q: What happens in the strangling moment? Lillie is in control so is it that she wants to be strangled?

A: Lisa McGee talked about the fact that Lillie wants danger because she's trapped in her room. She also talked about the fact that she has written a genre piece and so in a thriller you need a gasp moment that shocks the audience. If a production can surprise the audience with this section, then it will be successful.

Q: What is Bizzy reading?

A: Lisa McGee talked about the fact that Lillie has a problem with Bizzy because she can't just write whatever stories she likes; someone is reading them. She thinks that Bizzy is reading the play itself. Whatever your company decides for your production, the person playing Bizzy still needs to create a 'real' character.

Q: Do you consider this a thriller or a comedy?

A: A thriller is like a puzzle – it slowly lays the clues. A really good mystery tells you the answer in the first scene but you ignore it. A good storyteller makes you forget the clue and then you get to discover it again. In this play the first line tells us the ending but we don't realise until the end. It's a mystery with thriller elements, but it needs to be funny too.

Q: Why does the scene with Dara and the gun happen twice?

A: It's about suspense – you show what happens and then go and find out how you got there. You want to keep people watching and keep people guessing. It's a mystery.

Q: Does the relationship between Lillie and Dara go beyond platonic?

A: It probably does, it may not. McGee wanted to put two young female characters at the centre and put the focus on them. Lillie is obsessed with Dara – Dara represents everything that Lillie isn't. Lillie probably does fancy her, but that is just one interpretation. Jimmy's reaction may be relevant. There is some shame there – does he suspect it's more than platonic?

Q: Does Lillie have a medical condition? Why can't she leave her room?
A: Maybe it's her mum? Is Lillie the glass baby? Has the mum convinced her that she can't go out? That's up to each company to decide. Having been through the pandemic, some young people may be able to empathise with Lillie's situation.

Q: Can we change fat Pat and fat Matt so as to not use the word fat?
A: Lisa McGee said that the most important thing about Matt and Pat is that they're cartoonish. If you can do that and try to make it rhyme, then that could work. You'll have to look at other beats in the play to make sure it makes sense. Don't change their names from Matt and Pat.

Suggested references

Films by Alfred Hitchcock
Stranger Things (2016–)
Sunset Boulevard (1950), dir. Billy Wilder
The Usual Suspects (1995), dir. Bryan Singer
Vanilla Sky (2001), dir. Cameron Crowe
Fairy tales
Fantasy
Comedy twins in stories
Huge Italian paintings in galleries/online – very useful for thinking about how to
    compose a stage picture

Book recommendations from Des
The Director's Craft (2008), Katie Mitchell
A Director Prepares (2001), Anne Bogart

Music suggestions from the participants
Euphoria soundtrack
Aetherlight (instrumental) – Mt. Wolf
When the Detail Lost Its Freedom – Brian McBride

From a workshop led by Des Kennedy
With notes by Freyja Winterson

Tuesday

by Alison Carr

Alison Carr was recently a finalist for The Women's Prize for Playwriting and she is an Associate Artist with Silent Uproar. Her theatre credits include *Until It's Gone* for A Play, A Pie and A Pint/Stellar Quines; *The Last Quiz Night on Earth* for Box of Tricks Theatre Company; *Caterpillar* for Theatre503/Stephen Joseph Theatre, Finalist – Theatre503 Playwriting Award; IRIS for Live Theatre, Winner – Writer of the Year, Journal Culture Awards; *The Soaking of Vera Shrimp* for Winner, Live Theatre/The Empty Space Bursary Award. Audio credits include *We Step Outside and Start to Dance* for ACE, National Lottery, Winner – OnComm Award; *Stuff* performed by Olivier Award winner Sophie Thompson for Painkiller Podcast; *Drenched* for Finalist, Nick Darke Award; *Dolly Would* for BBC Radio 4. Online credits include *Last Quizmas* for Box of Tricks Theatre Company; *Armour* for Gala Theatre.

Characters

Note: for the purposes of writing the script the principal characters have been allocated a sex (5F and 4M) but this can be changed as required. Pronouns can also be altered as needed (he/him, she/her, they/them).

'Us'	*'Them'*
Alex (*F*)	**Jay** (*M*)
Ash (*F*)	**Magpie** (*F*)
Billy (*M*)	**Sam** (*F*)
Mack (*F*)	**Cam** (*M*)
Franky (*M*)	

Plus an ensemble of as many performers as you wish including:

Ali	**Figure One/Figure Two**
Remy	
Charlie	
Naz	
Lou	

The dialogue should be performed with pace.

Direct address to the audience telling them the story of what happened is in italics.

Dialogue between characters in the moment is not.

There are no breaks between the narration sections and the scenes, and there are no scene changes. Each section flows quickly and smoothly into the next.

Lines that are not allocated to named characters can be performed by individuals or multiple speakers. I'd encourage the performers to find characters in the unallocated lines too.

There is no set and there are minimal props.

≡ *It happened on a Tuesday.*

≡ *Which is surprising, cos nothing decent ever happens on a Tuesday.*

≡ *Everyone knows that.*

≡ *Tuesdays – they're nothing.*

≡ *They're grey.*

≡ *Beige.*

≡ *Lame.*

≡ *Boring.*

≡ *But this Tuesday . . .*

   It started off the same as any other.

   Wake up.

≡ *Alarm.*

≡ *Snooze.*

≡ *Alarm.*

≡ *Snooze.*

≡ *Alarm.*

≡ *Snooze.*

≡ *(as a parent shouting) Get up!*

All *Groan.*

≡ *Have a wash.*

≡ *Get dressed.*

≡ *Have breakfast.*

≡ *Brush teeth.*

≡ *Shoes on.*

≡ *Coat on.*

≡ *Bag on.*

All *And go to Lane End School.*

≡ *Even the name is dull. It's not even at the end of a lane.*

≡ *Old concrete buildings and plastic annexes. A sports field. A yard. A car park.*

≡ *Just a normal school.*

≡   *We do breakfast club before lessons. Have some cornflakes and then do aerobics. It's fun.*

≡   *It's knackering.*

≡   *Morning registration.*

≡   *Here, miss.*

≡   *Here, sir.*

≡   *A sneaky last look at our phones before we have to put them away for the day.*

≡   *(as a teacher) Is that a phone?*

All   *No.*

≡   *(as a teacher) Give it to me. Now. You'll get it back at the end of the day.*

All   *Groan.*

First lesson.

≡   *Physics.*

≡   *English.*

≡   *Art.*

≡   *PE.*

≡   *History.*

All   *Bell rings.*

Break.

≡   *(as a teacher) Wait. The bell is for me, not for you. You are dismissed.*

All   *Break.*

Second lesson.

≡   *Geography.*

≡   *Chemistry.*

≡   *French.*

≡   *Business Studies.*

≡   *Maths.*

All   *Lunchtime.*

≡   *And that's when it happened.*

≡   *It started off the same as every other Tuesday lunchtime.*

I was eating a Mars bar.

≡ *I was in detention.*

≡ *I was kicking the football with Josh and Tia.*

≡ *I was standing in the lunch queue.*

≡ *I was on the toilet.*

≡ *I was biting my nails.*

≡ *I was avoiding Mr Simmons.*

≡ *I was sneezing.*

≡ *I was crying.*

≡ *I was playing hockey.*

≡ *I was talking to Alex.*

Alex   Shhhhh. Can you hear that?

≡ What?

Alex   That.

≡ *It started off quiet. A low hum. You barely noticed it.*

   Just a scratching out of sight, an irritation in your ear.

≡ *Suddenly, though, everyone was pouring into the yard from all directions. Hundreds of us. All of us. From every year. Staff too. Flocking into the yard to see what that sound was.*

≡ *The sound that was building and growing to a loud squealing.*

≡ *A high screeching.*

≡ *A cracking.*

≡ *A breaking.*

≡ What is it? Where's it coming from?

Alex   The sky.

≡ Are you sure?

Alex   Positive.

≡ *We all looked up. We squinted.*

≡ *Peered.*

≡ *Stared.*

All   *Gasped.*

≡ *The sky over the school yard started changing colour. From turquoise to sapphire to aqua to navy, and every shade in between.*

≡   *It swirled and pulsed. It was beautiful.*

≡   *It was scary.*

≡   *Then suddenly it ripped apart. Loud scraping. Blue away from blue. Clouds torn in two. A fat, jagged tear across the sky.*

≡   *For a moment nobody moved. Nobody breathed.*

    Then whoosh. We started to be pulled up towards the tear.

≡   *A force. A strength that yanked us off our feet and dragged us up towards the rip in the sky.*

≡   *Those on the outskirts found themselves being dragged along on their toes towards it, lifting and falling.*

Ali (*being dragged along*)   I can't stop!

≡   *But those right underneath it were whipped straight up into the air.*

Remy (*is sucked up*)   Aaarghhhhhh!

≡   *Quick thinkers grabbed for the nearest thing to cling on to – a bollard.*

≡   *A drain cover.*

≡   *A railing.*

≡   *Some kept their grip.*

≡   *Others didn't.*

≡   *And not everyone had something nearby to grab on to.*

≡   *The sky groaned and creaked as pupils and staff disappeared up through the tear.*

≡   *The birch tree planted in memory of the old headteacher got unearthed, its roots flapping as it spun up into the sky.*

Ash   But – look – it's stuck. The trunk's gone through the tear but the leaves are blocking it.

≡   *The pull stopped. Those still in the air dropped out on to the ground. Piles of us – confused.*

≡   *Frightened.*

≡   *Relieved.*

≡   (*At the bottom of a pile?*) *Squashed.*

≡   *The birch tree quivered and shook, but it stayed plugging the hole.*

Alex   This is our chance. Now! Let's get inside.

≡   Come on. Don't look back.

≡   Hurry up!

≡   Come on!

Alex   Is everyone inside?

≡   I think so. Wait. Who's that?

≡   Where?

≡   Over there. It's Miss Moore. What's she doing?

≡   Making sure everyone's in, I suppose.

Alex   She needs to get inside. The tree's not going to hold.

≡   *And it didn't. It disappeared through the tear with a 'thwoop'.*

≡   *Miss Moore followed close behind, 'thwoop'. Gone.*

≡   *All of this on a Tuesday lunchtime.*

≡   *It was really, really weird.*

≡   *The teachers – those that were left – were wide-eyed and ashen as they ushered us along to the assembly hall. Even Mr Chandra who's always bragging about that time he dodged a stampeding cow –*

≡   *A stampeding cow?*

≡   *Yeah. He was on holiday and –*

≡   *Anyway.*

≡   *We all stood blinking and shivering in the hall as they called the registers.*

For this section the names and responses (or no responses for the missing) can overlap and extra names can be added if required until we get to Ash who is called last.

≡   Evie?

≡   Here.

≡   Mack?

Mack   Here.

≡   Franky?

Franky   Here.

≡   Yasmin?

≡   Here.

≡   Leon? Leon?

≡   *Mrs Turner took our class register cos Mr Humphries was gone, last seen spinning up through the sky.*

≡   I was meant to have detention with him later.

≡   Not anymore.

≡   Chloe?

≡   Here.

≡   Billy?

Billy   Here.

≡   Ash?

Ash   Here

⎫
⎬   *both at the same time*
⎭

Magpie   Here

Ash and **Magpie** *emerge. They are identical. This could be achieved by the two actors wearing the same outfits, having the same physicality, way of speaking, etc. Have fun with it.*

The reaction from the others will also play into this – is there pointing and whispering at the two of them? Does the group move away, isolating them?

Ash   Hang on.

Magpie   Hang on.

They stare at each other. Might they mirror each other's movements?

Ash   You're –

Magpie   You're –

Ash   No.

Magpie   No.

Ash   Stop copying me.

Magpie   Stop copying me.

Ash   Why do you look the same as me?

Magpie   Erm, it's you who looks the same as me.

Ash   Freckles here, here, here.

Magpie   Wonky ears. Trying to hide them under your hair.

Ash   Can you do that thing with your little finger?

Magpie   Yeah.

Have you got that scar on your knee?

Ash   Yeah.

Magpie   From falling off your bike?

Ash   Yeah. It hurt.

Magpie   Really hurt.

Ash   What's your favourite crisps?

Magpie   Pickled Onion Monster Munch.

What's your favourite colour?

Ash   Green.

Have you got a dog?

Magpie   No. A cat.

Both   Called Errol.

Cool.

≡   *Two identical people. One who hadn't been here before the sky tore in two.*

≡   *And as the sky swirled outside and the windows shook, we actually looked around us and realised that this was only the start of it.*

≡   *As well as Ash suddenly having a double and the people who were missing, there were new people too. People we hadn't seen before.*

≡   *There was at least one teacher I didn't know and quite a few kids.*

It's a big school, we don't all know everyone, but these kids – no one knew them. No one.

≡   *And then there were the ones who we did recognise – classmates, teammates, friends – who were acting different. Dressed different. Being just, different.*

Charlie   That was weird.

≡   Sorry?

Charlie   That, out there. One minute we're talking to Emma, the next the ground opens up.

≡   The ground?

Charlie   Yeah.

≡   Why are you talking to me, Charlie?

Charlie   We're best friends.

≡   No we're not. We haven't spoken since juniors.

Charlie   What?

≡   *And slowly the hall split in two. Split into Us and Them.*

Ash   *Faces that were the same as ours, but not us.*

≡   *Faces we didn't know, that we'd never seen before.*

≡   *Faces that we did know but were different. We stared.*

≡   *Blinked.*

≡   *Smiled.*

≡   *Frowned at each other across the hall.*

≡   (*Us*) Who are you?

≡   (*Them*) Who are you?

≡   (*Us*) We asked first

≡   (*Them*) What's going on?

≡   (*Us*) You tell us.

≡   (*Them*) We don't know.

One minute everything was normal and then an earthquake or, I don't know.
The ground opened up, a zig zag across the school yard. We got dragged towards
it and fell through.

≡   (*Us*) The ground didn't open, the sky opened.

≡   (*Them*) The ground.

≡   (*Us*) The sky.

≡   (*Them*) The ground.

≡   (*Us*) The sky.

≡   *And just when we thought things couldn't get any more bizarre –*

Sam   You haven't said my name, miss.

≡   Who said that?

Sam   Me. You haven't said me. I'm here.

Sam *pushes her way through from behind a group.*

Billy   Sam?

Sam   Billy. I'm so glad you're okay.

Billy   Sam, is that you?

Sam   I'm scared, what's going on?

Billy   It's you. (*He hugs her tight*)

≡   Is that . . .?

≡   It can't be.

≡   It is.

≡   I don't believe it. It's not possible.

≡   She's right there.

≡   But how?

≡   Who is it?

≡   Billy's sister Sam.

≡   Sam who died. Last year. Run over by a driver who was texting.

Sam   What? What are they saying?

≡   This can't be happening.

What . . . what if we're all dead?

≡   I don't think so.

≡   Is this heaven?

≡   I hope not.

Alex   We're not all dead.

≡   Good.

Alex   It's obvious really, what's happened.

≡   Is it?

Alex   Parallel universes.

All   What?!

Alex   Parallel universes. And our world and their world have collided.

What else could it be?

Everyone 'ums' and 'ahs' but can offer no alternative.

Alex   I've been waiting for something like this to happen. I'm surprised it's taken so long. The signs have been building up for a while.

≡   Have they?

Alex   Of course.

≡   Like what signs?

Alex   The friction from the different universes piling up and getting squashed together has obviously been causing build-ups of radiation –

≡   (*sarcastic*) Obviously.

Alex   Which has been making people act weird. Make odd decisions.

≡   But isn't that just everyone all the time?

Alex   Okay. Making people act weirder than normal. Make odder decisions.

Get more irritated and angrier with each other.

An increase in anxiety and depression.

Jay   Headaches?

Alex   Yeah.

Jay   Being tired but not being able to sleep?

Alex   Yeah.

Jay   I knew it.

Alex   This is all a bit of a relief, really. It's good to know there's been a reason for it all.

Jay   I was worried we were all just going mad.

Alex   Me too.

I'm Alex, by the way.

Jay   Jay.

Alex   Are you from up there?

Jay   Yeah.

Alex   But you knew this was coming too?

Jay   I knew something was going on, but no one would listen.

≡   Sorry to interrupt, but there's no such thing as parallel universes.

Both   Yes there is.

≡   Says who?

Alex   Me.

Jay   Us.

Alex   Isn't the fact that all this is happening all the proof you need?

≡   I don't understand.

≡   Me neither.

≡   It's just stupid.

Alex   No it's not. There's loads of different theories about parallel universes – what they are, where they are, if they are.

Jay   Some people say that déjà vu is evidence that parallel universes are real. Or the Mandela Effect.

≡   The what Effect?

Jay   People en masse remembering things differently. Google it.

≡   I'm still confused.

Alex   Okay. Clearly what's occurred is, the new people, the doubles, the different people – their universe and our universe have collided which caused a tear.

≡   As simple as that?

Alex   Why not?

Here the tear is in the sky and people got pulled up and out.

Jay   There the tear is in the ground and people got sucked down and in.

≡   But in all the chaos and everyone whizzing around in the sky, we didn't realise at first that people were falling in to our universe too?

Alex   Exactly.

≡   But how are there different universes? Where do they come from?

Alex   That's the question.

Jay   I'm sure between us . . . two heads are better than one.

Alex (*unsure?*)   Yeah. Okay.

Jay   We should start by making a list. Working out who is where.

Alex   That's exactly what I was going to suggest.

So first – who is missing from this universe?

≡   Miss Moore.

≡   Mr Humphries.

≡   Half the netball team.

≡   A whole load of Year 9s.

Mack *appears. She's clearly looking for somebody.*

Mack   Has anybody seen Ali and Remy?

≡   They're usually glued to you. Where you are, they are.

Mack   Exactly. So where are they?

≡   Where have you looked?

Mack   All over.

≡   They've gone.

Mack   I know that. Where?

≡   Where do you think? (*Points to the sky.*)

Mack   No.

≡   I saw them. They spiralled up into the sky, around and around each other so fast I couldn't tell which was which anymore, higher and higher. Then gone.

Mack   But what about me?

≡   You'd rather be up there?

Mack   Dunno. It depends what it's like.

They'll wish I was there. They're going to be lost without me.

≡   They've got each other. Who have you got, Mack?

Mack   What do you mean? Loads of people. Everyone knows me.

But **Mack** *is standing noticeably alone. She scurries away.*

Jay   And who do we have from the other universe who fell in?

≡   A few Year 7 boys. They're in a huddle in the corner.

≡   That teacher over there in the ugly cardigan.

≡   Yeah, that cardigan is definitely from another dimension.

≡   There's Ash and Other Ash –

Magpie   Can you not call me 'Other Ash'. My name's Magpie.

Ash   Why do they call you that? No one calls me Magpie.

Magpie   Cos I like shiny things.

Ash   What?

Magpie   My grandad called me it once as a joke but it stuck.

Ash   I don't get it.

Magpie   I take things. Sometimes. Things that aren't necessarily mine.

Ash   You steal things?

Magpie   Just little things. It's no big deal.

And actually it's not even accurate cos I Googled it and magpies are scared of shiny objects so, yeah.

Ash   What kind of things do you steal?

Magpie   Sweets. Crisps. Jewellery. Make-up. Anything.

Nothing big.

Everyone does it.

Ash   I don't.

Magpie   Don't look at me like that.

Alex   Is there anyone else from up there?

≡   Billy's sister, Sam.

Alex   Yes. Sam who died here but didn't die up there.

Jay   Is that everyone?

Alex   Well, there's you.

Jay   Me. Yes.

And although we're not doubles like Ash and Magpie or related like Billy and Sam, there's definitely some similarities between us.

Alex   Definitely.

Jay   Have you lived around here for a long time?

Alex   My whole life. You?

Jay   Just moved here last year, my mam got a new job.

Alex   What's your mam called?

Jay   Sue.

What's your dad called?

Alex   Tony. Yours?

Jay   I don't know my dad.

≡   And, you know, one of you is a girl and one of you is a boy.

Both   So?

Jay   It's only the chance of which sperm is the quickest that decides your sex.

Alex   In this universe a sperm carrying a X chromosome got to the egg first.

Jay   In my universe a Y chromosome won the race. That's all it is.

≡   *While we tried to work out what was happening, outside the sky continued to swirl and churn, changing colour like a bruise. But no one new fell in. We figured they'd probably all taken cover too.*

≡   *We could hear sirens wailing in the distance and catch the flicker of blue lights flashing, but no one came.*

Mack   Why is no one coming to help us?

≡   How can they? Anyone who comes near will get pulled up through the tear.

Mack   Urgh. My phone's totally dead. Is anyone's phone working?

≡   No.

≡   No.

≡   There's no dial tones or Wi-Fi on anything.

Mack   This is an actual nightmare.

≡   Do you think this is just happening here or everywhere?

Mack   I don't know.

I hope my brother's okay.

≡   I hope my dad's okay.

≡   I hope my step-sister's okay.

≡   I hope my mam's okay.

≡   I hope my nan's okay.

≡   I hope my hamster's okay.

≡   *The Them seemed alright. We were all just scared.*

≡   *Confused.*

≡   *Hungry.*

≡   *The two sides merged. We chatted.*

≡   *Laughed.*

≡   *Worried.*

≡   *Hoped.*

≡   *Waited. All we could do was wait.*

Cam *loiters. He's keeping to himself, but* **Mack** *sees him.*

Mack   You. You.

Cam   Me?

Mack   Yes. I don't know you. Are you from up there?

Cam   Yes.

Mack   Why didn't you speak up when they were asking who else fell through?

Cam *shrugs.*

Mack   Did you really fall through the ground from another universe?

Cam   S'pose so.

Mack   What's your name?

Cam   Cam.

Mack   Why don't we have a Cam here?

Cam *shrugs.*

Mack   Do you have a me up there?

Cam   Dunno.

Mack   Oh you'd know. Everybody knows me.

Cam *shrugs.*

Mack   What's that?

Cam   An orange.

Mack   A what?

Cam   An orange.

Mack   What's that?

Cam   You don't have oranges?

Mack   No

Cam   It's like, a fruit.

Mack   A what?

Cam   You don't have fruit?

Mack   No.

Cam   It's good for you.

Mack   What does an orange taste like?

Cam   Like . . . sort of like . . . it tastes like . . . An orange.

Mack   Like chicken?

Cam   No.

Mack   Like liquorice?

Cam   No.

Mack   Like cabbage?

Cam   No.

Mack   That's a shame.

Cam   Sorry.

Mack   I'm joking with you, stupid. I know what an orange is.
Why are you holding it?

Cam   It's all I've got from up there.

Mack   It'll get sorted out, they'll find a way to get you back.

Cam   I don't know if I want to go back.

Mack   Why not?

Cam   Here might be better.

Mack   Why do you say that?

Cam   You know when you just want the ground to open and swallow you up?

Mack   Yeah.

Cam   It did. And it was great.

Mack   What were you doing when it happened?

Cam   Eating my lunch behind the new science block.

Mack   What new science block?

Cam   Our school has a new science block.

Mack   Ours doesn't. Mind you, I hate science.

Why were you eating your lunch there?

Cam   It's quiet. And they leave me alone.

Mack   They?

Cam   I'd been off school for ages with glandular fever. Today was my first day back.

Mr Simmons pointed me out in registration, said 'welcome back' and made everyone turn around and say it too.

All   Welcome back, Cam.

Cam   He's horrible, Mr Simmons. I hate him. Do you have him here?

Mack   Yeah.

Cam   What's he like?

Mack   Horrible.

Cam   So everyone said 'welcome back' and I said 'thank you' and smiled. Tried to.

Sometimes in photos I think I'm smiling then when I see it I look like I'm having a really difficult poo.

Mack   I look great in photos.

Cam   The morning dragged so slowly but eventually it was lunchtime.

I was just starting my sandwich when they came around the corner –

Figure One *and* **Figure Two** *emerge.* **Cam***'s memory of the incident plays out*:

Figure One   What you doing?

Cam   Just having my lunch.

Figure Two   What you having it round here for?

Cam   Dunno.

Figure One   Do you think you're too good to sit with the rest of us?

Cam   No.

Figure Two   Have you got any crisps?

Cam   I'm not allowed crisps.

Figure One   Why not?

Cam   Mam says.

Figure Two (*mocking*)   Mam says.

Cam   I've got an orange.

Cam *hands* **Figure Two** *the orange, who takes it and throws it.*

Figure One   Go and get it, then. Go on.

Cam   It doesn't matter.

Figure Two   Course it does, it's your lunch. Look it's rolling into the yard.

Cam *goes for the orange but they kick it out of reach. The two* **Figures** *surround him, pushing him between them.*

Cam   Please, just leave me alone.

Figure One   We're not doing anything.

Figure Two   Stop running into us.

The pushing continues, until **Cam** *pushes one of them back. Hard. Hard enough for the* **Figure** *to fall over.*

Cam   Sorry. I'm sorry.

Figure One   You've had this coming for ages.

Figure Two   You're so stuck-up.

Figure One   Think you're better than us. You're not.

Cam   And then the ground started to shudder and shake.

Figure Two   What's happening?

Cam   I didn't even see the crack open. It must have been right underneath me.

I thought I was falling down cos they'd pushed me over, but I just kept falling and falling and falling. Straight down. Arms by my side, legs straight, like when I went down the log flume that time at Alton Towers.

It was blackness all around me, darker and darker until it spat me out and I landed in the yard.

Just me, though. Not them.

Then something bounced off my head and dropped with a thud beside me.

It was my orange.

A group walk past. Someone glances over.

Mack (*aggressive*)   What are you looking at?

The group hurry away.

Mack   Come over here, you can sit with me.

No one's sitting with me and I don't know why.

Cam *and* **Mack** *move away.*

Billy   Are you warm enough?

Sam   Yes.

Billy   Are you hungry?

Sam   No.

Billy   Thirsty?

Sam   No.

Billy   Do you need the toilet?

Sam   I'm not a baby. If I need the toilet I'll go to the toilet.

Billy   Sorry. I just want to make sure you're okay.

Sam   I'm fine.

Sam *stands up.*

Billy   Where are you going?

Sam   Nowhere. My foot's gone to sleep.

Billy   Is it okay?

Sam   It's just from sitting down for too long.

Urgh, you know when you get pins and needles.

Billy   It's horrible.

Sam?

Sam   What?

Billy   When Mam sees you she's going to . . . I don't know. Cry probably. Loads.

Sam   Yeah.

Billy   And swear. Loads.

Sam   It's funny, I only just saw her this morning.

Billy   It's been nearly a year since we saw you.

Sam?

Sam   What?

Billy   I love you.

Sam   What?

Billy   I love you. I want you to know that.

Sam   Okay.

Billy   I always wish I'd told you I love you more often. Every day.

And . . . I left Flopsy's cage open when he escaped that time but I let Mam blame you.

Sam   I knew it.

Billy   Sorry.

Sam   You don't need to say sorry.

Billy   I do, though. I always felt bad about that. She really shouted at you.

Sam   I know but it wasn't you, was it?

Billy   It was, I just said. I was feeding him and I didn't close the lock properly.

Sam   No, I mean it was my Billy, not you.

Billy   Oh.

Sam   I'm not being nasty.

Billy   I know.

Sam   Are you crying?

Billy   No. (*But he is upset.*)

Franky *appears, anxious. He accidentally bumps into* **Sam**. **Billy** *overreacts and squares up to him.*

Billy   Oi. Be careful.

Franky   Sorry.

Billy   Watch where you're going.

Franky   I'm sorry.

Billy   What use is sorry?

Sam   Stop it. It was nothing. I'm fine.

Billy   He's barging around like an idiot. Like he owns the place.

Sam   That's enough.

(*To* **Franky**.) Sorry about him.

Billy   Don't apologise for me.

Sam   You do it, then.

Franky   He doesn't have to.

Sam   He does.

Go on.

Billy (*quiet*)   I'm sorry.

Sam   I can't hear you.

Billy   I'm sorry.

Sam   I'm sorry who?

Billy   What? I don't know. I don't know who this is. Don't you?

Sam   Oh. You're from up there too?

Franky   Erm . . .

Sam   Sorry, I didn't realise. What's your name?

Franky   Franky.

Sam   I don't recognise you, sorry. Not that I know everyone, it's a big school.

There's quite a few of us fell through, isn't there.

Do you think it smells different here?

Franky   A don't know. A bit.

Sam   I do.

Billy   A bad smell?

Sam   No, just different. Like when you go round a friend's and their house smells different. Not bad, just different to your house.

Billy   I'm sorry you don't like the way we smell.

Billy *walks away.*

Sam (*calling after him*)   I didn't say that.

(*To* **Franky**.) He's in a mood.

Franky   Why?

Sam   Cos I didn't say I love him back.

Franky   Why didn't you say it?

Sam   Cos I don't. I love Billy, my Billy, but he isn't him.

I'm not being horrible but I might look the same and sound the same as his sister, but I'm not her.

And I'm sorry his Sam died, but it's not my fault.

The things that have happened here, they're not my problem, you know. They're not our problem, are they?

Billy *reappears.*

Billy   Mr Chandra is taking groups of us to the canteen for snacks.

I saved you a space in the first group.

Sam   Okay. Are you coming, Franky?

Billy   I only saved one space.

Franky   I can wait.

Sam   See you in a bit then.

Franky   Okay.

Sam *and* **Billy** *go.*

Franky   Not my problem.

Not. My. Problem.

A group nearby laughs between themselves.

Franky *moves over to them.*

Franky   Hi.

≡   Hello.

Franky   I'm Franky, Other Franky, from up there. Can I sit with you?

The group happily make a space for **Franky**.

Elsewhere **Mack** *and* **Cam** *sit together.*

Mack   I'm hungry.

Cam   It'll be our turn soon.

Mack   But I'm hungry now. Let's eat your orange.

Cam   I don't know.

Mack   Just holding it isn't helping anyone. Come on.

Mack *pulls some peel off.*

Mack   Urghh. It's all rotten inside.

Your mam's giving you rotten oranges to eat?

Cam   No.

Mack   It stinks. Go and throw it away.

She pushes **Cam** *away, although he doesn't get rid of the orange.*

Naz *approaches* **Mack.**

Naz   Where's your little friends, Mack?

Mack   You know where, they got pulled up.

Naz   I don't think I've ever seen you by yourself before.

Mack   Unlike you, Naz, I have friends.

Naz   I've got friends too.

Mack   Where?

Naz   Here.

A small group emerges.

Naz   I think you know them. You've made their lives miserable for years.

Mack   No I haven't.

Naz   You've made my life miserable.

Mack   It's not my fault you're such a loser.

Yeah, can you all take a step back please.

But they don't and **Mack** *is nervous although she's trying not to show it.*

Naz   Not so brave without Ali and Remy here, are you.

Do they tighten around **Mack**? *Do they start to push and jostle her?*

Cam (*quiet*)   Leave her alone.

(*a bit louder*) Leave her.

Naz   Get lost.

Cam (*louder*)   Leave her.

Naz   What do you care?

You don't know what she's like.

Cam   And this makes you just as bad.

Naz   It'll do her good to know what it's like to be on the receiving end.

It might make her think twice next time before she says or does something nasty.

Cam   How bad is she?

Naz   The worst.

Mack   Cam, I'm not. They're just soft. Can't take a joke.

Naz   This is our only chance.

Mack   Too scared to take me on normally.

Naz   No, you've always got your sidekicks with you.

Mack   They're my friends.

Naz   They're as scared of you as we are.

Mack   No they're not.

Naz   I bet they're glad to be up there, free of you.

Mack   Don't say that.

Naz   What do you say, Cam?

Cam   I don't know.

The group tighten around **Mack** *but* **Cam** *tries to pull* **Naz** *back.*

Cam   No.

Naz   Too late.

Cam (*calling to a teacher*)   Miss! Miss!

The group scatter leaving **Mack** *shaken.*

Cam   Are you okay?

Mack   Course I am. I could have taken them on.

Cam   It's scary, isn't it. Being one against a group, all with angry eyes and clenched fists.

Mack   I wasn't bothered.

Cam   You look bothered.

Mack   How come you'll stand up to that lot, but up there you hide behind the science block?

Cam   I don't know. It's different.

Mack   No it isn't.

Cam   You could just say thank you.

Mack *doesn't reply.*

Magpie *appears.*

Magpie   I don't know if this is really obvious, but why don't we just go outside?

≡   What?

Magpie   All of us from up there, why don't we just go outside into the yard and get sucked back up into our universe?

Replies of 'oh yeah', 'of course', 'it's obvious', etc.

Magpie   Come on then, let's go.

Alex   Wait, wait, wait.

You can't just go outside and get pulled back up.

Sam   Why not?

Alex   Who knows where you'll end up?

Billy   Yeah, Sam, it's not safe.

Sam   We'll end up back home.

Jay   Not necessarily.

This might not be the only breach.

If universes are colliding there could be tears all over. They might be moving and shifting all the time. You might get pulled up and land in a universe where the dinosaurs never got wiped out or which is entirely submerged in water.

Sam   Or we might end up back home.

Jay   Are you willing to take the risk?

And if it's that easy, why have none of our people up there just jumped back down? Or maybe they've tried and ended up in a different universe entirely. One where cats make the rules and keep humans as pets.

Sam   I don't want to be a cat's pet but I wouldn't mind seeing a dinosaur.

Alex   Let's all just wait for now until I work something better out.

Ash *appears, furtive. She beckons to* **Magpie**.

Ash   Come here.

Magpie   What?

Ash   Here.

Magpie *does.* **Ash** *holds open her bag –* **Magpie** *sees inside.*

Magpie   Where did you get all that?

Ash   Everyone's bags are just lying about. No one's paying attention.

Magpie   You stole it all?

Ash   Yeah. It was easy.

Magpie   You should put it back.

Ash   Why? I thought you'd be pleased.

Magpie   Why would I be pleased?

Ash   I thought it would be fun.

Magpie   Was it?

Ash   Not now it isn't, you've spoiled it.

Magpie   You don't want to be like me, Ash.

You're good. People like you, respect you.

Ash   I'm boring.

Magpie   I'm jealous of boring. Being boring means your parents don't look so tired and disappointed all the time.

Ash   Being boring means my parents expect everything to be perfect. Top of the class, good at everything.

Magpie   The first thing I stole was two eyeshadows and a blusher from Topshop.

I was with my friend Katie. She took a denim jacket – walked out wearing it – but I was too scared to take anything that big. We got out of the shop and a security guard appeared. Katie legged it but I was too slow. The security guard brought me back inside and rang my mam.

Ash   I remember Katie.

Magpie   Yeah?

Ash   Her and her dad moved away years ago.

But I remember going to town with her most Saturdays, she was always trying to get me to nick stuff.

Magpie   You didn't, though.

Ash   No.

Magpie   Well, I did.

Mam came. She kept asking why I'd done it, I didn't have to steal. The shop didn't call the police, and she took me home and grounded me. But that time we spent, from the shop to home, it was the most time we'd spent together in ages.

I liked it.

I kept stealing. Sometimes I'd get away with it, sometimes I wouldn't. When I'd get caught Mam or Dad or both of them would come and shout at me.

They don't now, though. They've given up. But I can't stop myself cos maybe, maybe next time I do something wrong they'll be bothered again.

Ash   I'd love my parents to not be bothered about what I do, to leave me alone.

Magpie   You wouldn't if it happened.

Ash   Were they nice – the eyeshadows and blusher?

Magpie   No. Horrible.

Ash   You can still change.

Magpie   I don't know.

Ash   Do you want to?

Magpie   I think so. I don't really like who I am.

Ash   I don't think we're meant to, are we? Not yet.

Lou *approaches, angry.*

Lou   Oi, Ash. I saw you in my bag. Give me my money back.

Ash   I haven't got your money.

Lou   I saw you.

Ash   It was her. (*Pointing at* **Magpie**.)

Magpie   What? No it wasn't. It was her.

Ash   It was her.

Magpie   It was her.

Lou   I don't know which one's which.

Ash   She took it. Magpie. The clue's in the name.

Magpie   Don't do this, Ash.

Ash   She stole your money, Lou.

Lou   I've told sir.

Ash   Good.

Lou   You lot, the Them. You can't be trusted.

≡   *And so it started. The divide.*

≡   *Suspicion.*

≡   *Accusation.*

≡   I've got money missing, too.

≡   And me.

≡   And my phone.

≡   And my headphones.

≡   Me too.

Lou   Magpie can't be trusted. She needs to be separated from the rest of us.

Magpie   I didn't take your stuff.

Lou   Ash says you did.

Magpie   She's lying.

Lou   Ash wouldn't lie. She's not like that.

Put Magpie in a classroom on her own.

Sir says. Sir says you're to sit in there on your own and he'll guard outside.

≡   *The Year 7 boys from up there started to cry that they wanted to go home. It was really sad.*

≡   *It was really annoying.*

≡   *We were all getting tired.*

≡   *Cold.*

≡   *Bored.*

≡   *Scared that this wasn't stopping, that things weren't going back to normal.*

≡   *The novelty had worn off and it wasn't exciting anymore.*

≡   *These people, these strangers.*

≡   *Outsiders.*

≡   *Aliens.*

≡   *Asking so many questions and looking lost. Moaning. Complaining.*

≡   *Eating our snacks and drinking our drinks.*

≡   How long are they going to be here?

≡   Are they going to have to come home with us, cos we haven't got any room.

≡   What about the new ones – where will they go?

Mack   What will I tell Ali and Remy's parents about where they've gone?

≡   Are our people okay up there? Will your lot be treating them well?

≡   Our lot?

≡   Why did you have to fall into our school yard? Why us?

≡   I just want things to go back to normal.

Sam *starts to cough.*

Billy   Are you okay?

Sam   Yes.

But she keeps coughing.

Billy   You don't sound okay.

Sam   There's just a tickle in my throat.

≡   *Then they all started to cough. Just a little at first, a tickle in their throats, but it didn't stop.*

≡   *Then another started.*

≡   *And another.*

≡   *And another.*

≡   *And another.*

≡   *Until all of them from up there were coughing and coughing and coughing.*

Billy   I'll get you some water.

Exit **Billy**.

Jay   I was worried this might happen.

Alex   Me too.

≡   What's going on?

Jay   The first clue was Cam's rotten orange. It was the first sign that our atmosphere isn't compatible –

Alex (*interrupting*)   It isn't compatible –

Jay   That's what I was saying.

Alex   I know.

Jay   Then why did you butt in? You never let me do the explaining.

Alex   I do. Loads.

Jay   You're always saying 'I'. I did this, I worked out. It's never 'we'.

Alex   Sorry, I'm not used to working with someone else.

Jay   Neither am I. But it's nice to have someone who understands, who 'gets it' like I do. Don't you think?

Alex   I don't know. It's . . . different.

Jay   Fine. Go ahead.

Alex   What?

Jay   Explain it.

You tell everyone what's happening and then you work out what to do if you're so amazing.

Alex   Jay . . .

But **Jay** *turns away.*

Alex   Our atmosphere and their atmosphere having exactly the same mixture of nitrogen, oxygen, carbon dioxide and argon is really unlikely. Similar, maybe, but not the same.

Something in our atmosphere isn't compatible for them. Is bad for them, even.

≡   Are they going to be okay?

Alex   I don't know.

≡   Are they going to rot like Cam's orange?

Alex   I don't know.

≡   What's their atmosphere like up there?

Alex   I don't know.

≡   Are our people okay?

Alex   I don't know.

Jay   You don't know much, do you.

Billy *returns with a glass of water for* **Sam**.

Billy   Here you go.

Sam   Thanks.

Sam *drinks.*

Billy   What's this?

Sam   What?

Billy   On your arm, let me see.

It's a rash. All red spots up your arm. Does it hurt?

Sam   It's itchy.

Magpie   Really itchy.

Alex   You're having an allergic reaction to the atmosphere.

Our air is irritating your skin.

≡   A rash is worse than a cough.

≡   A rash is contagious. Are we going to catch it?

Alex   Probably not.

≡   Probably isn't very certain. Are you sure?

Alex   Well, no.

≡   She said we're going to catch it.

Jay   She didn't.

≡   She said it's contagious.

Alex   I didn't.

≡   It's definitely contagious. Stay away.

≡   Move away.

≡   Get over there. Further.

Mack   Further.

Cam   Help me.

Mack   Don't touch me.

Cam   I helped you.

Mack   So?

≡   Further.

≡   Further.

≡   Further.

The sides separate again into Us and Them.

Franky *is resisting being put with the Them.*

≡   You too, Franky. Get over there with Them, where you belong.

Franky   I'm not one of them.

≡   Yes you are.

Franky   I'm not.

≡   You said you are.

Franky   I lied. I'm Here Franky, not There Franky. I'm from here.

≡   There is no Here Franky.

Franky   Yes there is, just none of you notice me.

≡   Impossible. You're lying.

Franky   I'm not.

≡   That's what a liar would say.

Franky   I swear. I'm not coughing, I've not got a rash. Look.

≡   Why would you say you're from up there if you're not?

Franky   For a fresh start.

≡   What?

Franky   A do-over.

You don't know me cos I'm off school so much looking after my dad. He needs so much help.

I look after him and my little brother – I do the washing, the shopping, cooking, cleaning, all of it. And no matter how hard I try there's always more to do, it never stops. And if they think I can't cope, if they think I'm not doing well enough, we might get split up and I can't let that happen.

I love my dad and I know it's not his fault, but when you thought I was from up there it was such a weight off my shoulders. Other Franky doesn't have all that responsibility.

She said – Sam – she said it's not my problem.

I just wanted it not to be my problem for a little bit. Just so I could have a rest.

≡   I'm so sorry, Franky.

≡   I don't believe him.

≡   What?

≡   He's lying. He's one of them.

Franky   I'm not. Please.

≡   I believe him.

≡   So do I.

≡   I don't.

≡   Me neither. And do we really want to take the risk?

Franky *is pushed across with the rest of the them.*

Billy *is in with the them, with* **Sam**.

≡   Billy, come away.

Billy   No.

≡   Come over here to us where it's safe.

Billy   I'm staying with Sam.

Sam   They're right. You should go over there.

Billy   No.

Sam   You might catch it, whatever it is.

Billy   I don't care.

Sam   I'm scared.

Billy   So am I.

They wrap their arms around each other and won't be parted.

≡   *We didn't take our eyes off them.*

≡   *We didn't blink, didn't dare.*

≡   *How could we trust them? One was a thief.*

Magpie   It wasn't me.

≡   *One was a liar.*

Franky   I'm not lying.

≡   *Who knew what the rest of them were capable of?*

≡   *They cowered in a corner and we took turns to stand guard. Teachers too; it wasn't just us wanting to make sure we were kept apart.*

≡   *They coughed their dry coughs. Their skin got paler. Their eyes drooped.*

≡   *Outside it was starting to get dark but we could still hear the pull and the rattle from the tear in the sky.*

Billy *cradles* **Sam** *who – along with the rest of the them – has gotten progressively worse. She's pale, weak.*

Billy   I'll get you some more water.

He gets up to go but is stopped by **Lou**.

Billy   Let me past.

Lou   You can't leave. You might have it, might spread it.

Billy   I haven't.

Lou   You might.

Billy   I can't let her die again. You have to let me through.

Billy *tries to barge past* **Lou** *but is pushed back.*

Sam *is itching her arm.*

Billy   Try not to scratch it. You're making it bleed.

Sam   Tell me the story about the chicken.

Billy   What?

Sam   Sorry, I forgot. My head's a bit fuzzy.

Mam used to tell me and my Billy this story when we were little –

Billy   About the chicken who felt *cooped* up so went on an *egg*-cellent holiday?

Sam   That's right.

Tell it to me.

Billy   It was silly, for babies.

Sam   Please.

Billy   I don't know if I can remember it very well.

Sam   Try.

Billy   It was a cold and rainy day on the farm –

Sam   On Sunnydale Farm.

Billy   Yes, Sunnydale Farm. It was cold and rainy but out in the field Farmer Giles was –

But **Sam** *descends into another coughing fit.*

Billy   I don't know what to do.

What do we do?

We can't just sit here doing nothing.

Alex   He's right. We have to do something.

Ash   But what?

Alex   Think. Think, Alex, if you're so clever.

Cam's orange was the first sign. Where is it? Can I see it?

Alex *tries to go to* **Cam** *but* **Lou** *stops her.*

Alex   This could help them. Help all of us.

Cam   Here.

Cam *throws the orange across to* **Alex***. She studies it.*

Alex   What do oranges have? Vitamin C. What does Vitamin C do?

Jay   Fights infection.

Alex   Yes. Fights infection.

Go to the kitchens, look for anything full of Vitamin C – oranges, broccoli, cauliflower, brussel sprouts –

Jay   Urgh, no Brussels sprouts

Alex   Yes Brussels sprouts. Go on, quickly.

≡   Not all of it, though. We need to keep enough back for us. Just in case.

≡   *The fruit and veg worked. A bit.*

≡   *It perked them up. A bit.*

≡   *But they were still coughing. Still had a rash.*

≡   *They needed to get back to their universe. And quickly.*

Alex   Okay, let's think.

Jay, can you help me? I really need you to help me.

Franky   We can all help.

Jay   Let's go back to the beginning.

What do we know for sure?

Sam   That there's another universe.

Ash   With different versions of us in it.

Billy   Or people we lost here.

Cam   Or people who aren't here at all.

Alex   That's right. Yes.

Magpie stole something, Ash didn't.

A driver texted, a driver didn't.

A school built a new science block, a school didn't.

Jay   Our mam met my dad. Our mam met someone else.

Alex   And so on.

Different outcomes from different choices.

Jay   And for every choice we make, the option we don't take happens in another universe that exists in its own time and space.

Mack   Okay, so how does that help us now?

Alex   I don't know.

Magpie   Can we undo what we did today? The choices we made? Stop it happening?

Ash   How?

Magpie   I don't know.

Jay   The choices we've made can't be undone.

It's not what we *did* that matters –

Jay & Alex   It's what we do *now*.

Billy   And that shouldn't be us sitting here separately glaring at each other.

Ash   He's right. It needs all of us, together.

The two sides merge. They're talking animatedly, throwing around ideas.

≡   *We got all of the whiteboards out of the nearby classrooms and put them around the hall.*

≡   *We got all of the Bunsen burners and microscopes.*

≡   *All of the art supplies.*

≡   *All of the textbooks we could find, library books too – fiction and non-fiction, desperately looking for ideas.*

≡   *Crash mats.*

≡   *Music stands.*

≡   *One of those clicky wheels for measuring distance.*

≡   *Everything we could find to try and help us work out what to do.*

From all of the activity, **Cam** *emerges. But no one can hear him.*

Cam   All of us together.

≡   What about –?

Cam   All of us together.

≡   What if we –?

Cam   All of us together.

Mack   What are you saying? Shhh, Cam's saying something.

Cam   All of us together.

Ash   Yeah, it needs all of us working together. That's what I said. And we are.

Cam   A human chain.

Jay   Explain.

Cam   We make a human chain, one long enough to reach right up to the tear.

Then someone can climb up it and go through.

Magpie   I suggested going up through the tear earlier.

Cam   Yes but if the person is attached to the human chain and there's dinosaurs or giant cats it means they're not stuck in that universe with no way back.

There is a beat as everyone thinks about this, then a clamour of 'no', 'no way', 'not a chance', etc.

Jay   Has anyone got a better idea?

That shuts everyone up.

Jay   Okay. We'll make the chain and then I'll go through.

Alex   You're not well enough.

Franky   I'll do it. I've let my dad down and my brother, wanting to be away from them. I'll go through, it's the least I can do.

≡   Franky, your dad needs you. And your brother. You can't risk it.

Franky   Who can risk it? We all have people who need us, who'll miss us.

Ash   I'll do it.

Alex   Why?

Ash   It's the least I can do.

Jay   What do you mean?

Ash   Magpie knows.

Creation of the human chain –

≡   *We started by creating the anchor, two teachers in the assembly hall tied to a pillar with bicycle chains.*

≡   Secure?

≡   Secure.

≡   *From there we snaked out to the door, gripping each other around our waists and tied together by whatever we could find – jumpers, tights, headphone cables. Anything to help us stay together.*

≡   *As soon as we edged the door open to outside we felt the pull.*

≡   Deep breath. We can do this. We have to.

≡   *The chain continued to right under the tear where we started to be lifted off the ground. Grips tightened.*

≡   *It was hard to tell how high we'd need to go. On and on we went, each new link crawling over the ones in front to add themselves to the human chain.*

Cam   Mack, your turn.

Mack   No way.

Magpie   We need everyone.

Mack   I can't.

Billy   You can.

Mack   I'm scared.

Sam   We're all scared.

Mack   I can't do it on my own.

Franky   You're not on your own, look at everyone.

You're next after Naz.

Naz *holds a hand out to* **Mack** *but* **Mack** *doesn't take it.*

Mack   I can't.

≡   *Up and up we went – Us and Them, one after another – reaching up towards the tear in the sky.*

ASH   Is it high enough?

CAM   I don't know, but there's no one left but us two.

≡   *Cam crawled up first, Ash close behind.*

The nearer they got to the tear, the stronger the pull.

Cam   It's still not quite long enough.

Ash   I could jump?

Cam   No. We need to all stay connected for this to work.

≡   *All seemed lost, but then –*

Cam   Mack!

Mack   It was boring down there on my own, there was no one to talk to.

≡   *Finally everyone was connected and Ash was able to stick her head up through the tear.*

All   Well?

Ash   It looks like our yard. It's not submerged in water. There's no dinosaurs or giant cats.

Hang on, someone's coming. They've got . . . it's a rope. They've got a rope. Why didn't we think of that?

≡   *Ash took the rope, pulled it through the tear and passed it down the human chain to the teachers at the bottom who tied it to the pillar in the assembly hall.*

≡   Secure?

≡   Secure.

≡   *The human chain climbed down and the rope held fast, joining our two universes together. It was time to swap back.*

Ash   I'm really sorry.

Magpie   Forget it.

Ash   I should have admitted it was me.

Magpie   You should, yeah. Maybe I'm not the one who needs to change.

≡   *As they climbed up the rope we smiled, waved, said bye, but we struggled to look them in the eye.*

Mack   See you.

Cam   Yeah.

Mack   You can do it, you know. You can speak up. I've seen it.
Be braver. Remember how it felt standing up for yourself.

Cam   Be kinder. Remember how it felt being scared.

≡   *As ours came down there was hugging and crying.*

≡   *Ours had a rash too and a cough. We asked how they'd been treated.*

≡   Really well.

≡   They were so kind. So worried.

≡   They really looked after us.

≡   *No one said anything.*

≡   *I looked at the floor.*

≡   *I looked at my shoes.*

Alex   Bye then. I couldn't have done it without you.

Jay   I know you couldn't.

Ali   Hiya.

Remy   Hi.

Mack   I missed you.

Both   Did you?

Mack   Yeah. It's good to have things back to normal.

Ali   Yeah, about that.

Remy   We're not going to walk two steps behind you all the time anymore.

Ali   Or agree with everything you say.

Remy   Or do everything you tell us to do.

Mack   Okay.

Both   Really?

Mack   Yeah.

Ali *and* **Remy** *walk away together, leaving* **Mack** *behind.*

Mack   Hold on, wait for me.

Mack *follows them.*

≡   *Eventually everyone was back where they started except for –*

Billy   Please don't go.

Sam   I have to.

Billy   No you don't. Stay. Come home with me and we can be a family again.

Sam   But what about my Billy? What about my mam?

Do you want them to lose me too, when you know what it feels like?

Billy *shrugs.*

Sam   I know this is hard.

But let me go so my Billy doesn't feel as bad as you do.

Billy   I'm your Billy.

Sam   You're not. You know you're not.

You are like him, though. Kind. Annoying. Always looking after me.

Billy   I didn't look after you well enough, though.

Sam   It wasn't your fault.

Billy   I want my Sam back.

Sam   I know you do. But you can't have her, she's gone.

What you can do is give the Billy up there his Sam back.

Billy   I love you.

Sam   I love you too.

They hug.

Alex   *And just like that, everything was back to normal.*

≡   *Normal apart from the swirling, yawning tear in the sky.*

Alex   *Apart from that, yeah.*

≡   *We blocked the tear up with a trestle table briefly. Mr Chandra and Miss Moore lugged it up the rope. It lasted long enough to evacuate everyone from the area.*

≡   *The police and ambulance and fire engines and parents and neighbours and carers and mysterious figures in black suits were waiting at a cordon far back from the school gates.*

≡   *The mysterious figures in black looked quite annoyed when they heard we had saved the day with some rope and a trestle table.*

   They swarmed on the building while our worried loved ones enveloped us in more hugs and tears.

≡   *School was closed for ages which was great at first and then it got quite boring.*

Ash   *I think about Magpie all the time. About what she's doing up there. If she's okay. Will I see her again, if it happened again? Could it happen again?*

Alex   *At least we know the signs to look out for. Remember – tiredness, headaches, weird behaviour, odd decisions.*

≡   *The official announcement was that the strange sky was some rare, freak weather phenomenon.*

≡   *Climate change.*

≡   *Anything we tried to post on social media disappeared straight away.*

≡   *There was nothing on the news or in the papers, and we never found out if it was worldwide or just us.*

≡   *No one believed us about what really happened.*

Billy   *I haven't told Mam about Sam. Not without any proof. But I know. And it helps me feel better that she's happy and thriving up there, and at least one Billy hasn't lost her.*

Mack   *I wonder about my choices every day now. Everything, even as simple as what to have for breakfast. If I have porridge rather than toast, is a whole new universe created? A porridge-verse? And is that better or worse? What if me in the porridge-verse is having more fun than me here?*

Franky   *I started to doubt that it had ever happened at all. It all seemed so far-fetched. That I would even think about leaving my dad. Cos when I saw him outside the school, so worried, I realised that I need him as much as he needs me.*

Billy   *And if you ever need a break, want to hang out.*

Franky   *I'd like that, thanks.*

≡   *When school finally re-opened we all ran straight into the yard and looked up into the sky. We squinted.*

≡   *Peered.*

≡   *Stared.*

All   *Gasped.*

≡   *It was normal. Totally normal.*

≡   *Blue.*

≡   *Calm.*

≡   *Serene.*

≡   *Still.*

   But if you looked really closely –

Alex   There, can you see it?

≡   *Where?*

Alex   There. If you look you can see a faint line, where the sky's been stitched back together. The two blues don't quite match up.

≡   Can you see it?

≡   Yeah.

≡   Me too.

≡   Where?

≡   I can see it. So it did happen?

≡   Definitely.

≡   100 per cent.

≡   We were right.

≡   *It happened on a Tuesday.*

≡   *At Lane End School.*

≡   *And it was really, really weird.*

End.

Tuesday

BY ALISON CARR

*Notes on rehearsal and staging, drawn from a workshop with the writer,
held on Zoom and at the National Theatre, October 2022, facilitated by director
Adam Penford and movement director Jess Williams*

How the writer came to write the play

Alison Carr is a playwright based in Newcastle, and after an attachment with the National Theatre was commissioned to write her first play for young people. Carr wrote *Tuesday* in 2019 (at a time when she hadn't even heard of Zoom). Lead director Adam Penford observed how resonant the themes in the play had become since it was first written.

Alison Carr said that she can sometimes go down internet rabbit holes, and this time the Mandela Effect caught her imagination. She was intrigued by the idea of collective misremembering of information. For example, she could have sworn that 'chartreuse' was a dark red, but she was disconcerted to discover it is a sickly green. There are lots of examples of the Mandela Effect; some are tiny and some are more significant. One of the theories to explain why these incidents of collective misremembering happen is that they are evidence of the existence of parallel worlds. Carr was struck by the idea that the walls of the universe are thin, and other realities might permeate our universe. She said that she uses the terms 'parallel worlds' and 'multiverse' interchangeably when thinking about these themes. The starting point for writing this play was an idea, as opposed to a location or a specific character. She wanted the focus to be on *what happens in that place*.

Fundamentally, Carr was drawn to writing something about choices and consequences. She felt that the age groups of those working with this play will be making choices that have knock-on effects that will set them off on different life paths.

What if this choice breaks off into a different universe, and you get the chance to meet the person who made the other choice?

Warm-up excercises (can be used in person and on Zoom)

1 Does anybody else

Think of something that you like; for example, 'I like chocolate' or 'I love swimming'. On Zoom, everyone switches off their camera, the first person (e.g. the facilitator) says the first statement, and anyone else who likes that thing switches their camera on. The first person then chooses the next person, everyone turns their cameras off again, and the game repeats. In person, instead of turning your camera on, cross the room into an empty space, so everyone who likes that thing is standing together.

2 Sign name

In British Sign Language (BSL), speakers have a 'sign name', which is a physical gesture to communicate their name. In thirty seconds, everyone thinks of a sign name for themselves. Go round the group, with participants saying their name and performing their 'sign name'. The rest of the group repeats the name and the gesture.

3 Two truths and a lie

Participants have ninety seconds to think of two things that are true, and one thing that is a lie. Be as inventive as you want! One at a time, participants list their three statements, and the rest of the group has to vote on which one is a lie. On Zoom, you can vote by holding up your fingers to show which one you think is a lie.

This game encourages creativity and imagination, but also encourages people to lie! This is a useful way to initiate conversations about speaking truthfully in fictional circumstances, which is the heart of acting. Adam also said that young people tend to leave the lie to last, which reveals something about strategy.

Approaching the play

Day one: do a read-through of the play. At this point, maybe the main characters have been cast, but the ensemble lines probably haven't been allocated. Sit in a circle and read it a line at a time round in a circle. This means that you don't necessarily get the through-line of the characters, but everyone gets a chance to hear the play without worrying about who has which part.

Themes

After the read-through, it could be useful to discuss the themes of the play. This engages the performers in the question of 'what is this play really about?'. What is it that you think your audience might take away from this? This discussion makes the actors care more about the shared objective of the production.

In one minute, the group listed as many themes as possible they could think of that were contained in the play, and typed the answers in the chat box. The themes were:

Reflection, loss of identity, bigger picture, otherness, routine, friendship, letting go, identity, grief, sibling love/relationships, relationships, belonging, family, loss, same person/different lives, choices, cause/effect, actions have consequences, social pressure on youth, you can't always get what you want, us and them, regret.

Alison Carr then chose five themes to discuss in more detail:

1 Us and them
2 Actions have consequences
3 Sibling love and relationships

4   Social pressure on young people

5   You can't always get what you want

In breakout rooms, groups discussed: How is the theme explored in the play? How does the theme resonate in the world we live in, and in the performers' lives?

Carr stressed that you have complete control over choosing the themes that you will work with in rehearsal.

The following notes are a summary of the feedback from the discussions that were had in breakout rooms:

1 Us/Them

What counts as 'us'? When you're younger, you experience different 'tribes'. This can result in rumours and a fear of the unknown. The group reflected that the experience of refugees is relevant, and how we might be manipulated by the media to fear the other. The war in Ukraine was considered a resonant theme. We are becoming more divided as a society; the influence of social media can mean that debates are split along binaries.

Considering another world coming into our lives may spark conversations around empathy, as the play asks us to consider other ways of living. New people coming into an environment can be a novelty, until people get tired of it, and then fear and separation set in; people get tired of being nice. It was observed that there was an 'Us and Them' culture within schools post-Covid, as students had lived and learnt in smaller groups. There was some reflection on how the process of building a unified ensemble with the cast may mirror the themes in the play.

2 Actions have consequences

Magpie as a character was considered to strongly embody this theme. Ash also makes the wrong choices in blaming Magpie. The situation between Cam and Mack resonates; seeing that Cam was bullied makes Mack look at their own choices and their consequences. This theme is also explored through the death of Sam; a driver was texting when they killed her, which has a huge and lasting effect on Billy. The consequences of the events of the play leave the lingering desire for them to pull together and become a community.

The group also reflected on the consequence of *not* taking action. It was felt that some students in difficult circumstances feel that they don't have choices, but that it was important to help them see that their actions do matter. Negative actions have consequences, but so do positive actions.

3 Sibling love and relationships

The play deals with loss, grief and acceptance that things happen. The group reflected on how resilient young people are and the lessons that teachers and practitioners can take from them. The group considered status and power within those relationships. It was felt that Sam's death is very powerful, and considering that everyone has suffered some form of loss, it will be a good opportunity to navigate this theme with a duty of care and in a safe way. The group reflected that family relationships can change through separation, which gives a fresh insight into the nature of the relationships. It is important to be able to let go in relationships, and learn not to be possessive.

4 Social pressure on youth

The play deals with peer pressure and bullying. There is pressure on Frankie, who needs to take on adult responsibility. There is also pressure on young people now to adapt and cope in a post-Covid world. Young people are dealing with a lot, quickly, in a way they haven't had to before. It was reflected that the scale of the ways in which we have asked them to adapt has not been seen since the Second World War.

5 You can't always get what you want

The acceptance that is required when things don't go how you want them to requires resilience. The characters in the play want to escape the mundane Tuesday-ness of Tuesday, but what they get as an alternative is not necessarily better! This introduces the idea of being careful what you wish for. The group reflected that Magpie shoplifts to get attention, even if the attention is negative.

There could be a discussion with the young people about the importance of being able to handle disappointment. Adam Penford reflected that 'the grass is always greener' is a great theme of children's literature.

Penford flagged up the themes of mental health and the environment, as what happens in the play is environmental.

Characters and characterisation

In this play there are named characters, as well as ensemble dialogue which isn't allocated to a particular character.

Adam Penford offered a Stanislavski-inspired approach to building a character, which asks the fundamental questions, and is about analysing the text:

What do I say about myself? (e.g. I am tired, I am bored)

What do others say about me? (e.g. I am lazy, I am late)

What do I say about other characters? (e.g. Ash is stupid, Mack is brave)

What does the playwright say about me? (e.g. I have red hair, I enter running)

Focusing on each character, write the quotations out in first person: 'I am tired, I am bored'. Avoid interpretation, just mine what is in the text; you are not extrapolating or diagnosing.

Three ways were suggested for how to deliver this exercise:

- Ask the young people to look at it at home, and then have a discussion in an hour. This will get the students thinking about the characters in detail and identifying choices.

- Use the exercise as you're doing the read-through to include those who don't want to read; every character has one person reading and one scribe who sits with a big piece of A3 split into the four questions.
- You can read the play with an inner circle and an outer circle; one group's role is to be the fact gatherers, who writes them all down, and everyone else writes down the questions; things they don't understand, or things they don't know about. At the end of each unit, you can interrogate those things.

The following notes are a summary of the discussions about each character:

Alex: Alex sees himself as clever, but has high expectations of himself. He experiences self-doubt and insecurity, but is also responsible.

Jay: Jay is anxious and less dominant than Alex. Jay has just moved in and didn't know their dad, so felt a bit more of an outsider. It was noticed that other characters don't say much about Jay, and sometimes the absence of something reveals as much as the presence of something. Is this because Jay stands back in the shadows more? Jay is good at noticing things.

Ash: Ash has freckles, they're not a thief, they have wonky ears, their favourite colour is green and they like Pickled Onion Monster Munch. They think they're boring, and their parents expect them to be perfect. Ash says, 'I'd love my parents not to be bothered about what I do.' Most of what is said about Ash is by Magpie.

Magpie: Their name comes from their granddad. They are firm in their decision in the play to come together. They talk about wrongs and rights and are clear that actions have consequences.

Billy: The tragedy of Sam has had a large impact on Billy. He feels guilty and wants to be protective. Other characters don't quite know how to deal with him, which could be to do with anxiety about how to deal with someone who's gone through a painful experience. Billy wants to keep Sam safe and undo the damage. He wonders if he could have stopped it.

Sam: Sam speaks in a lot of sentences that begin 'I'm'. She feels the need to clarify how she's feeling and what kind of person she is. There is a choice to be made about whether Sam or Billy is older. Billy feels protective, but this could be a psychological need rather than a reference to their ages. Sam hasn't experienced a tragedy, so she is blasé, but Billy has the mark of someone who has experienced a tragedy, which creates an interesting dynamic.

Mack: Other characters see Mack as manipulative and unkind. Mack sees themselves as a leader who is confident and knows what they want but is also sensitive. Mack struggles to create conversation. Mack says that Cam is stupid.

Cam: Cam shrugs when we first meet him. Cam says 'I don't know if I want to go back' and wonders if 'here might be better'. Could it be that Cam is used to being invisible, unnoticed and unhappy, but in this world it's Cam's orange that acts as a catalyst? Maybe switching worlds was a brilliant thing for Cam.

Alison reflected that Ash, Magpie, Billy and Sam go on the biggest journeys in the play. One of the fundamentals of drama is that characters end the play differently to how they started.

Adam reflected on the importance of status, and on the work that can be done by the director in terms of how each character fits into the group. What is the hierarchy of the group? And does that change from moment to moment within the journey of the play? There should be specific detail in terms of the nature of these relationships.

Building character physicality

Once named characters have been cast, get everyone to walk around the space. Start to build the character; get them walking as their character and get them listening. Ask questions like 'How old is your character; your age, or older or younger?' and 'If your character was a colour, what colour would they be?' and instruct the students to allow that to infect how they're walking through the space; let it seep through their body, let it affect how they're moving, how they're reacting to the space, to other people in the space. That will change their pace, eye contact, whether they take up space, whether they hide and so on.

After a time, bring them to a halt, stand up, sit down, grab a chair, go to sleep as their character, have breakfast as their character, go to the park as their character. The park provocation is interesting and revealing because some will play sport, some will daydream, some sit in a corner. Use this exercise to get them to think about who they're playing and how that character may differ from themselves.

Status

The group read the exchange between Naz and Mack on page 509 and Adam Penford asked them to consider: On a scale of 1–10, where would you rank both Naz and Mack's status in this scene? The group observed Naz has a higher status than Mack.

Penford asked the group to identify **what it is that each character wants in this scene**. That could be described as their objective or their intention. Distil your thoughts into one active word that an actor can play. If it's something a character wants, it should be something that they can be given. Ask the question: how do you know if you've managed to get it? For example, 'an apology' is interesting, because you either get it or you don't and therefore you know quite clearly when you've achieved your objective.

- In pairs, answer the question, 'What does this character want?' Try the idea that came to you first, then try out the less obvious version.
- Work on scenes in pairs, thinking about specific intentions. Identify your character's objective and explore how to play it.

Production, staging and design

This is a play with big theatrical moments, which requires decisions about how to realise those. Carr said that she had a preference for little to no design in terms of built structural elements. There could be levels, but there is no need to be encumbered, and don't waste time sourcing props. Ensure that the scene changes don't slow it down in any way.

There doesn't need to be a set, but there should be design; for example, how do you differentiate between the Us and Them through costume? Do they wear uniform? How are those differences conveyed? Are they marked or are they subtle?

There are big asks; people fall from the sky, a human chain is sucked up into the sky, which offers up theatrical challenges. Each group will do it differently, and there is no prescribed way that any of these things should be created. Carr didn't have anything specific in her head when she wrote it.

The play doesn't hinge on moments feeling naturalistic. The direct address supports with telling the audience what is happening, so you don't have to be bogged down with creating those environments in a realistic way. Find ways to make it move and paint the stage with actors in a space without having to rely on literal physical elements.

Lead director Adam Penford was joined by movement director Jess Williams for a physical workshop, held at the National Theatre, October 2022

Warm-ups

1 Sign name

In-person version: Go round once as described on page 530. Then, go round the circle again, and do your sign name as small as possible (tiny mouse version). Go round again and do the biggest, loudest version you can.

2 Pass the click

Adam Penford demonstrated using a click, combined with gesture and facial expression, to mime throwing a ball in the air and bouncing it on the floor. He then threw the click across the circle, using gesture and eye contact. Keep passing the click around the circle. Penford then added another click, so there were two going round the circle. With a smaller group, you can walk round the space and continue the game.

If the group isn't responding or is being talkative, this is a great game to bring silence and focus back to a room, because it requires concentration and eye contact – if you throw it to someone who's not looking at you, it falls apart. Creative students will also recognise that it supports imagination.

3 Count one, two, three

In pairs, count to three, alternating who is speaking. For example, A says 'one', B says 'two', A says 'three' and so on. Then, take out the number two and replace it with a clap, so the sequence is 'one', clap, 'three'. Next, take out the number three and replace it with a stamp. Replace number one with a nod of the head. After each development, you can ask them to rate the difficulty out of ten.

Adam Penford observed that the last round is often the easiest, because you get into a rhythm with a partner. This game doesn't match everyone's access needs, so Penford tends to get a sense of the group before playing it.

4 Overlapping rhythms

In three groups, count with a gesture: on 'one' stick your arm out, palm flat with thumb towards the ceiling (as if you were going to shake hands) and on 'two' onwards, clench your fist and move your arm as if you were counting for rock paper scissors. (There is another version where you can stamp your feet to count.)

Group One: Count one, two, three

Group Two: Count one, two, three. four

Group Three: Count one, two, three, four, five

All three groups start together. The groups' counting will then split off, but if everyone stays in the same tempo, the groups will come back together and eventually all get to the first gesture at the same time again. No one is allowed to count out loud. See if you can keep the set rhythm going.

When everyone gets back to the gesture for 'one' simultaneously, switch rhythms, so Group One counts to five, Group Two counts to three, and Group Three counts to three.

The game is tricky, but when you do it with young people, the sense of achievement when they complete a round is massive.

Characters and characterisation

In smaller groups, participants looked at specific characters, and fed back the highlights of their discoveries to catch the rest of the group up. As each character was being discussed, the group was asked to consider how that character relates to the one they had been looking at: What is the relationship between them? Would they be friends, would they be scared of them? This exercise is a shortcut, and a quick way to tackle the play.

Mack

She is dependent on others but doesn't like to admit it. When we first meet her she is desperately looking for someone. She thinks she has lots of friends but she's always on her own. As a character, she contains contradictions. In the play, she is keen to know when someone is going to help them, and she panics when the phone is dead, which somewhat contradicts her tough and confident outer shell. In her perception, Ali and Remi are glued to her. She is a multi-layered character (like an onion) and the play reveals her layers. She is very attached to Cam, who is the opposite of her. The play reveals her security and allows her to see herself for who she really is, inviting her to redeem herself at the end.

Jay

Jay is the 'beta male'. He wants to be a collaborator, but Alex won't allow him to be his equal. Within the text, Jay says that they just moved to the upstairs world, and he doesn't know his dad; he is not familiar with the upstairs world. He is bright and analytical and has lots of ideas to solve things, but Alex is reluctant to work with him. Jay and Alex subvert traditional gender roles.

Magpie

She is an attention seeker with a turbulent relationship with her parents. She likes shiny things and she likes to take things. She is very aware of her situation, and she sees herself in Ash. Of all the characters, she is the most aware that actions have consequences. Her love of shiny, reflective things could be a metaphor for her self-awareness, as she can see her own reflection.

Billy

Billy is defined by the loss of his sister. He is quite ostracised, maybe because others don't know how to deal with the tragedy. He has to mature quite quickly, which separates him because he's been through something that they haven't been through. He wasn't the brother that he wanted to be and he's trying to make up for lost time. Initially he is looking for Sam to overcome this trauma, but he realises it's up to him. Ultimately, he experiences some degree of closure – she was taken from him once, but at the end he lets her go.

Alex

Alex defines herself by her knowledge and intelligence, but has a lot of self-doubt. Alex tends to take charge and is responsible. She is very aware of things, and is the thinker whereas Jay is the doer. Alex comes up with ideas and is thoughtful.

Ash

Ash and Magpie are the most obvious examples of a 'mirror image' between the two worlds. Ash lives under the weight of heavy parental expectation but is unsure of herself. Magpie is self-aware, but Ash is not quite there yet. She tries out being more like Magpie and it doesn't go very well. Her parents expect her to be perfect, which contributes to her view that she is boring. She wishes her actions were not scrutinised.

Cam

Cam keeps himself to himself, has short lines and shrugs. Cam is unsure of himself, self-conscious and eats behind the science block. Cam experienced a long illness and has only just returned to school, which the teacher makes a big deal of. Cam doesn't want to go back because he thinks 'here' might be better.

Sam

Sam doesn't have much of a filter, and states things as she sees them: 'the people down here aren't my problem'. At the start of the play she is dismissive to Billy 1, but at the end of the play she compares him to her Billy. In the end, she says that she loves him too. People don't really know who she is outside of what happened to her. Did people know who she was prior to the tragedy?

After what can be quite an academic approach, it's useful to take a physical approach.

Bomb/Shield/Target

- Thinking as the character your group has been looking at, in your own head, choose another character you want to keep a distance from. Choose someone who is in that character's group that you are avoiding.
- Now do the opposite – choose the character your character is most drawn to. You don't have to reveal this at any point, so there's no right or wrong.
- Lastly, who do you think could offer your character the most protection?

It may help to think of them as a bomb (stay away), a shield (protect you) and a target (drawn to).

Walk around the space at your own tempo. If you see a space, fill it. As you walk, look for your bomb person. Stay as far away from your bomb as is physically possible, whilst staying in the space. Find your bomb, keep moving and stay as far away from them as possible. Keeping your bomb in your eye line, identify your shield, and keep the shield between you and the bomb. Whilst doing that, identify your target, and try to get close to them.

Adam Penford reflected that when you relate this exercise to character, it could be the case that the person you're trying to stay away from is the person who is the most drawn to you, which generates instant dramatic conflict.

This practical, goal-driven exercise is a useful way to physicalise relationships, and it can be used as a tool for staging – it's quick to put something on its feet.

Movement exercises for use in rehearsals: style and staging

1 One to six

- Move through the space.
- Pick up the pace – as if you're on your way somewhere important. Make eye contact as you pass someone and give them a friendly face. Drop your shoulders, lift your focus, let the connection build up, use the whole room and try to balance the space

- On 'one', freeze as still and as quickly as you can.
- On 'go', start again with a change of direction. Use these commands, push the pace.
- On 'two' find the nearest person and greet them. Greet them and then immediately carry on walking.
- On 'three' touch a wall or pillar – go to the walls and clear the middle of the space.
- On 'four' make the centre of the space as busy as possible. Get as close to each other as you feel comfortable.
- Mix up the order of the instructions and move through the commands.
- On 'five' go to the floor and come up again, however you feel comfortable.
- On 'six' put the beat somewhere in your body.
- The game calls for efficiency – don't run around and panic, use your eyes to see what everyone else is doing.
- Alternating between 'one' and 'six' can be successful.
- Try 'a secret six', and then 'even more of a secret', then 'less of a secret', bigger again, bigger again, the biggest, most confident 'six' anyone has ever seen.
- Try a 'six' with someone, then an awkward 'six' with the same person, then a joyful 'six' with that person.

There are a lot of different versions of this exercise; think about how to pull out the movement qualities of the play to give the actors simple instructions.

2 Walk to the beat

- Using music, walk in time to the track for eight counts, freeze for eight counts, then repeat.
- Walk for six, freeze for six, repeat.
- Walk for four, freeze for four, repeat.
- Walk for two, freeze for two, repeat.
- Then join it together: eight sequence, six, four, two, repeat.

The approach is about working in layers: start with the simplest thing, then add layers and choreography will emerge.

- Now, rather than freezing, bounce when you stop walking.
- Now when you bounce, bounce with someone else.
- Make physical contact with someone. This can be in twos or it can be in groups. Each time find someone new.

This gets groups working as a team and gets young people to make contact without thinking about it. You can also mix it up and have different groups in counterpoint to each other.

- Split the group into As and Bs.
- As do the sequence as before (eight, six, four, two, repeat). Bs do the same sequence but in the opposite order (two, four, six, eight, repeat).
- Final version: fake it till you make it! If you get lost, keep walking in the space until you find someone to join in with. From the outside you have no idea who's right and who's wrong.

3 Leader and follower

Find a partner, and both put your right hands out flat in front of you, palms facing down, with one person's hand flat on top of the other. The leader pushes down, and the follower pushes up. The leader can use pressure to push both hands to the ground, and if they use less pressure, the follower will push both hands up. This way, the leader can control the movement. The leader should stay fairly static and get the follower to do most of the moving. It's really important that the follower pushes upwards all the time.

While you're doing this work, consider detail; think about pace, dynamic, movement, stopping and starting. Check your free arm and make sure it's free and not holding any tension. After some time with the leader controlling the pair's movement, swap the leader and follower.

Then, the follower should close their eyes. The safest thing for the follower to do is to push up hard. The leader then has a duty of care to the follower. Having eyes closed can make the task easier, because you are focusing on one thing.

Additional layer: try the exercise in threes so there's an outside eye who can observe. They can put their hand underneath and become the follower; the follower becomes the leader and so on.

Contact work is underpinned by the push; this can be tried with the back, knees or with a stick. There is a version where you don't decide who is the leader and who is the follower, but let it play out organically.

4 Making shapes

Working alone, pick two body parts, and think about them being pulled in opposite directions; for example, your left index finger is being pulled to the ceiling and your right knee is being pulled to the floor. Come up with four shapes that each have two body parts being pulled in opposite directions. If you ask someone to create a shape with their body, they will stand like a star. If you ask them to think about tension, they will create something more dynamic. Once you have your four shapes, start to practise going from one shape to the next. The quality to use is a slow morphing or melting from one shape to the next.

Groups of five: all slowly go into your first shape together, and then think about how you can link together. Slowly morph there and think about how you might link your shapes. You can use the 'push' idea from the contact exercise to move from one shape to the next.

Make a big chain and keep morphing and changing. Then choose a point of focus in the room and look towards it.

Acting exercises for use in rehearsals

1 Stakes

Take ten people out of the group. Each of these actors has lost an item, ranging in value. They've each been told what the object is, and a number from one to ten, which reflects the stakes of the loss. The ten actors then stand in a jumbled-up order and each do short, thirty-second improvisations.

The rest of the group must decide what it is that they've lost, and how valuable it is to them, putting them in order from one to ten. Then reveal the correct order!

The stakes of an object can depend on context: a train ticket might be very high stakes if it's the last Eurostar and you have to get to a funeral. This leads to a conversation about specificity. If you try to get cheap laughs and clown around to pull focus, you impede the story that you're trying to tell.

Objects and stakes used for this exercise:

1   dirty tissue
2   pencil
3   20p
4   homework
5   train ticket
6   house keys
7   £50
8   phone
9   passport
10 child

2 Objectives

Sometimes called intentions or actions, an 'objective' is what your character wants. This is connected to **stakes**.

- One person wants to leave the room because she's left the light on outside. The other person doesn't want them to leave the room because they're watching a film and it's coming up to the best bit. Improvise the scene and play to win. Don't feel the need to entertain, just play the reality of that situation.

- Version one: parent and child

- Version two: romantic relationship

- After each time, those watching should rate from one to ten where each character was in terms of stakes and decide who achieved the objective.

- Consider: what tactics did each actor employ to achieve their objective? For example, avoidance or changing the subject.

- Something like turning the light off can be high stakes if there's a fire risk, or the character has OCD.

- As soon as you stop playing the objective, you lose the dramatic tension.

Obstacles: the thing that's stopping you achieving the thing you want to achieve. Technically you can just walk out, but the obstacle has to be big enough to stop you doing that, otherwise it's not very interesting dramatically.

- This time, try the same objective but with a different set of **given circumstances**.

- A wants to leave the room because B has killed their pet hamster. B needs A to stay because they are agoraphobic, and A is the only thing in their life.

In the example the group watched, the stakes escalated, and the scene went from being about the hamster in the toilet to being about whether A loved B, and the future of their relationship. B was able to sustain the scene because she kept changing the tactics: emotional blackmail, physical blocking, guilt, etc. For a long time B was physically obstructing the door, but it was compelling when she changed tactics, moved away from the door and broke down in tears.

The stakes kept changing, because the scene exposed different consequences. What does it mean for that character after that moment?

Stakes being sustained at the same level becomes boring; scenes that stay on a 3 are as disengaging as scenes that start on a 9 and stay there.

The chair game

- Bring your chair into the space and sit down. Spread the chairs evenly around the space.

- Choose one volunteer who has to move across the space and sit in the empty chair. However, they have to move as though their knees have been tied together, or like a penguin.

- If you get up from your chair, you're not allowed to go back to your chair.

- Try to work as a team and think of tactics.

Movement work: staging the play

Stage one

In teams of six or seven, spread yourselves out and face the same way. Whoever is at the front of the cluster becomes the leader (i.e. if you can't see anyone in front of you, you're the leader). The leader moves very slowly, and the rest of the group copies what the leader is doing, at Tai Chi speed. You are aiming for group synchronicity, accuracy and detail; for the leader, it's the opposite of trying to catch them out. If you start to move fast, you lose the detail behind you in the rest of the group. If you can't see the leader from where you are, copy the person in front of you that you can see.

After a while, the leader can choose to turn slowly turn in either direction, and then when a new person can't see anyone in front of them, they become the leader, and the movement continues. As a group, try to move seamlessly from one leader to the next. Consider the detail you can find in your body, for example in your posture and the way you're moving your legs.

When you take the movement of the arms away, movement becomes more pedestrian; arms can make movement seem more abstract. For the development of this exercise, arms aren't banned but they're not important.

Stage two
Choose a point of focus, like a clock on a wall, and begin the ensemble movement. Rather than turning, at any point someone can choose to weave their way forward and become the leader.

Stage three
Stand two groups across the space from each other, facing one another. The point of focus then becomes the leader of the other team. The intention is not squaring up to each other, but inspecting them, trying to get a better view of them, or trying to understand them. At any point, you can swap the leader by having another member of the group come forward and take their place at the front. Set a minimum distance that the groups are allowed to be from each other.

Development: try to make the movement 50 per cent smaller/50 per cent more pedestrian.

An easy way to set something is to give someone one or two movements to create, and then set it. With this movement work, you can experiment with combining it with text; either alternating between movement and text or combining them.

The playwright Alison Carr is keen on pace in her plays. Try not to put a ten-minute ballet in the middle of your production, but use the physical work to support the narrative.

For this play: you could cluster the group together and find a point of contact. Look at a point on the ceiling and use the pushing exercise from earlier where one person pushes down and one pushes up on a point of contact and imagine the tear in the sky. Start with an improvised version, create a set version, and then put the text on top. The movement could also be used as an echo of the character's experience.

In pairs, choose the same four areas of your body, e.g. nose, front of left hip, right shoulder blade. Imagine that each one of those body parts is being pulled forwards and up. Create a sequence moving through each body part. Vary the pace and length of each movement; try to ensure that each movement or 'event' doesn't take the same amount of time.

Then, take two sets of pairs and mix up the pairs so they're not standing next to each other. The pairs then travel from one end of the room going through their sequence of four movements. Think about the joins; don't show where one movement begins and another ends. Add more pairs in, and cluster them closer together.

If you treat that as your base phrase, you can add lots of other things to it. You can change pace, scale and so on. The movement can start small and get bigger. For example, imagine that the pull is getting stronger and the force is accumulating. Start the journey in cinematic slow motion before speeding up. Then, find a point of focus that the whole group looks out, and it doesn't matter if you're out of time with your partner.

You can build the side of the group, and add events during the journey: one person falls over, everyone falls over, add emotions to it, add moment of stillness, or a snap where it starts slow and then it snaps into speed, or a pair manages to resist the force and then gets sucked up.

On a smaller stage, it could be like a whirlwind, in a circle. A smaller version could still give us the same impression of where the tear is. You could also incorporate props into push/pull dynamics, like an item of clothing or a stick.

Top tips:

- Working on material with your group that they have made will encourage them to own it. If they are struggling to commit to tension or resistance on their own, you can do a push/pull with a person in place and then take them away.

- Don't necessarily tell them when you're 'working on the thing'; move from the warm-up to creating material.

- You can set additional challenges to add to this work; for example, maintain contact, break contact, layer on bomb/shield/target.

- Reversing material is difficult but it is possible. If you do the going up in a really physical way, you might just want to describe the coming back down again. You could do it with two groups, and they could see each other.

Staging ideas

In groups, participants staged the first page and a half of the play in the following ways:

1 In the round
This is a challenge in terms of projection, which can be an issue for younger performers. This configuration lends itself to heightened physicality because of the inherent theatricality of the configuration.

2 Promenade
Looking up as a group is one way to bring in the tear moment. It captures the audience's imagination because you don't know what they're talking about yet. Getting the audience involved in physical action makes you listen closely to what was being said.

3 Design-led (using props/costume)
Character emerged through the differentiation of how actors interacted with props and costumes. It may not be props, but it was felt that the play can 'take *something*'.

4 Movement-based
This version was very atmospheric, and anonymous in terms of character because of the ensemble.

Additional ideas

The 'tree moment' could be delivered by finding a focal point; invite the audience to feel the tree with the focus. Find the level of the focal point and the movement of the performers. It could also be delivered with puppetry or props; for example, a stack of bags with strings attached for branches.

Question and answer with Alison Carr

Q: Can we change stage directions or gender?
A: Go ahead with small things, but don't make fundamental changes to the text or story.

Q: Can changes be made to reflect location in terms of names of places and dialect?
A: Yes!

Q: Can characters be created out of the ensemble text, and given names?
A: Yes.

Q: Can ensemble lines be given to the named characters?
A: Yes.

Q: Can lines be reallocated from named characters to ensemble characters?
A: In general moments yes, but nothing that's specific to the storytelling.

Q: Can a school change the circumstances of Sam's death? (In an instance where a student had experienced a similar event)
A: Yes.

Q: Can we integrate music into the show?
A: As long as no one's bursting into song or doing a dance number.

Q: Can students compose music to underscore the piece, as part of their GCSE coursework?
A: Yes! Bespoke underscoring would be brilliant.

Q: Can voiceover and film be used?
A: Yes.

Q: Can the staging be a mixture of naturalism and physical theatre, with abstract moments?
A: This is a play that leans into physical theatre and has scope for that. It is asking you to create people flying in the air and human chains. As long as those elements are weaved in to propel the story as it is, as opposed to bringing the story to a stop.

Suggested references

Directing Young People in Theatre (2015), Samantha Lane

Music used by Jess Williams:
Prince – 'Controversy' (warm-up)
Jain – 'Heads Up' (warm-up)
Kiasmos – 'Held'
Hot Chip – 'Motion Sickness'
Underworld – 'Boy Boy Boy'
Wet Leg – 'Chaise Longue'
Bonobo – 'No Reason'
Imogen Heap – 'Mic Check'
Elbow – 'Lippy Kids'
Cat Power – 'Manhattan'

From a workshop led by Adam Penford and Jess Williams
With notes by Lucy Allan

Participating Companies

#TeamDrama
9 to 12 Collective HWS
20Twenty Connections
Aberystwyth Arts Centre Youth Theatre
Acorn Young People's Theatre
Act2 Academy
Actors Workshop
Alderbrook
Alderwood School
Amersham School
Angmering Connections
Apollo Theatre Arts
The Archbishop Lanfranc Academy
Ardclough Youth Theatre
Arts1 Actors Company
artsdepot Young Company
Astor Secondary School
Atlantic Coast Theatre Co.
Aurora Theatre Arts Co.
Beacon Young Company
Bedford College
Benjamin Britten Music Academy
BHASVIC Theatre Company
Bilborough Sixth Form College
Birkenhead High School Academy
Bishops High School
Black Cherry Youth Theatre
The Boaty Theatre Company
Bourne Academy
Brewery Youth Theatre
Bristol Free School
Bristol Institute of Performing Arts
Brockhill Park Performing Arts College
Brunton Young Company
Burton College
Bury Grammar School
Buxton Opera House Young Company
Byre Youth and Community Arts
Cabot Learning Federation Post 16
Caerphilly Youth Theatre
CAPA College
Capital City Academy
The Carlton Academy
Carmel Performing Arts
CAST Performance Academy
Cast Youth Theatre
Cavendish School

The Chantry School
The Charter School East Dulwich
Crescent Arts Youth Theatre
Chase High School
Chelsea Academy
Cheltenham's Bournside School
Chesterton Youth Theatre
CHS South
Churchill Theatre Young Company
City of London Academy Shoreditch Park
City of London Academy Southwark
City of Oxford college
CJCA
Cockburn School
The College, Merthyr Tydfil
Colne Primet Academy
Company of Teens
Corn Exchange Newbury Youth Theatre
Corn Exchange Young Performers
The Cotswold School
County Limerick Youth Theatre
Cox Green School
Craven College
Croydon Youth Theatre
Curious Connections
The Customs House Youth Theatre
City of Westminster College Company
The Deaf Academy
Delanté Détras Theatre Company
Derby Theatre Connections Company
Devizes School
Dorset Drama Academy
The Drama Studio
DSA
Duckegg North Lincolnshire
Dudley College Performing Arts
East London Theatre School – Young Actors
    Company
Eastbury Drama group
Everyman Youth Theatre
Felpham Community College
Fisher Youth Theatre Group
Flying High Young Company
Framingham Earl High School
Fred Longworth High School
The Garage Norwich
Gateshead College

Ghost Light Young Performers
Glasgow Acting Academy SCIO
GLJ Theatre
Gordano School
Griese Youth Theatre
Group 64 Theatre for Young People
Gulbenkian Young Company
Hackney Shed Collective
Harris Academy Beckenham
Hatton Youth Theatre
Haywards Heath Performing Arts
Hayworth Players
Heles School
Helsby High School
High Definition Drama
Hopwood Hall College
Huntingdon Youth Theatre
ILEX Theatre
Ilkley Players Greenroom
Imaginarium Young Actors Company
In the Round Theatre
InterACT Youth Theatre (Neston)
Inverclyde Youth Theatre (Kayos)
Ipswich School
The Island Free School
Jarrow School
JCoSS
Kensington Arts
Kesteven and Grantham Girls' School
Kildare Youth Theatre
The King's Company
King Edward VI Five Ways School
Kings Theatre Arts Academy: Youth
Kingsdale Foundation School
Kingsford Drama Seniors
Kingsthorpe College
Knightswood Secondary School
Kola Nuts
KPYT
The Langley Academy
Lathom High School
Lipson Cooperative Academy
LORIC Players – South Wirral High School
Love Theatre Jersey
The Lowry Artists
Lowry Young Company
Lowther Youth Theatre
Lumos Theatre
Mark Rutherford School
MHCHS Theatre Group

The Mill Youth Theatre
Mishmak Youth Theatre
MKT Young Company
Mr. Sands Youth Theatre
Multiplicity Theatre Company
Murray Park Community School
New City College Epping Forest Campus
Nine Lives Theatre Company
NMPAT Young Actors
Norbury High School for Girls
Norlington School
Northampton High School
Nottingham College Actors
The Nottingham Emmanuel School Academy
Nottingham Playhouse Connections Company
Nower Hill High School
NUSA Young Company
Oasis Academy Coulsdon
Octagon Theatre
Oldham College
On Point Theatre Company
One Act Theatre Company
Ormiston Rivers Academy
Ousedale School
Over & Under Theatre Company
OX2 Collective
PACT Theatre
Page2stage youth theatre
Patrician Youth Theatre
Peake Productions
Peanuts Rep
Penketh Youth Theatre
Perfect Circle Youth Theatre
Plympton Academy
Plymstock School
Point Ensemble
Poole High School
Port Talbot Youth Theatre
PQA Wolverhampton
Prendergast Players
Proteus Theatre Company
Pump House CYT
Pure Drama
Plough Youth Theatre
QEGS
Queen Elizabeth's School
Queen's Park High School
Ratzcool
RAW Academy
REC Youth Theatre Company

Red Rose Chain
The Repertory Theatre Project
The Ridgeway School & Sixth Form College
Robert Barclay Academy
Roundwood park school
Royal & Derngate Young Company: Connect
Ruislip High School
Rushden Academy Performing Arts
Saracens High School
Shazam Theatre Company SCIO
Shenfield Sixth Form Performing Arts
  Academy
Silverdale Youth Theatre
Simon Langton Grammar School for Boys
Sir Henry Floyd Grammar School
The Sir John Colfox Academy
The Sixth Form Bolton
Solihull Sixth Form College
South Hunsley School Theatre Company
Southwark Playhouse Young Company
The Spires College
Springwest Academy
SRWA Theatre Company
St Bartholomew's School
St Brendan's Sixth Form College
St Christopher's School
St Ives Youth Theatre
St John Plessington Catholic College
St Laurence School
St Mary's Catholic College
St Saviour's and St Olave's School
St Thomas the Apostle School and Sixth Form
St Patrick's College, Ballymena
Stag Youth Theatre
Stage Goons
stage@LeedsYoungCompany
Stagecoach East Kilbride
Stagedoor Learning
Stockport Academy
Stockton Riverside College
Store Room Youth Theatre
Straffan Drama Club
Stratford School Academy
Strike A Light Youth Theatre
Strive Drama
Suffolk New College Performing Arts
The Swanage School

TADAA
Telford Priory School
Theatre Arts Starlight Theatre Company
Theatre by the Lake
Theatre Royal Bury St Edmunds' Young
  Company
Theatre Royal Plymouth
TheatreWorks Deal
The Thetford Academy
Through The Wardrobe
Tibby's Theatre Troop
Titchfield Festival Youth Theatre
Towers School and Sixth Form
Tramshed Young Company
Trinity Academy Bristol
Trinity Youth Theatre
Twyford CofE High School
TYT Company
University of Worcester
Urock
Vyners School
Warminster School
Waterford Youth Arts
West Lakes Academy
West Yorkshire Drama Academy
Westacre Theatre Company
Westborough High School
Westfield Arts College
White City Youth Theatre
Wildern School
William Howard School
Wiltshire Creative FE
Wimbledon College Theatre Company
Winstanley College
Wollaston School Theatre Company
Woodrush High School
Worcester Theatres
Worcester Youth Theatremakers
The Workshop Theatre Class
Worthing College
Yew Tree Youth Theatre
York Theatre Royal Youth Theatre
Young Actors Company
Young Dramatic Arts
The Young Rep
Ysgol Aberconwy
Ysgol Penglais School Drama Department

Partner Theatres

Aberystwyth Arts Centre
artsdepot
Beacon Arts Centre
Bristol Old Vic
Buxton Opera House
Cast Doncaster
Chichester Festival Theatre
Crewe Lyceum
Derby Theatre
The Fire Station Sunderland
The Garage Norwich
The Grand Theatre Blackpool
HOME Manchester
Lighthouse Poole
The Lowry Salford
Lyric Theatre Belfast
Lyric Theatre Hammersmith
Marlowe Theatre Canterbury
North Wall Oxford
Nottingham Playhouse
Pitlochry Festival Theatre
Queen's Theatre Hornchurch
Reading Rep Theatre
Riverbank Arts Centre
Royal & Derngate
Sheffield Theatres
Soho Theatre
Theatr Brycheiniog
Theatre by the Lake
Theatre Peckham
Theatre Royal Plymouth
Tramshed
Trinity Theatre, Tunbridge Wells
Wiltshire Creative
Worcester Theatres
York Theatre Royal

National Theatre Connections Team

The National Theatre

National Theatre
Upper Ground
London SE1 9PX

Registered charity no: 224223

Director of the National Theatre
Rufus Norris
Executive Director
Kate Varah

The Mohn Westlake Foundation supports nationwide
Learning programmes for young people.

Connections is supported by The Mohn Westlake Foundation,
Buffini Chao Foundation, Bank of America, The EBM Charitable Trust,
Andrew Lloyd Webber Foundation, Katie Bradford Arts Trust, Susan Miller
and Byron Grote, Henry Oldfield Trust, The Broughton Family Charitable Trust,
Mulberry Trust, The Peter Cundill Foundation, The D'Oyly Carte Charitable
Trust and The John Thaw Foundation.

Nationwide learning is supported by Buffini Chao Foundation,
Garfield Weston Foundation, Clore Duffield Foundation, Tim and Sarah Bunting,
Behrens Foundation, Cleopatra Trust and Milton Grundy Foundation.

Performing Rights

Application for permission to perform, etc. should be made before rehearsals begin to the following representatives:

For *Tuesday, Is This Good Enough?* and *Samphire*:
Permissions Department
Bloomsbury Publishing Plc
50 Bedford Square
London WC1B 3DP
performance.permissions@bloomsbury.com

For *Strangers Like Me*:
Berlin Associates
7 Tyers Gate
London SE1 3HX
agents@berlinassociates.com

For *Old Times*:
Independent Talent Group Ltd
40 Whitfield Street,
London W1T 2RH
alexrusher@independenttalent.com

For *Innocent Creatures*:
United Agents
12–26 Lexington Street
London W1F 0LE
gsmart@unitedagents.co.uk

For *The Heights*:
United Agents
12–26 Lexington Street
London W1F 0LE
nbarron@unitedagents.co.uk

For *(Circle Dreams Around) The Terrible, Terrible Past*:
Judy Daish Associates
2 St Charles Place
London WI0 6EG
howard@judydaish.com

For *Model Behaviour*:
Curtis Brown Group Ltd
Haymarket House
28–29 Haymarket
London SW1Y 4SP
lily@curtisbrown.co.uk

For *Is My Microphone On?*:
Casarotto Ramsay & Associates
Waverley House
7–12 Noel Street
W1F 8GQ
imogen@casarotto.co.uk